'O' LEVEL

INTRODUCTION TO MULTIMEDIA

STRICTLY AS PER NEW DOEACC SYLLABUS M4.2-R4

Dr. R.K. Jain

KHANNA BOOK PUBLISHING CO. (P) LTD.

ISBN: 978-81-80016-74-0

Published by:
Khanna Book Publishing Co. (P) Ltd.
4C/4344, Ansari Road, Darya Ganj, New Delhi-110 002
Phone: 011-23244447 Telefax: 011-23244448
E-mail: contact@khannabooks.com
Website: www.khannabooks.com

Regd. Off: 1694-95, 1st Floor, Nai Sarak, Delhi-110006 (India)
Phone: 011-23283211 Telefax: 011-23256658

Printed in India by:
ZN Printers, Delhi

Preface

The new syllabus of DOE's various levels of courses, popularly called O-level, A-level, B-level and C-level is out. Keeping in mind the various developments taking place around the world in the field of computers, these syllabus include most of them. While keeping in mind the level of students studying the various levels, the degree of difficulties of the syllabus have been very well designed. I hope that after the new syllabus the courses would be as popular as they were before.

There had been a long struggle between Training Institutes and Government Organizations, since these organizations would not recognize the degree/diploma given by them. Students passing out from these institutions were not given jobs based upon the said diplomas/degrees. Ultimately, the Government formed a society under the Department of Electronics, called DOEACC, who conducts tests and gives grades to the students irrespective of the institutes where they have studied. It is also possible to give the test without having any proper institutional studies. This is more or less on the terms of SAT and GRE conducted by USA. The only difference is that this is not online. There are fixed dates for the exams.

The course for this has been designed for students to appear in the exams at various levels. These levels are O-level, A-level, B-level, C-level. The most popular among these is the O-level, since it is the entry level. Once you have cleared the O-level, you are eligible for a government job. Each course has been divided into various modules. Various books are available for various modules. This book is also made for you to prepare for the O-level course.

This book has been written totally in accordance with the syllabus provided. Each chapter has been embedded with the screen shots for you to know what to expect on the screen, while running the application. Each chapter contains examples which can be attempted to supplement the reading. At the end of the chapter, there is a thorough revision of the text read. Not to mention of the questions provided in the beginning, both in the form of objective and subjective. The book also contains Sample papers which are based on the samples provided by DOEACC society. These would help you in preparing for the exams.

Author

Syllabus

M4.2-R4: INTRODUCTION TO MULTIMEDIA

Outline of Course

S.No.	*Topic*	*Minimum No. of Hours*
1.	Introduction to Multimedia	08
2.	Computer Fonts and Hypertext	10
3.	Audio Fundamentals and representations	10
4.	Image Fundamentals and representations	10
5.	Video and Animation	10
6.	Multimedia Authoring	12

Lectures	=	60
Practicals /Tutorials	=	60
Total	=	120

DETAILED SYLLABUS

1. **Introduction to Multimedia** **08 Hrs.**

   What is multimedia, Components of multimedia, Web and Internet multimedia applications, Transition from conventional media to digital media.

2. **Computer Fonts and Hypertext** **10 Hrs.**

   Usage of text in multimedia, Families and faces of fonts, outline fonts, bitmap fonts, International character sets and hypertext, Digital fonts techniques.

3. **Audio fundamentals and representations** **10 hrs.**

   Digitization of sound, frequency and bandwidth, decibel system, data rate, audio file format, Sound synthesis, MIDI wavetable, Compression and transmission of audio on Internet, Adding sound your multimedia project, Audio software and hardware.

4. **Image fundamentals and representations** **10 Hrs.**

   Colour Science, Colour, Colour Models, Colour palettes, Dithering, 2D Graphics, Image Compression and File Formats: GIF, JPEG, JPEG 2000, PNG, TIFF, EXIF, PS, PDF, Basic Image Processing (can use Photoshop), Use of image editing software, White balance correction, Dynamic range correction, Photo retouching.

5. **Video and Animation** **10 Hrs.**

   Video Basics: How Video Works, Broadcast Video Standards, Analog video, Digital video, Video Recording and Tape formats, Shooting and Editing Video (Use Adobe Premier for editing), Video Compression and File Formats, Video compression based on motion compensation, MPEG-1, MPEG-2, MPEG-4, MPEG-7, MPEG-21, Animation: Cell Animation, Computer Animation, Morphing.

6. **Multimedia Authoring** **12 Hrs.**

   Multimedia Authoring Basics, Some Authoring Tools, Micromedia Director and Flash.

Introduction to Multimedia 1

1.1 What is Multimedia?

First thing first, let us understand what Multimedia means. Multi- means many, i.e., not one, more than one. Media means medium to communicate or talk. Now how would a computer talk to you. It would either create a sound, show a picture or some text on the screen. All this would be communicated to you by computer using medium like Monitor to show the text and picture, speaker to broadcast sound. All these mediums of the computer, like monitor and speaker are collectively called Computer Media.

Now what we make of Multimedia. It is a process by which computer communicates with you using more than one computer medium like sound, text, graphics, animation or video. Any two or more combinations from the above can be used and the net result can be displayed on the monitor screen or transferred to your web or the web site which you may create.

Among the various applications of multimedia are the dazzling effects you can see in most of the advertisements on the TV. How about Pepsi advertisement of Oh Bubbly. It makes good use of sound, graphics, and animation. Most of the advertisements which you see on the TV are the results of computer created animation (using software called Flash, about which you would be reading in a later chapter) and combinations of pictures shot by either still or video camera. These pictures are then changed to suit according to needs using a software called Photoshop, about which too you will read in a later chapter.

A perfect example of Multimedia is the creation of a motion picture called Toy, which was totally made in the studio using the various animations and live actors. It used live pictures and merged them with animations and fit in the sound to create an effect which had been highly appreciated by many. Some time back Japanese made a complete film on Ramayan, totally animated with Hindi sound.

1.1.1 Advantages of Multimedia

Not comparing with any other media, the major advantages of multimedia are:

- **Make the Text more attractive:** You can design your multimedia project in such a way that the text, its readability is enhanced and is easier to read and look. This can be done by using the various applications of fonts, which are later discussed in the book.
- **Adding Video and Audio:** Have you ever wondered why TV is more popular than Radio. Simple, because in TV you can see and hear, whereas in Radio you can just listen. So by adding both audio and video in your multimedia project, you can enhance the viewability and hearability of your project.
- **Merging of the media:** Multimedia is a great way of combining; text, audio, video, animation,

graphics, etc., to make it more attractive not only in seeing but even in catching your eye on your multimedia project.

- **Easier to understand:** Multimedia makes it easier to understand the various topics which you are trying to explain.
- **Entertaining while learning:** Multimedia is such a process which makes you learn in a easier and entertaining way.

1.2 Components of Multimedia

Most multimedia and Web projects must be undertaken in stages. Some stages should be completed before other stages begin and some stages may be skipped or combined.

Here are the four basic stages in multimedia project:

1.2.1 Planning and Costing

A project always begins with an idea or a need that you refine by outline its messages and objectives. Identify how you will make each message and objective work within your authoring system. Before you begin developing, plan what writing skills, graphic art, music, video and other multimedia expertise will be required. Develop a creative graphic look and feel, as well as a structure and navigation system that will let the viewer visit the messages and content. Estimate the time needed to do all elements, and prepare a budget. Work up a short prototype of proof-of-concept. The more time you spend getting your arms around your project and defining its content and structure, the faster you can later build it and less reworking and rearranging will be required midstream.

Make a mental flow of the project before beginning to assemble.

1.2.2 Designing and producing

Perform each of the planned tasks to create a finished product.

1.2.3 Testing

Always test your programs to make sure they meet the objectives of your project, they work properly on the intended delivery platforms and they meet the needs of your client or client user.

1.2.4 Delivering

Package and deliver the project to the end user.

1.2.5 Multimedia Needs

Needless to say that you need a good computer to start with. You also need software to match it too. Not that since somebody told you to use a particular software, you will use that. You must use the software with which you are familiar with. This will help you in saving time and energy.

You also need to stay organized, because as the construction work gets under way, all the little bits and pieces of multimedia content will get lost under growing piles of paper, cassettes, videotapes, disks, phone messages, permissions and releases, cookie crumbs, photocopies and mail. Even in offices, where the floors are swept every morning, you are bound to loose some important paper which accidentally drops in the night. You must forget about time management. A project which you estimate to complete in 24 hours would normally take 48 hours. You will need time in abundance so that you are not racing against time, which would effect your output. Budgeting is another factor you should look into.

You cannot create a project all alone. It is very difficult though not impossible. You will need the help of other people. Multimedia is often a team effort: artwork is performed by graphic artists, video shoots by video producers, sound editing by audio producers and programming by programmers. You might have to do some dirty work like carrying things for others.

Let us look a look at the major factors like Hardware and Software. We would however discuss them in details in a later chapter.

1.2.5.1 Hardware

For all practical purposes we would be talking about PCs in general. This however, does not rule out the possibility of running the end product on any other computer. It can even be running on a TV with the help of a television set-top box such as Sega, Nintendo or Sony.

1.2.5.2 Operating System

When Windows is discussed in this book, it means Windows 95/98/ME/2000. The basic principles for creating and editing multimedia elements are the same for Apple Macintosh and PCs. A bitmap is a bitmap, a digitized sound is a digitized sound regardless of the methods or tools used to make and display it or play it back.

Indeed, many software tools readily convert picture, sound and other multimedia files (and even whole functioning projects) from Macintosh to Windows format, and vice versa, using known file formats or even binary compatible files that require no conversion at all. While there is a lot of talk about platform-independent delivery of multimedia on the Internet, with every new version of a browser there remain annoying failures on both platforms.

1.2.5.3 Software

Multimedia software tells the hardware what to do. Display the color red. Move that tiger three leaps to the left. Slide in the words "Now You've Done It!" from the right and blink them on and off. Play the sound of cymbals crashing. Run the digitized movie of Captain Hook. Turn down the volume on that MP3 file!

You do not have to be a programmer or a computer scientist to make multimedia work for you, but you do need some familiarity with terms and building blocks; even the simplest multimedia tools require an iota of knowledge to operate.

If someone sends you a file in Macintosh AIF format, you should know that you're getting digitalized sound. Then load up your tools and open the help files' your learning curve will be easier to manage because you have the bigger picture.

1.3 Web and Internet Multimedia Applications

Some time back, a publisher in New Delhi issued Model Test Papers of class XI and XII in the form of CD-ROMs. You had to put the CD in the computer and it would ask you the question. You have to replay choosing one of the options given there and the result would come on the screen immediately. It is another form of training. Though the concept is quite new in India, but, is catching up fast in other countries.

The teaching method is more and more interactive using the multimedia concepts and instead of teacher asking the questions the questions are asked by the computer and students have to reply on the computer itself by pressing various keys. Thus, the result is compiled on the spot.

1.3.1 Science and Technology

Over the years Multimedia with the help of Internet has taken the Science and Technology to a new height. An experiment being done in USA can be watched in India. Of course, if the surgeon allows it to be seen. Similarly all the new information is passed over the thousands of computers in few seconds, to keep every user know about it. I know of cases where doctors in India send x-ray and other reports to the corresponding doctors in USA via Internet and ask for the possible treatments.

The same thing happens in other spheres of research. All the possible research materials are shared. The most important part which the Multimedia and Internet have given to the mankind is the communication. It takes hardly few seconds to transfer the sound and graphics from one part of the world to another.

1.3.2 Kiosks

Kiosks are like booths, wherein you feed the data to get the information. These are very useful in places like Exhibitions, where you press a button to know where you are. All the relative informaton about the other places, which you can visit are shown along with maps, etc. We have one placed at Ashoka Hotel to help tourists know more about Delhi. Supposing you have to go to Karol Bagh from Ashoka Hotel, it would not just tell you the distance, but will also tell you the route and how much the Taxi and Scooter would charge.

In other countries similar types are available on railway stations, shopping malls, museums and grocery stores. These are stand-alone terminals or kiosks to provide information and help. Such installations reduce demand on traditional information booths and personnel, add value and they can work round the clock, even in the middle of the night, when live help is off duty.

1.3.3 Business

I am quite sure that you must have seen a sales conference of a company. if not atleast must have heard about it. There the speaker while talking about the sales has the various charts and graphs displayed on the board using the overhead projector. This becomes the part of the sales display and supports the figures given by the speaker. The same can now be done using the various facilities of the multimedia with graphs and sounds. The most common software used here is the presentation software from Microsoft named as Microsoft PowerPoint.

Multimedia is enjoying widespread use in training programs. The teacher replaces speaker in the above example. Flight attendants learn to manage international terrorism and security through simulation. Mechanics learn to repair engines. Sales people learn about product lines and leave behind software to train their customers. Fighter pilots practice full-terrain sorties before spooling up for the real thing.

1.3.4 Games

There is no limit to the number of games available in the market for playing on computers. These games are quite similar to the ones you see in so called Video Parlours. Most of them are interactive, i.e., they react to what you do or how you play. All of them are part of multimedia application, since all of them make good use of sound and graphics.

1.4 Transition from Conventional Media to Digital Media

Let us now learn about the Computer which you would need to create Multimedia. Not only computer, you also need software to match it too. You must use the software with which you are familiar. This will help you in saving time and energy. It is not that you would see the hardware which is needed now but you would also make mentally sure that the same would last atleast 3 years.

Let us look at the two major factors like Hardware and Software in little details.

1.4.1 Hardware

For all practical purposes we would be talking about Personal Computers in general. This, however, does not rule out the possibility of running the multimedia product on any other computer. It can even be running on a TV with the help of a television set-top box such as Sega, Nintendo or Sony. These are becoming popular overseas though have a little presence in India.

1.4.2 Software and Operating System

The most important software which a personal computer has, is Operating System. And the most popular operating system now-a-days is Windows. It is upto you to use the version which suits you the best since Windows XP is the latest, but other versions like Windows 95/98/ME/2000 are also available in the market.

A graphic is first converted into bitmaps in computer. Sound is converted to digitized sound. For these whichever tools you use would not make a difference since the end product is the same. Indeed, many software tools readily convert picture, sound and other multimedia files (and even whole functioning projects) from Macintosh to Windows format, and vice versa, using known file formats or even binary compatible files that require no conversion at all.

Multimedia software tells the hardware what to do. Display the colour red. Move that tiger three leaps to the left. Slide in the words "Now You've Done It!" from the right and blink them on and off. Play the sound of cannibals crashing. Run the digitized movie of Captain Hook. Turn down the volume on that MP3 file!

You do not have to be a programmer or a computer scientist to make multimedia work for you, but you do need some familiarity with terms and building blocks; even the simplest multimedia tool requires an iota of knowledge to operate. If someone sends you a file in Macintosh AIF format, you should know that you're getting digitalized sound. Then load up your tools and open the help files' learning curve. It will be easier to manage because you have the bigger picture.

1.4.3 OCR (Optical Character Recognition) Devices

It is not that you would be typing the text in all the cases. You may enter the text in computer by scanning it from the matter already available. In fact, while using scanner you can not even scan the text, but would scan the images too, which can be stored in the computer. For this you need to have what is called an OCR software, meaning Optical Character Reader software, which reads all the characters on the image character by character. OCR software turns bitmapped characters into electronically recognizable ASCII text.

A scanner is typically used to create the bitmap. Then the software breaks the bitmap into chunks according to whether it contains text or graphics, by examining the texture and density of areas of the bitmap and by detecting edges. The text areas of the image are then converted to ASCII characters using probability and expert system algorithms.

Most OCR applications claim about 99% accuracy when reading 8- to 30- point characters at 300 dpi and can reach processing speeds of about 150 characters per second. These programs, however, have difficulty in reading poor copies of originals where the edges of characters have bled; these and poorly received faxes in small print may yield more recognition errors than it is worthwhile to correct after the attempted recognition.

1.4.4 Touch-Screen

A touch screen registers input when a finger or other object comes in beams and ultrasonic acoustic waves. Infrared beams criss-cross the surface of the screen and when a light beam is broken, that location is recorded. It is widely used as Kiosks as mentioned in Chapter1.

1.4.5 Scanners

Whereas a keyboard, mouse or trackball requires manual input of data, scanners allow input of printed data. A scanner reads text, photographs and graphics from paper which are then converted into bit patterns for processing, storage or output. Scanner is a device that examines a spatial pattern one part after another and generates analog or digital signals corresponding to the pattern. Scanners are often used in mark sensing, pattern recognition or character recognition. Practically scanner uses light for examining the spatial patterns.

In a scanner, as the image is scanned, it is converted into light and dark picture elements, or pixels, similar to newspaper photo. Colour scanners can assign a specific colour to a pixel. The pixel are then stored as bit patterns. This technique makes the images usable by word processing, desktop publishing, and graphic packages.

There are two types of scanners, Hand-held scanner and Flat-bed scanner.

1.4.6 Hand-Held Scanner

These devices read data on price tags, shipping labels, inventory part number, book ISBNs, and the like. Hand-held scanner, sometimes called wand scanners, use either contact or laser technology.

It has a set of light emitting diodes. It is placed over the material to be scanned and slowly dragged from the top to the bottom. The light emitted by the diodes is not reflected by black lines and is reflected by whole areas. The material is converted and stored in a bitmap.

Typical applications are to store images and reproduce them in publications.

1.4.7 Flat-bed Scanner

It consists of a box with glass plate on top, which is used for placing the document to be scanned. The light beam is situated below the glass plate and is moved from left to right horizontally. After scanning one line the beam moves up little and scans the next line.

The scanner can also store colour images.

1.4.8 Digital Cameras

In recent years, source-data automation has expanded to allow the direct entry of graphic information, as well as text-based information via scanners. In a process called imaging, a scanner converts a drawing, a picture, or any document into computer- recognizable form by shinning a light on the image and sensing the intensity of the reflection at each point of the image.

That is, the hard-copy image is translated into an electronic format that can be interpreted by and stored on computers. The electronic version of the image can then be stored, probably on disk, and reproduced on the screen when needed. The image to be stored can be handwritten notes, a photograph, a drawing, an insurance form - anything that can be digitized. Once an image has been digitized and entered to the computer system, it can be retrieved, displayed, altered, merged with text, stored, and sent via data communications to one or several remote locations.

Businesses find imaging particularly useful for documents, since they can view an exact replica of the original document at any time. Professional photo agencies are the another area where imaging is useful. Here the film that was shot with a conventional camera is processed onto optical disk instead of prints or slides. Professional photo agencies keep thousands of images on file, ready to be leased for a fee. Typically a couple of dozen small-size images can be displayed on the screen at one time; a particular image can be enlarged to full screen size with a click of a mouse button.

A digital camera can store many more pictures than an ordinary camera, Pictures taken using a digital camera are stored inside its memory and can be transferred to a computer by connecting the camera to it. A digital camera takes pictures by converting the light passing through the lens at the front into a digital image. It does that by using a grid of tiny light sensors which convert the light that is falling on them into binary patterns of 0s and 1s. Different binary patterns are used to represent the different colours and shades of light that make up a picture. Pictures taken using a digital camera can be easily saved and transferred from one computer to another where they can be edited using special graphics software.

Some digital camera can also capture short clips of moving images but for longer video clips a digital video camera is needed. However, both of these types of camera are still quite expensive.

1.4.9 Speakers

Computers can output music, voices and many other complicated sounds using speakers. To be able to output sound a computer needs a special circuit board inside it called a sound card. Most PCs have at least one small speaker built into them which generates sound from the audio input signal generated by the sound card.

The quality and volume of the sound produced can be improved by connecting external speakers into a port at the back of the computer. Headphones can also be attached to this port so that any sound can only be heard by the person using the computer.

1.4.10 Printers

They are hardcopy output devices and can be divided into two distinct categories:

1. Impact Printers

2. Non-impact Printers

1.4.11 Impact Printers

A printer in which printing is the result of mechanically striking the printing medium is an impact printer. An impact printer makes contact with the paper to produce an image. The impact may be produced by a print hammer character, like that of a typewriter key striking a ribbon against the paper or by a print hammer hitting paper and ribbon against a character.

An impact printer must be used if printing a multiple copy report so that the duplicate copies will receive the imprint.

Impact printers are of following types:

1.4.11.1 Dot-Matrix Printer

In Dot Matrix Printer the individual characters are formed by a matrix of wires or styluses. Dot-matrix printers are also called serial printers. The images are formed by a print head that is composed of a series of little print hammers that look like the heads of pins. The print head usually has nine pins or 24 pines. The bottom 2 pins are used to form the descenders of lower case letters viz., p, q, g and y. Many expensive dot-matrix printers do not provide descenders, but print quality is improved when they are used.

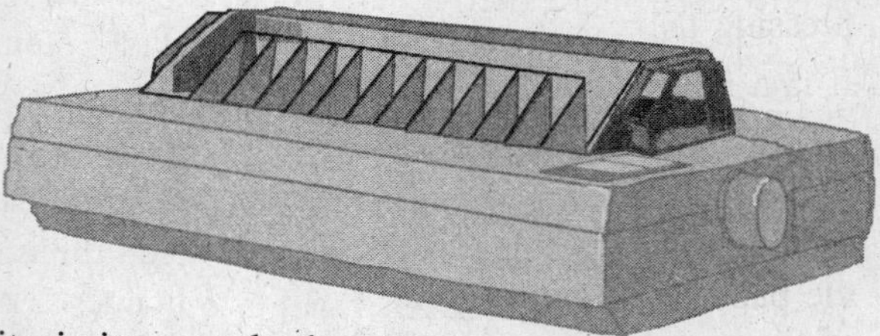

1.4.11.2 Daisywheel Printers

A serial impact printer in which the printing element is a plastic hub that has a large number of flexible radial spokes, each spoke having one or more different raised printing characters. The wheel is rotated as it is moved horizontally step by step under computer control, and stops when a desired character is in a desired print position so a hammer can drive that character against an inked ribbon.

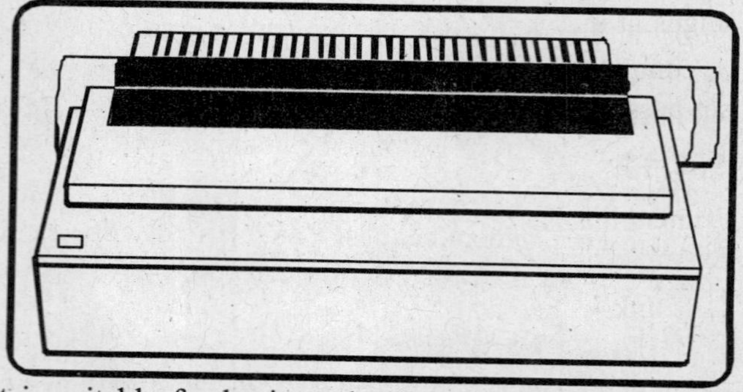

Daisy Wheel Printers are slower than dot-matrix printers, but they produce a high-resolution output. This high-resolution output is often called letter quality printing because it is suitable for business letters and memos. You can print in as many type fonts or foreign languages on a daisywheel printer as there are print wheels to fit your particular model of machine.

It is also called as a smart printer because of its bi-directional printing and built-in microprocessor control features.

1.4.11.3 Line Printers

It prints an entire line in a single operation without necessarily printing one character at a time. These are generally electro-mechanical devices which print complete lines of print up to 160 characters in width, at speeds about 300 to 2000 lines per minute. Line printers are used primarily in the mini/mainframe processing environment. Examples of line-at-a-time impact printers are:

1. Chain Printers
2. Band Printers and
3. Drum Printers

Chain Printers: It is a high-speed printer in which the type are carried by the links of a revolving chain. As the characters on the print chain revolve in a horizontal loop, a desired character eventually aligns in a given column. At this instant, the hammer strikes the paper forcing the page into the inked ribbon and the ribbon against the character thus creating the desired symbol on the print page. The chain is cycled continuously until a complete print line has been formed. The print page is then advanced one line and the process is repeated.

Band Printers: On a band printer, several similar sets of fully formed characters are embossed on a horizontal band that is continuously moving in front of the print hammers. In band printer, the paper is momentarily stopped and, as the desired character passes over a given column, the hammer activates, pressing the ribbon against the paper to form the image.

It is a line printer that uses band of type characters as its printing mechanism.

Drum printers or (Barrel Printers): A printer in which all the characters for printing are placed round the surface of a cylinder (the barrel), the entire character set being placed round the cylinder at each print position. Print hammers opposite each print position can be activated by the computer striking the paper and bringing it in contact with a continuous ink ribbon between the paper and the surface of the barrel. The barrel rotates at high speed, the appropriate character being selected as it reaches a position immediately opposite the print hammers.

A drum printer uses 80 or more character sets embossed on a cylindrical drum. A separate hammer for each character set forces the print page into an inked ribbon and the character when the character aligns at the print position.

A complete line of output is printed for each revolution of the drum since all the characters in each set pass their print stations during revolution.

1.4.12 Non-Impact Printers

Printers that do not strike characters against ribbon or paper when they print, are non-impact printers. Example of non-impact printers include

1. Ink-jet printers
2. Laser printers

These printers make much less noise than impact printers. If you are using a non-impact printer, do not try to print on multiple-part carbon forms: because no impact is being made on the paper, you will end up with no copies.

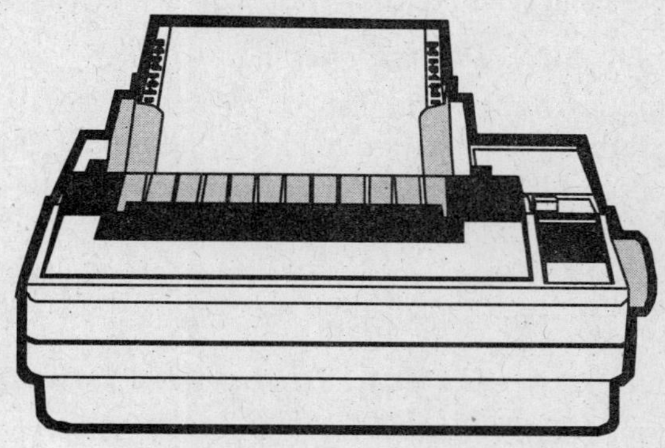

1.4.12.1 Ink-jet Printers

It uses a technique of projecting droplets of ink at paper to form the required image. Ink-jet printer creates an image directly on paper by spraying ink through as many as 64 tiny nozzles. It provides a print resolution of around 360 dots per inch.

1.4.12.2 Laser Printers

The physical properties of LASERS (Light Amplification by Stimulate Emission of Radiation) allows for the very precise positioning of narrow beam of light, transferring a high energy source to a very small area. This property is used to control printing, i.e., laser printers, to read information from bar codes and to read and write information in optical storage devices.

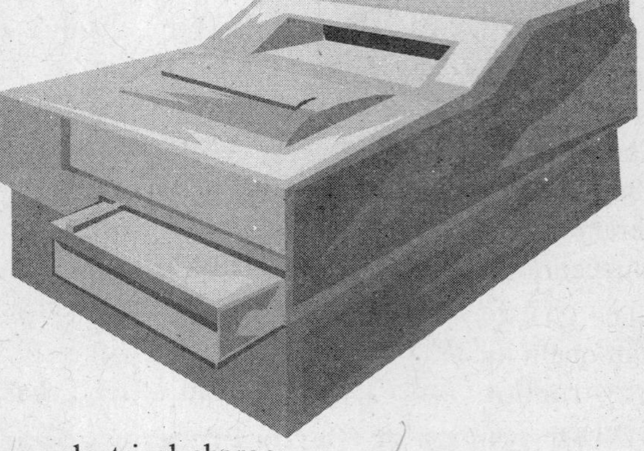

Laser printer is a non-impact printer that creates, by means of a laser beam directed on a photosensitive surface, a latent image which is then made visible by a toner and transferred and fixed on paper.

A separate computer is built into the printer to interpret the data that it receives from the computer and to control the laser. Just as electron gun in a graphic monitor can target any pixel, the laser in a laser printer can aim at any point on a drum creating an electrical charge.

Toner which is composed of tiny particles of oppositely charged ink, sticks to the drum in the places the laser has charged. Thus, with pressure and heat, the toner is transferred off the drum to paper. Also laser printers contain special memory to store the images they print. The resolution of laser printers is 600 DPI both horizontally and vertically; some high-end models have resolution of 1200 DPI.

1.4.13 Plotters

It is an output unit that directly produces a hard copy record of data on a removable medium, in the form of a two-dimensional graphic representation. Plotters are designed to produce large drawings or images such as construction plans for buildings or blueprints for mechanical objects.

There are two major types of pen plotters:

1. Flatbed plotters
2. Drum plotters

1.4.13.1 Flatbed Plotters

It uses a bed or tray to hold paper in a fixed position. A movable pen is usually held by a single arm that can move the pen both horizontally and vertically. The computer instructs the flatbed plotter by directing the pen to x-y position on the page.

1.4.13.2 Drum Plotter

It has a single arm that can only move across the drum horizontally. The drum itself moves the paper forward or backward to enable the pen to draw in any vertical direction. Any type of diagonal line is drawn by combining a horizontal movement of the pen arm with a vertical page movement via the drum.

Drum plotters are used to produce continuous output, such as plotting earthquake activity, or for long graphic output, such as the structural view of a 'skyscraper'.

1.4.14 Optical Disks and Drivers as CDROM and DVD

Introduced in 1980 for stereo buffs, the extraordinarily successful compact disk, is an optical disk designed to enhance the reproduction of recorded music. To make a CD recording, the analog sounds of music are translated into their digital equivalents and stored on a 5.25 inches optical disk. In fact, anything that can be digitized can be stored on optical disk: data, text, voice, still pictures, music, graphics, and video.

CD-ROM (Compact disk-read only memory) a spinoff of audio CD technology, is created at a mastering facility, just as audio CDs are created at a recording studio. The master copy is duplicated or "pressed" at the studio to distribute large amounts of data, such as an online encyclopedia or multimedia presentations. Computer programs and associated user manuals are often distributed on CD-ROMs video sequences and library references are also recorded for educational applications.

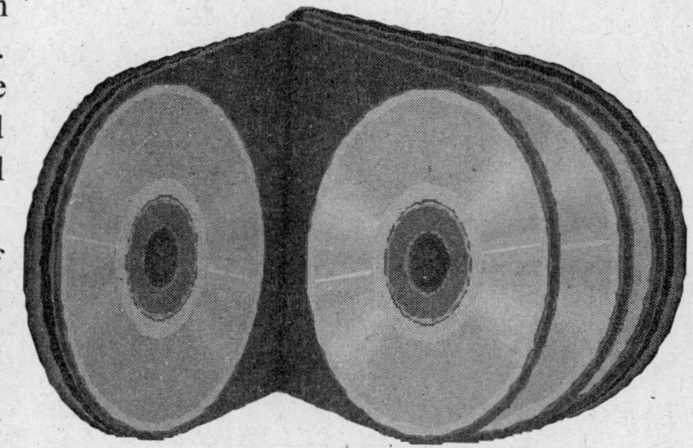

Since CD-ROMs have the capacity to hold lots of high-quality images, this type of storage is well suited for structural drawings used by architects and engineers. Unlike an audio CD player, however, a CD-ROM drive is nearly devoid of buttons and LCD readouts, excepts for a button to load and unload a disk and few lights to tell you when the drive is reading a disk or playing music. The drive is controlled by a software in your PC that sends instructions to controller circuitry that is either a part of the computer's motherboard or on a separate board installed in an expansion slot.

Over the year CD-ROM drive performance has improved as the hardware technology provided faster access speeds. The original single-speed 150 KBps CD-ROM drives are now considerably obsolete. Double-speed 2x(300 KBps) and quad-speed 4x(600 KBps) CD-ROM drives currently offer the best performance for the price, with access speeds at 300 msec or less.

Faster drives viz., 6x and 8x (1.2 MBps) are on the drawing board multimedia disks. The most demanding CD-ROMs of all, are written only for 2x or 4x drives. So going faster won't increase the performance of video and audio until multimedia software titles are written specifically for the faster CD-ROM drives. This is no doubt the latest and the best medium for storing data.

Though they look very similar to music CDs, so to differentiate from them, the computer ones are called CD-ROMs. They are round in shape and are about 5" in diameter. Till recently they used to be Read Only but now writeable CDs are also available with the relevant drives to write on them. With capacity to write data of about 600 floppies, it has become very popular over the recent times.

In the form of videodisks or compact disks (CDs), optical disks represent a new trend in small, high-capacity storage of images and sound. A single optical disk stores nearly 1 GB of data on one side. To put this storage capacity into perspective, an optical disk can hold 800 television quality images or 60 minutes of high fidelity music.

The explosive growth in storage needs has driven the computer industry to provide cheaper, more versatile storage devices with greater capacity. New storage technologies using optical disks exceed the storage capacities currently available with magnetic disks of the same size. Optical storage techniques used by computers are basically the same as those used to record music on compact disks.

Optical disks differ from magnetic disk storage by the way data is stored and read from the storage media. A laser beam is used to write and read data on these reflective disks, so they are also known as laser disks. In this technology a laser hits a layer of metallic material spread over the surface of a disk. When data is being entered heat from the laser produces tiny spots on the disk surface. To read the data, the laser scans the disk, and a lens picks up different light reflections from the various spots.

Optical disks are becoming a very inviting option for users. They are less sensitive to environmental fluctuations, and they provide more direct-access storage at a cost that is much less per megabyte of storage than the magnetic disk alternative.

Optical disk technology is still emerging and has yet to stabilize; however, at present there are three different types of optical disks in common use:

read-only

recordable, and

erasable.

1.4.15 Digital Versatile Disc (DVD)

Nine major electronics companies (Toshiba, Matsushita, Sony, Philips, Time Warner, Pioneer, JVC, Hitachi and Mitsubishi Electric) have agreed to formulate optical disc technology for distribution of multimedia and feature-length movies called DVD, as per the following specifications.

DVD Features	***DVD Specifications***
Disc diameter	120 mm (5 inches)
Disc thickness	1.2 mm (0.6 mm thick disc x 2)
Memory capacity	4.7 gigabytes/single side
Track pitch	0.74 micrometer
Wave length of laser diode	650 nanometer/635 nanometer
Numerical aperture (NA)	0.6
Error correction	RS-PC (Reed Solomon Product Code)
Signal modulation	8-16
Data transfer rate	Variable speed data transfer at an average rate of 4.69 mega bits/second for image and sound
Image compression	MPEG2 digital image compression
Audio	Dolby AC-3 (5.1 ch), LPCM for NTSC and MPEG Audio, LPCM for PAL/SECAM (a maximum of 8 audio channels and 32 subtitle channels can be stored)
Running time (movies)	133 minutes a side (at an average data rate of 4.69 mega bits/second for image and sound, including three audio channels and four subtitle channels)
File management structure	Micro UDF and ISO-9660

With the new medium capable not only of gigabyte storage capacity but also full-motion video (MPEG2) and high-quality audio in surround sound, the bar has again risen for multimedia developers. Commercial multimedia projects will become more expensive to produce as consumers' performance expectations rise. There are two types of DVD-DVD Video and DVD-ROM; these reflect marketing channels, not the technology.

DVD can provide 720 pixels per horizontal line, whereas current televisions (NTSC) provide 240 — television pictures will be sharper and more detailed. With Dolby AC-3 Digital Surround Sound as part of the specification, six discrete subwoofer channel, developers can program the low-frequency doom and gloom music popular with Hollywood. DVD also supports Dolby Pro-Logic Surround Sound, standard stereo and mono audio.

Users can randomly access any section of the disc and use the slow-motion and freeze-frame features during movies. Audio tracks can be programmed for as many as 8 different languages, with graphic subtitles in 32 languages. Some manufacturers such as Toshiba are already providing parental control features in their players.

1.4.16 Multimedia Networks

There are five basic types of communication network that are used to provide multimedia communication services:

1. Telephone networks
2. Data networks
3. Broadcast television networks
4. Integrated services digital networks
5. Broadband multiservice networks.

As the name signifies, the first three network types were initially designed to provide just a single type of service: telephony, data communications and broadcast television respectively. The last two network types, however, were designed from the outset to provide multiple services. In the case of the first three network types, the technological developments have enabled them to provide additional services.

1.4.16.1 Telephone networks

Public switched telephone networks have been in existence for many years and have gone through many changes during this time. They were designed to provide a basic switched telephone service which, with the advent of the other network types, has become known as a plain old telephone service or POTS.

The term "switched" is used to indicate that a subscriber can make a call to any other telephone that is connected to the total network. Initially, such networks spanned just a single country but later the telephone networks of different countries were interconnected so that they now provide an international switched service.

1.4.16.2 Data networks

Data networks were designed to provide basic data communication services such as electronic mail (e-mail) and general file transfers. The user equipment connected to these networks, therefore, is computer such as a PC, a workstation, or an email/file server. The two most widely deployed networks of this type are the X.25 network and the Internet. Because of its operational mode, however, the X.25 network is restricted to relatively low bit rate data applications and hence is unsuitable for most multimedia applications.

1.4.16.3 Broadcast television networks

Broadcast television networks were designed to support the diffusion of analog television (and radio) program throughout wide geographical areas. In the case of a large town or city, the broadcast medium is normally a cable distribution network while for larger areas, a satellite network or sometimes terrestrial broadcast network is used.

Since their introduction, digital television services have become available with these networks which, together with a low bit rate return channel for interaction purposes, provide a range of additional services such as games playing and home shopping.

1.4.16.4 Integrated services digital networks

Integrated services digital networks started to be deployed in the early 1980s and were originally designed to provide PSTN users with the capability of having additional services. This was achieved firstly, by converting the access circuits that connect user equipment to the network — a telephone for example — into an all-digital form and secondly, by providing two separate communication channels over these circuits.

These allow users either to have two different telephone calls in progress simultaneously or two different calls such as a telephone call and a data call.

1.4.16.5 Broadband multiservice networks

Broadband multiservice networks were designed in the mid-1980s for use as public switched networks to support a wide range of multimedia communication applications. The term broadband was used to indicate the circuits associated with a call could have bit rates in excess of the maximum bit rate of 2 Mbps — 30x64 kbps — provided by an ISDN.

As such, they were designed to be an enhanced ISDN and hence were called broadband integrated services digital networks or B-ISDN. Also, for the same reason, an ISDN is sometimes referred to as narrowband ISDN or N-ISDN.

1.5 Transition from Conventional Media to Digital Media

We have the music all around us. Even the animals sometimes make sound in the form of music. Though of the birds are known to have musical notes. Their sound, specially made in the morning, is very pleasing to the ears. You can hear music from various types of speakers, attached to your Tape recorders, TV, or even to the music station. When a music is coming out of the speakers the surrounding atmospheric air is actually compressed or decompressed at various rates depending up on the source signal, and this process carries the sound through the media from the source to the destination.

Without going into the various frequency details at this stage, it can be said that at any point of time, only two states can be represented by computer, viz., low level (zeros) and high level (ones). These signals are called digital signals. When the original analog light waves of an image or sound waves of a sound are sampled and converted to binary digits is called digitization. Traditional multimedia systems us specialized equipment that records sounds and graphics in an analog format such as cassette tapes, records, or video cassette tapes. Analog equipment relies on waves to record information such as sounds or video. Technology has changed the hardware used to develop multimedia from the traditional analog equipment tocomputer-based or digital multimedia systems. Digital systems sample analog waves and convert them into a series of numbers, 0s and 1s (digital) for processing by a computer.

Let us Revise

1. Multimedia combines text, sound and video to give multimedia projects.
2. Hypertext is where the text of the document is linked in between for an easy access.
3. Hypergraphics allows students to easily interact with their teachers.
4. Animation is created using frames and running them.
5. Multimedia is quite widely used for teaching and training.
6. Technology has used text and graphics to make communication easy.
7. Multimedia is used to create Kiosks.
8. Multimedia is widely used to create Games.
9. Personal Computers are mainly used for creating multimedia applications.
10. Hardware to be used for multimedia should be such that you are not short of memory or hard disk space.
11. Software used be the one which you are familiar with.
12. Sound files are available in computer under Windows.
13. You can create your own sound and save it in your computer.
14. MIDI means Musical Instrument Digital Interface.
15. Digital format is more in use now.
16. For video you can use available video clips or shoot your own.
17. OCR reads the characters and saves them as text in ASCII format.
18. Touch screen allows you to get information by just touching the screen.
19. There are two types of scanners: Hand-held and Flat-bed.
20. Digital cameras are used to take digital pictures which can be transferred to computers.
21. Speakers can be used to get the sound from the computer.
22. Printers are mainly of two types: Impact and Non-impact.
23. Plotters can be used to plot the information.
24. DVD means Digital Versatile Disc.
25. Among the types of multimedia networks in use are: Telephone networks, Broadcast television networks, Integrated services digital networks and Broadband multiservice networks.

Multiple Choice Questions

1. Of the following which is not used in Multimedia:

   (a) text (b) sound (c) odour
   (d) video.

2. In Animation, you run ________ at a very high speed.

   (a) frames (b) text (c) sound
   (d) food.

3. Hypertext allows you to have _________ from one section to another.

   (a) animation (b) anchors (c) games.

4. Multimeida Kiosks are like _________.

   (a) Touch screen (b) Keyboard (c) Mouse

   (d) Speaker.

5. Video Parlours have multimedia ________.

   (a) Text (b) Games.

6. DVD is a :

   (a) sound device. (b) optical disk. (c) video device.

7. You can add your own sound to the computer.

   (a) Yes. (b) No.

8. For putting the printed text to the computer, besides keyboard, we use:

   (a) monitor. (b) mouse. (c) OCR.

9. A touch screen is like a:

   (a) Kiosks. (b) Printer. (c) Keyboard.

10. Sound format more in use now-a-days is:

    (a) MIDI. (b) Digital.

11. Popular operating system these days is:

    (a) DOS. (b) Windows.

12. NTSC is a _________ format.

    (a) sound (b) video (c) text

13. CD ROMs are high-density memory devices.

    (a) Yes (b) No

14. Data on the CD-ROM will be affected by humidity and dust.

    (a) True (b) False

15. Laser beam is used to store data on CD-ROM/

    (a) True (b) False

True/False Questions

1. Hypertext is where the text of the document is linked in between for an easy access.
2. Animation is created using frames and running them.
3. Technology has used text and graphics to make communication difficult.
4. Multimedia is widely used to create Games.
5. Hardware to be used for multimedia should be such that you are not short of memory or hard disk space.
6. Sound files are not available in computer under Windows.
7. MIDI means Musical Instrument Digital Interface.
8. For video you can use available video clips or shoot your own.
9. Touch screen does not allow you to get information by just touching the screen.
10. Digital cameras are used to take digital pictures which can be transferred to computers.
11. Printers are mainly of two types: Impact and Non-impact.
12. DVD means Digital Verify Disc.

Matching Columns

In the following case, commands are given in the left hand columns and their actions in the right hand column. Match them.

Column A	Column B
A. Graphics	1. Combination of more than one media
B. Text	2. High speed printer using laser beam
C. CD-ROM	3. Optical Character Reader
D. Multimedia	4. Public places information provider
E. Laser Printer	5. Line drawing and images
F. OCR	6. Moving images
G Multimedia Kiosks	7. Alpha numeric characters
H. Animation	8. Optical disk to store data

Fill in the Blanks with appropriate words

a. Graphics b. Microphone c. Multimedia d. OCR!
e. Dot Matrix Printer

1. Computer activity where more than one media is involved is called ________________.
2. Printer which uses dots to print characters is called ________________.
3. Sound is recorded through ______________.
4. Text having line drawings and images is called _______________.
5. Device which converts text into computer media is called ________________.

Descriptive Type Questions

1. What do you understand by Multimedia?
2. Define the terms: Hypertext and Hypergraphics.
3. What is the process of Animation?
4. How is multimedia used in Education and Training?
5. How is multimedia used in Science and Technology?
6. What role does multimedia play in development of games?
7. What is Flight Simulator?
8. What type of Hardware and Software is used for creating Multimedia?
9. What are sound files known as?
10. What is the difference between MIDI and Digital sound formats?
11. What is OCR used for?
12. What is the use of scanners?
13. How is Digital Camera used?
14. Describe the various types of printers used.
15. Describe the various types of multimedia networking used.
16. What is the use of Touch screen?

17. Describe the various types of Optical disks available?
18. Describe the working of speakers.

Answers to Objective Type Questions

Multiple Choice Questions

1. c	2. a	3. b	4. a
5. b	6. b	7. a	8. c
9. a	10. b	11. b	12. b.
13. a	14. b	15. a	

True False Questions

1. T	2. T	3. F	4. T
5. T	6. F	7. T	8. T
9. F	10. T	11. T	12. F

Matching Columns

A. 5	B. 7	C. 8	D. 1
E. 2	F. 3	G 4	H. 6

Fill in the Blanks

1. c	2. e	3. b	4. a
5. d			

Computer Fonts and Hypertext

2

2.1 Usuage of text in Multimedia

Alphanumeric characters are used to present information in the text form. By alphanumeric I mean that characters are either Alpha (i.e., from a to z) or Numeric (i.e., from 1 to 9). In computer most of the files are text files or graphic files. Multimedia uses both and sometimes even combines them to make the presentation look more attractive. Text can be of various types such as plaintext, formatted text, and hypertext.

2.1.1 Plain Text

It is the unformatted text, consisting of fixed sized characters from a limited character set, all having the same type of appearance.

2.1.2 Formatted Text

It is the text where appearance of text can be changed using font parameters, i.e., bold, italics, underlined varying shapes, sizes and coolurs, etc. The text of the book for example.

2.1.3 Hypertext

How do you read a book, for example, this one. Chapter by chapter, page by page. While you are on page 43, do you have any idea what is there on page 28. No. The solution to this lies in linkage which is provided by Hypertext. Thus, Hypertext is a process which puts links or anchors, as they are called, for easy accessing to another page while reading one page.

It may not be very clear here, since these things do not happen in the printed book like this one, which you are reading. But, it is very common in web pages. There while on a page, you can refer to any other page by just a click, using so called Anchors.

Let us see how it is done. While publishing material on the web site page, the information is divided into various small "chunks". These are called nodes. Then links are put into these nodes. These links in the language of the web are called Hyperlinks. The process of finding a node among other nodes is called Browsing, which is sometimes referred for searching on the net. What are you doing? Browsing the Internet. That is you are searching something on the Internet. The World Wide Web (WWW) is a hypertext system accepted throughout the World.

Hypertext applications are particularly useful while working with massive amounts of text such as encyclopaedias and multi volume case law reports .

2.2 Families and Faces of Fonts

Fonts are typically measured in a unit specific to the printing industry called the point. A point (abbreviated "pt") is the traditional printer's typographer's unit for specifying the size of fonts, the spacing between adjacent lines and the thickness of rules – among other things. It is still used a log, although some countries and some publishers now prefer to use the metric system (specifically the millimeter – mm – and centimeter – cm). CSS uses only the Anglo-American point. It does so because that point's value is in between the other two values. Also, it conforms to the point size used in PostScript printers, the most common type of printer.

To understand how type is sized, you first need some information about what makes up a letter. The x-height is the size of the body or main part of the letter and is approximately equal to the height of the x of the font. The ascender is that part of the lowercase letter that extends above the x-height. The descender is that part of the lowercase letter that extends below the x-height.

The size of type is usually obtained by measuring from roughly the top of its ascenders to the bottom of its descenders. (In the days of metal type, the font size was the size of the letter body). The measurement is expressed in points. The difference of a point is more noticeable in smaller sizes than in larger sizes. Text type, used for running text, is generally 14pt or less. Common sizes are 10 pt and 12 pt. Display type, type used for headings, is generally bigger than 14pt.

2.2.1 Length units

The point unit is the traditional measurement of length is typography, but not always the best for Web design. CSS accepts a range of different units which fall into three categories.

- absolute units – this category includes the point unit described above as well as other units (mm, cm, in, pc) which describe physical distances that can be measured with a measuring band.
- relative units – these units describe distances relative to other distances. The "em" unit, is the foremost member of this group which also includes the ";ex" unit.
- the pixel unit – the pixel unit as defined in CSS, forms a group of its own since it has some unique characteristics. On normal computer screens, the pixel unit will do what you expect. On printers and other high-resolution devices it will do what you hope!

The three groups their units are described in more detail below. Common for all the units is the way they are combined with numbers to form values.

2.2.2 Absolute units

An absolute unit is a unit of measure that specifies a fixed length – a length which can be measured with a measuring band. The units are:

- **`millimeter:mm`**
- **`centimeter: command (1cm = 10 mm)`**
- **`inch: in (1in = 25.4mm)`**
- **`point: pt (72pt = 1 in)`**
- **`pica: pc (1pc = 12pt)`**

The mm and command units come from the metric system of measurements. The other units are all defined as fraction of an inch. A pica is 12 pints. Six picas equal one inch. Absolute units have limited usefulness because they cannot be scaled. In general, they should only be used if you know the physical properties of the output medium. For example, if you write a style sheet for a document you know will only be printed on A4-sized paper, absolute units may be the right choice. In most cases, however, you will be better off using relative units.

2.2.3 Relative units

A relative unit is a unit of measure that specifies a value that is relative to the font size. There are two relative units in CSS: "em" and "ex". Usually the font size they refer to is the font size of the element itself. (The only exception is the font-size property, which we discuss later in the chapter where the value scales to the font size of the element's parent.) Relative units have the advantage over absolute unit sin that they scale automatically. When you choose a different font, all properties that were expressed in em or ex don't have to be changed. The em unit was heavily promoted earlier and we will not repeat all the good arguments for using the em unit here, but merely state the facts. In CSS, the em is exactly equal to the font size (i.e. the height of the font). For example, in a 12pt font, the em is 12pt wide, while in a 15pt font the em is 15pt wide.

The ex unit is also relative to the font size but in a different way. It is called "ex" because it is defined as the x-height. The em can be set explicitly in CSS1, but the ex is a characteristic of the font, so it cannot be set explicitly. This means you can determine how big it is only by inspecting the font. For example, Times Roman has a relatively large ex (x-height) compared to Baskerville. So even though a 12pt Times Roman and a 12 pt Baskerville both have an em of 12pt, their ex values will vary because their x-heights vary. Times Roman's will be somewhat larger than Baskerville's.

2.2.4 The pixel unit

The term pixel is derived from Picture Element. The pixel is the smallest element on a video display screen, such as a computer monitor or a television. It also applies to the output from certain types of printers, such as laser printers. The pixel unit in CSS is based on pixels, but is slightly more refined than the name implies. On computer screen, the pixel unit behaves as you expect it to. Consider these two rules:

```
H1 { border-width: 4px }
H2 { border-width: 3px }
```

In the example above, the width of the border surrounding H1 element is set to four pixels and the border around H2 elements is set to three pixels. On a normal computer screen, these values will be used as specified. That is the border around H1 elements will actually be four pixels wide and the border around H2 elements will be three pixels wide. Another seemingly obvious fact is that the H1 border will be exactly one pixel thicker than the H2 border.

2.2.5 Stroke-based fonts

A glyph's outline is defined by the vertices of individual strokes and stroke's profile. Its advantages over outline fonts include reducing number of vertices needed to define a glyph, allowing the same

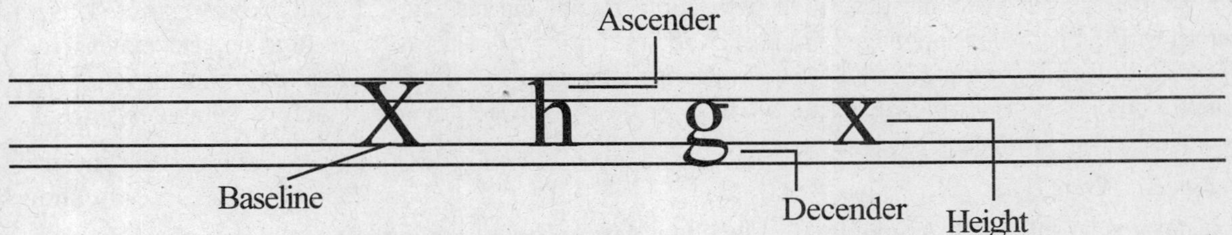

vertices to be used to generate a font with a different weight, glyph width, or serifs using different stroke rules, and the associated size savings.

For a font developer, editing a glyph by stroke is easier and less prone to error than editing outlines. A stroke-based system also allows scaling glyphs in height or width without altering stroke thickness of the base glyphs. Stroke-based fonts are heavily marketed for East Asian markets for use on embedded devices, but the technology is not limited to ideograms.

Commercial developers included Agfa Monotype (iType), Type Solutions, Inc. (owned by Bitstream Inc.) (Font Fusion (FFS), btX2), Fontworks (Gaiji Master), which have independently developed stroke-based font types and font engines.

Although Monotype and Bitstream have claimed tremendous space saving using stroke-based fonts on East Asian character sets, most of the space saving comes from building composite glyphs, which is part of the TrueType specification and does not require stroke-based approach.

The various formats supported by are:

Bold

Italics

Underline

These are the main styles and we had earlier used them in our letter. But, if you go deep into the working of the software, you would see that it allow you to convert the character to:

Strikethrough

Double strikethrough

Superscript

Subscript

Shadow

Outline

Emboss

Engrave

Small Caps

All Caps

Hidden

2.2.6 Font formats

2.2.6.1 Type 1 and Type 3 fonts

Type 1 and Type 3 fonts were developed by Adobe for professional digital typesetting. Using PostScript, the glyphs are outline fonts described with cubic Bezier curves. Type 1 fonts were restricted to a subset of the PostScript language, and used Adobe's hinting system, which used to be very expensive. Type 3 allowed unrestricted use of the PostScript language, but didn't include any hint information, which could lead to visible rendering artifacts on low-resolution devices (such as computer screens and dot-matrix printers).

2.2.6.2 TrueType font

TrueType is a font system originally developed by Apple, Inc. It was intended to replace Type 1 fonts, which many felt were too expensive. Unlike Type 1 fonts, TrueType glyphs are described with quadratic Bezier curves. It is currently very popular and implementations exist for all major operating systems.

2.2.6.3 OpenType font

OpenType is a smartfont system designed by Adobe and Microsoft. OpenType fonts contain outlines in either the TrueType or Type 1 (actually CFF) format together with a wide range of metadata.

2.2.6.4 METAFONT

METAFONT uses a different sort of glyph description. Like TrueType, it is a vector font description system. It draws glyphs using strokes produced by moving a polygonal or elliptical pen approximated by a polygon along a path made from cubic Bézier splines and straight line segments, or by filling such paths. Although when stroking a path the envelope of the stroke is never actually generated, the method causes no loss of accuracy or resolution.

This is a Proportional font

This is a courier font

This is an Ornamental font

This is Sans serif font

This is Serif font

2.3 Outline Fonts

Outline fonts or vector fonts are collections of vector images, i.e. a set of lines and curves to define the border of glyphs. Early vector fonts were used by vector monitors and vector plotters using their own internal fonts, usually with thin single strokes instead of thick outlined glyphs. The advent of desktop publishing brought the need for a universal standard to integrate the graphical user interface of the first Macintosh and laser printers. The term to describe the integration technology was WYSIWYG (What You See Is What You Get). The universal standard was (and still is) Adobe PostScript. Examples are PostScript Type 1 and Type 3 fonts, TrueType and OpenType.

The primary advantage of outline fonts is that they can be easily transformed by applying a mathematical function to each vector point, scaling them without causing pixellation. Outline font characters can be scaled to any size and otherwise transformed with more attractive results than bitmap fonts, but requires considerably more processing and may yield undesirable rendering, depending on the font, rendering software, and output size.

The following examples would show how the font size make the difference:

A	**12 point**
A	**16 point**
A	**20 point**
A	**24 point**
A	**30 point**
A	**40 point**
A	**48 point**

Outline fonts have a major problem, in that Bézier curves cannot be rendered accurately onto a raster display (such as most computer monitors and printers), and their rendering can change shape depending on the desired size and position. Measures such as font hinting have to be used to reduce the visual impact of this problem, which require sophisticated software that is difficult to implement correctly. Many modern desktop computer systems include software to do this, but they use considerably more processing power than bitmap fonts, and there can be minor rendering defects, particularly at small font sizes. Despite this, they are frequently used because people often consider the processing time and defects to be acceptable when compared to the ability to scale fonts freely.

2.4 Bitmap Fonts

A computer font (or font) is an electronic data file containing a set of glyphs, characters, or symbols such as dingbats. Although the term font first referred to a set of metal type sorts in one style and size, since the 1990s most fonts are digital, used on computers.

There are three basic kinds of computer font file data formats:

- Bitmap fonts consist of a series of dots or pixels representing the image of each glyph in each face and size.
- Outline fonts (also called vector fonts) use Bézier curves, drawing instructions and mathematical formulae to describe each glyph, which make the character outlines scalable to any size.
- Stroke fonts use a series of specified lines and additional information to define the profile, or size and shape of the line in a specific face, which together describe the appearance of the glyph.

Bitmap fonts are faster and easier to use in computer code, but inflexible, requiring a separate font for each size. Outline and stroke fonts can be resized using a single font and substituting different measurements for components of each glyph, but are somewhat more complicated to use than bitmap fonts as they require additional computer code to render the outline to a bitmap for display on screen or in print.

A bitmap image can be displayed in a different size only with some distortion, but renders quickly; outline or stroke image formats are resizable but take more time to render as pixels must be drawn from scratch each time they are displayed.

Fonts are designed and created using font editors. Fonts specifically designed for the computer screen and not printing are known as screenfonts.

An assortment of bitmap fonts from the first version of the Macintosh operating system.

A bitmap font is one that stores each glyph as an array of pixels (that is, a bitmap). It is less commonly known as a raster font. Bitmap fonts are simply collections of raster images of glyphs. For each variant of the font, there is a complete set of glyph images, with each set containing an image for each character. For example, if a font has three sizes, and any combination of bold and italic, then there must be 12 complete sets of images.

Advantages of bitmap fonts include:

* Extremely fast and simple to render
* Unscaled bitmap fonts always give exactly the same output
* Easier to create than other kinds.

The primary disadvantage of bitmap fonts is that the visual quality tends to be poor when scaled or otherwise transformed, compared to outline and stroke fonts, and providing many optimized and purpose-made sizes of the same font dramatically increases memory usage. The earliest bitmap fonts were only available in certain optimized sizes such as 8, 9, 10, 12, 14, 18, 24, 36, 48, 72, and 96 points, with custom fonts often available in only one specific size, such as a headline font at only 72 points.

The limited processing power and memory of early computer systems forced exclusive use of bitmap fonts. Improvements in hardware have allowed them to be replaced with outline or stroke fonts in cases where arbitrary scaling is desirable, but bitmap fonts are still in common use in embedded systems and other places where speed and simplicity are considered important.

Bitmap fonts are used in the Linux console, the Windows recovery console, and embedded systems. Older dot matrix printers used bitmap fonts; often stored in the memory of the printer and addressed by the computer's print driver. Dot matrix printers are still used on carbon paper business forms. Bitmap fonts may be used in cross-stitch.

To draw a string using a bitmap font, means to successively output bitmaps of each character that the string comprises, performing per-character indentation. Also true type fonts, bitmap fonts can be monospaced (i.e.. every character is plotted a constant distance from the previous character that it is next to, while drawing) or proportional (each character has its own width). However, the particular font-handling application determines how each font will be displayed.

2.4.1 Monochrome fonts vs. fonts with shades of gray

Digital bitmap fonts (and the final rendering of vector fonts) may use monochrome or shades of gray. The latter is anti-aliased. When displaying a text, typically an operating system properly represents the "shades of gray" as intermediate colors between the color of the font and that of the background.

However, if the text is represented as an image with transparent background, "shades of gray" require an image format allowing partial transparency.

2.4.2 Scaling

Bitmap fonts look best at their native pixel size. Some systems using bitmap fonts can create some font variants algorithmically. For example, the original Apple Macintosh computer could produce bold by widening vertical strokes and oblique by shearing the image. At non-native sizes, many text rendering systems perform nearest-neighbor resampling, introducing ugly jagged edges. More advanced systems perform anti-aliasing on bitmap fonts whose size does not match the size that the application requests. This technique works well for making the font smaller but not as well for increasing the size, as it tends to blur the edges. Some graphics systems that use bitmap fonts, especially those of emulators, apply curve-sensitive nonlinear resampling algorithms such as 2xSaI or hq3x on fonts and other bitmaps, which avoids blurring the font while introducing little objectionable distortion at moderate increases in size.

The difference between bitmap fonts and outline fonts is similar to the difference between bitmap and vector image file formats. Bitmap fonts are like image formats such as Windows Bitmap (.bmp), Portable Network Graphics (.png) and Tagged Image Format (.tif or .tiff), which store the image data as a grid of pixels, in some cases with compression. Outline or stroke image formats such as Windows Metafile format (.wmf) and Scalable Vector Graphics format (.svg), store instructions in the form of lines and curves of how to draw the image rather than storing the image itself.

A "trace" program can follow the outline of a high-resolution bitmap font and create an initial outline that a font designer uses to create an outline font useful in systems such as PostScript or TrueType. Outline fonts scale easily without jagged edges or blurriness.

2.4.3 Bitmap font formats

A bitmap color font for the Amiga OS.

- Portable Compiled Font (PCF)
- Glyph Bitmap Distribution Format (BDF)
- Server Normal Format (SNF)
- DECWindows Font (DWF)
- Sun X11/NeWS format (BF, AFM)
- Microsoft Windows bitmapped font (FON)
- Amiga Font, ColorFont, AnimFont
- ByteMap Font (BMF)
- PC Screen Font (PSF)

2.5 International Character Sets and Hypertext

Pronounced "ass-key." It is a binary code for data that is used in communications, mostly in minicomputers and all personal computers. ASCII is a 7-bit code providing 128 possible character combinations, the first 32 of which are used for printing and transmission control.

Since the common storage unit is an 8-bit byte (256 combinations) and ASCII uses only 128, the extra bit is used to hold a parity bit or special symbols. For example, the PC uses the additional values for foreign language and graphics symbols. In the Macintosh, the additional values can be user-defined to enhance a font. Following is the list of complete ASCII codes.

Character	*Hex code for ASCII*	*ANSI code*	*Description*
NUL	0000	0	Null
SOH	0001	1	Start of heading
STX	0002	2	Start of text
ETX	0003	3	End of text
EOT	0004	4	End of transmission
ENQ	0005	5	Enquiry
ACK	0006	6	Acknowledge
BEL	0007	7	Bell
BS	0008	8	Backspace
HT	0009	9	Horizontal tabulation
LF	000A	10	Line feed
VT	000B	11	Vertical tabulation
FF	000C	12	Form feed
CR	000D	13	Carriage return
SO	000E	14	Shift out
SI	000F	15	Shift in
DLE	0010	16	Data link escape
DC1	0011	17	Device control 1
DC2	0012	18	Device control 2
DC3	0013	19	Device control 3
DC4	0014	20	Device control 4
NAK	0015	21	Negative acknowledge
SYN	0016	22	Synchronous idle
ETB	0017	23	End of transmission block
CAN	0018	24	Cancel
EM	0019	25	End of medium
SUB	001A	26	Substitute
ESC	001B	27	Escape
FS	001C	28	File separator
GS	001D	29	Group separator
RS	001E	30	Record separator
US	001F	31	Unit separator
SP	0020	32	Space
!	0021	33	Exclamation point
“	0022	34	Quotation mark
#	0023	35	Number sign
$	0024	36	Dollar sign
%	0025	37	Percent

Character	*Hex code for ASCII*	*ANSI code*	*Description*
&	0026	38	Ampersand
‘	0027	39	Apostrophe
(	0028	40	Left parenthesis
)	0029	41	Right parenthesis
*	002A	42	Asterisk
+	002B	43	Plus sign
,	002C	44	Comma
-	002D	45	Hyphen
.	002E	46	Full stop
/	002F	47	Solidus
0	0030	48	Digit zero
1	0031	49	Digit one
2	0032	50	Digit two
3	0033	51	Digit three
4	0034	52	Digit four
5	0035	53	Digit five
6	0036	54	Digit six
7	0037	55	Digit seven
8	0038	56	Digit eight
9	0039	57	Digit nine
:	003A	58	Colon
;	003B	59	Semicolon
<	003C	60	Less-than sign
=	003D	61	Equals sign
>	003E	62	Greater-than sign
?	003F	63	Question mark
@	0040	64	Commercial at
A	0041	65	Latin capital letter A
B	0042	66	Latin capital letter B
C	0043	67	Latin capital letter C
D	0044	68	Latin capital letter D
E	0045	69	Latin capital letter E
F	0046	70	Latin capital letter F
G	0047	71	Latin capital letter G
H	0048	72	Latin capital letter H
I	0049	73	Latin capital letter I
J	004A	74	Latin capital letter J
K	004B	75	Latin capital letter K
L	004C	76	Latin capital letter L

Character	Hex code for ASCII	ANSI code	Description
M	004D	77	Latin capital letter M
N	004E	78	Latin capital letter N
O	004F	79	Latin capital letter O
P	0050	80	Latin capital letter P
Q	0051	81	Latin capital letter Q
R	0052	82	Latin capital letter R
S	0053	83	Latin capital letter S
T	0054	84	Latin capital letter T
U	0055	85	Latin capital letter U
V	0056	86	Latin capital letter V
W	0057	87	Latin capital letter W
X	0058	88	Latin capital letter X
Y	0059	89	Latin capital letter Y
Z	005A	90	Latin capital letter Z
[	005B	91	Left square bracket
\	005C	92	Reverse solidus
]	005D	93	Right square bracket
^	005E	94	Circumflex accent
_	005F	95	Low line
`	0060	96	Grave accent
a	0061	97	Latin small letter a
b	0062	98	Latin small letter b
c	0063	99	Latin small letter c
d	0064	100	Latin small letter d
e	0065	101	Latin small letter e
f	0066	102	Latin small letter f
g	0067	103	Latin small letter g
h	0068	104	Latin small letter h
i	0069	105	Latin small letter i
j	006A	106	Latin small letter j
k	006B	107	Latin small letter k
l	006C	108	Latin small letter l
m	006D	109	Latin small letter m
n	006E	110	Latin small letter n
o	006F	111	Latin small letter o
p	0070	112	Latin small letter p
q	0071	113	Latin small letter q
r	0072	114	Latin small letter r
s	0073	115	Latin small letter s
t	0074	116	Latin small letter t
u	0075	117	Latin small letter u

Character	Hex code for ASCII	ANSI code	Description
v	0076	118	Latin small letter v
w	0077	119	Latin small letter w
x	0078	120	Latin small letter x
y	0079	121	Latin small letter y
z	007A	122	Latin small letter z
{	007B	123	Left curly bracket
|	007C	124	Vertical line
}	007D	125	Right curly bracket
~	007E	126	Tilde
DEL	007F	127	Delete
	0080	128	Reserved
	0081	129	Reserved
	0082	130	Reserved
	0083	131	Reserved
IND	0084	132	Index
NEL	0085	133	Next line
SSA	0086	134	Start of selected area
ESA	0087	135	End of selected area
	0088	136	Character tabulation set
	0089	137	Character tabulation with justification
	008A	138	Line tabulation set
PLD	008B	139	Partial line down
PLU	008C	140	Partial line up
	008D	141	Reverse line feed
SS2	008E	142	Single shift two
SS3	008F	143	Single shift three
DCS	0090	144	Device control string
PU1	0091	145	Private use one
PU2	0092	146	Private use two
STS	0093	147	Set transmit state
CCH	0094	148	Cancel character
MW	0095	149	Message waiting
	0096	150	Start of guarded area
	0097	151	End of guarded area
	0098	152	Start of string
	0099	153	Reserved
	009A	154	Single character introducer
CSI	009B	155	Control sequence introducer

Character	*Hex code for ASCII*	*ANSI code*	*Description*
ST	009C	156	String terminator
OSC	009D	157	Operating system command
PM	009E	158	Privacy message
APC	009F	159	Application program command
	00A0	160	No-break space
¡	00A1	161	Inverted exclamation mark
¢	00A2	162	Cent sign
£	00A3	163	Pound sign
¤	00A4	164	Currency sign
¥	00A5	165	Yen sign
¦	00A6	166	Broken bar
§	00A7	167	Section sign
¨	00A8	168	Diaeresis
©	00A9	169	Copyright sign
ª	00AA	170	Feminine ordinal indicator
«	00AB	171	Left-pointing double angle quotation mark
¬	00AC	172	Not sign
-	00AD	173	Soft hyphen
®	00AE	174	Registered sign
¯	00AF	175	Macron
°	00B0	176	Degree sign
±	00B1	177	Plus-minus sign
^{2}	00B2	178	Superscript two
^{3}	00B3	179	Superscript three
´	00B4	180	Acute accent
µ	00B5	181	Micro sign
¶	00B6	182	Pilcrow sign
·	00B7	183	Middle dot
¸	00B8	184	Cedilla
^{1}	00B9	185	Superscript one
º	00BA	186	Masculine ordinal indicator
»	00BB	187	Right-pointing double angle quotation mark
¼	00BC	188	Vulgar fraction one quarter
½	00BD	189	Vulgar fraction one half

Character	*Hex code for ASCII*	*ANSI code*	*Description*
¾	00BE	190	Vulgar fraction three quarter
¿	00BF	191	Inverted question mark
À	00C0	192	Latin capital letter A with grave
Á	00C1	193	Latin capital letter A with acute
Â	00C2	194	Latin capital letter A with circumflex
Ã	00C3	195	Latin capital letter A with tilde
Ä	00C4	196	Latin capital letter A with diaeresis
Å	00C5	197	Latin capital letter A with ring above
Æ	00C6	198	Latin capital ligature AE
Ç	00C7	199	Latin capital letter C with cedilla
È	00C8	200	Latin capital letter E with grave
É	00C9	201	Latin capital letter E with acute
Ê	00CA	202	Latin capital letter E with circumflex
Ë	00CB	203	Latin capital letter E with diaeresis
Ì	00CC	204	Latin capital letter I with grave
Í	00CD	205	Latin capital letter I with acute
Î	00CE	206	Latin capital letter I with circumflex
Ï	00CF	207	Latin capital letter I with giaeresis
Ð	00D0	208	Latin capital letter ETH
Ñ	00D1	209	Latin capital letter N with tilde
Ò	00D2	210	Latin capital letter O with grave
Ó	00D3	211	Latin capital letter O with acute
Ô	00D4	212	Latin capital letter O with circumflex

Character	Hex code for ASCII	ANSI code	Description
Õ	00D5	213	Latin capital letter O with tilde
Ö	00D6	214	Latin capital letter O with diaeresis
×	00D7	215	Multiplication sign
Ø	00D8	216	Latin capital letter O with stroke
Ù	00D9	217	Latin capital letter U with grave
Ú	00DA	218	Latin capital letter U with acute
Û	00DB	219	Latin capital letter U with circumflex
Ü	00DC	220	Latin capital letter U with diaeresis
Ý	00DD	221	Latin capital letter Y with acute
Þ	00DE	222	Latin capital letter thorn
ß	00DF	223	Latin small letter sharp s
à	00E0	224	Latin small letter a with grave
á	00E1	225	Latin small letter a with acute
â	00E2	226	Latin small letter a with circumflex
ã	00E3	227	Latin small letter a with tilde
ä	00E4	228	Latin small letter a with diaeresis
å	00E5	229	Latin small letter a with ring above
æ	00E6	230	Latin small ligature ae
ç	00E7	231	Latin small letter c with cedilla
è	00E8	232	Latin small letter e with grave
é	00E9	233	Latin small letter e with acute
ê	00EA	234	Latin small letter e with circumflex

Character	Hex code for ASCII	ANSI code	Description
ë	00EB	235	Latin small letter e with diaeresis
ì	00EC	236	Latin small letter i with grave
í	00ED	237	Latin small letter i with acute
î	00EE	238	Latin small letter i with circumflex
ï	00EF	239	Latin small letter i with giaeresis
ð	00F0	240	Latin small letter eth
ñ	00F1	241	Latin small letter n with tilde
ò	00F2	242	Latin small letter o with grave
ó	00F3	243	Latin small letter o with acute
ô	00F4	244	Latin small letter o with circumflex
õ	00F5	245	Latin small letter o with tilde
ö	00F6	246	Latin small letter o with diaeresis
÷	00F7	247	Division sign
ø	00F8	248	Latin small letter o with stroke
ù	00F9	249	Latin small letter u with grave
ú	00FA	250	Latin small letter u with acute
û	00FB	251	Latin small letter u with circumflex
ü	00FC	252	Latin small letter u with diaeresis
ý	00FD	253	Latin small letter y with acute
þ	00FE	254	Latin small letter thorn
ÿ	00FF	255	Latin small letter y with diaeresis

2.6 Digital Fonts Techniques

It can be defined as a specific collection of graphics characters, with associated descriptive, character-positioning, and character-shape information required by a computer system to represent a specific type family and one or more typefaces and type sizes. To create a difital font, we only have to:

1. draw the shapes
2. export them as a .TTF or a .PFB and .PFM file.

Graphics can be created using any of the graphics creating software like Photoshop, CorelDRAW, etc. These software also allow you to convert them to easy to use graphics for the font-making programs.

Let us Revise

1. Alphanumeric characters are used to present information in the text form.
2. Plain text is the unformatted text.
3. Fomatted text is formatted for bold, italics, etc.
4. Hypertext has a link to other text.
5. Fonts are typically measured in a unit specific to the printing industry called the point.
6. The point unit is the traditional measurement of length is typography.
7. An absolute unit is a unit of measure that specifies a fixed length – a length which can be measured with a measuring band.
8. A relative unit is a unit of measure that specifies a value that is relative to the font size.
9. The term pixel is derived from Picture Element.
10. A glyph's outline is defined by the vertices of individual strokes and stroke's profile.
11. Type 1 and Type 3 fonts were developed by Adobe for professional digital typesetting.
12. TrueType is a font system originally developed by Apple, Inc.
13. OpenType is a smartfont system designed by Adobe and Microsoft.
14. Outline fonts or vector fonts are collections of vector images, i.e. a set of lines and curves to define the border of glyphs.
15. Bitmap fonts consist of a series of dots or pixels representing the image of each glyph in each face and size.

Multiple Choice Questions

1. A family of graphic characters that usually include many type sizes and styles is called:

   (a) typeface (b) font (c) point.

2. Commonly known sans serif font is:

   (a) Arial (b) Helvitica (c) Both.

3. A font style has the following:

   (a) Bold (b) Italics (c) Underlined

   (d) All of them.

4. Hypermedia structures are navigated through
   (a) Keys (b) Panels (c) Buttons.

True/False Questions

1. Plain text is the unformatted text.
2. Hypertext has no link to other text.
3. The point unit is the traditional measurement of length is typography.
4. A relative unit is not a unit of measure that specifies a value that is relative to the font size.
5. A glyph's outline is defined by the vertices of individual strokes and stroke's profile.
6. TrueType is a font system originally developed by Apple, Inc.
7. Outline fonts or vector fonts are not collections of vector images, i.e. a set of lines and curves to define the border of glyphs.

Matching Columns

In the following case, commands are given in the left hand columns and their actions in the right hand column. Match them.

Column A	Column B
A. WWW	1. Adobe Type Manager
B. ASCII	2. A unique number for every character
C. Scaling	3. Scalable font system
D. ATM	4. Space between lines
E Postscript	5. Non-linear access to text
F. Unicode	6. World Wide Web
G Leading	7. Changing the size of the font
H. Hypertext	8. 7 bit code format

Fill in the Blanks with appropriate words

a. bip-mapped b. HTML c. kerning d. OCR
e. hypertext f. units g. font h. leading
i. baseline j. typeface k. serif

1. The little decoration at the end of a letter stroke is a ___________.
2. A _______________ typeface is a family of graphic characters that usually includes many type sizes and styles.
3. Type sizes are usually expressed in __________.
4. An imaginary horizontal line on which characters rest is called ___________.
5. The space between the lines is called __________.
6. A _________ is a collection of characters of a single size and style belonging to a particular typeface family.
7. _________ font come in predefined sizes and weights.
8. ___________ is the space between individual characters.

9. The standard document format used for pages on the web is called ____________.
10. The text in which the user has the facility to navigate in a non-linear fashion for the desired information is called _______________.
11. ________ are used to codigy printed text for direct input of printed text to computers.

Descriptive Type Questions

1. How is text used in the Multimedia?
2. Define the terms: Plain Text, Formatted Text, and Hypertext.
3. Define the following terms:

Length units	Absolute units
Relative units	Pixel units
Type 1 and Type 3 fonts	TrueType fonts
OpenType font	Metafont

4. Define Outline fonts.
5. What are Bitmap fonts?
6. In the context of bitmap fonts, define the following:

Scaling	Font formats

7. What are Internation Character Sets?
8. What are digital fonts?

Answers to Objective Type Questions

Multiple Choice Questions

1. a	2. c	3. d	4. c

True False Questions

1. T	2. F	3. T	4. F
5. T	6. T	7. F	

Matching Columns

A. 6	B. 8	C. 7	D. 1
E. 3	F. 2	G. 4	H. 5

Fill in the Blanks

1. k	2. j	3. f	4. i
5. h	6. g	7. a	8. c
9. b	10. e	11. d	

Audio Fundamentals and Representations 3

3.1 Fundamentals of Sound

Sound is perhaps the most important part of the multimedia project. It is one of the basics of the project. Well, sound can be very distinctive. Any sound can make a pleasant listening or it can sound disturbing too if made at a little higher pitch. So while making the multimedia project it is imperative that the sound should be perfect. It should not disturb but should give pleasant listening.

Sound is like waves. When something vibrates in the air by moving back and forth, it creates waves of pressure. These waves are spread like the ripples tossed into a still pool, and when they reach your eardrums, you experience the changes of pressure, or vibrations, as sound. Sound is defined as the audiotry sensation produced by the mechanical vibrations of objects. Sound is usually represented as waves, periodic waves corresponding to musical sound and a periodic waves corresponds to noise. Acoustics is the branch of science dealing with the sutdy of sound and isconcerned with the gereation, transmission and reception of sound waves. There are different methods to produce mechanical vibrations, such as beating a drum, ringing a bell and breaking a glass on the floor.

Acoustics is the branch of science that studies sound. Sound pressure levels are measured in decibels. A decibel measurement is actually the ratio between a chosen reference point on a logarithmic scale and the level that is actually experienced. When you increase the sound output power, there is only a 6 dB increase; when you make the sound 100 times more intense, the increase in dB is not hundredfold, but only 20 dB.

For your knowledge some decibel scale examples are given below:

Db	*Watts*	*Example*
195	25-40 million	Saturn rocket
170	100,000	Jet engine with afterburner
160	10,000	Turbojet engine at 7,000 pounds thrust
150	1,000	ALSETEX splinterless stun grenade
140	100	2 HBL2226 speakers pulling 2400 watts inside an automobile
130	10	75-piece orchestra, at fortissimo
120	1	Large chipping hammer
110	0.1	Riveting machine
100	0.01	Automobile on highway
90	0.001	Subway train; a shouting voice

80	0.0001	Inside a 1952 Corvette at 60 mph
70	0.00001	Voice conversation; freight train 100 feet away
60	0.000001	Large departmental store
50	0.0000001	Average residence or small business office
40	0.00000001	Residential areas of Chicago at night
30	0.000000001	Very soft whisper
20	0.0000000001	Sound studio

3.1.1 Categories of Sound

To reproduce sound you need to record it so that the recorded sound can be played back when required. The two categories of sound are:

- Analog Sound
- Digital Sound

3.1.1.1 Analog Sound

Any recorded sound is known as analog sound an it is represented by the fluctuations in the amplitude. Amplitude of a wave is the maximum displacement of a particle in the path of a wave and is a measure of the peek-to-peek height of the wave. In analog sound recording, the fluctuations in the amplitude are recorded continuously on a recording media. The continuously recording of the amplitude fluctuations on a recording media provides the information necessary for the reproduction of the sound waves.

3.1.1.2 Digital Sound

Digital sound is a term applied to sound that has been digitized into binary code. The reprsentation of sound waves in the binary format, which means representation using only zeros and ones, enables the computers to use digital sound. Sound waves are converted to digital form by means of a circuit that assigns a value or binary set of numbers that correspond to the shape of the incoming electrical wave or current. As computer cannot understand analog data, it must be converted to digital. When analog sound is conveted to digital, it is generally saved as a wave file.

3.2 Digitization of Sound

A digital recorder firstly requires the input of an analog signal; this signal may come directly from a microphone pre-amp, but any analog audio signal can be converted. Measurements of the signal intensity are then made at regular intervals (sampling) by the analog-to-digital converter. At each sampling point, the signal must be assigned a specific intensity from a set range of values (quantization). For doing this, the original sound wave can now be described using only numbers—as digital information. Each sample can be given an ordinal number which signifies the point in relative time that it represents, and the magnitude of the sample is an analog of pressure at the microphone (Watkinson 1994) (or, for an artificial sound signal, the pressure that would be at the microphone to correspond to that sound.) When the original signal is converted into numbers (usually binary numbers, 1's and 0's, called 'bits') further additions of noise and distortion, provided they are not great enough to cause digital errors, can be rejected at every stage of processing; this is what is referred to as the regenerative nature of digital signals. Digital errors, called bit errors in binary digital systems, are events of noise and/or distortion which cause one number (or bit) to appear more like another number than like the number they started out as. As long as a digital symbol appears closer to being what it began as than to anything else, it can be regenerated. When raw digital errors cannot be avoided, error correction coding can allow some of them to be detected and fixed. Error correction, essential when transferring digital audio over noisy channels, helps to eliminate bit errors by comparing extra data against the main data to detect limited numbers of digital errors, figure out which digital symbols (numbers) were changed, and change them back. When playing back a digital recording, the digital information is converted back into a continuous, analog signal by a digital-to-analog converter. This electronic signal is then amplified and converted back into a sound wave by a loudspeaker (just as would be done with the analog signal produced by an analog machine from an analog recording).

3.3 Frequency and Bandwidth

The number of pressure variation per second is called frequency of sound. The sampling rate is measured in terms of Hertz (Hz), which is the term for cycles per second. The sampling rate determines the frequency at which samples will be drawn for the recording. Sampling at higher rates more accurately captures the high-frequency content of the sound. In other words, the higher sampling rate implies that more samples are taken during the given time interval and the quality of reconstruction is better.

Bandwidth is how much data, expressed in bits per second (bps), you can send from one computer to another in a given amount of time. The greater the bandwidth of your connection, the less time you will spend waiting for text, images, sounds and animated illustrations to upload and download from computer to computer.

3.4 Decibel System

Sound which is measured in terms of sound pressure level is called decibels. A decibel measurement is actually the ratio between a chosen reference point on a logarithmic scale and the leel that is actually experienced. So, it can be said that decibel is a unit for measuring loundness of sound.

3.5 Data Rate

Data rate is the rate at which information being transferred. It is expressed in terms of amount of information per unit of time. For example, a common type of data rate used when describing the speed of ahard drive is Megabits/second. Bit rate based formats are the simplest when it comes to calculating a file size. This is because a "bitrate" is actually a data rate. Specially a bitrate is a data rate that is specified in terms of number of bits/unit of time.

Many popular formats store data in terms of bitrate.Some example include DV, MPEG-1, MPEG-2, MPEG-4, RealMedia, and Windows Media. Some of these formats support variable bitrate and quality-based encoding. However, as long as you know the averate bitrate, you can use it to calculate the firle size.

3.6 Audio File Format

When you create multimedia, it is likely that you will deal with file formats and translators for text, sounds, images, animations or digital video clips. A sound file's format is simply a recognized methodology for organizing the digitized sound's data bits and bytes into a data file. The structure of the file must be known, of course, before the data can be saved or later loaded into a computer to be edited and/or played as sound. The following table shows some of the common sound formats used for multimedia.

Purpose	*Extension*	*MIME Type*
669 MOD Music	.669	
AIFF Audio	.aifc	audio/aiff
AIFF Audio	.aiff	audio/aiff
AIFF Sound	.aiff	audio/x-aiff
AIFF Sound Compressed	.aife	audio/x-aiff
AIFF Sound	.aif	audio/x-aiff
aLAW Sound	.al	
Amiga 8-bit sound	.8svx	
Amiga IFF Sound	.svx	
Amigra MD Sound	.med	
Amiga OctaMed music	.8med	
AU Audio	.snd	audio/basic
AU Audio	.ulw	audio/basic
Beatnik	.rmf	audio/rmf
Beatnik	.rmf	audio/x-rmf
MIDI	.kar	audio/mid
MIDI	.kar	audio/midi
MIDI	.kar	audio/x-midi
MIDI	.mid	audio/mid
MIDI	.mid	audio/midi
MIDI	.mid	audio/x-midi
MIDI	.midi	audio/mid
MIDI	.midi	audio/midi
MIDI	.midi	audio/x-midi
MIDI	.smf	audio/mid
MIDI	.smf	audio/midi
MIDI	.smf	audio/x-midi
μLaw Sound	.au	audio/basuic
μLaw Sound	.ul	audio/basic
MP3 Audio	.mp3	audio/mpeg
MP3 Audio	.mp3	audio/x-mpeg
MPEG audio stream	.mla	audio/mpeg
MPEG audio stream	.mls	audio/mpeg
MPEG audio stream	.mls	audio/x-mpeg
MPEG audio stream	.mp2	audio/x-mpeg

MPEG audio stream	.mpa	audio/mpeg
MPEG audio stream	.mpeg	audio/x-mpeg
MPEG audio stream	.mpg	audio/mpeg
MPEG audio stream	.mpg	audio/x-mpeg
MPEG audio stream	.mpm	audio/mpeg
MPEG audio stream	.mpm	audio/x-mpeg
MPEG audio stream	.mpv	video/mpeg
MPEG-I Audio Movie	.mp2	audio/x-mpeg
MPEG-I Audio Movie	.mpa	audio/x-mpeg
MPEG-I Audio Movie	.ml5	
MPEG-I Audio Movie	.mla	audio/x-mpeg
MPEG-I Audio Movie	.m75	
MPEG-I Layer 3	.mp3	
QCP Audio	.qcp	audio/vnd.qcelp
Real Time Steaming Protocol	.rtsp	application/x-rtsp
RealAudio	.ra	audio/x-pn-realaudio
RealAudio	.ra	audio/vnd.rn-realaudio
RealAudio	.ram	audio/x-pn-realaudio
RealAudio	.rm	audio/x-pn-realaudio
Sound Designer 2 File	.sd2	
Sound of various types	.snd	
SoundEdit Sound ex SOX	.hcom	
VOC Sound	.voc	
WAV Audio	.wav	audio/wav

In Windows, digitized sounds are most commonly stored as WAV files. For the Internet, new formats are emerging as companies develop solutions for streaming and playing sound on the Web. There are many ways to store the bits and bytes that describe a sampled waveform sound. The method used for Red Book Audio data files on consumer-grade music CDs is Linear Pulse Code Modulation.

The wave format (WAV) was introduced by Microsoft and IBM with the introduction of Windows. Windows make use of MIDI files. A MIDI interface is built into many sound boards on the PC.

3.6.1 AIFF (Audio Interchange File Format)

Audio Interchange File Format (AIFF) is an audio file format standard used for storing sound data for personal computers and other electronic audio devices. The format was co-developed by Apple Computer in 1988 based on Electronic Arts' Interchange File Format (IFF, widely used on Amiga systems) and is most commonly used on Apple Macintosh computer systems.

The audio data in a standard AIFF file is uncompressed pulse-code modulation (PCM). There is also a compressed variant of AIFF known as AIFF-C or AIFC, with various defined compression codecs.

Standard AIFF is a leading format (along with SDII and WAV) used by professional-level audio and video applications, and unlike the better-known lossy MP3 format, it is non-compressed (which aids rapid streaming of multiple audio files from disk to the application), and lossless. Like any non-compressed, lossless format, it uses much more disk space than MP3—about 10MB for one minute of stereo audio at a sample rate of 44.1 kHz and a sample size of 16 bits. In addition to audio data, AIFF can include loop point data and the musical note of a sample, for use by hardware samplers and musical applications.

The file extension for the standard AIFF format is .aiff or .aif. For the compressed variants it is supposed to be .aifc, but .aiff or .aif are accepted as well by audio applications supporting the format.

3.6.2 Musical Instruments Digital Interface (MIDI)

MIDI (Musical Instrument Digital Interface), is an industry-standard protocol that enables electronic musical instruments such as keyboard controllers, computers, and other electronic equipment to communicate, control, and synchronize with each other. MIDI allows computers, synthesizers, MIDI controllers, sound cards, samplers and drum machines to control one another, and to exchange system data. MIDI does not transmit an audio signal or media — it transmits event messages such as the pitch and intensity of musical notes to play, control signals for parameters such as volume, vibrato and panning, cues, and clock signals to set the tempo. As an electronic protocol, it is notable for its widespread adoption throughout the music industry.

All MIDI compatible controllers, musical instruments, and MIDI-compatible software follow the same MIDI 1.0 specification, and thus interpret any given MIDI message the same way, and so can communicate with and understand each other. MIDI composition and arrangement takes advantage of MIDI 1.0 and General MIDI (GM) technology to allow musical data files to be shared among many different files due to some incompatibility with various electronic instruments by using a standard, portable set of commands and parameters. Because the music is stored as instructions rather than recorded audio waveforms, the data size of the files is quite small by comparison. Individual MIDI files can be traced through their own individual key code. This key code was established in early 1994 to combat piracy within the sharing of .mid files.

The original physical MIDI connection uses DIN 5/180° connectors. Opto-isolating connections are used, to prevent ground loops occurring among connected MIDI devices.

Logically, MIDI is based on a ring network topology, with a transceiver inside each device. The transceivers physically and logically separate the input and output lines, meaning that MIDI messages received by a device in the network not intended for that device must be re-transmitted on the output line (MIDI-OUT) by means of a "soft through". This can introduce a delay, one that is long enough to become musically significant on larger MIDI rings.

MIDI-THRU ports started to be added to MIDI-compatible equipment soon after the introduction of MIDI, in order to improve performance. The MIDI-THRU port avoids the aforementioned retransmission delay by linking the MIDI-THRU port to the MIDI-IN socket almost directly. The difference between the MIDI-OUT and MIDI-THRU ports is that data coming from the MIDI-OUT port has been generated on the device containing that port. Data that comes out of a device's MIDI-THRU port, however, is an exact duplicate of the data received at the MIDI-IN port.

Such chaining together of instruments via MIDI-THRU ports is unnecessary with the use of MIDI "patch bay," "mult" or "Thru" modules consisting of a MIDI-IN connector and multiple MIDI-OUT connectors to which multiple instruments are connected. Some equipment has the ability to merge

MIDI messages into one stream, but this is a specialized function and is not universal to all equipment. MIDI Thru Boxes clean up any skewing of MIDI data bits that might occur at the input stage. MIDI Merger boxes merge all MIDI messages appearing at either of its two inputs to its output, which allows a musician to plug in several MIDI controllers (*e.g.*, two musical keyboards and a pedal keyboard) to a single synth voice device such as an EMU or Proteus.

All MIDI compatible instruments have a built-in MIDI. Some computers' sound cards have a built-in MIDI, whereas others require an external MIDI which is connected to the computer via the newer D-subminiature DA-15 game port, a USB connector or by FireWire, ethernet or by MADI (RME standard). MIDI connectors are defined by the MIDI standard. In the 2000s, as computer equipment increasingly used USB connectors, companies began making USB-to-MIDI audio interfaces which can transfer MIDI channels to USB-equipped computers. As well, due to the increasing use of computers for music-making and composition, some MIDI keyboard controllers were equipped with USB jacks, so that they can be plugged into computers that are running "software synths" or other music software.

3.6.2.1 File formats

Standard MIDI File (SMF) Format: MIDI messages (along with timing information) can be collected and stored in a computer file system, in what is commonly called a MIDI file, or more formally, a Standard MIDI File (SMF). The SMF specification was developed by, and is maintained by, the MIDI Manufacturers Association (MMA). MIDI files are typically created using computer-based sequencing software (or sometimes a hardware-based MIDI instrument or workstation) that organizes MIDI messages into one or more parallel "tracks" for independent recording and editing. In most sequencers, each track is assigned to a specific MIDI channel and/or a specific instrument *patch*; if the attached music synthesizer has a known instrument palette (for example because it conforms to the General MIDI standard), then the instrument for each track may be selected by name. Although most current MIDI sequencer software uses proprietary "session file" formats rather than SMF, almost all sequencers provide export or "Save As..." support for the SMF format.

An SMF consists of one header chunk and one or more track chunks. There exist three different SMF formats; the format of a given SMF is specified in its file header. A Format 0 file contains a single track and represents a single song performance. Format 1 may contain any number of tracks, enabling preservation of the sequencer track structure, and also represents a single song performance. Format 2 may have any number of tracks, each representing a separate song performance. Sequencers do not commonly support Format 2. Large collections of SMFs can be found on the web, most commonly with the extension .mid but occasionally with the .smf. These files are most frequently authored with the (rather dubious) assumption that they will be only ever be played on General MIDI players.

MIDI Karaoke File (.KAR) Format: MIDI-Karaoke (which uses the ".kar" file extension) files are an "unofficial" extension of MIDI files, used to add synchronized lyrics to standard MIDI files. SMF players play the music as they would a .mid file but do not display these lyrics unless they have specific support for .kar messages. These often display the lyrics synchronized with the music in "follow-the-bouncing-ball" fashion, essentially turning any PC into a karaoke machine. None of the MIDI-Karaoke file formats are maintained by any standardization body.

XMF File Formats: The MMA has also defined (and AMEI has approved) a new family of file formats, XMF (eXtensible Music File), some of which package SMF chunks with instrument data in

DLS format (Downloadable Sounds, also an MMA/AMEI specification), to much the same effect as the MOD file format. The XMF container is a binary format (not XML-based, although the file extensions are similar).

RIFF-RMID File Format: On Microsoft Windows, the system itself uses proprietary RIFF-based MIDI files with the ".rmi" extension. Note, Standard MIDI Files are not RIFF-compliant. A RIFF-RMID file, however, is simply a Standard MIDI File wrapped in a RIFF (Resource Interchange File Format) chunk. For compatibility reasons many digital musicians overlook this format. One solution to this incompatibility is to extract the data part of the RIFF-RMID chunk, the result will be a regular Standard MIDI File. RIFF-RMID is not an official MMA/AMEI MIDI standard.

Extended RMID File Format: In recommended practice RP-29, the MMA defined a method for bundling one Standard MIDI file (SMF) image with one Downloadable Sounds (DLS) image using the RIFF container technology. However, this method was deprecated when the MMA introduced the Extensible Music Format (XMF), which because of its many additional features is generally preferred for MIDI-related resource bundling purposes going forwards.

Extended MIDI File (.XMI) Format: The XMI format is a proprietary extension of the SMF format introduced by the Miles Sound System, a middleware driver library targeted at PC games. XMI is not an official MMA/AMEI MIDI standard.

3.6.3 Wave Form (WAV)

WAVE or **WAV**, short for **Waveform Audio File Format**, is a Microsoft and IBM audio file format standard for storing an audio bitstream on PCs. It is an application of the RIFF bitstream format method for storing data in "chunks", and thus is also close to the 8SVX and the AIFF format used on Amiga and Macintosh computers, respectively. It is the main format used on Windows systems for raw and typically uncompressed audio. The usual bitstream encoding is the Linear Pulse Code Modulation (LPCM) format. Both WAVs and AIFFs are compatible with Windows, Macintosh, and Linux operating systems. The format takes into account some differences of the Intel CPU such as little-endian byte order. The RIFF format acts as a "wrapper" for various audio compression codecs.

Though a WAV file can hold compressed audio, the most common WAV format contains uncompressed audio in the linear pulse code modulation (LPCM) format. The standard audio file format for CDs, for example, is LPCM-encoded, containing two channels of 44,100 samples per second, 16 bits per sample. Since LPCM uses an uncompressed storage method which keeps all the samples of an audio track, professional users or audio experts may use the WAV format for maximum audio quality. WAV audio can also be edited and manipulated with relative ease using software. The WAV format supports compressed audio, using, on Windows, the Audio Compression Manager. Any ACM codec can be used to compress a WAV file. The UI for Audio Compression Manager may be accessed through various programs that use it, including Sound Recorder in some versions of Windows.

Beginning with Windows 2000, a WAVE_FORMAT_EXTENSIBLE header was defined which specifies multiple audio channel data along with speaker positions, eliminates ambiguity regarding sample types and container sizes in the standard WAV format and supports defining custom extensions to the format chunk.

There have been some WAVE format inconsistencies reported, for example how 8-bit data is unsigned, but 16-bit data is signed; and many chunks duplicate the same information found in other chunks. WAV file can contain embedded IFF "List"s, that may contain several "sub-chunks".

Uncompressed WAV files are quite large in size, so, as file sharing over the Internet has become popular, the WAV format has declined in popularity. However, it is still a commonly used file type, suitable for retaining "first generation" archived files of high quality, for use on a system where disk space is not a constraint, or in applications such as audio editing, where the time involved in compressing and uncompressing data is a concern. More frequently, the smaller file sizes of compressed but lossy formats such as Ogg Vorbis, MP3, ATRAC, AAC, Musepack and WMA are used to store and transfer audio. Their small file sizes allow faster Internet transmission, as well as lower consumption of space on memory media. However, lossy formats trade off smaller file size against loss of audio quality, as all such compression algorithms compromise available signal detail. There are also lossless codecs, such as FLAC, Shorten, Monkey's Audio, ATRAC Advanced Lossless, Apple Lossless, WMA Lossless, TTA, and WavPack, but none of these is yet a ubiquitous standard for either professional or home audio.

The usage of the WAV format has more to do with its familiarity, its simplicity and simple structure, which is heavily based on the RIFF file format. Because of this, it continues to enjoy widespread use with a variety of software applications, often functioning as a 'lowest common denominator' when it comes to exchanging sound files between different programs. In spite of their large size, uncompressed WAV (though that format can be different from the Microsoft WAV) files are sometimes used by some radio broadcasters, especially those that have adopted the tapeless system. BBC Radio in the UK uses 44.1 kHz 16 bit two channel .wav audio as standard in their VCS system. The ABC "D-Cart" system, which was developed by the Australian broadcaster, uses 48 kHz 16 bit two channel .wav files, which is identical to that of Digital Audio Tape.

This is a reference to compare the monophonic (not stereophonic) audio quality and compression bitrates of the different codecs available for .wav files including PCM, ADPCM, Microsoft GSM 06.10, CELP, SBC, Truespeech and MPEG Layer-3.

Format	*Bitrate*	*1 Minute =*	*Sample*
11,025 Hz 16 bit PCM	176.4 kbit/s[17]	1292 KB[18]	11k16bitpcm.wav
08,000 Hz 16 bit PCM	128 kbit/s	0938 KB	8k16bitpcm.wav
11,025 Hz 8 bit PCM	088.2 kbit/s	0646 KB	11k8bitpcm.wav
11,025 Hz μ-Law	088.2 kbit/s	0646 KB	11kulaw.wav
08,000 Hz 8 bit PCM	064 kbit/s	0469 KB	8k8bitpcm.wav
08,000 Hz μ-Law	064 kbit/s	0469 KB	8kulaw.wav
11,025 Hz 4 bit ADPCM	044.1 kbit/s	0323 KB	11kadpcm.wav
08,000 Hz 4 bit ADPCM	032 kbit/s	0234 KB	8kadpcm.wav
11,025 Hz Microsoft GSM 06.10	018 kbit/s	0132 KB	11kgsm.wav
08,000 Hz MP3 16 kbit/s	016 kbit/s	0117 KB	8kmp316.wav
08,000 Hz GSM6.10	013 kbit/s	0103 KB	8kgsm.wav
08,000 Hz Lernout & Hauspie SBC 12 kbit/s	012.0 kbit/s	0088 KB	8ksbc12.wav
08,000 Hz DSP Group Truespeech	009 kbit/s	0066 KB	8ktruespeech.wav
08,000 Hz Mp3 8 kbit/s	008 kbit/s	0060 KB	8kmp38.wav
08,000 Hz Lernout & Hauspie CELP	004.8 kbit/s	0035 KB	8kcelp.wav

The above are WAV files; even those that use the MP3 codec have the ".wav" extension.

3.6.4 Moving Pictures Expert Group Layer 3 (MP3)

MPEG-1 Audio Layer 3, more commonly referred to as **MP3**, is a patented digital audio encoding format using a form of lossy data compression. It is a common audio format for consumer audio storage, as well as a de facto standard of digital audio compression for the transfer and playback of music on digital audio players.

MP3 is an audio-specific format that was designed by the Moving Picture Experts Group as part of its MPEG-1 standard. The group was formed by several teams of engineers at Fraunhofer IIS, AT&T-Bell Labs, Thomson-Brandt, CCETT, and others. It was approved as an ISO/IEC standard in 1991.

The use in MP3 of a lossy compression algorithm is designed to greatly reduce the amount of data required to represent the audio recording and still sound like a faithful reproduction of the original uncompressed audio for most listeners. An MP3 file that is created using the setting of 128 kbit/s will result in a file that is about 11 times smaller than the CD file created from the original audio source. An MP3 file can also be constructed at higher or lower bit rates, with higher or lower resulting quality.

The compression works by reducing accuracy of certain parts of sound that are deemed beyond the auditory resolution ability of most people. This method is commonly referred to as perceptual coding. It uses psychoacoustic models to discard or reduce precision of components less audible to human hearing, and then records the remaining information in an efficient manner.

This technique is often presented as relatively conceptually similar to the principles used by JPEG, an image compression format. The specific algorithms, however, are rather different: JPEG uses a built-in vision model that is very widely tuned (as is necessary for images), while MP3 uses a complex, precise masking model that is much more signal dependent.

From the first half of 1994 through the late 1990s, MP3 files began to spread on the Internet. The popularity of MP3s began to rise rapidly with the advent of Nullsoft's audio player Winamp, released in 1997. In 1998, the Rio PMP300, one of the first portable MP3 players was released, despite legal suppression efforts by the RIAA.

In November 1997, the website mp3.com was offering thousands of MP3s created by independent artists for free. The small size of MP3 files enabled widespread peer-to-peer file sharing of music ripped from CDs, which would have previously been nearly impossible. The first large peer-to-peer filesharing network, Napster, was launched in 1999.

In 1996, the song 'Until it sleeps' by Metallica became the first track to be illegally copied from CD, encoded as an MP3, and made available on the Internet by a user operating under the nickname 'NetFrack'. The ease of creating and sharing MP3s resulted in widespread copyright infringement. Major record companies argue that this free sharing of music reduces sales, and call it "music piracy". They reacted by pursuing lawsuits against Napster and against individual users who engaged in file sharing.

Despite the popularity of the MP3 format, online music retailers often use other proprietary formats that are encrypted or obfuscated in order to make it difficult to use purchased music files in ways not specifically authorized by the record companies. Attempting to control the use of files in this way is known as Digital Rights Management. Record companies argue that this is necessary to prevent the files from being made available on peer-to-peer file sharing networks. This has other side effects, though, such as preventing users from playing back their purchased music on different types of devices. However, the audio content of these files can usually be converted into an unencrypted format. For instance, users are often allowed to burn files to audio CD, which requires conversion to an unencrypted audio format.

Unauthorized MP3 file sharing continues on next-generation peer-to-peer networks. Some authorized services, such as Beatport, Bleep, Juno Records, eMusic, Zune Marketplace, Walmart.com, and Amazon.com sell unrestricted music in the MP3 format.

3.6.4.1 Encoding audio

The MPEG-1 standard does not include a precise specification for an MP3 encoder, but does provide example psychoacoustic models, rate loop, and the like in the non-normative part of the original standard. At the present, these suggested implementations are quite dated. Implementers of the standard were supposed to devise their own algorithms suitable for removing parts of the information from the audio input. As a result, there are many different MP3 encoders available, each producing files of differing quality. Comparisons are widely available, so it is easy for a prospective user of an encoder to research the best choice. It must be kept in mind that an encoder that is proficient at encoding at higher bit rates (such as LAME) is not necessarily as good at lower bit rates.

During encoding, 576 time-domain samples are taken and are transformed to 576 frequency-domain samples. If there is a transient, 192 samples are taken instead of 576. This is done to limit the temporal spread of quantization noise accompanying the transient.

3.6.4.2 Decoding audio

Decoding, on the other hand, is carefully defined in the standard. Most decoders are "bitstream compliant", which means that the decompressed output – that they produce from a given MP3 file – will be the same, within a specified degree of rounding tolerance, as the output specified mathematically in the ISO/IEC standard document (ISO/IEC 11172-3). Therefore, comparison of decoders is usually based on how computationally efficient they are (i.e., how much memory or CPU time they use in the decoding process).

3.6.4.3 Audio quality

When performing lossy audio encoding, such as creating an MP3 file, there is a trade-off between the amount of space used and the sound quality of the result. Typically, the creator is allowed to set a bit rate, which specifies how many kilobits the file may use per second of audio. The higher the bit rate, the larger the compressed file will be, and, generally, the closer it will sound to the original file.

With too low a bit rate, compression artifacts (i.e. sounds that were not present in the original recording) may be audible in the reproduction. Some audio is hard to compress because of its randomness and sharp attacks. When this type of audio is compressed, artifacts such as ringing or pre-echo are usually heard. A sample of applause compressed with a relatively low bit rate provides a good example of compression artifacts.

Besides the bit rate of an encoded piece of audio, the quality of MP3 files also depends on the quality of the encoder itself, and the difficulty of the signal being encoded. As the MP3 standard allows quite a bit of freedom with encoding algorithms, different encoders may feature quite different quality, even with identical bit rates. As an example, in a public listening test featuring two different MP3 encoders at about 128 kbit/s, one scored 3.66 on a 1–5 scale, while the other scored only 2.22.

Quality is dependent on the choice of encoder and encoding parameters. However, in 1998, MP3 at 128 kbit/s was providing quality only equivalent to AAC at 64 kbit/s and MP2 at 192 kbit/s.

The simplest type of MP3 file uses one bit rate for the entire file — this is known as Constant Bit Rate (CBR) encoding. Using a constant bit rate makes encoding simpler and faster. However, it is also possible to create files where the bit rate changes throughout the file. These are known as Variable Bit Rate (VBR) files. The idea behind this is that, in any piece of audio, some parts will be much easier to compress, such as silence or music containing only a few instruments, while others will be more difficult to compress. So, the overall quality of the file may be increased by using a lower bit rate for the less complex passages and a higher one for the more complex parts. With some encoders, it is possible to specify a given quality, and the encoder will vary the bit rate accordingly. Users who know a particular "quality setting" that is transparent to their ears can use this value when encoding all of their music, and not need to worry about performing personal listening tests on each piece of music to determine the correct bit rate.

Perceived quality can be influenced by listening environment (ambient noise), listener attention, and listener training and in most cases by listener audio equipment (such as sound cards, speakers and headphones).

3.6.5 Advanced Streaming Format (ASF)

Advanced Systems Format (formerly **Advanced Streaming Format, Active Streaming Format**) is Microsoft's proprietary digital audio/digital video container format, especially meant for streaming media. ASF is part of the Windows Media framework.

ASF is based on serialized *objects* which are essentially byte sequences identified by a GUID marker.

The format does not specify how (*i.e.*, with which codec) the video or audio should be encoded; it just specifies the structure of the video/audio stream. This is similar to the function performed by the QuickTime, AVI, or Ogg container formats. One of the objectives of ASF was to support playback from digital media servers, HTTP servers, and local storage devices such as hard disk drives.

The most common filetypes contained within an ASF file are Windows Media Audio (WMA) and Windows Media Video (WMV). Note that the file extension abbreviations are different from the codecs which have the same name. Files containing only WMA audio can be named using a .WMA extension, and files of audio and video content may have the extension .WMV. Both may use the .ASF extension if desired.

ASF files can also contain objects representing metadata, such as the artist, title, album and genre for an audio track, or the director of a video track, much like the ID3 tags of MP3 files. It supports scalable media types and stream prioritization; as such, it is a format optimized for streaming.

The ASF container provides the framework for digital rights management in Windows Media Audio and Windows Media Video. An analysis of an older scheme used in WMA reveals that it is using a combination of elliptic curve cryptography key exchange, DES block cipher, a custom block cipher, RC4 stream cipher and the SHA-1 hashing function.

ASF container-based media is usually streamed on the internet either through the MMS protocol or the RTSP protocol.

3.6.6 Real Media (RM)

RealMedia is a multimedia container format created by RealNetworks. Its extension is ".rm". It is typically used in conjunction with RealVideo and RealAudio and is used for streaming content over the Internet.

Typically these streams are in CBR (constant bitrate).

Recently, RealNetworks has developed a new container for VBR (variable bitrate) streams, named RMVB (RealMedia variable bitrate).

Support of RealMedia is available in a wide variety of multimedia players for different architectures/ platforms, including RealPlayer and the Real Alternative codec pack. The open source DAP firmware Rockbox has added support for reading RM containers as of 6 July 2009, although only certain codecs contained in RM files are playable.

3.6.7 Audio Video Interleave

Audio Video Interleave, known by its acronym AVI, is a multimedia container format introduced by Microsoft in November 1992 as part of its Video for Windows technology. AVI files can contain both audio and video data in a file container that allows synchronous audio-with-video playback. Like the DVD video format, AVI files support multiple streaming audio and video, although these features are seldom used. Most AVI files also use the file format extensions developed by the Matrox OpenDML group in February 1996. These files are supported by Microsoft, and are unofficially called "AVI 2.0".

AVI is a derivative of the Resource Interchange File Format (RIFF), which divides a file's data into blocks, or "chunks." Each "chunk" is identified by a FourCC tag. An AVI file takes the form of a single chunk in a RIFF formatted file, which is then subdivided into two mandatory "chunks" and one optional "chunk".

The first sub-chunk is identified by the "hdrl" tag. This sub-chunk is the file header and contains metadata about the video, such as its width, height and frame rate. The second sub-chunk is identified by the "movi" tag. This chunk contains the actual audio/visual data that make up the AVI movie. The third optional sub-chunk is identified by the "idx1" tag which indexes the offsets of the data chunks within the file.

By way of the RIFF format, the audio/visual data contained in the "movi" chunk can be encoded or decoded by software called a codec, which is an abbreviation for (en)coder/decoder. Upon creation of the file, the codec translates between raw data and the (compressed) data format used inside the chunk. An AVI file may carry audio/visual data inside the chunks in virtually any compression scheme, including Full Frame (Uncompressed), Intel Real Time (Indeo), Cinepak, Motion JPEG, Editable MPEG, VDOWave, ClearVideo / RealVideo, QPEG, and MPEG-4 Video.

Since its introduction in the early 90s, new computer video techniques have been introduced which the original AVI specification did not anticipate.

- AVI does not provide a standardised way to encode aspect ratio information, with the result that players cannot select the right one automatically (though it may be possible to do so manually).
- There are several competing approaches to including timecode in AVI files, which affects usability of the format in film and television postproduction (although it is widely used). An equivalent of the Broadcast Wave extensions, designed to standardise postproduction metadata for wave audio files, has not emerged.
- AVI is not intended to contain variable frame rate material. Workarounds for this limitation increase overhead dramatically.
- AVI was not intended to contain video using any compression technique which requires access to future video frame data beyond the current frame. Approaches exist to support modern video

compression techniques (e.g. MPEG-4) which rely on this functionality, although this is beyond the intent of the original specification and may cause problems with playback software which does not anticipate this use.

- AVI cannot contain some specific types of VBR data (such as MP3 audio at sample rates below 32KHz) reliably.
- Overhead for AVI files at the resolutions and frame rates normally used to encode feature films is about 5 MB per hour of video, the significance of which varies with the application.

More recent container formats (such as Matroska, Ogg and MP4) solve all these problems, although software is freely available to both create and correctly replay AVI files which use these more recent techniques.

3.6.7.1 DV AVI

DV AVI (aka DV-AVI) is a type of AVI file where the video has been compressed to conform with DV standards. There are two types of DV-AVI files:

- Type 1: The multiplexed Audio-Video is kept in its original multiplexing and saved together into the Video section of the AVI file
- Does not waste much space (audio is saved uncompressed, but even uncompressed audio is tiny compared to the video part of DV), but Windows applications based on the VfW API do not support it.
- Type 2: Like type 1, but audio is also saved as an additional audio stream into the file.
- Supported by VfW applications, at the price of little increased file size.

Type 1 is actually the newer of the two types. Microsoft made the "type" designations, and decided to name their older VfW-compatible version "Type 2", which only furthered confusion about the two types. In the late 1990s through early 2000s, most professional-level DV software, including non-linear editing programs, only supported Type 1. One notable exception was Adobe Premiere, which only supported Type 2. High-end FireWire controllers usually captured to Type 1 only, while "consumer" level controllers usually captured to Type 2 only. Software is and was available for converting Type 1 AVIs to Type 2, and vice-versa, but this is a time-consuming process.

Many current FireWire controllers still only capture to one or the other type. However, almost all current DV software supports both Type 1 and Type 2 editing and rendering, including Adobe Premiere. Thus, many of today's users are unaware of the fact that there are two types of DV AVI files. In any event, the debate continues as to which – Type 1 or Type 2 – if either, is better.

3.7 Sound Synthesis

The process by which a sound card creates music is called the sound synthesis or audio synthesis. Dialogue, music or other sound effects can be achieved either through audio means or through sound synthesis. Captured audio in digital form provides high quality sound reproduction and is useful for dialogue and music sequences. There are two fundamental types of sound syntheis technology.

1. The FM Synthesis
2. The Wavetable Synthesis

3.7.1 The FM Synthesis

It is an outdated technique which is not very commonly used now-a-days.

3.7.2 The Wavetable Synthesis

Wavetable synthesis is used in certain digital music synthesizers to implement a restricted form of real-time additive synthesis. The technique was first developed by Wolfgang Palm of PPG in the late 1970s and published in 1979, and has since been used as the primary synthesis method in synthesizers built by PPG and Waldorf Music and as an auxiliary synthesis method by Sequential Circuits, Ensoniq, Korg, Access and Dave Smith Instruments among others.

Wavetable synthesis is fundamentally based on periodic reproduction of an arbitrary, single-cycle waveform. The distinction to other synthesis methods employing single-cycle waveforms is twofold:

1. multiple single-cycle waveforms are used while
2. one or several wave modulators control the change between those multiple waveforms or mixtures thereof.

The wave modulation rate is usually significantly smaller than the sampling rate.

The particular sound associated with wavetable synthesis is unique, since only perfect harmonics are produced. Depending on the details of the actual implementation the sound also contains recognizable artefacts, especially aliasing, quantization and phase truncation noise.

3.7.2.1 Comparison with other digital synthesis techniques

Wavetable synthesis is closely related to additive synthesis, however unlike additive synthesis the user does not have to work with single harmonics, since each waveform in a wavetable represents a combination of multiple harmonics.

- Sample-based synthesis uses multiple-cycle waveforms and intricate algorithms for pitch-shifting.
- LA synthesis uses short PCM samples for the attack portion of the sound and looped samples (most of them single-cycle loops) for the sustain/release portion of the sound.
- Granular Synthesis uses many overlapping windowed samples. While these samples are very short, they are never periodic.

3.8 Compression and Transmission of Audio on Internet

It is a subject of debate whether analog audio is superior to digital audio or vice versa. The question is highly dependent on the quality of the systems (analog or digital) under review, and other factors which are not necessarily related to sound quality. Arguments for analog systems include the absence of fundamental error mechanisms which are present in digital audio systems, including aliasing, quantization noise, and the absolute limitation of dynamic range. Advocates of digital point to the high levels of performance possible with digital audio, including excellent linearity in the audible band and low levels of noise and distortion (Sony Europe 2001).

Accurate, high quality sound reproduction is possible with both analog and digital systems. Excellent, expensive analog systems may outperform digital systems, and vice versa; in theory any system of either type may be surpassed by a better, more elaborate and costly system of the other type, but in general it tends to be less expensive to achieve any given standard of technical signal quality with a digital system, except when the standard is very low. One of the most limiting aspects of analog technology is the sensitivity of analog media to minor physical degradation; however, when the degradation is more pronounced, analog systems usually perform better, often still producing recognizable sound, while digital systems will usually fail completely, unable to play back anything from the medium. The principal advantages that digital systems have are very uniform source fidelity, inexpensive media duplication (and playback) costs, and direct use of the digital 'signal' in today's popular portable storage and playback devices. Analog recordings by comparison require comparatively bulky, high-quality playback equipment to capture the signal from the media as accurately as digital.

Early in the development of the Compact Disc, engineers realized that the perfection of the spiral of bits was critical to playback fidelity. A scratch the width of a human hair (100 micrometres) could corrupt several dozen bits, resulting in at best a pop, and far worse, a loss of synchronization of the clock and data, giving a long segment of noise until resynchronized. This was addressed by encoding the digital stream with a multi-tiered error-correction coding scheme which reduces CD capacity by about 20%, but makes it tolerant to hundreds of surface imperfections across the disk without loss of signal. In essence, "error correction" can be thought of as "using the mathematically encoded backup copies of the data that was corrupted." Not only does the CD use redundant data, but it also mixes up the bits in a predetermined way (see CIRC) so that a small flaw on the disc will affect fewer consecutive bits of the decoded signal and allow for more effective error correction using the available backup information.

Error correction allows digital formats to tolerate quite a bit more media deterioration than analog formats. That is not to say poorly produced digital media are immune to data loss. Laser rot was most troublesome to the Laserdisc format, but also occurs to some pressed commercial CDs, and was caused in both cases by inadequate disc manufacture. (Note that Laserdisc, despite using a laser optical system that has become commonly associated with digital disc formats, is an old analog format, except for its optional digital audio tracks; the video image portion of the content is always analog.) There can occasionally be difficulties related to the use of consumer recordable/rewritable compact discs. This may be due to poor-quality CD recorder drives, low-quality discs, or incorrect storage, as the information-bearing dye layer of most CD-recordable discs is at least slightly sensitive to UV light and will be slowly bleached out if exposed to any amount of it. Most digital recordings rely at least to some extent on computational encoding and decoding and so may become completely unplayable if not enough consecutive good data is available for the decoder to synchronize to the digital data stream, whereas any intact fragment of any size of an analog recording is usually playable.

Unlike analog duplication, digital copies are usually exact replicas, which can be duplicated indefinitely without degradation, unless imposed DRM restrictions apply or mastering errors occur. Digital systems often have the ability for the same medium to be used with arbitrarily high or low quality encoding methods and number of channels or other content, unlike practically all analog systems which have mechanically pre-fixed speeds and channels. Most higher-end analog recording systems offer a few selectable recording speeds, but digital systems tend to offer much finer variation in the rate of media usage.

There are also several non-sound related advantages of digital systems that are practical. Digital systems that are computer-based make editing much easier through rapid random access, seeking, and scanning for non-linear editing. Most digital systems also allow non-audio data to be encoded into the digital stream, such as information about the artist, track titles, etc., which is often convenient. (However, it is technically possible, and not difficult, to implement analog systems with integrated digital metadata channels. In fact, it is possible to record digital metadata onto one track of an analog multitrack recording using any home computer from the 1980s, such as a Commodore 64, that can record data on cassettes.)

3.9 Adding Sound your Multimedia Project

Apple was the first company to have sound and video interleaved into the computer. It outpaced Microsoft's Audio/Video Interleaved technology, with the release of QuickTime. QuickTime has become a standard file format for displaying digitized motion video from hard disk or CD-ROM without special hardware.

Digital audio data is interleaved with video information in the file and when it is played back the audio stays synchronized to the motion picture. You can use QuickTime just to play stereo sounds and MIDI; the video part of QuickTime is not required. QuickTime will display many graphic image formats as well.

Whether you're working on a Macintosh or in Windows, you will need to follow certain steps to bring an audio recording into your multimedia project. Here is a brief overview of the process:

1. Decide what kind of sound is needed (such as background music, special sound effects and spoken dialog). Decide where these audio events will occur in the flow of your project. Fit the sound cues into your storyboard or make up a cue sheet.
2. Decide where and when you want to use either digital audio or MIDI data.
3. Acquire source material by creating it from scratch or purchasing it.
4. Edit the sounds to fit your project.
5. Test the sounds to be sure they are timed properly with the project's images. This may involve repeating steps 1 through 4 until everything is in sync.

When it's time to import your compiled and edited sounds into your project, you'll need to know how your particular multimedia software environment handles sound data. Each program handles it a bit differently, but the process is usually fairly straightforward: just tell your software which file you want to play and when to play it. This is usually handled by an importing or "linking" process during which you identify the files.

Scripting languages such an OpenScript (ToolBook), Lingo (Director) and ActionScript (Flash) provide a greater level of control over audio playback, but you'll need to know about the programming language and environment. In authoring environments, it is usually a simple matter to play a sound when the user clicks a button, but this may not be enough.

If the user changes screens while a long file is playing, for example, you may need to program the sound to stop before leaving the current screen. If the file to be played cannot be found on the hard disk, you may need to code an entire section for error handling and file location. Sample code is generally provided in both printed and online documentation for software that includes sound playback.

3.9.1 Recording Sound using Sound Recorder

If you have a microphone attached to sound card in your PC, you can use Sound Recorder available in Windows to make voice recordings, which can then be added to other documents. And if your sound card has a Line in Connector, then you can connect a stereo receiver or other sound sorce to it and use Sound Recorder to make recordings from that source. Sound stimulates the sense of hearing. In humans, hearing takes place whenever vibrations of frequencies from 15 hertz to about 20,000 hertz reach the inner ear. Such vibrations reach the inner ear when they are transmitted through air. The speed of sound varies, but at sea level it travels through cool, dry air at about 1,190 km/h (740 mph).

To make sound recording, do this:

1. To Open Sound Recorder, click Start, and then highlight Programs, Accessories, Entertainment and then Sound Recorder.
2. Choose Properties from the File menu. In the Properties dialog box that appears, click Convert Now... to display the Sound Selection dialog box, choose the file format and attributes, i.e., sampling rates you want. Click to close the Sound Selection dialog box and then click Ok to close the properties dialog box.
3. Click the Record button and start recording. As you record, the green line expands to indicate sound levels. You can see how much time has elapsed. The maximum recording length is 60 seconds.
4. When you finish the recording, click the Stop button.
5. To save the recording as a file, open the File menu, and choose Save and then name the file if you have not already given.

3.10 Audio Software and Hardware

or all practical purposes we would be talking about Personal Computers in general. This, however, does not rule out the possibility of running the multimedia product on any other computer. It can even be running on a TV with the help of a television set-top box such as Sega, Nintendo or Sony. These are becoming popular overseas though have a little presence in India.

3.10.1 Software and Operating System

The most important software which a personal computer has, is Operating System. And the most popular operating system now-a-days is Windows. It is upto you to use the version which suits you the best since Windows XP is the latest, but other versions like Windows 95/98/ME/2000 are also available in the market.

A graphic is first converted into bitmaps in computer. Sound is converted to digitized sound. For these whichever tools you use would not make a difference since the end product is the same. Indeed, many software tools readily convert picture, sound and other multimedia files (and even whole functioning projects) from Macintosh to Windows format, and vice versa, using known file formats or even binary compatible files that require no conversion at all.

Multimedia software tells the hardware what to do. Display the colour red. Move that tiger three leaps to the left. Slide in the words "Now You've Done It!" from the right and blink them on and off. Play the sound of cannibals crashing. Run the digitized movie of Captain Hook. Turn down the volume on that MP3 file!

You do not have to be a programmer or a computer scientist to make multimedia work for you, but you do need some familiarity with terms and building blocks; even the simplest multimedia tool requires an iota of knowledge to operate. If someone sends you a file in Macintosh AIF format, you should know that you're getting digitalized sound. Then load up your tools and open the help files' learning curve. It will be easier to manage because you have the bigger picture.

3.10.2 Playing MIDI Files Using Media Player

Media files can be played using Media Player in the following manner.

1. Start Media Player by clicking the Start button, and then highlighting Programs, Accessories, Entertainment and Media Player.

2. Open the File menu and choose Open and use the Open dialog box to open the file you want play. If the file you open is a video clip, a window displaying the first frame of the video appears.
3. Click the Start button to begin playing the media file.

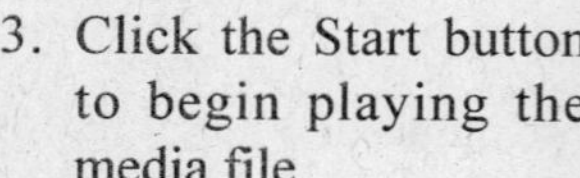

3.10.3 Playing Sound Files with Sound Recorder

To play the sound files using Sound Recorder, do the following:

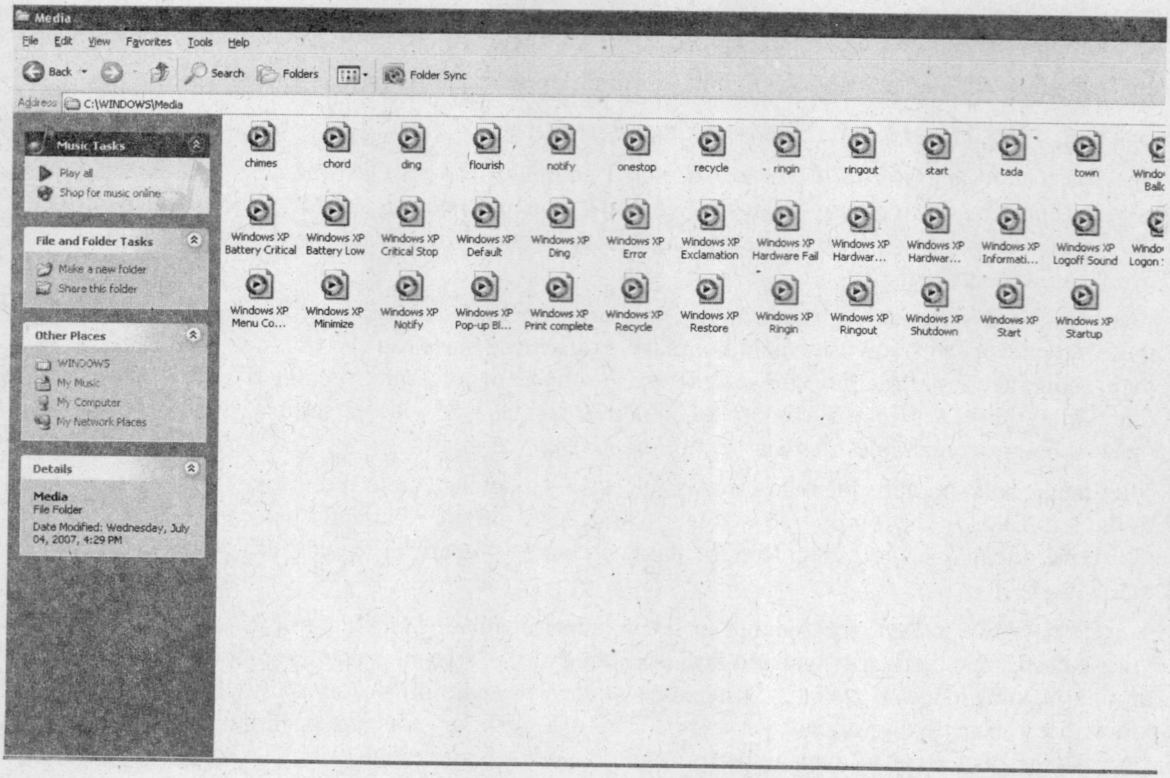

1. Start Sound recorder, as done earlier.
2. Click File menu, and choose Open or press Ctrl + O. The open dialog box appears.
3. In the dialog box, open the folder (containing the sound file) you want to play, then click Open command button.
4. Click the Play button in the sound recorder window to play the sound.
5. Click the Stop button to stop playing the sound.
6. If you want to move sound file from end to beginning, then you have to click Seek to Start button or move from beginning to end. Click Seek to End button.

Let us Revise

1. Sound is perhaps the most important part of the multimedia project.
2. Acoustics is the branch of science that studies sound.
3. Any recorded sound is known as analog sound an it is represented by the fluctuations in the amplitude.
4. Digital sound is a term applied to sound that has been digitized into binary code.
5. The number of pressure variation per second is called frequency of sound.
6. Bandwidth is how much data, expressed in bits per second (bps), you can send from one computer to another in a given amount of time.
7. Data rate is the rate at which information being transferred.
8. When you create multimedia, it is likely that you will deal with file formats and translators for text, sounds, images, animations or digital video clips.
9. Audio Interchange File Format (AIFF) is an audio file format standard used for storing sound data for personal computers and other electronic audio devices.
10. MIDI (Musical Instrument Digital Interface), is an industry-standard protocol that enables electronic musical instruments such as keyboard controllers, computers, and other electronic equipment to communicate, control, and synchronize with each other.
11. WAVE or WAV, short for Waveform Audio File Format, is a Microsoft and IBM audio file format standard for storing an audio bitstream on PCs.
12. MPEG-1 Audio Layer 3, more commonly referred to as MP3, is a patented digital audio encoding format using a form of lossy data compression.
13. When performing lossy audio encoding, such as creating an MP3 file, there is a trade-off between the amount of space used and the sound quality of the result.
14. Advanced Systems Format (formerly Advanced Streaming Format, Active Streaming Format) is Microsoft's proprietary digital audio/digital video container format, especially meant for streaming media. ASF is part of the Windows Media framework.
15. RealMedia is a multimedia container format created by RealNetworks.
16. Audio Video Interleave, known by its acronym AVI, is a multimedia container format introduced by Microsoft in November 1992 as part of its Video for Windows technology.
17. The process by which a sound card creates music is called the sound synthesis or audio synthesis.

18. Wavetable synthesis is used in certain digital music synthesizers to implement a restricted form of real-time additive synthesis.
19. Accurate, high quality sound reproduction is possible with both analog and digital systems.
20. QuickTime has become a standard file format for displaying digitized motion video from hard disk or CD-ROM without special hardware.
21. Scripting languages such an OpenScript (ToolBook), Lingo (Director) and ActionScript (Flash) provide a greater level of control over audio playback, but you'll need to know about the programming language and environment.

Multiple Choice Questions

1. Which of the following statements about MIDI audio is not true:
   (a) Files are smaller than digital audio sound.
   (b) MIDI can easily be used to playback spoken dialog.
   (c) MIDI data is completely editable.
   (d) MIDI data is device dependent.
2. ASF stands for:
   (a) advanced systems format (b) advanced streaming format (c) advanced systems file
   (d) asynchonous sound format.
3. Human hearing frequency range is:
   (a) 0 to 20 Hz (b) 20 Hz to 20 KHz (c) 20 KHz to 1 GHz
   (d) 1 GHz to 10 THz.
4. We can record the sound by:
   (a) Windows Media Player (b) Sound Recorder (c) both (a) and (b)
   (d) none of the above.
5. Removing blank space or dead air at the beginning or end of a recording is sometimes called:
   (a) quantizing (b) trimming (c) flashing
   (d) quieting.
6. Which is true about MIDI files:
   (a) MIDI files aremuch more compact than digital audio files.
   (b) MIDI files embedded in web pages load and play more quickly than their digital equivalents.
   (c) MIDI files may sound better than digital audio files.
   (d) all of the above.
7. Which of the following is a combination of text, audio and graphics?
   (a) Images (b) Video (c) Multimedia
   (d) Unimedia

True/False Questions

1. Acoustics is the branch of science that studies sound.
2. Digital sound is a term applied to sound that has been digitized into binary code.

3. Bandwidth is how much data, expressed in bits per second (bps), you can send from one computer to another in a given amount of time.
4. When you create multimedia, it is not likely that you will deal with file formats and translators for text, sounds, images, animations or digital video clips.
5. MIDI (Musical Instrument Digital Interface), is an industry-standard protocol that enables electronic musical instruments such as keyboard controllers, computers, and other electronic equipment to communicate, control, and synchronize with each other.
6. MPEG-1 Audio Layer 3, more commonly referred to as MP3, is a non-patented digital audio encoding formát using a form of lossy data compression.
7. RealMedia is a multimedia container format created by RealNetworks.
8. The process by which a sound card creates music is called the sound synthesis or audio synthesis.
9. Accurate, high quality sound reproduction is possible with both analog and digital systems.

Matching Columns

In the following case, commands are given in the left hand columns and their actions in the right hand column. Match them.

Column A	Column B
A. Microphone	1. Branch of physics that studies sound
B. AIFF	2. KHz (Kilohertz)
C. DSP	3. removing dead aire or blank space
D. Audio File Format	4. Sound format
E. Acoustics	5. Transducer device
F. Trimming	6. Digital Sound Processing
G Sampling rate	7. .wav

Fill in the Blanks with appropriate words

a. sampling rate b. decibels c. sampling size d. trimming

e. Transducer f. sound

1. _________ is produced by the vibration of matter.
2. _________ is a device capable of changing signals from one form to another.
3. The process of removing the blank spaces before or after the required signals is called _______.
4. Sound pressure levels (loudness or volume) are measured in ___________.
5. The number of computer zeros and ones (bits) required to represent a given signal in digital form is called ___________.
6. The time interval taken between two samples of the original analog data, during digitizing is called ___________.

Descriptive Type Questions

1. What do you understand by Sound?
2. Define the various types of sound.
3. How is sound digitized?

4. Define Frequency and Bandwidth
5. What is Decibel System?
6. Define the followings:

Audio Interchange File Format	Musical Instruments Digital Interface
Wave Form	MP3
Advanced Streaming Format	Audio Video Interleave

7. Describe the various types of sound synthesis.
8. How would you add sound to your multimedia project?
9. Describe the various software used for multimedia.
10. Describe how would you do the following:
    Play MIDI files using Media Player
    Play Sound files using Sound Recorder

Answers to Objective Type Questions

Multiple Choice Questions

1. b	2. b	3. b	4. b
5. b	6. d	7. c	

True False Questions

1. T	2. T	3. T	4. F
5. T	6. F	7. F	8. T
9. T			

Matching Columns

A. 5	B. 4	C. 6	D. 7
E. 1	F. 3	G 2	

Fill in the Blanks

1. f	2. e	3. d	4. b
5. c	6. a		

Image Fundamentals and Representations

4

4.1 Introduction

During the late 1970s, personal computers became more powerful, capable of drawing both basic and complex shapes and designs. In the 1980s, artists and graphic designers began to see the personal computer, particularly the Commodore Amiga and Macintosh, as a serious design tool, one that could save time and draw more accurately than other methods. 3D computer graphics became possible in the late 1980s with the powerful SGI computers, which were later used to create some of the first fully computer-generated short films at Pixar. The Macintosh remains one of the most popular tools for computer graphics in graphic design studios and businesses.

4.1.1 Colour Science

Modern computer systems, dating from the 1980s and onwards, often use a graphical user interface (GUI) to present data and information with symbols, icons and pictures, rather than text. Graphics are one of the five key elements of multimedia technology.

3D graphics became more popular in the 1990s in gaming, multimedia and animation. In 1996, Quake, one of the first fully 3D games, was released. In 1995, Toy Story, the first full-length computer-generated animation film, was released in cinemas worldwide. Since then, computer graphics have become more accurate and detailed, due to more advanced computers and better 3D modelling software applications, such as Cinema 4D.

4.1.2 Image types

4.1.2.1 2D Computer Graphics

2D computer graphics are the computer-based generation of digital images—mostly from two-dimensional models, such as 2D geometric models, text, and digital images, and by techniques specific to them. The word may stand for the branch of computer science that comprises such techniques, or for the models themselves.

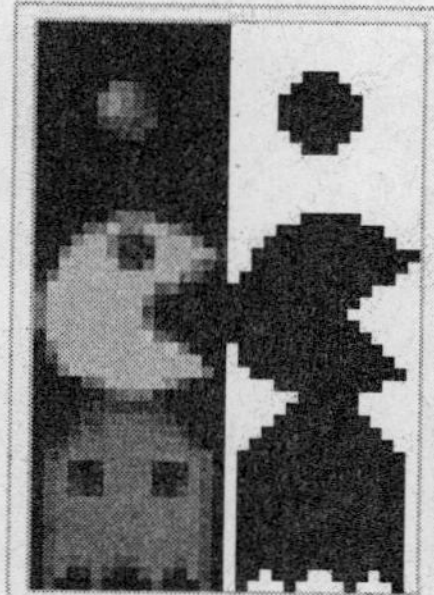

Raster graphic sprites (left) and masks (right)

2D computer graphics are mainly used in applications that were originally developed upon traditional printing and drawing technologies, such as typography, cartography, technical drawing, advertising, etc.. In those applications, the two-dimensional image is not just a representation of a real-world object, but an independent artifact with added semantic value; two-dimensional models are therefore preferred, because they give more direct control of the image than 3D computer graphics, whose approach is more akin to photography than to typography.

4.1.2.2 *Pixel art*

Pixel art is a form of digital art, created through the use of raster graphics software, where images are edited on the pixel level. Graphics in most old (or relatively limited) computer and video games, graphing calculator games, and many mobile phone games are mostly pixel art.

4.1.2.3 *Vector Graphics*

Vector graphics formats are complementary to raster graphics, which is the representation of images as an array of pixels, as it is typically used for the representation of photographic images. There are instances when working with vector tools and formats is best practice, and instances when working with raster tools and formats is best practice. There are times when both formats come together. An understanding of the advantages and limitations of each technology and the relationship between them is most likely to result in efficient and effective use of tools.

4.1.2.4 *3D Computer Graphics*

3D computer graphics in contrast to 2D computer graphics are graphics that use a three-dimensional representation of geometric data that is stored in the computer for the purposes of performing calculations and rendering 2D images. Such images may be for later display or for real-time viewing.

7x Magnification

Vector

Bitmap

Ice Cream

Example showing effect of vector graphics versus raster graphics.

Despite these differences, 3D computer graphics rely on many of the same algorithms as 2D computer vector graphics in the wire frame model and 2D computer raster graphics in the final rendered display. In computer graphics software, the distinction between 2D and 3D is occasionally blurred; 2D applications may use 3D techniques to achieve effects such as lighting, and primarily 3D may use 2D rendering techniques.

3D computer graphics are often referred to as 3D models. Apart from the rendered graphic, the model is contained within the graphical data file. However, there are differences. A 3D model is the mathematical representation of any three-dimensional object (either inanimate or living). A model is not technically a graphic until it is visually displayed. Due to 3D printing, 3D models are not confined to virtual space. A model can be displayed visually as a two-dimensional image through a process called 3D rendering, or used in non-graphical computer simulations and calculations.

4.1.2.5 *Computer Animation*

Computer animation is the art of creating moving images via the use of computers. It is a subfield of computer graphics and animation. Increasingly it is created by means of 3D computer graphics, though 2D computer graphics are still widely used for stylistic, low bandwidth, and faster real-time rendering needs. Sometimes the target of the animation is the computer itself, but sometimes the target is another medium, such as film. It is also referred to as CGI (Computer-generated imagery or computer-generated imaging), especially when used in films.

An example of Computer animation produced using Motion capture

To create the illusion of movement, an image is displayed on the computer screen then quickly replaced by a new image that is similar to the previous image, but shifted slightly. This technique is identical to the illusion of movement in television and motion pictures.

4.2 Colour and Colour Models

Colours are everywhere around us. But, how does one colour differ from another. There are a number of colour libraries and each one of them have different shades. There is so much to colours that it may need one book to study each one of them.

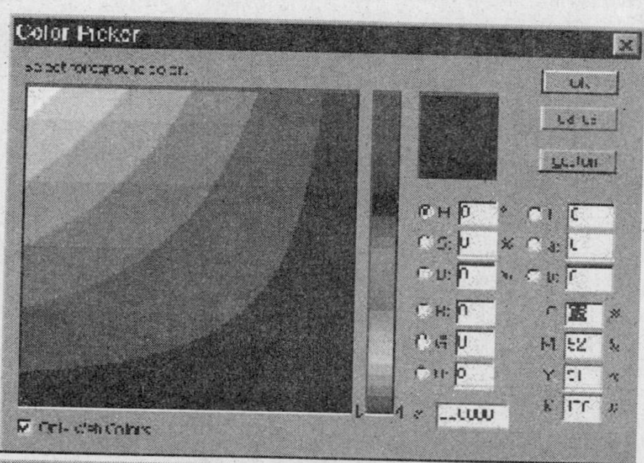

Let us concentrate on what is available under Photoshop.

We would be talking about 4 different type of colour modes:

- RGB (Red, Green and Blue)
- CYMK (Cyan, Yellow, Magenta and Black)
- HSB (Hue, Saturation and Brightness)
- CIE Lab

Let us study them one by one.

4.2.1 RGB Model

This is made up of three primary colours, i.e., Red, Green and Blue. Most of the colours are the mixture of all these. For example a pure Red will be 255, maximum for a colour, of Red and 0 of Green and Blue each. While the White would be 255 of each and Black would be 0 of each.

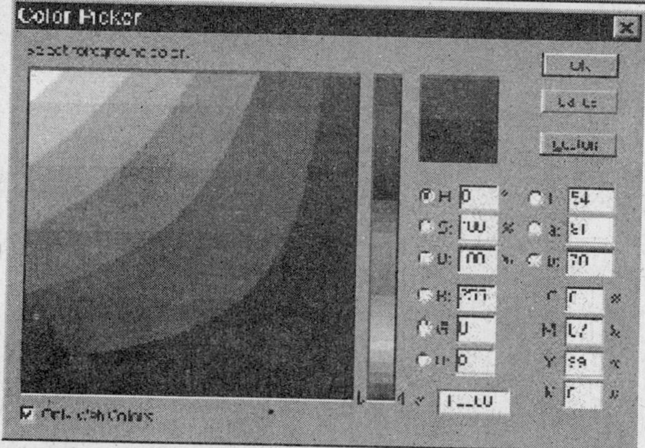

4.2.2 CYMK Model

As said earlier CYMK stands for Cyan, Yellow, Magenta and Black. These 4 also make a set of combinations to form different colours. Here you have to add them according to percentages of each one of them. This set of colours are used by the high-end laser printers and are mostly used by commercial printers.

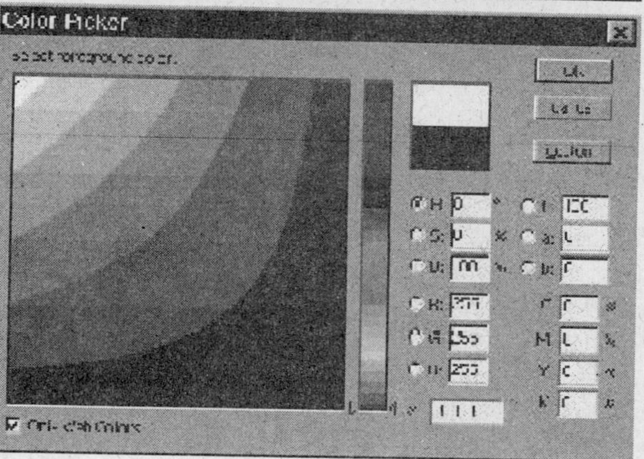

4.2.3 HSB Model

This is another colour combination where H stands for Hue, S for Saturation and B for Brightness. Here Hue is the basic colour from the colour wheel, which is expressed in terms of degrees from 0 to 360. It represents the position of the colour on the colour wheel. Saturation is the strength of the colour. It is measured in percentage of colour minus the amount of gray in it. Brightness is also measured in terms of percentage. It varies from 0 where it is black and to 100 where it is white.

4.2.4 CIE Lab

Photoshop uses the CIE mode, because its gamut is so broad, to convert from one colour model to another.

4.2.5 Bitmap and Grayscale Mode

The Bitmap mode uses only two colour values to display images—black and white, while the Grayscale mode offers 256 shades of gray that range from white to black.

Whenever a picture is printed in black and white or Grayscale, for instance, as part of a newsletter or brochure, it makes sense for you to work on it in Grayscale mode. To convert a color image to Grayscale, simply choose Image; Mode, Grayscale. You will asked for permission to discard the colour information. Click Ok to confirm, and picture is converted to grays.

4.2.6 Indexed Colours

Indexed Colour is a palette or rather a collection of palettes—256 to be exact. With this mode, you know exactly what you are getting, and you do not like any of the palettes Photoshop supplies, you can build your own. This type of colours are perfect for World Wide Web.

Dithering means that certain colours are combined, that is, adjacent pixels are interspersed, visually blending onscreen to create a new colour although they retain their original colour—or the closest index equivalent—when viewed at a large magnification.

4.3 Colour palettes

The HDR Color Picker allows you to accurately view and select colors for use in 32 bit HDR images. As in the regular Adobe Color Picker, you select a color by clicking a color field and adjusting the color slider. The Intensity slider allows you to adjust the brightness of a color to match the intensity of the colors in the HDR image you're working with. A Preview area lets you view swatches of a selected color to see how it will display at different exposures and intensities.

4.3.1 Change the Color Picker

Instead of using the Adobe Color Picker, you can choose colors from your computer operating system's standard color picker or from a third party color picker.

1. Choose Edit > Preferences > General (Windows) or Photoshop > Preferences > General (Mac OS).
2. Choose a color picker from the Color Picker menu, and click OK.

4.3.2 About Foreground and Background Colors

Photoshop uses the foreground color to paint, fill, and stroke selections and the background color to make gradient fills and fill in the erased areas of an image. The foreground and background colors are also used by some special effects filters. You can designate a new foreground or background color using the Eyedropper tool, the Color palette, the Swatches palette, or the Adobe Color Picker. The default foreground color is black, and the default background color is white. (In an alpha channel, the default foreground is white, and the background is black.)

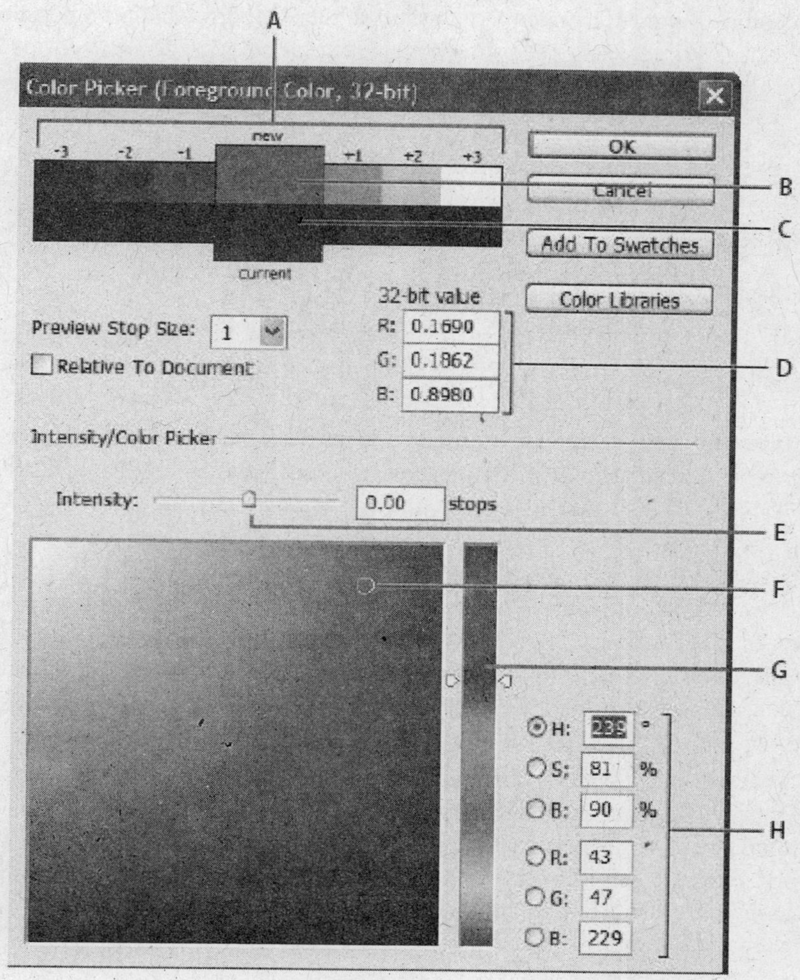

Colour Picker

A. Preview area B. Adjusted color C. Original color D. 32-bit floating point value E. Intensity slider F. Picked color G. Color slider H. Color values

4.3.3 Customize Color Settings

For most color-managed workflows, it is best to use a preset color setting that has been tested by Adobe Systems. Changing specific options is recommended only if you are knowledgeable about color management and very confident about the changes you make.

After you customize options, you can save them as a preset. Saving color settings ensures that you can reuse them and share them with other users or applications.

- To save color settings as a preset, click Save in the Color Settings dialog box. To ensure that the application displays the setting name in the Color Settings dialog box, save the file in the default location. If you save the file to a different location, you must load the file before you can select the setting.

- To load a color settings preset that's not saved in the standard location, click Load in the Color Settings dialog box, select the file you want to load, and click Open.

Thus, we have the following set of standard number of colours that could be deployed for multi-colour display purposes:

Colour depth	Colours available
1 - bit per pixel	2 Colours
4 - bits per pixel	16 Colours
8 - bits per pixel	256 Colours (known as 8 bit colour)
16 - bits per pixel	65,536 Colours (known as 16 bit colour)
24 - bits per pixel	16.7 million colours (known as 24 bit colour or 'True Colour' as it almost resembles the actual world, also with millions of colours)

Colour depth defines the number of bits required to store the information of each pixel in the image, and in turn determines the total number of possible colours that can be displayed in the image. For example, an 8-bit number and can display a total of 2^8 or 256 colours.

4.4 Dithering

A technique used in computer graphics to create the illusion of varying shades of gray on a monochrome display or printer, or additional colors on a color display or printer. Dithering relies on treating areas of an image as groups of dots that are colored in different patterns. Akin to the print images called halftones, dithering takes advantage of the eye's tendency to blur spots of different colors by averaging their effects and merging them into a single perceived shade or color.

Depending on the ratio of black dots to white dots within a given area, the overall effect is of a particular shade of gray. Dithering is used to add realism to computer graphics and to soften jagged edges in curves and diagonal lines at low resolutions. In the half tone process, patterns of dot used to build scanned or printed image create the illusion of continuous shades of gray or continuous shades of colour. In a half-tone process, half-tone dots vary in size according to their gray or colour value. The darker the gray value, the larger the dot size.

4.5 2D Graphics

See section 4.2.1.1

4.6 Image Compression and File Formats:

Encoding data to take up less storage space. For example, short names in fixed length fields waste a lot of space. A simple method called run length encoding converts the spaces into a code that indicates how many blanks follow. There are two major methods used for data compression, statistic and dictionary and two widely-used examples of each: Huffman coding and LZW (Lempel-Ziv-Welch). Text files can be compressed the most. Dense, machine language files can be compressed about third. While some graphics files leave little room for compaction, others compress well.

The data compression technique is used on a graphical image. Uncompressed graphics files tend to use up large amounts of storage, so image compression is useful to conserve space. Image compression is minimizing the size in bytes of a graphic files without degrading the quality of the image to an unacceptable level. The reduction in the file size allows more images to be stored in a given amount of disk or memory space. It also reduces the time required for images to be sent over the Internet or download from web pages.

In information technology, lossy compression is a data compression method which discards (loses) some of the data, in order to achieve its goal, with the result that decompressing the data yields content that is different from the original, though similar enough to be useful in some way. Lossy compression is most commonly used to compress multimedia data (audio, video, still images), especially in applications such as streaming media and internet telephony. By contrast, lossless compression is required for text and data files, such as bank records, text articles, etc. In many cases it is advantageous to make a master lossless file which can then be used to produce compressed files for different purposes; for example a multi-megabyte file can be used at full size to produce a full-page advertisement in a glossy magazine, and a 10 kilobyte lossy copy made for a small image on a web page

4.6.1 Lossy and Lossless Compression

It is possible to compress many types of digital data in a way which reduces the size of a computer file needed to store it or the bandwidth needed to stream it, with no loss of the full information contained in the original file. A picture, for example, is converted to a digital file by considering it to be an array of dots, and specifying the colour and brightness of each dot. If the picture contains an area of the same colour, it can be compressed without loss by saying "200 red dots" instead of "red dot, red dot, ...(197 more times)..., red dot".

The original contains a certain amount of information; there is a lower limit to the size of file that can carry all the information. As an intuitive example, most people know that a compressed ZIP file is smaller than the original file; but repeatedly compressing the file will not reduce the size to nothing, and will in fact usually increase the size.

In many cases files or data streams contain more information than is needed for a particular purpose. For example, a picture may have more detail than the eye can distinguish when reproduced at the largest size intended; an audio file does not need a lot of fine detail during a very loud passage. Developing lossy compression techniques as closely matched to human perception as possible is a complex task. In some cases the ideal is a file which provides exactly the same perception as the original, with as much digital information as possible removed; in other cases perceptible loss of quality is considered a valid trade-off for the reduced data size.

4.6.2 Compression ratio

The compression ratio (that is, the size of the compressed file compared to that of the uncompressed file) of lossy video codecs is nearly always far superior to that of the audio and still-image equivalents.

- Video can be compressed immensely (e.g. 100:1) with little visible quality loss;
- Audio can often be compressed at 10:1 with imperceptible loss of quality;
- Still images are often lossily compressed at 10:1, as with audio, but the quality loss is more noticeable, especially on closer inspection.

4.6.3 Compabilities and Limitations of Bitmap Images

When a bitmap displays a coloured image, such as a mountain, there are several shades of gradation in colours and lighting. In this case, each pixel in the bitmap might have 16, 24, or 48 bits of information associaged with it. The more bits, the greater the resolution of the bitmap and the larger the file.

- Compression techniques are used to shrink the file size of the bitmap while maintaining as much data as is necessary to render a good picture. One such format is the 8-bit .gif format, while uses a palletter of 256 colours. The advantage of the compressed .gif is that is smaller file that can be resized with satisfactory results, as it uses lossless compression. The disadvantage is that it cannot faithfully reproduce images containing more than 256 colours.

- Bitmaps are an image type most appropriate for photo-realistic images and complex drawings requiring fine detail.
- Limitation of bitmapped image include large file sizes and the inability to scale or resize the image easily while maintaining quality. A bitmap image when magnified to larger sizes leads to increase in distance betwen pixels. At a certain stage individual pixel become visible as single — coloured squares and image takes on a boxy apprearance with degradation in quality. This phenomenon, is called pixelation.
- You can grab a bitmap image from a screen, scan it with a scanner, download it from a website, or capture it from a video capture device.
- You can then manipulate and adjust many of its properties, and cut and paste among many bitmaps using specialized image editing programs.
- You can import a colour or gray scale bitmap from the Windows, the colours will seem darker and richer.
- Because bitmap images are built pixeel by pixel, they can be easily edited. Zooming in on a bitmap image in any graphics program allows the user to add, delete, or change the colour of individual pixels.

4.6.4 Capabilities and Limitations of Vector Images

Vector images are a collection of individual objects rather than pictures elements. A vector image can be composed of points connected by lines, or nodes (control points) connected by Bezier curves.

- Each individual object contained in a vector image is defined by a mathematical equation. This means that vector images are not resolution dependent. Thus, each vector object is scalable and can generally be resized without any loss of image quality. As such, vector images are ideal for graphics usch as maps and company logos that often equire scaling.
- A vector object cna be filled with colour and patterns, and you can select it as a single object.
- Each individual object may be edited to contain attributes such as outline, colour and fill. Modifying the object's attributes will not change the basic object. The size of the object can also be transformed or shaped by using and adjusting its control points.
- Vector images are most appropriate for lines, boxes, circles, polygons and other graphic shapes that can be mathematically expressed in angles, coordinates and distances.
- Vector images cannot be used for photo realistic images and photos
- For the web pages, that use vector graphics in plug-ins such as Flash, download faster and when used for animation, draw faster than bitmaps.
- Vector images have no white pixel backgrounds. This means that you can put a vector object above another without blocking out the object underneath.
- Vector drawn objects use a fraction of the memory space required to describe and store the same object form.

- Vector images typically have small file size because one such file contains only the mathematical equations that determine the Bezier curves that efine the image. A vector image file does not contain the image itself.
- Converting bitmaps to vector drawn objects is difficult, however, autotracing programs can compute the bounds of shapes and colours in bitmapped mages require a plug (such as a Flash player) for display on a web page.

4.7 GIF

GIF stands for Graphics Interchange Format. It is another format that is widely used for picture displayed on the World Wide Web. GIF file format is commonly used to display indexed colour graphics and images in hypertext markup language (HTML) documents overe the World Wide Web. GIF files have .gif extension.

GIF graphics file format developed by CompuServe and used for transmitting raster images on the Internet. An image may contain up to 256 colors, including a transparent color. The size of the file depends on the number of colors actually used. The LZW compression method is used to reduce the file size still further.

4.8 JPEG

The primary programs for lossless editing of JPEGs are jpegtran, and the derived exiftran (which also preserves Exif information), and Jpegcrop (which provides a Windows interface).

These allow the image to be

- cropped,
- rotated, flipped, and flopped, or
- converted to grayscale (by dropping the chrominance channel).

While unwanted information is destroyed, the quality of the remaining portion is unchanged.

JPEGjoin allows different JPEG images which have the same encoding to be joined without re-encoding.

Some changes can be made to the compression without re-encoding:

- optimize the compression (to reduce size without change to the decoded image),
- convert between progressive and non-progressive encoding,

The freeware Windows-only IrfanView has some lossless JPEG operations in its JPG_TRANSFORM plugin.

4.9 JPEG 2000

It is a format that provides grater flexibility than the standard JPEG format. Using JPEG 2000, you can produce images with better compression and quality for both web and print publishing. Unlike traditional JPEG files, which are lossy. The JPEG 2000 format supports optional lossless compression. The JPEG 2000 format also supports using a region of interes (ROI) to minimize file size and preserve quality in critical regions of an image.

4.10 PNG

It handles 1 to 48 bit images, and is a lossless, well-compressed format like GIF. However, it is still not very popular format. It supports a large set of techical features; including superior lossless compression feature. Compression in PNG is called the ZIP method. PNG comes in two formats, PNG-8 and PNG-24.

PNG-8: It is similar to the GIF format. The difference is that in the PNG format, images can be stored with a maximum of 256 colours and brilliantly supports 1-bit transparency. It is because of efficient colour data saving of PNG format.

PNG-24: It comes with 24-bit colour support and is much efficient to JPEG because, PNG-24 is a lossless compression format and is more suitable for the creations of larger files in comparision to JPEG. The files of PNG format have .png extension.

4.11 TIFF

Tagged Image File Format – Widely-used raster graphics file format developed by Aldus and Microsoft that handles monochrome, gray scale, 8-and 24-bit color. It uses several compression methods: LZW provides ratios of about 1.5:1 to 2:1. Ratios of 10:1 to 20:1 are possible for documents with lots of white space using CCITT Group III sIV compression methods (fax). It is widely used for transferring bitmap images between application programs. TIFF images have .tiff and .tif extension. It is used in desktop publishing, faxing, 3-D applications and medical imaging applications. It is a file format designed by Microsoft.

4.12 EXIF (Exchangeable Image File Format)

It is a standard for storing interchange information in image files, especially those using JPEG compression. Most digital cameras now use the EXIF format. The format is part of the DCF standard created by JEITA to encourage interperability between imaging devices.

4.13 PS (Postscript)

Page description language from Adobe Systems, Inc., used in a wide variety of printers, image setters and display systems. PostScript Commands do not drive the printer directly. They are language statements (ASCII text) that are translated into the printer's machine language by a PostScript interpreter built into the printer. Fonts are scaled to size by the interpreter, thus eliminating the need to store a variety of font sizes on disk. PostScript fonts come in Type 1 and Type 3 formats and Adobe makes only Type 1. Type 1 fonts are widely used and are made by other companies as Adobe later made the format public. Type 1 fonts are encrypted and compressed and also allow for hints which improve the appearance of text, especially at desktop laser printer resolutions. Type 1 fonts use a simpler, more efficient command language than Type 3. With Adobe Type Manager, Type 1 fonts can also be used on non PostScripts printers. Type 3 fonts do not use encryption or hints, but can use the entire PostScript language to create complex designs that include fills and patterns. Type 3 fonts can also be bitmaps. In order to speed up printing small fonts on PostScript printers, Windows 3.1 creates Type 3 bitmaps from its TrueType outlines. Originally developed as a device-independent imaging language, PostScript is used extensively on Macs and PCs. It has also migrated to workstations, minis and mainframes.

4.14 PDF

A richly formatted document which may contain graphics as well as text that can be transferred to another type of computer system without losing the rich formatting. To create portable documents, you need portable document software (PDS), such as Adobe Acrobat that is designed to save the formatting information to a file that can be easily transferred to a different type of computer system. To read the document, you need a file viewer program that is specifically designed to work on the type of computer you are using. For example, you can create an Adobe Acrobat document on a Macintosh and give the file to somebody using a Sun workstation. To read the file, the Sun user needs a copy of the Adobe Acrobat reader program.

4.15 Basic Image Processing

In 1987, Thomas Knoll, a PhD student at the University of Michigan, began writing a program on his Macintosh Plus to display grayscale images on a monochrome display. This program, called Display, caught the attention of his brother John Knoll, an Industrial Light & Magic employee, who recommended Thomas turn it into a full-fledged image editing program. Thomas took a six month break from his studies in 1988 to collaborate with his brother on the program, which had been renamed ImagePro.

Later that year, Thomas renamed his program Photoshop and worked out a short-term deal with scanner manufacturer Barneyscan to distribute copies of the program with a slide scanner; a "total of about 200 copies of Photoshop were shipped" this way. During this time, John traveled to Silicon Valley and gave a demonstration of the program to engineers at Apple Computer Inc. and Russell Brown, art director at Adobe. Both showings were successful, and Adobe decided to purchase the license to distribute in September 1988. While John worked on plug-ins in California, Thomas remained in Ann Arbor writing program code. Photoshop 1.0 was released in 1990 for Macintosh exclusively.

4.15.1 Photoshop CS3

Photoshop CS3 is marketed with three main components of improvement over previous versions: "Work more productively, edit with unrivalled power, and composite with breakthrough tools." New features

propagating productivity include streamlined interface, improved Camera Raw, better control over print options, enhanced PDF support, and better management with Adobe Bridge. Editing tools new to CS3 are the Clone Source palette and nondestructive Smart Filters, and other features such as the Brightness/ Contrast adjustment and Vanishing Point module were enhanced. The Black and White adjustment option improves users control over manual grayscale conversions with a dialog box similar to that of Channel Mixer. Compositing is assisted with Photoshop's new Quick Selection and Refine Edge tools and improved image stitching technology. CS3 Extended contains all features of CS3 plus tools for editing and importing some 3D graphics file formats, enhancing video, and comprehensive image analysis tools, utilizing MATLAB integration and DICOM file support.

4.15.2 Starting Photoshop CS 3

You can start Photoshop CS 3 by one of the following methods:

4.15.2.1 Using the Start Menu

1. Click on **Start** button. The start menu will appear.
2. Click at **Programs**.
3. Click on **Adobe Photoshop CS 3**.

4.15.2.2 Using Shortcut

You can use this feature if the icon of the software has been created and is put on the desktop.

1. First, locate the Photoshop CS 3 shortcut icon.
2. When you find it, position the mouse over the icon and click it to open the software.

Using any of the above options you will start the software and get the opening screen first, and then the main screen on which you have to work.

Both the screens are shown on the next pages.

4.15.3 Minimum System Requirements

- Intel® Pentium® 4, Intel Centrino®, Intel Core™ Duo (or compatible) processor
- Microsoft® Windows® XP with Service Pack 2, Windows Vista™ Home Premium, Business, Ultimate, or Enterprise (certified for 32-bit editions only)
- 512MB of RAM minimum (1GB recommended)
- 2.0GB of available hard-disk space (additional free space required during installation)
- 1,024x768 minimum monitor resolution with 16-bit or greater video card
- DVD-ROM drive
- QuickTime 7 software required for multimedia features
- Internet or phone connection required for product activation
- Broadband Internet connection required for Adobe Stock Photos* and other services

4.15.3.1 Installing the Software

Before you install Illustrator, close all of your Adobe applications and any browser windows.

Do one of the following:

- Insert DVD in your drive, and follow the on-screen instructions. (If the installer does not launch automatically, then double-click Setup.exe (Windows) or Setup (Mac OS) at the root level of your disk to start the installation process.)

- If you downloaded the software from the web, then open the folder and double-click Setup.exe (Windows) or Setup (Mac OS), and then follow the on-screen instructions.

After original installation in order to install additional components or reinstall your software, you will need access to the original installer (CD, DVD or the download from the web). Before you begin additional installations or reinstallations, please make sure that the installer is in the same drive or location that it was in during the original installation. By default, templates, sample files, and a reduced set of fonts are installed with Illustrator CS3. You'll find additional fonts, stock photo and clip art content, as well as back-up copies of the installed fonts, in the Goodies folder of the installation DVD.

4.15.3.2 Uninstalling the Software

Before you uninstall Illustrator, close all of your Adobe applications and any browser windows.

Do one of the following:

- Open the Windows Control Panel and double-click Add or Remove Programs. Select the product that you want to uninstall, click Change/Remove, and then follow the on-screen instructions.
- Before uninstalling you may want to deactivate Illustrator CS3 by choosing Help > Deactivate and following the on-screen instructions, assuming you will be installing Illustrator on a different machine. You may run up to two activated copies of the software at any one time.

4.15.3.3 Activating Software

If the Activation dialog box is not already open, choose Help > Activate.

Follow the on-screen instructions.

- If you want to install the product on a different computer, you must first deactivate the software on your computer. To deactivate, choose Help > Deactivate.

4.15.3.4 Registration Information

When you install your software, be sure to register to get up-to-date product information, training, newsletters and invitations to Adobe events and seminars. You will also receive a complimentary benefit for registering.

4.16 Menu Commands

One look at these menu commands and you know what is where.

4.16.1 File menu

New: The New command lets you create a blank, untitled Photoshop image. You can also use this command to create a new image with the exact same pixel dimensions as an image or selection that has been copied to the Clipboard.

Open: It allows you to open an existing file from either the hard disk or other media attached to the computer, floppy drive, CD drive, etc. This also gives rise to a dialog box, from where you can select the file, which you want to open.

Browse: This command allows you to browse through files before opening them.

Open As: It allows you to open a file in another format.

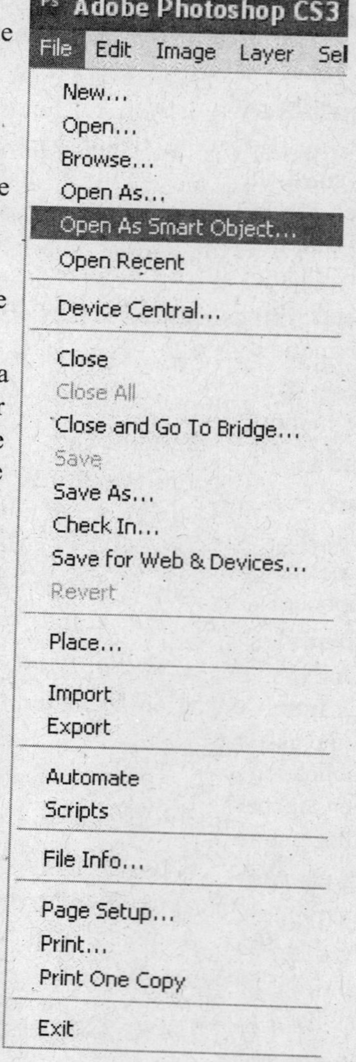

Open Recent: It allows you to open a recently opened file.

Edit in ImageReady: It allows you to edit the image in the ImageReady mode.

Close: It allows you to close the current photoshop file.

Close All: Closes all the open files.

Close and Go To Bridge: Closes the curent file and open the Bridge.

Save: It saves the current photoshop file.

Save As: It allows you to save the current file under a new name or overwrite the current file.

Save a Version: It allows you to save the current file under as a new version. Adobe Version Cue integrates design management into your existing workflows within and across the Adobe Creative Suite applications, including Adobe GoLive CS, Adobe Illustrator CS, Adobe InDesign CS, and Adobe Photoshop CS.

Save for Web: It allows you to save the current file as a Web page.

Revert: This command is used to restore the most recently saved version of your file deleting all changes made since the last time you saved it.

Place: This command is used to place the text into the file.

Import: This command is active only if you have the scanner attached to your computer. This will help you in getting the scanned picture into the file.

Export: Using this command you can export the selected text of the publication into a document file in the format selected by you.

Automate: The Automate commands simplify complex tasks by combining them into one or more dialog boxes.

Scripts: This command has 4 different features of scripts which allow you to export layers to files, Layer Comps To Files, Layer Comps to PDF and Layer Comps to WPG. It also allows you to browse for more files.

File Info: Adobe Photoshop supports the information standard developed by the Newspaper Association of America (NAA) and the International Press Telecommunications Council (IPTC) to identify transmitted text and images. This standard includes entries for captions, keywords, categories, credits, and origins. The captions and keyword entries can also be searched by some third-party image browsers.

Page Setup: You can define here various options for your new photoshop file.

Print with Preview: You can change the various options by seeing the preview before printing.

Print: This gives rise to a dialog box, where you can set the options for printing the publication.

Print One Copy: You can print one copy of the image on the screen.

Exit: Closes your session with Photoshop.

4.16.2 Edit menu

Undo/Redo: This command is used to reverse the last action taken by you. However, you can't undo all the actions. If the action can be reversed, the command read Undo on the Edit menu and names the action such as Undo Pasting. If the action cannot be reversed the command is off and thus can be read as cannot Undo. After you have do undo, you can Redo too if it is allowed.

Step Forward: This command is used to move a step forward in the motion.

Step Backward: This command is used to trace back the step in the motion.

Fade: Allows the object to fade.

Cut: This command is used to cut the selected text or graphics from your file and keep it available for pasting it later to any other place in the same file or any other file or even any other software which supports the clipboard text.

Copy: This command is also used to copy the selected text or graphics from your file and keep it available for pasting it later. Only difference it has from Cut command is that it leaves the original text as it is whereas in the case of Cut the original text is lost. When you have more than one publication open, you can copy objects between publications without using the Clipboard. Select an object in one publication, drag it to position in the other publication window and release the mouse button to create a copy.

Copy Merged: This command makes a merged copy of all the visible layers in the selected area.

Paste: This command is used to place the selected text or graphics from clipboard, where the text using the above Cut or Copy command has been kept.

Paste Into: This command pastes a cut or copied selection inside another selection in the same image or different image. The source selection is pasted onto a new layer, and the destination selection border is converted into a layer mask.

Clear: This command is used to delete the current selection from your file without storing it in the Clipboard. This has the same effect as pressing Delete or Backspace.

Check Spelling: This is one of the new command of Photoshop and allows you to spell check the text in your drawings using the in-built dictionary.

Find and Replace Text: Another of the the new commands of Photoshop, which allows you to find particular text and replace it with another.

Fill: This command is used to fill foreground and background colour.

Edit Image Layer Select
Undo Print
Step Forward
Step Backward
Fade...
Cut
Copy
Copy Merged
Paste
Paste Into
Clear
Check Spelling...
Find and Replace Text...
Fill...
Stroke...
Free Transform
Transform
Auto-Align Layers...
Auto-Blend Layers
Define Brush Preset...
Define Pattern...
Define Custom Shape...
Purge
Adobe PDF Presets...
Preset Manager...
Color Settings...
Assign Profile...
Convert to Profile...
Keyboard Shortcuts...
Menus...
Preferences

Stroke: Photoshop provides a variety of ways to fill a selection or a layer with colors, images, or patterns. You can also paint a border around a selection or a layer using the Stroke command. To increase the contrast between your image and the surrounding work canvas, you can fill the canvas with a specified color.

Free Transform: When an image is resampled, Adobe Photoshop uses an interpolation method to assign color values to any new pixels based on the color values of existing pixels in the image. The more sophisticated the method, the more quality and detail from the original image are preserved.

Transform: You can use rulers and guides to lay out your work, and you can copy and move selections within an image and between applications. You can also transform objects using specific transformations or using the transform bounding box.

Define Brush Preset: You can define a brush setting here.

Define Pattern: The pattern you define here is repeated as tiles within the selection. Each new pattern replaces the current pattern. If you want to reuse patterns, save a file of swatches for defining patterns. You can also use the pattern stamp tool to paint with a pattern.

Define Custom Shape: This command allows you to select a custom shape from the options bar.

Purge: The Purge command permanently clears from memory the operation stored by the command or buffer, and cannot be undone. Use the Purge command when information held in memory is so large, Photoshop cannot perform the next operation.

Adobe PDF Presets: Although the default PDF presets are based on best practices, you may discover that your workflow requires specialized PDF settings that aren't available using any of the built-in presets. In this case, you can create and save your own custom presets for reuse in Photoshop or any product in the Adobe Creative Suite. In Photoshop, you can save the preset using the Adobe PDF Presets command or clicking the Save Preset button in the Save Adobe PDF dialog box. Adobe PDF presets are saved as files with a .joboptions extension. This is useful, for example, if you want your vendor or printer to send you a .joboptions file with the Adobe PDF presets that work best with their workflow.

Preset Manager: This command allows you to preset a set of gradients to be used later and called.

Color Settings: The settings in these dialog boxes are used for the following:

- To convert images between standard color modes (such as from RGB to CMYK).
- When opening an RGB, Grayscale, or CMYK file, to compare the file's color space to the color space defined in the appropriate Setup dialog box. If the two color spaces are not the same, you can convert the file.
- When viewing a file on-screen, to convert the file to the monitor's color space. This only affects the display, not the file—Photoshop assumes that the file's true color space is the one defined in the appropriate Setup dialog box.

Assign Profile: Lets you select a different profile. The application assigns the new profile to the document without converting colors to the profile space. This may dramatically change the appearance of the colors as displayed on your monitor.

Convert to Profile: Allows to convert colors in a document to another profile.

Keyboard Shortcuts: This command allows you to see the various keyboard shortcuts associated with various commands.

Menus: You can customize menus using this command.

Preferences: You can choose to set preference of various options as shown next.

4.16.3 Image menu

Mode: The modes available under Photoshop's this command are: Bitmap; Grayscale; Dutone; Indexed Color; RGB Color; CMYK Color; Lab Color; Multichannel; 8Bits/ Channel; 16 Bits/Channel; Color Table; Assign Profile and Convert to Profile.

Adjustments: This command is used to adjust the various colours of your image. You will read more about them later. Various options available under this are shown here.

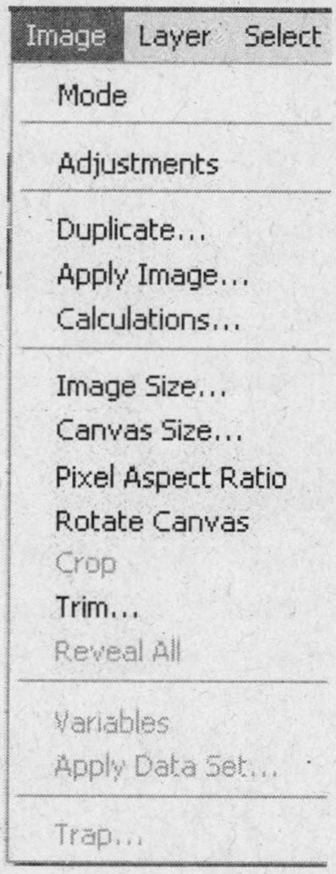

Duplicate: You can copy an entire image (including all layers, layer masks, and channels) into available memory without saving to disk by using the Duplicate command or by dragging and dropping.

Apply Image: The Apply Image command lets you blend one image's layer and channel (the source) with a layer and channel of the active image (the destination).

Calculations: The Calculations command lets you blend two individual channels from one or more source images. You can then apply the results to a new image or to a new channel or selection in the active image. You cannot apply the Calculations command to composite channels.

Image Size: When preparing images for online distribution (on a Web site, for example), it's useful to specify image size in terms of the pixel dimensions. Keep in mind that changing pixel dimensions affects not only the size of an image on-screen but also its image quality and its printed characteristics—either its printed dimensions or its image resolution.

Canvas Size: The Canvas Size command lets you add or remove work space around an existing image. You can crop an image by decreasing the canvas area. Added canvas appears in the same color or transparency as the background.

Pixel Aspect Ratio: An image on a computer monitor is made up of pixels that are essentially square. An image displayed on a video monitor is analog and does not involve pixel shape. Nonsquare pixels are the most commonly used by encoding devices for video. When importing an image created by a square-pixel graphics program into a video editing program like Adobe Premiere, the square pixels are scaled to the nonsquare pixels for video encoding. This scaling results in a distorted image.

Rotate Canvas: The Rotate Canvas commands let you rotate or flip the entire image. It does not work on individual layers or parts of layers, paths, or selection borders.

Crop: Photoshop provides two ways to crop an image:

- The Image > Crop command discards the area outside of a rectangular selection and keeps the same resolution as the original.
- The crop tool lets you crop an image by dragging over the area you want to keep. The advantage of using the crop tool is that you can rotate and resample the area as you crop.

Trim: This command is used to discard a border area around the edge of the image, based on transparency or edge colour.

Reveal All: This command is used to reveal all images on the screen.

Variables: You use variables to define which elements in a template change. You can define three types of variables. Visibility variables show or hide the content of a layer. Pixel Replacement variables replace the pixels in the layer with pixels from another image file. Text Replacement variables replace a string of text in a type layer.

Apply Data Set: You can apply a data set's contents to the base image while leaving all the variables and data sets intact. This changes the look of the PSD document to contain the values of the data set. You can also preview how each version of your graphic will look with each data set.

Trap: After you have converted the image to CMYK, you can adjust the color trap. Trap is the overlap needed to ensure that a slight misalignment or movement of the plates while printing does not affect the final appearance of the print job. If any distinctly different colors in your image touch, you may need to overprint them slightly to prevent tiny gaps from appearing when the image is printed. This technique is known as trapping. In most cases, your print shop will determine if trapping is needed and tell you what values to enter in the Trap dialog box.

4.16.4 Layer menu

New: This command creates a new layer which can be via Copy or Cut menu.

Duplicate Layer: This command duplicates the selected layer.

Delete: This command deletes the selected picture, layer, etc.

Layer Properties: The layer properties allow you to lock layers of an image so that they cannot be changed.

Layer Styles: When applying layer styles, you can specify a number of common options for each effect. Various options of the layer styles are on next few pages.

Smart Filter: Any filter applied to a Smart Object is a Smart Filter. Smart Filters appear in the Layers palette below the Smart Object layer to which they are applied. Because you can adjust, remove, or hide Smart Filters, they are nondestructive. You can apply any Photoshop filter—except for Extract, Liquify, Pattern Maker, and Vanishing Point—as a Smart Filter. In addition, you can apply the Shadow/ Highlight and Variations adjustments as Smart Filters.

New Fill Layers: A new layer is added with the optional fill selected by you.

New Adjustment Layer: A new layer is added with the option selected by you. Various available options are: Levels, Curves, Color Balance, Brightness/Contrast, Hue/Saturation, Selective Color, Channel Mixer, Gradient Map, Photo Filter, Invert, Threshold and Posterize.

Change Layer Content: This command allows you to change the contents of a layer.

Layer Content Options: This command allows you to change the various options of a layer.

Layer Mask: When you finish creating a layer mask, you can either apply the mask and make the changes permanent or delete the mask without applying changes. Because layer masks are stored as alpha channels, applying and deleting layer masks can help reduce file size..

Vector Mask: A vector mask creates a sharp-edged shape on a layer and is useful any time you want to add a design element with clean, defined edges. Once you create a layer with a vector mask, you can apply one or more layer styles to it, edit them if needed, and instantly have a usable button, panel, or other Web design element.

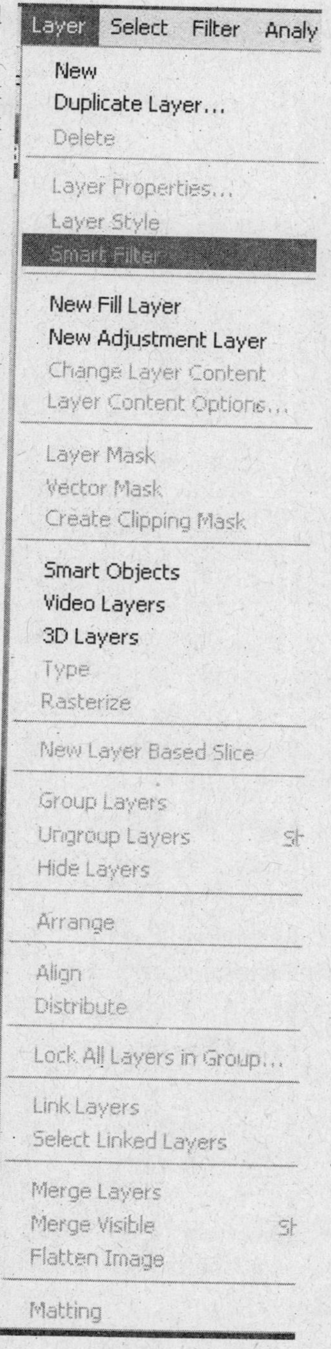

Create Clipping Mask: You can use the content of a layer to mask the layers above it. The transparent pixels of the bottom or base layer mask out the content of layers above it that are part of a clipping mask. For example, you might have a shape on one layer, a texture on the overlying layer, and some text on the topmost layer. If you define all three layers as part of a clipping mask, the texture and the text appear only through the shape on the base layer, and take on the opacity of the base layer.

Smart Objects: A Smart Object is a container in which you can embed raster or vector image data, for instance, from another Photoshop or Adobe Illustrator file. The embedded data retains all its original characteristics and remains fully editable. You can create a Smart Object in Photoshop by converting one or more layers. In addition, you can paste or place the data in Photoshop from Illustrator. Smart Objects give you the flexibility to scale, rotate, and warp layers nondestructively in Photoshop. Once a Smart Object stores source data inside a Photoshop document, you can then work on a composite of that data in the image. When you want to modify the document (for example, scale it), Photoshop re-renders the composite data based on the source data.

Video Layers: You can use Photoshop Extended to edit individual frames of video and image sequence files. In addition to using any Photoshop tool to edit and paint on video, you can also apply filters, masks, transformations, layers styles, and blending modes. After making edits, you can save the document as a PSD file (that can be played back in other Adobe applications such as Premiere Pro and After Effects or accessed as a static file in other applications), or you can render it as a QuickTime movie or image sequence.

3D Layers: You can place a 3D model against a background image and change its position or viewing angle to match the background.

Type: This command is used to create type in a layer.

Rasterize: This command is used to rasterize the image in the layer.

New Layer Based Slice: When you create a slice from a layer, the slice area encompasses all the pixel data in the layer. If you edit the layer's content, the slice area automatically adjusts to encompass the new pixels.

Group Layers: Layers are grpuped together using this.

Ungroup Layers: Once grouped by the above command, you can ungroup them.

Hide Layers: You can hide a layer using this command.

Arrange: This command is used for the followings:

- Bring to Front to make the layer the topmost layer.

- Bring Forward to move the layer one level up in the stacking order.
- Send Backward to move the layer one level down in the stacking order.
- Send to Back to make the layer the bottommost layer in the image (except for the background).

Align: This command is used for the followings:

- To align a single layer to a selection, make the layer active.
- To align multiple layers to a selection or to the active layer, link together two or more layers.
- To distribute multiple layers, link together three or more layers.
- Top to align the topmost pixel on the linked layers to the topmost pixel on the active layer or the topmost edge of the selection border.
- Vertical Center to align the vertical centermost pixel on the linked layers to the vertical centermost pixel on the active layer or the vertical center of the selection border.
- Bottom to align the bottommost pixel on the linked layers to the bottommost pixel on the active layer or the bottommost edge of the selection border.
- Left to align the leftmost pixel on the linked layers to the leftmost pixel on the active layer or the leftmost edge of the selection border.
- Horizontal Center to align the horizontal centermost pixel on the linked layers to the horizontal centermost pixel on the active layer or the horizontal center of the selection border.
- Right to align the rightmost pixel on the linked layers to the rightmost pixel on the active layer or the rightmost edge of the selection border.

Distribute: This command allows you to position the contents of linked layers at evenly spaced intervals.

Lock All Layers in Group: This command locks all the layers in the particular set.

Link Layers: You can link two or more layers or groups. Unlike multiple layers selected at the same time, linked layers retain their relationship until you unlink them. You can move, apply transformations, and create clipping masks from linked layers.

Select Linked Layers: Linked layers can be selected using this command.

Merge Layers: This command allows you to merge two or more layers.

Merge Visible: This command makes sure that the merged layers are visible.

Flatten Image: In a flattened image, all visible layers are merged into the background, greatly reducing file size. Flattening an image discards all hidden layers and fills the remaining transparent areas with white. In most cases, you won't want to flatten a file until you have finished editing individual layers.

Matting: When you move or paste an anti-aliased selection, some of the pixels surrounding the selection border are included with the selection. This can result in a fringe or halo around the edges of the pasted selection. These three Matting commands let you edit these unwanted edge pixels:

4.16.5 Select menu

All: This command selects all the items on the screen.

Deselect/Reselect: This command deselects/reselcts the items already selected.

Reselect: You can reselect the items deselected above.

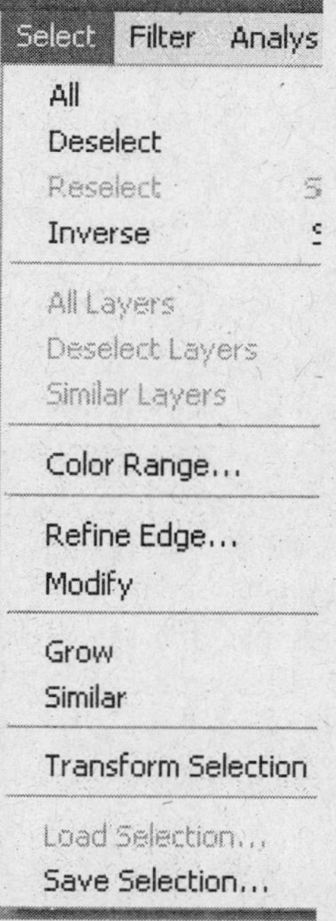

Inverse: The inverted command inverts the colours in an image. You might use this command to make a positive black-and-white image negative or to make a positive from a scanned black-and-white negative.

All Layers: The command allows you to select all layers.

Deselect Layers: The command deselects all the layers.

Similar Layers: The similar layers are selected.

Colour Range: The Color Range command selects a specified color or color subset within an existing selection or an entire image. If you want to replace a selection, be sure to deselect everything before applying this command.

Refine Edge: You can define feathering for the marquee, lasso, polygon lasso, or magnetic lasso tool as you use the tool, or you can add feathering to an existing selection. Feathering effects become apparent when you move, cut, or copy the selection.

Modify: You can use the following Select commands to increase or decrease the pixels in an existing selection.

Grow: Grow and Similar commands are used to expand a selection to include areas similar in color.

Similar: Select the similar layers.

Transform Selection: The Free Transform command lets you use the Scale, Rotate, Skew, Distort, and Perspective commands without having to select them from the menu. To access the various transformation modes, you use different shortcut keys as you drag the handles of the transform bounding box.

Load Selection: When you have finished modifying an alpha channel or simply want to use a previously saved selection, you can load the selection into the image.

Save Selection: You create a new alpha channel as a mask. For example, you can create a gradient fill in a blank channel, and then use it as a mask. Or you can save a selection to either a new or existing channel.

4.16.6 Filter Menu

Last Filter: This command allows you to call the last filter used.

Convert for Smart Filters: Any filter applied to a Smart Object is a Smart Filter. Smart Filters appear in the Layers palette below the Smart Object layer to which they are applied. Because you can adjust, remove, or hide Smart Filters, they are nondestructive. You can apply any Photoshop filter—except for Extract, Liquify, Pattern Maker, and Vanishing Point—as a Smart Filter. In addition, you can apply the Shadow/Highlight and Variations adjustments as Smart Filters. To work with Smart Filters, select a Smart Object layer, choose a filter, and then set filter options. After you apply a Smart Filter, you can adjust, reorder, or delete it.

Extract: The Extract command provides a sophisticated way to isolate a foreground object and erase its background on a layer. Even objects with wispy, intricate, or undefinable edges may be clipped from their backgrounds with a minimum of manual work.

Filter Gallery: The Filter Gallery provides a preview of many of the special effects filters. You can apply multiple filters, turn on or off the effect of a filter, reset options for a filter, and change the order in which filters are applied. When you are satisfied with the preview, you can then apply it to your image. Not all filters in the Filter menu are available in the Filter Gallery.

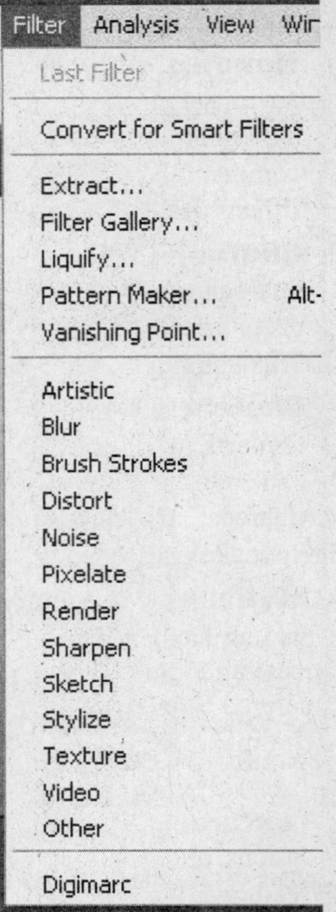

Liquify: Several tools in the Liquify dialog box distort the brush area when you hold down the mouse button or drag. The distortion is concentrated at the center of the brush area, and the effect intensifies as you hold down the mouse button or repeatedly drag over an area.

Pattern Maker: The Pattern Maker lets you create an infinite variety of patterns based on a selection or the contents of the Clipboard. Because the pattern is based on the pixels in a sample, it shares visual characteristics with the sample. For example, if you sample an image of grass, the Pattern Maker generates a tileable pattern that is different from the sample but still appears to be grass.You can generate multiple patterns from the same sample, and save pattern tiles as preset patterns for future use in Photoshop and ImageReady.

Vanishing Point: The Vanishing Point feature lets preserve correct perspective in edits of images that contain perspective planes, for instance, the sides of a building or any rectangular object.

Artistic: Apply a painterly or special effect for a fine-arts or commercial project. For example, use the Cutout filter for collages or type treatment. These filters replicate natural or traditional media effects. Various options available under this command are: Coloured Pencil, Cutout, Dry Brush, Film Grain, Fresco, Neon Glow, Paint Daubs, Palette Knife, Plastic Wrap, Poster Edges, Rough Pastels, Smudge Stick, Sponge, Underpainting and Watercolor.

Blur: Soften a selection or an image. Blur filters are useful for retouching. They smooth transitions by averaging the pixels next to the hard edges of defined lines and shaded areas in an image. Various options available under this command are: Blur, Blur More, Gaussian Blur, Motion Blur, Radial Blur, Smart Blur.

Brush Strokes: Like the Artistic filters, the Brush Strokes filters give a painterly or fine-arts look using different brush and ink stroke effects. Some of the filters add grain, paint, noise, edge detail, or texture to an image for a pointlist effect. Various options available under this command are: Accented Edges, Angled Strokes, Crosshatch, Dark Strokes, Ink Outlines, Spatter, Sprayed Strokes and Sumi-e.

Distort: Geometrically distort an image, creating 3-D or other reshaping effects. Note that these filters can be very memory intensive. This command has the following options: Diffuse Glow, Displace, Glass, Ocean Ripple, Pinch, Polar Coordinates, Ripple, Shear, Spherize, Twirl, Wave and ZigZag.

Noise: Add or remove noise, or pixels with randomly distributed color levels. This helps to blend a selection into the surrounding pixels. Noise filters can create unusual textures or remove problem areas, such as dust and scratches, from an image. The Add Noise filter can be used to reduce banding in feathered selections or graduated fills or to give a more realistic look to heavily retouched areas. This command has the following options: Add Noise, Despeckle, Dust & Scratches and Median.

Pixelate: Sharply define a selection by clumping pixels of similar color values in cells. This command has the following options: Color Halftone, Crystallize, Facet, Fragment, Mezzotint, Mosaic and Pointillize.

Render: Create 3-D shapes, cloud patterns, refraction patterns, and simulated light reflections in an image. You can also manipulate objects in 3-D space, create 3-D objects (cubes, spheres, and cylinders), and create texture fills from grayscale files to produce 3-D-like effects for lighting. This command has the following options: 3D Transform, Clouds, Difference Clouds, Lens Flare, Lighting Effects and Texture Fill.

Sharpen: Focus blurry images by increasing the contrast of adjacent pixels. They include the Sharpen Edges and Unsharp Mask filters, which find and sharpen areas where significant color changes occur (such as at the edges). The Unsharp Mask filter is commonly used for high-end color correction This command has the following options: Sharpen, Sharpen Edges, Sharpen More and Unsharp Mask.

Sketch: Add texture to images, often for a 3-D effect. The filters also are useful for creating a fine-arts or hand-drawn look. Many of the Sketch filters use the foreground and background color as they redraw the image. Various options under this command are: Bas Relief, Chalk & Charcoal, Charcoal, Chrome, Conte Crayon, Graphic Pen, Halftone Pattern, Note Paper, Photocopy, Plaster, Reticulation, Stamp, Torn Edges and Water Paper.

Stylize: Produce a painted or impressionistic effect on a selection by displacing pixels and by finding and heightening contrast in an image. After using filters like Find Edges and Trace Contour that highlight edges, you can apply the Invert command to outline the edges of a color image with colored lines or to outline the edges of a grayscale image with white lines. Various options under this command are: Diffuse, Emboss, Extrude, Find Edges, Glowing Edges, Solarize, Tiles, Trace Contour and Wind.

Texture: Give images the appearance of depth or substance, or to add an organic look. Various options under this command are: Craquelure, Grain, Mosaic Tiles, Patchwork, Stained Glass and Texturizer.

Video: Include the NTSC (National Television Standards Committee) Colors filter, which restricts the gamut of colors to those acceptable for television reproduction, and the De-Interlace filter, which smooths moving images captured on video. This command has the following options: De-Interlace and NTSC Colors.

Other: Let you create your own filters, use filters to modify masks, offset a selection within an image, and make quick color adjustments. This command has the following options: Custom, DitherBox, High Pass, Maximum, Minimum and Offset.

Digimarc: Embed a digital watermark into an image to store copyright information. This command has the following options: Embed Watermark and Read Watermark.

4.16.7 View menu

Proof Setup: Select this command to choose the output display that you want to simulate:

Custom: To soft proof colours as displayed on a specific output device.

Working CYMK: To soft-proof colours using the current CYMK working space.

Working Cyan Plate, Working Magenta Plate, Working Yellow Plate, Working Black Plate, or Working CMY Plate: To soft-proof specific CYMK ink colour using the current CYMK working space.

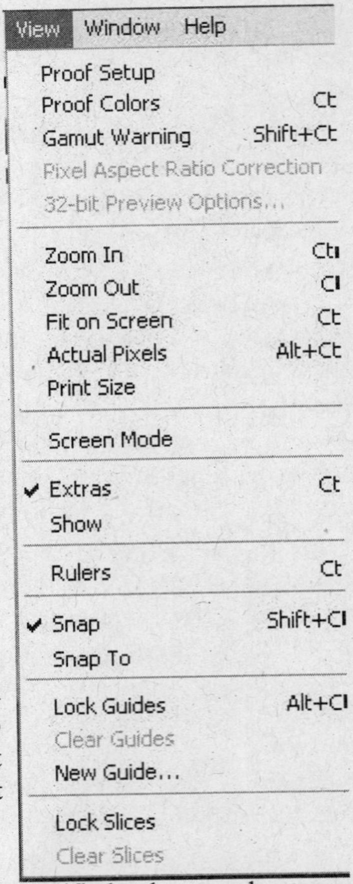

Windows RGB: To soft-proof colours using either a standard Windows monitor as the proof profile space that you want to simulate.

Monitor RGB: To soft-proof colours using your current monitor colour space as the proof profile space.

Simulate Paper: To preview the specific shade of white exhibited by the print medium.

Simulate Ink Black: To preview the amount of black pigment absorbed by the print medium.

Proof Colours: Use this command to toggle the soft-proof display on or off.

Gamut Warning: The gamut is the range of colors that can be displayed or printed in a color system. A color that can be displayed in RGB or HSB models may be out-of-gamut, and therefore unprintable, for your CMYK setting. Photoshop automatically brings all colors into gamut when you convert an image to CMYK. But you might want to identify the out-of-gamut colors in an image or correct them manually before converting to CMYK.

Pixel Aspect Ratio Correction: The preset file sizes in the Preset menu of the New file dialog let you create images at a size and pixel aspect ratio to compensate for scaling when incorporated into video. The presets also create a document with nonprinting guides that delineate the action safe and title safe areas of the image. Using the preset file sizes, you can produce images for specific video systems—NTSC, PAL, or HDTV.

View Window Help
Proof Setup
Proof Colors Ct
Gamut Warning Shift+Ct
Pixel Aspect Ratio Correction
32-bit Preview Options...
Zoom In Ct
Zoom Out Cl
Fit on Screen Ct
Actual Pixels Alt+Ct
Print Size
Screen Mode
✓ Extras Ct
Show
Rulers Ct
✓ Snap Shift+Cl
Snap To
Lock Guides Alt+Cl
Clear Guides
New Guide...
Lock Slices
Clear Slices

32-bit Preview Options: The Color Range command selects a specified color or color range within an existing selection or an entire image. If you want to replace a selection, be sure to deselect everything before applying this command. The Color Range command is not available for 32 bits-per-channel images.

Zoom In: Select the zoom tool, and click the area you want to magnify. Each click magnifies the image to the next preset percentage, centering the display around the point you click. At maximum magnification, the center of the zoom tool appears empty.

Zoom Out: Select the zoom tool. Hold down Alt (Windows) or Option (Mac OS) to activate the zoom-out tool, and click the area of the image you want to reduce. Each click reduces the view to the previous preset percentage.

Fit on Screen: These options scale both the view and the window size to match the monitor size.

Actual Pixels: This command displays the image at 100%.

Print Size: The magnification of the image is adjusted to display its approximate printed size, as specified in the Print Size section of the Image Size dialog box.

Screen Mode: The blending mode specified in the options bar controls how pixels in the image are affected by a painting or editing tool. It's helpful to think in terms of the following colors when visualizing a blending mode's effect:

- The base color is the original color in the image.
- The blend color is the color being applied with the painting or editing tool.
- The result color is the color resulting from the blend.

To select a blending mode for a tool. Choose from the Mode pop-up menu in the options bar.

Normal: Edits or paints each pixel to make it the result color. This is the default mode. (Normal mode is called Threshold when you're working with a bitmapped or indexed-color image.)

Dissolve: Edits or paints each pixel to make it the result color. However, the result color is a random replacement of the pixels with the base color or the blend color, depending on the opacity at any pixel location.

Behind: Edits or paints only on the transparent part of a layer. This mode works only in layers with Lock Transparency deselected and is analogous to painting on the back of transparent areas in a sheet of acetate.

Clear: Edits or paints each pixel and makes it transparent. This mode is available for the Line tool (when fill region is selected), the Paint Bucket tool , the Brush tool , the Pencil tool , the Fill command, and the Stroke command. You must be in a layer with Lock Transparency deselected to use this mode.

Darken: Looks at the color information in each channel and selects the base or blend color—whichever is darker—as the result color. Pixels lighter than the blend color are replaced, and pixels darker than the blend color do not change.

Multiply: Looks at the color information in each channel and multiplies the base color by the blend color. The result color is always a darker color. Multiplying any color with black produces black. Multiplying any color with white leaves the color unchanged. When you're painting with a color other than black or white, successive strokes with a painting tool produce progressively darker colors. The effect is similar to drawing on the image with multiple magic markers.

Color Burn: Looks at the color information in each channel and darkens the base color to reflect the blend color by increasing the contrast. Blending with white produces no change.

Linear Burn: Looks at the color information in each channel and darkens the base color to reflect the blend color by decreasing the brightness. Blending with white produces no change.

Lighten: Looks at the color information in each channel and selects the base or blend color—whichever is lighter—as the result color. Pixels darker than the blend color are replaced, and pixels lighter than the blend color do not change.

Screen: Looks at each channel's color information and multiplies the inverse of the blend and base colors. The result color is always a lighter color. Screening with black leaves the color unchanged. Screening with white produces white. The effect is similar to projecting multiple photographic slides on top of each other.

Color Dodge: Looks at the color information in each channel and brightens the base color to reflect the blend color by decreasing the contrast. Blending with black produces no change.

Linear Dodge: Looks at the color information in each channel and brightens the base color to reflect the blend color by increasing the brightness. Blending with black produces no change.

Overlay: Multiplies or screens the colors, depending on the base color. Patterns or colors overlay the existing pixels while preserving the highlights and shadows of the base color. The base color is not replaced but is mixed with the blend color to reflect the lightness or darkness of the original color.

Soft Light: Darkens or lightens the colors, depending on the blend color. The effect is similar to shining a diffused spotlight on the image. If the blend color (light source) is lighter than 50% gray, the image is lightened as if it were dodged. If the blend color is darker than 50% gray, the image is darkened as if it were burned in. Painting with pure black or white produces a distinctly darker or lighter area but does not result in pure black or white.

Hard Light: Multiplies or screens the colors, depending on the blend color. The effect is similar to shining a harsh spotlight on the image. If the blend color (light source) is lighter than 50% gray, the image is lightened, as if it were screened. This is useful for adding highlights to an image. If the blend color is darker than 50% gray, the image is darkened, as if it were multiplied. This is useful for adding shadows to an image. Painting with pure black or white results in pure black or white.

Vivid Light: Burns or dodges the colors by increasing or decreasing the contrast, depending on the blend color. If the blend color (light source) is lighter than 50% gray, the image is lightened by decreasing the contrast. If the blend color is darker than 50% gray, the image is darkened by increasing the contrast.

Linear Light: Burns or dodges the colors by decreasing or increasing the brightness, depending on the blend color. If the blend color (light source) is lighter than 50% gray, the image is lightened by increasing the brightness. If the blend color is darker than 50% gray, the image is darkened by decreasing the brightness.

Pin Light: Replaces the colors, depending on the blend color. If the blend color (light source) is lighter than 50% gray, pixels darker than the blend color are replaced, and pixels lighter than the blend color do not change. If the blend color is darker than 50% gray, pixels lighter than the blend color are replaced, and pixels darker than the blend color do not change. This is useful for adding special effects to an image.

Difference: Looks at the color information in each channel and subtracts either the blend color from the base color or the base color from the blend color, depending on which has the greater brightness value. Blending with white inverts the base color values; blending with black produces no change.

Exclusion: Creates an effect similar to but lower in contrast than the Difference mode. Blending with white inverts the base color values. Blending with black produces no change.

Hue: Creates a result color with the luminance and saturation of the base color and the hue of the blend color.

Saturation: Creates a result color with the luminance and hue of the base color and the saturation of the blend color. Painting with this mode in an area with no (0) saturation (gray) causes no change.

Color: Creates a result color with the luminance of the base color and the hue and saturation of the blend color. This preserves the gray levels in the image and is useful for coloring monochrome images and for tinting color images.

Luminosity: Creates a result color with the hue and saturation of the base color and the luminance of the blend color. This mode creates an inverse effect from that of the Color mode.

Extras: This command allows you to show all images on the screen.

Show: From here you can select the various options to be seen on the screen.

Rules: Shows or hides rulers on the screen.

Snap: This command snaps the various guides on the screen.

Snap To: From the sub-menu you can select the various guides which you want to snap to.

Lock Guides: This command locks all the column and ruler guides so that you cannot move them accidentally.

Clear Guides: This command clears all guides from the screen.

New Guide: This command allows you to have a new guide on the screen.

Lock Slices: Using this command you can lock the varies slices on the screen.

Clear Slices: The above locked slices can be unlocked using this command.

4.16.8 Window Menu

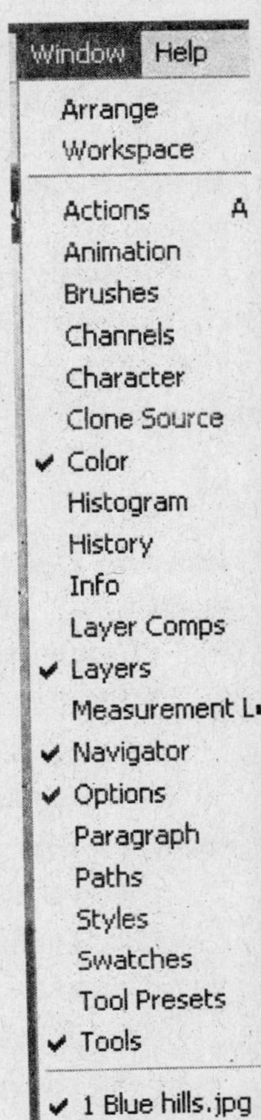

Arrange: It has the following commands under it.

- **Cascade:** This command opens another window of the current image.
- **Tile:** Using this command you can see on the screen more than one image.
- **Arrange Icons:** This command arranges icons on the screen.
- **Close All:** This command closes all the open windows.
- **New Window:** This command opens a new window of the screen image.

Workspace: This command allows you to save the current workspace.

Actions: Hides/Shows the Actions dialog box on the screen.

Brushes: Hides/Shows the brushes dialog box on the screen.

Channels: Hides/Shows the Channels dialog box on the screen.

Character: Hides/Shows the Character dialog box on the screen.

Colour: Hides/Shows the Color dialog box on the screen.

Histogram: Hides/Shows the Histogram dialog box on the screen.

History: Hides/Shows the History dialog box on the screen.

Info: Hides/Shows the Info dialog box on the screen..

Layer Comps: Hides/Shows the Layer Comps dialog box on the screen.

Layers: Hides/Shows the Layers dialog box on the screen.

Navigator: Hides/Shows the Navigator dialog box on the screen.

Options: Hides/Shows the various options on the screen.

Paragraph: Hides/Shows the Paragraph dialog box on the screen.

Paths: Hides/Shows the Paths dialog box on the screen.

Styles: Hides/Shows the Styles dialog box on the screen.

Swatches: Hides/Shows the Swatches dialog box on the screen.

Tools Presets: Hides/Shows the Tools Presets dialog box on the screen.

Tools: Hides/Shows the tools dialog box on the screen.

List of open: Shows the open files.

4.16.9 Help Menu

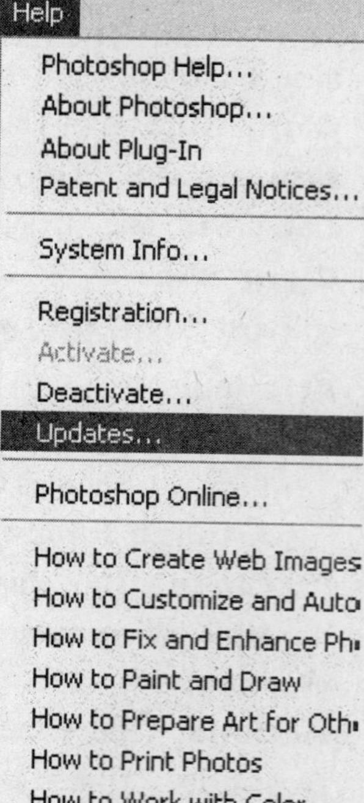

Photoshop Help: Shows the Photoshop Help on the screen.

About Photoshop: Shows the Copyright page of Photoshop.

About Plug-In: Shows the status of Plug-Ins.

Patent and Legal Notices: Shows the various legal notices.

System Info: It gives the information about the system you are working on.

Registration: You can register your software copy.

Activate: It allows you to activate your software.

Deactivate: It allows you to deactivate your software.

Updates: You can see the various updates of the software.

Photoshop Online: You can get Photoshop online for any problems which you may be facing.

How to Create Web Images: It has the following options under it.

- Create a gallery of images for the Web
- Create a rollover button
- Create a Web animation
- Optimize an image for the Web in ImageReady
- Resize and optimize an image for the Web in Photoshop
- Save a file to e-mail

How to Customize and Automate: It has the following options under it.

- Automate a task
- Batch rename files
- Customize palettes
- Customize tool presets

How to Fix and Enhance Photos: It has the following options under it.

- Add a texture to an image
- Add contrast to a photo
- Choose a scanning resolution
- Crop, straighten, or rotate a photo
- Fix red eyes
- Lighten or darken a photo

- Lighten or darken an area in a photo (dodge or burn)
- Make a photo frame
- Remove a color cast
- Remove an object from a photo
- Sharpen a photo
- Touch up spots, scratches, and wrinkles

How to Paint and Draw: It has following options under it.

- Create a custom brush
- Draw a circle or square
- Draw a custom shape
- Draw a doughnut or wheel shape
- Draw a path
- Edit a brush
- Get the brush cursor back
- Set brush pressure sensitivity for digitizing tablet
- Set options for the shape tools
- Stroke a path
- Use a clipping path to create transparency

How to Prepare Art for Other Applications: It has the following options under it.

- Export to Macromedia® Flash™ (SWF)
- Prepare images to place in page layout programs
- Put Adobe Illustrator artwork into Photoshop
- Put Photoshop artwork into Adobe Illustrator

How to Print Photos: It has the following options under it.

- Print multiple photos on a page
- Resize an image for printing

How to Work with Color: It has the following options under it.

- Convert a color photo to black and white
- Replace a color in an image

How to Work with Layers and Selections: It has the following options under it.

- Align objects on different layers
- Blend two images
- Hide and show a combination of layers
- Mask part of an image
- Move single and multiple objects
- Organize layers into layer sets
- Rotate a layer
- Soften the edge of a selection

- Unlock the background layer

How to Work with Type: It has the following options under it.

- Add a drop shadow
- Bend type
- Change the color of individual letters
- Change the font on multiple layers
- Fill type with an image
- Put type on a path

4.17 Tools of Photoshop

Photoshop has lots of tools to work with. These tools are available on the left side of the screen in the form of a toolbar, as shown here. These tools are for various purposes such as Selection, Painting, and Drawing, Erasing, etc.

For each tool when selected you would see the various options on the top of the toolbar in the form of another toolbar.

Let us see how these tools one by one.

4.17.1 Rectangular Marquees

This is the first tool on the toolbar. If pressed it gives rise to the various tools available under it.

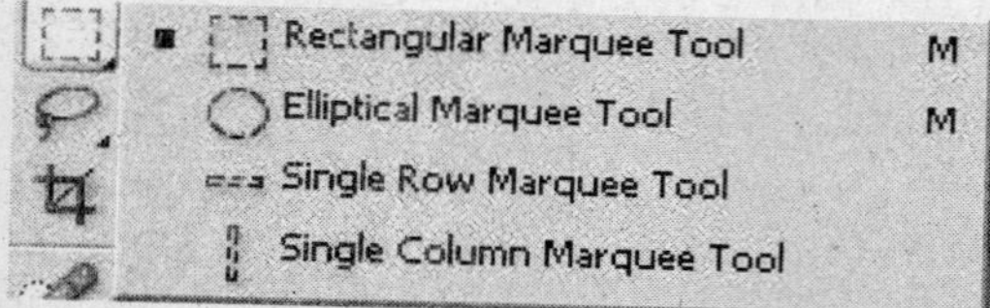

Click the Marquee tool in the toolbox. Move the tool over the blank canvas of your file and see the result. You can create a rectangular marquee with it as shown on the next page.

Various type of styles which can be used are Normal, Constrained Aspect Ratio, and Fixed Size. If you press and hold Shift key after you have made your first selection before you click again, you can make additional selections.

4.17.2 Move Tool

This tool is used to move the objects from one place to another. Click the Move tool in the toolbox. It gives rise to various options of the tool on screen, as shown here.

The move tool lets you drag a selection or layer to a new location in the image. With the Info palette open, you can track the exact distance of the move.

To specify move tool options:

1. Select the move tool.

2. Select any of the following:

Select Pixel Doubling to speed the preview of the move tool's effect by temporarily doubling the size of the pixels in the preview. This option has no effect on the pixels in the file; it simply provides faster previews with the tool. Auto Select Layer to select the topmost layer that has pixels under the move tool, rather than the selected layer.

To move a selection or layer:

1. Select the move tool.

To activate the move tool when another tool is selected, hold down Ctrl.

2. Do one of the following:

Move the pointer inside the selection border, and drag the selection to a new position. If you have selected multiple areas, all move as you drag. Select the layer you want to move. Then drag the layer to a new position.

4.17.3 Lasso Tool

These tools are used when you have to select irregular shapes. Using the Lasso tool to select an object requires a steady hand and good hand-eye coordination, as well as a clean mouse and mousepad or trackball. When selected it gives rise to the following options on the screen.

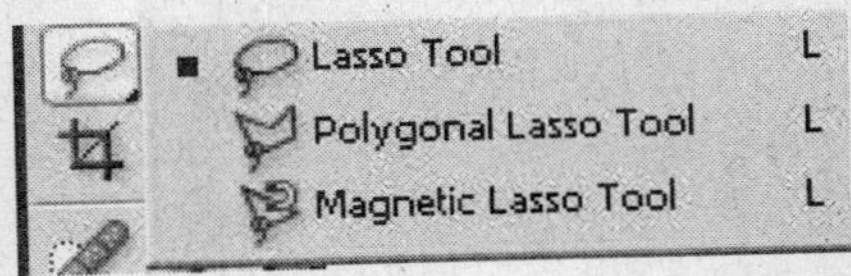

To select all pixels on a layer within the canvas boundaries:

1. Select the layer in the Layers palette.
2. Choose Select > All.

To deselect selections:

1. Do one of the following:

Choose Select > Deselect. If you are using the rectangle marquee, rounded rectangle marquee (ImageReady), elliptical marquee, or lasso tool, click anywhere in the image outside the selected area.

4.17.4 Magic Wand Tool

This tool is little different from the other selection tools. The Magic Wand selects pixels somewhat differently, it selects them based on colour values. This enables you to cut foreground objects, out of the background.

When selected it gives rise to the following options.

You cannot use the magic wand tool on an image in Bitmap mode.

To use the magic wand tool:

1. Select the magic wand tool.

2. In the options bar, specify a selection option. You can create a new selection, add to, subtract from, or restrict the selection. The magic wand cursor changes indicating which option is selected.
3. For Tolerance, enter a value in pixels, ranging from 0 to 255. Enter a low value to select colors very similar to the pixel you click or a higher value to select a broader range of colors.
4. To define a smooth edge, select Anti-aliased.
5. To select all areas using the same colors, select Contiguous. Otherwise only the adjacent pixels will be selected.
6. To select colors using data from all the visible layers, select Use All Layers. Otherwise, the magic wand tool selects colors from the active layer only.
7. In the image, click the color you want to select. All adjacent pixels within the tolerance range are selected.

4.17.5 Cropping Tool

This tool helps you in getting rid of unwanted parts of the picture. It forms part of the marquee tools submenu. You can also crop by making a selection with the rectangular marquee and then using the menu command Image, Crop to crop the image.

When selected this tool gives the following options.

You can use the following methods to crop images:

— Use the Crop command or the crop tool set to Delete to discard the area outside of a rectangular selection. Use the Crop command or the crop tool set to Hidden or Hide to hide the area outside of a rectangular selection. Use this feature when creating animations with elements that move from offscreen into the live image area.

— An image with the Crop command applied using the Hidden option and repositioned using the move tool.

— An image with the Crop command applied using the Delete option and repositioned using the move tool.

— Use the Trim command to discard a border area around the edge of the image, based on transparency or edge color.

— When using the crop tool, you can rotate the selected area before you perform the cropping operation. You can also specify a fixed size for the target image created from the cropped selection.

To use the crop tool:

1. Select the crop tool.
2. In the options bar, select an option to remove the cropped area:

Delete to permanently discard the cropped area. Hide to hide the cropped area but preserve the area in the image file.

3. Drag over the part of the image you want to keep.

   When you release the mouse button, the crop marquee appears as a bounding box with handles at the corners and sides.

4. Adjust the crop marquee:

   To move the marquee to another position, position the pointer inside the bounding box and drag. To scale the marquee, drag a handle. To constrain the proportions, hold down Shift as you drag a corner handle. To rotate the marquee, position the pointer outside the bounding box (the pointer turns into a curved arrow), and drag. To adjust the point around which the marquee is rotated, drag the circle at the center of the bounding box.

5. To crop the image, press Enter (Windows) or Return (Mac OS). To cancel the cropping operation, press Esc.

To specify the size of the cropped area:

1. Select the crop tool.
2. In the options bar, select Fixed Target Size.
3. To begin with the size values of the current image, click Front Image.
4. Enter values for the size you want for the cropped area.

   In Photoshop, you can also set the resolution you want for the cropped area. If you specify size but not resolution, the resolution changes automatically to compensate for the size change. If you specify resolution but not size, the size changes automatically to compensate for the resolution change.

5. Drag over the area you want to keep with the crop tool, and then press Enter.

To crop an image using the Crop command:

1. Use the rectangle marquee tool to select the part of the image you want to keep. Make sure the Feather option in the options bar is set to 0 pixels.
2. Choose Image > Crop.
3. Choose an option to hide or delete the cropped area:

   Select Hidden to hide the cropped areas of the image. The cropped areas are still in the image file and can be made visible by moving the layer with the move tool. Select Deleted to delete the cropped areas.

4. Click OK.

To crop an image using the Trim command:

1. Choose Image > Trim.
2. Crop the border:

   Select Transparent Pixels to remove an area of transparent pixels from the image. Select Top Left Pixel Color to remove an area the color of the upper left pixel from the image. Select Bottom Right Pixel Color to remove an area the color of the lower right pixel from the image.

3. Select one or more areas of the image to be trimmed: Top, Bottom, Left, or Right.

4. Click OK.

4.17.6 Slice Tool

You can create user-slices with the slice tool, from a layer, from a selection (ImageReady), or from guides (ImageReady). When you create a slice from a layer, the slice area encompasses all the pixel data in the layer. If you edit the layer's content, the slice area automatically adjusts to encompass the new pixels.

When selected it gives rise to the following options:

When defining an area for use as a rollover, place the rollover element on a separate layer, and create a slice from that layer. If you apply an effect to the layer—such as a drop shadow or glow—to create a rollover state, the slice automatically adjusts to encompass the new pixels.

To create a slice with the slice tool:

1. Select the slice tool. Any existing slices automatically display in the document window.
2. Choose a style setting in the options bar:

   Normal to determine slice proportions by dragging. Constrained Aspect Ratio to set a height-to-width ratio. Enter whole numbers or decimals for the aspect ratio. For example, to create a slice twice as wide as it is high, enter 2 for the width and 1 for the height. Fixed Size to specify the slice's height and width. Enter pixel values in whole numbers.
3. Drag over the area where you want to create a slice. Hold down Shift as you drag to constrain the slice to a square. Hold down Alt to draw from the center.

To create a slice from a layer:

1. Select a layer in the Layers palette.
2. Do one of the following: Choose Layer > Make Slice From Layer.

4.17.7 The Airbrush Tool

The airbrush tool applies gradual tones (including sprays of color) to an image, simulating traditional airbrush techniques. The edges of the stroke are more diffused than those created with the paintbrush tool. The pressure setting for the airbrush tool controls how quickly the spray of paint is applied. If you hold down the mouse button without dragging, you can build up color.

When selected it gives rise to the following options.

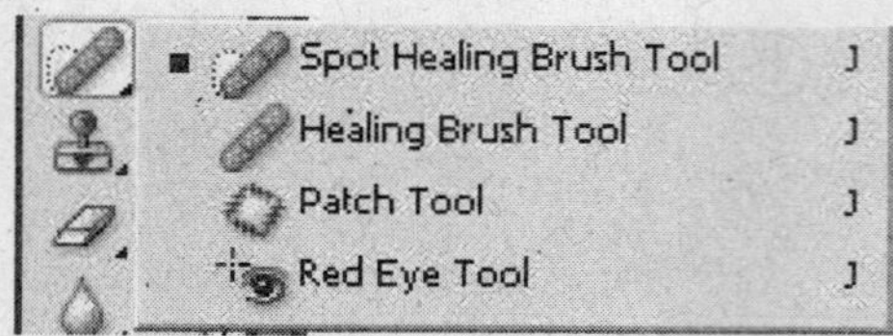

To use a painting brush:

1. Specify a foreground color.

2. Select airbrush tool.
3. Choose a size for the brush from the brush menu in the options bar. If a brush is too large to fit in the menu, it appears as a smaller brush with a number indicating the actual diameter in pixels.
4. Specify a blending mode to control how painting affects existing pixels in the image.
5. Specify pressure for the airbrush tool.
6. Specify the rate at which a brush stroke fades dynamically.
7. Drag in the image to paint.

4.17.8 Brush Tool

This tool is the most important of all brush tools in Photoshop. It is quite similar to the Airbrush but here the paint is applied quite evenly.

The paintbrush tool creates soft strokes of color.

When selected it gives rise to the following options.

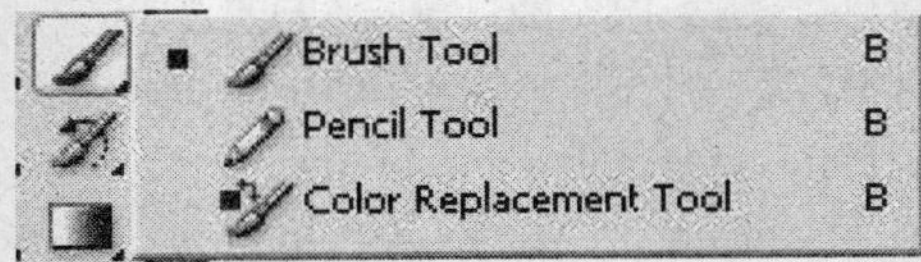

To use a paintbrush tool:

1. Specify a foreground color.
2. Select the brush tool.
3. Choose a size for the brush from the brush menu in the options bar. If a brush is too large to fit in the menu, it appears as a smaller brush with a number indicating the actual diameter in pixels.
4. Specify a blending mode to control how painting affects existing pixels in the image.
5. Specify opacity for the brush.
6. Set additional options:
   For the paintbrush tool, select Wet Edges to paint with a watercolor effect. The paint builds up along the edges of the brush stroke.
7. Specify the rate at which a brush stroke fades dynamically.
8. Drag in the image to paint.

To draw a straight line with one of the painting tools, click a starting point in the image. Then hold down Shift, and click an ending point.

4.17.9 Clone Stamp Tool

The clone stamp tool takes a sample of an image, which you can then apply over another image or part of the same image. Each stroke of the tool paints on more of the sample. Cross hairs mark the original sampling point.

When selected this gives the following options:

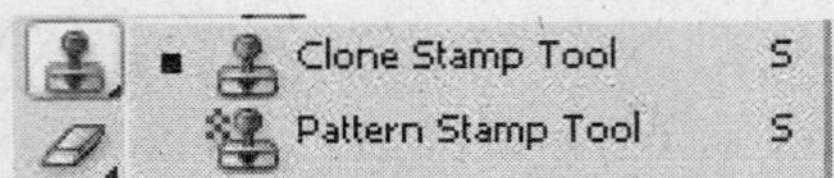

To use the clone stamp tool:

1. Select the clone stamp tool.
2. Choose a size for the brush from the brushes menu in the options bar. If a brush is too large to fit in the menu, it appears as a smaller brush with a number indicating the actual diameter in pixels.
3. Specify a blending mode and opacity.
4. Select Aligned to apply the entire sampled area once, regardless of how many times you stop and resume painting. This option is useful when you want to use different sized brushes to paint an image. You can also use the Aligned option to duplicate two halves of a single image and place them at different locations.

   If Aligned is deselected, the sampled area is applied from the initial sampling point each time you stop and resume painting. Because the clone stamp tool samples the entire image, this option is useful for applying multiple copies of the same part of an image to different images.
5. Select Use All Layers to sample data from all visible layers. If this is deselected, the tool samples only from the active layer.
6. If you are using a pressure-sensitive drawing tablet, specify the effects of stylus pressure.
7. Position the pointer on the part of any open image you want to sample, and Alt-click. This sample point is the location from which the image is duplicated as you paint.
8. Drag to paint with the tool.

If you are sampling from one image and applying to another, both images must be in the same color mode.

4.17.10 History Brush Tool

The history brush tool lets you paint a copy of one state or snapshot of an image into the current image window. This tool makes a copy, or sample, of the image and then paints with it.

For example, you might make a snapshot of a change you made with a painting tool or filter. After undoing the change to the image, you could use the history brush tool to apply the change selectively to areas of the image. Unless you select a merged snapshot, the history brush tool paints from a layer in the selected state to the same layer in another state.

The history brush tool works similarly to the clone stamp tool, but on any state or snapshot of the image, not just the current one.

When selected it gives rise to the following options:

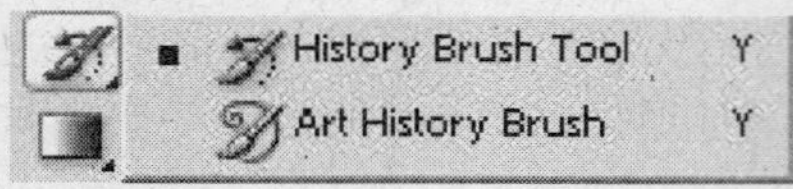

To paint with a state or snapshot of an image:

1. Select the history brush tool.

2. Specify the opacity and blending mode.
3. Choose a brush size.
4. If desired, select Impressionist to paint with an "impressionistic" copy of the source state or snapshot. This option drags and smears the pixels as you paint.
5. In the History palette, click the left column of the state or snapshot to use as the source for the history brush tool.
6. Drag to paint with the history brush tool.

4.17.11 Eraser Tools

You can also use the eraser to return the affected area to a state selected in the History palette.

When selected it gives the following options:

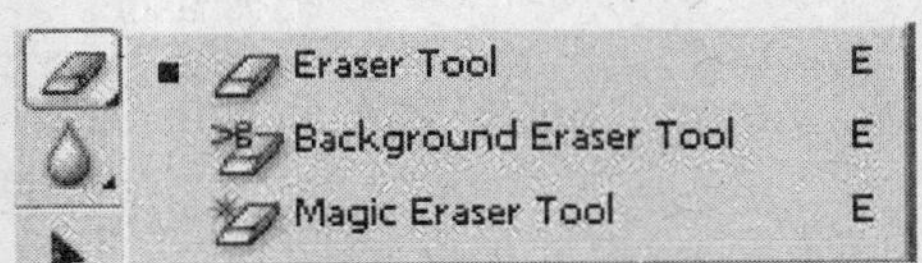

To use the eraser tool:

1. Select the eraser tool (icon).
2. Choose a size for the brush from the brush menu in the options bar. If a brush is too large to fit in the menu, it appears as a smaller brush with a number indicating the actual diameter in pixels.
3. Choose the tool type you want to use as an eraser—paintbrush, airbrush, pencil, or block.
4. Specify an opacity to define the strength of the erasure. An opacity of 100% erases pixels to complete transparency. A lower opacity erases pixels to partial transparency.
5. If you're using the paintbrush eraser, select Wet Edges to paint with a watercolor effect. When this is selected, the erased effect builds up along the edges of the brush stroke.
6. To erase to a saved state or snapshot of the image, select Erase to History. To use the eraser tool in Erase to History mode, hold down Alt as you drag in the image.
7. Specify how a brush strokes fades dynamically.
8. Drag through the area you want to erase.

4.17.12 Paint Bucket Tool

The paint bucket tool fills adjacent pixels that are similar in color value to the pixels you click.

When selected it gives rise to the following options:

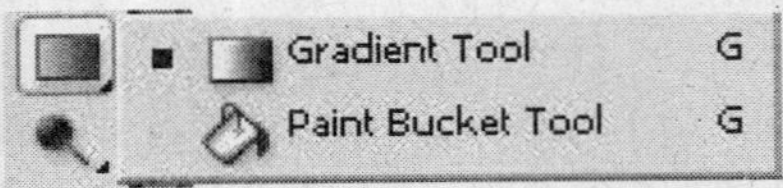

The paint bucket tool cannot be used with images in Bitmap mode.

To use the paint bucket tool:

1. Specify a foreground color.

2. Select the paint bucket tool.
3. Specify whether to fill the selection with the foreground color or with a pattern.
4. Specify a blending mode and opacity for the paint. (See Setting options for painting and editing.)
5. Enter the tolerance for the fill. The tolerance defines how similar in color a pixel must be to be filled. Values can range from 0 to 255. A low tolerance fills pixels within a range of color values very similar to the pixel you click. A high tolerance fills pixels within a broader range.
6. To smooth the edges of the filled selection, select Anti-aliased.
7. To fill pixels based on the merged color data from all visible layers, select Use All Layers.
8. To fill only pixels contiguous to the one you click, select Contiguous; leave unselected to fill all similar pixels in the image.
9. Click the part of the image you want to fill. All adjacent pixels within the specified tolerance are filled with the foreground color or pattern.

If you're working on a layer and don't want to fill transparent areas, make sure that the layer's transparency is locked in the Layers palette.

4.17.13 Blur and Sharpen Tool

The focus tools consist of the blur tool and the sharpen tool. The blur tool softens hard edges or areas in an image to reduce detail. The sharpen tool focuses soft edges to increase clarity or focus.

When Blur tool is selected you get the following options:

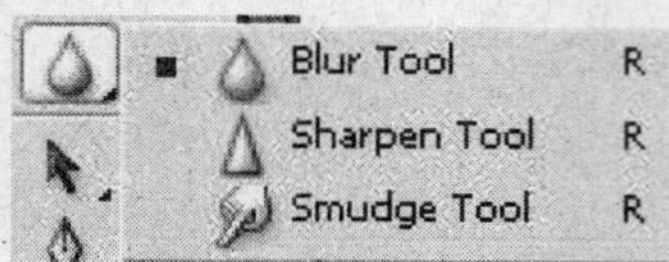

To use the blur or sharpen tool:

1. Select the blur tool or sharpen tool.
2. Choose a size for the brush from the brushes menu in the options bar. If a brush is too large to fit in the menu, it appears as a smaller brush with a number indicating the actual diameter in pixels.
3. Specify a blending mode and pressure.
4. Select Use All Layers to blur or sharpen using data from all visible layers. If this is deselected, the tool uses data from only the active layer.
5. If you are using a pressure-sensitive drawing tablet, specify the effects of stylus pressure.
6. Drag over the part of the image you want to blur or sharpen.

4.17.14 Dodge Tool

The toning tools consist of the dodge tool and the burn tool. Used to lighten or darken areas of the image, the dodge and burn tools are based on a traditional photographer's technique for regulating exposure on specific areas of a print. Photographers hold back light to lighten an area on the print (dodging) or increase the exposure to darken areas on a print (burning).

When selected it gives rise to the following options:

To use the dodge or burn tool:

1. Select the dodge tool or burn tool.
2. Choose a size for the brush from the brushes menu in the options bar. If a brush is too large to fit in the menu, it appears as a smaller brush with a number indicating the actual diameter in pixels.
3. Select what to change in the image:

   Midtones to change the middle range of grays. Shadows to change the dark areas. Highlights to change the light areas.
4. Specify the exposure for the tool.
5. If you are using a pressure-sensitive drawing tablet, specify the effects of stylus pressure.
6. Drag over the part of the image you want to modify.

4.17.15 Path Component Selection Tool

Since there are two different types of data in your image, rasterized and vector, you need to use separate sets of tools to make each type of selection. You can select pixels or make non-pixel selections. When you select pixels, you are selecting resolution dependent information in the image. Additionally, you can also select resolution independent paths and vector objects (or layer masks) in an image using the vector selection tools.

You can select paths and vector objects by clicking with the path component selection tool or the direct selection tool.

Selecting a path or segment displays all of the anchor points on the selected portion, including any direction lines and direction points if the selected segment is curved. Direction points appear as filled circles, selected anchor points as filled squares, and unselected anchor points as hollow squares.

When selected this gives rise to the following options:

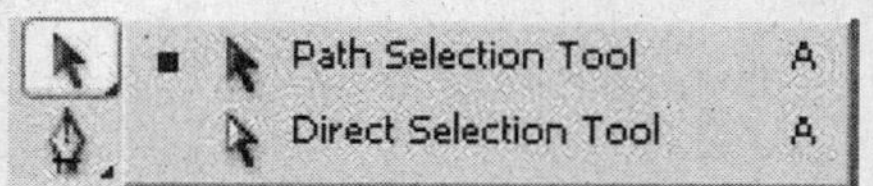

To select a path or vector object:

1. Select the path name in the Paths palette, or select the layer containing the vector object in the Layers palette.
2. Do one of the following:

   To select the entire path or subpath, select the path component selection tool (icon), and click anywhere inside the path. If the path consists of several subpaths, only the subpath under the pointer is selected.

   To display the bounding box along with the selected path, select Show Bounding Box in the options bar.

To select a segment of the path, select the direct selection tool, and click one of the segment's anchor points or drag a marquee over part of the segment.

Marquee-drag to select segments. When the direct selection tool is selected, you can select the entire path or subpath by holding down Alt and clicking inside the path.

3. To add selections, select the path component selection tool or the direct selection tool, then hold down Shift while selecting additional paths or segments. To activate the direct selection tool when any other tool is selected, position the pointer over an anchor point, and press Ctrl .

To add, subtract, restrict, or invert the filled areas in selections:

1. Using the path component selection tool, choose one of the following options in the options bar, then drag a marquee to select existing path areas.

   Add to Path Area adds the area in the new selection. Subtract from Path Area removes the overlapping area in a new selection from the existing path selection. Restrict Path Area, restricts the area to the overlapped range of the new selection and the existing path selection. Invert Path Area, inverts the overlap area of the new path selection within the new selection.

4.17.16 Type Tool

You can insert new text, change existing text, and delete text in type layers.

When selected this tool gives rise to the following options:

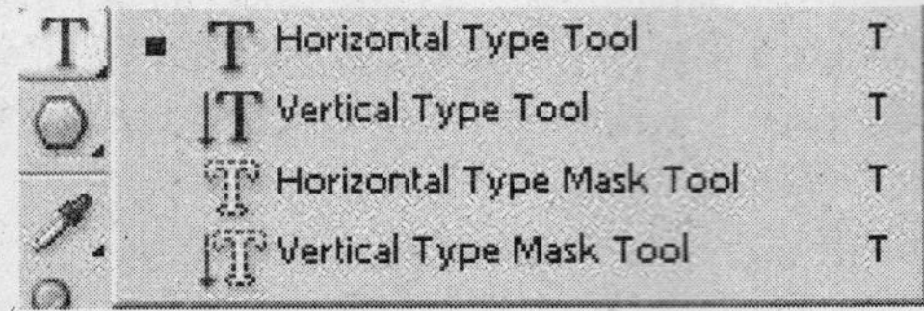

To edit text in a type layer:

1. Select the type tool.
2. Select the type layer in the Layers palette or click in the text to automatically select a type layer.
3. Position the cursor in the text and do one of the following:

   Click to set the insertion point. Select one or more characters you want to edit.
4. Enter text as desired.
5. Commit the changes to the type layer.

4.17.17 Pen Tool

The Info palette displays information about the color values beneath the pointer and, depending on the tool in use, other useful measurements. Various shown by the tool when selected are:

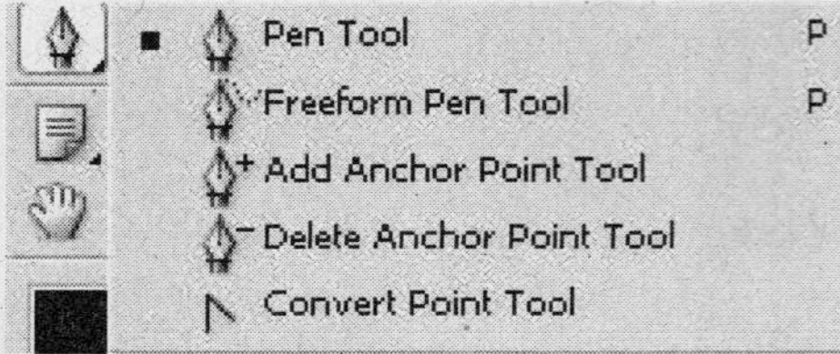

It is used to draw various curvical lines on the screen.

4.17.18 Rectangular Marquee Tools

The marquee tools let you select rectangles, ellipses, rounded rectangles, and 1-pixel rows and columns. By default, the selection border is dragged from its corner.

When selected it gives rise to the following options.

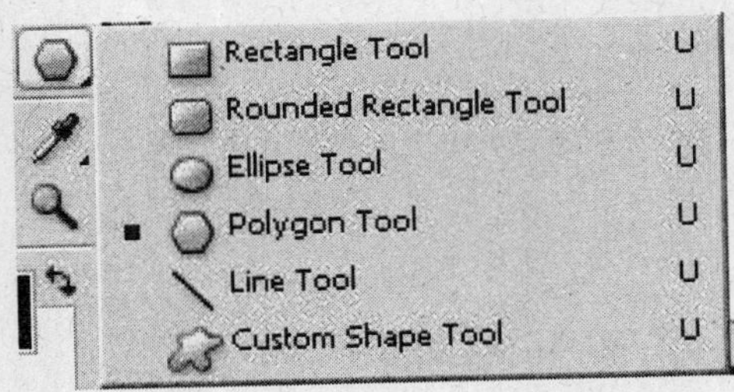

To use the marquee tools:

1. Select one of the following tools:

   Rectangle marquee to make a rectangular selection.

   Rounded rectangle marquee to select a rounded rectangle such as a Web-page button.

   Elliptical marquee to make an elliptical selection.

   Single row or single column marquee to define the border as a 1-pixel-wide row or column.
2. In the options bar, specify a selection option.
3. In the options bar, specify a feathering setting. Turn anti-aliasing on or off for the rounded rectangle or elliptical marquee.
4. For the rectangle, rounded rectangle, or elliptical marquee, choose a style in the options bar:

   Normal to determine marquee proportions by dragging. Constrained Aspect Ratio to set a height-to-width ratio. Enter the values (including decimal values) for the aspect ratio. For example, to draw a marquee twice as wide as it is high, enter 2 for the width and 1 for the height. Fixed Size to specify set values for the marquee's height and width. Enter pixel values in whole numbers. Keep in mind that the number of pixels needed to create a 1-inch selection depends on the resolution of the image.
5. Do one of the following to make a selection:

   With the rectangle, rounded rectangle, or elliptical marquee, drag over the area you want to select. Hold down Shift as you drag to constrain the marquee to a square or circle. To drag a marquee from its center, hold down Alt after you begin dragging. With the single row or single column marquee, click near the area you want to select, and then drag the marquee to the exact location. If no marquee is visible, increase the magnification of your image view.

4.17.19 Notes Tool

This tool is used to write notes on the image. This note is only visible and would not be printed while printing.

When selected this gives rise to the following options.

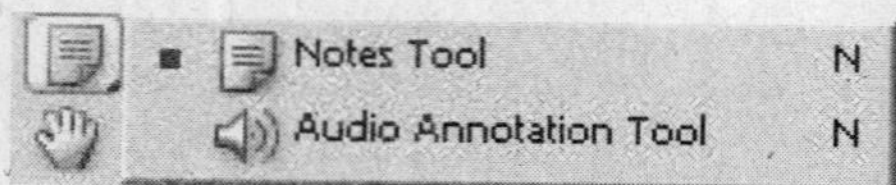

As is clear from above you can select font, colour, size, etc, for the note text from here.

4.17.20 Eyedropper Tool

You can view the color of a single area using the eyedropper tool, or you can use up to four color samplers to display color information for one or more locations in the image. These samplers are saved in the image, so you can refer to them repeatedly as you work, even if you close and reopen the image.

When selected it gives rise to the following options:

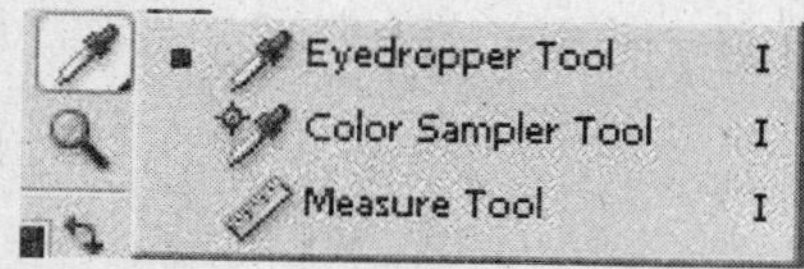

To use the Info palette and the eyedropper or color sampler tool to see color values:

1. Choose Window > Show Info to open the Info palette.
2. Select the eyedropper tool or color sampler tool, and choose what to sample from the pop-up menu in the eyedropper or color sampler tool options:

   Point Sample to read the value of a single pixel. 3 by 3 Average to read the average value of a 3-by-3 pixel area. 5 by 5 Average to read the average value of a 5-by-5 pixel area.

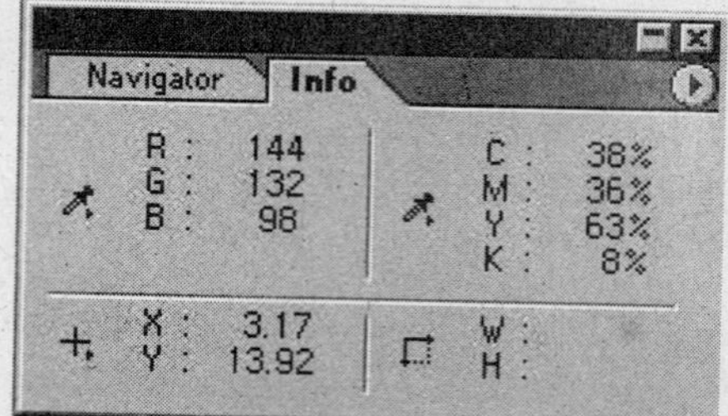

3. If you selected the color sampler tool, place up to four color samplers on the image. Click where you want to place a sampler.
4. Open a color adjustment dialog box.
5. Make your adjustments in the dialog box, and before applying them, view the before and after color values in the Info palette:

To view color values using the eyedropper tool, move the pointer over the area of the image you want to examine. Opening a color adjustment dialog box activates the eyedropper tool outside the dialog box. You still have access to the scroll controls and to the hand and zoom tools when using keyboard modifiers. To view the color values under the color samplers, look at the bottom half of the Info palette.

To move or delete a color sampler:

To move a color sampler, select the color sampler tool, and drag the sampler to the new location. To delete a color sampler, select the color sampler tool. Drag the sampler out of the document window, or hold down Alt and click the sampler.

To change the display of color sampler information in the Info palette:

To display or hide color sampler information in the Info palette, choose Show Color Samplers or Hide

Color Samplers from the palette menu. To change the color space in which a color sampler displays values, move the pointer onto the color sampler icon in the Info palette, hold down the mouse button, and choose another color space from the menu.

To use the eyedropper tool and Color palette to see color values:

1. Choose Window > Show Color to open the Color palette.
2. Open a color adjustment dialog box. This activates the eyedropper tool outside the dialog box.
3. Click the pixel you want to check in the image.
4. Make the adjustments in the dialog box, and before applying them, view the adjusted color values in the Color palette.

4.17.21 Hand Tool

This tool is used if the entire image is not visible in the document window, you can navigate to bring another area of the image into view. In Photoshop, you can also use the Navigator palette to quickly change the view of an image. When selected this gives the following options:

To view another area of an image:

Do one of the following:

1. Use the window scroll bars. Select the hand tool and drag to pan over the image.

To use the hand tool while another tool is selected, hold down the spacebar as you drag in the image.

To move the view of an image using the Navigator palette (Photoshop):

1. Choose Window > Show Navigator.
2. Do one of the following:

   Drag the view box in the thumbnail of the image, which represents the boundaries of the image window. Click in the thumbnail of the image. The new view includes the area you click.

To change the color of the Navigator palette view box:

1. Choose Palette Options from the Navigator palette menu.
2. Choose a color:

   To use a preset color, choose an option for Color. To specify a different color, click the color box, and choose a color as described in Using the Adobe Color Picker.

3. Click OK.

4.17.22 Zoom Tool

You can magnify or reduce your view using various methods. The window's title bar displays the zoom percentage (unless the window is too small for the display to fit), as does the status bar at the bottom of the window. The options of the tool are:

The 100% view of an image displays an image as it will appear in a browser (based on the monitor resolution and the image resolution). To zoom in, do one of the following:

1. Select the zoom tool.
2. The pointer becomes a magnifying glass with a plus sign in its center.
3. Click the area you want to magnify. Each click magnifies the image to the next preset percentage, centering the display around the point you click. When the image has reached its maximum magnification level of 6400%, the magnifying glass appears empty.
4. Choose View > Zoom In to magnify to the next preset percentage. When the image has reached its maximum magnification level, the command is dimmed.
5. Enter a magnification level in the Zoom text box at the lower left of the window.

To zoom out, do one of the following:

1. Select the zoom tool.
2. Hold down Alt to activate the zoom-out tool.
3. The pointer becomes a magnifying glass with a minus sign in its center.
4. Click the center of the area of the image you want to reduce. Each click reduces the view to the previous preset percentage. When the file has reached its maximum reduction level of 3.13%, the magnifying glass appears empty.
5. Choose View > Zoom Out to reduce to the previous preset percentage. When the image reaches its maximum reduction level, the command is dimmed. Enter a reduction level in the Zoom text box at the lower left of the window.

To magnify by dragging:

1. Select the zoom tool.
2. Drag over the part of the image you want to magnify.

   The area inside the zoom marquee is displayed at the highest possible magnification. To move the marquee around the artwork in Photoshop, begin dragging a marquee and then hold down the space bar while dragging the marquee to a new location.

To display an image at 100%, do one of the following:

1. Double-click the zoom tool.
2. Choose View > Actual Pixels.

To change the view to fit the screen, do one of the following:

1. Double-click the hand tool.
2. Choose View > Fit on Screen.

These options scale both the view and the window size to fit the available screen space. If the image is smaller than the monitor size, the image is displayed at 100%. To automatically resize the window when magnifying or reducing the view: With the Zoom tool active, select Resize Windows to Fit in the options bar. The window resizes when you magnify or reduce the view of the image. When Resize Windows to Fit is deselected (the default), ImageReady maintains a constant window size regardless of the image's magnification. This can be helpful when using smaller monitors or working with tiled views.

4.17.23 Healing Brush Tool

Photoshop CS 3 onwards there is a new tool called Healing Brush Tool. This tool lets you correct imperfections, causing them to disappear into the surrounding image. Like the cloning tools, you use the healing brush tool to paint with sampled pixels from an image or pattern. However, the healing brush tool also matches the texture, lighting, and shading of the sampled pixels to the source pixels. As a result, the repaired pixels blend seamlessly into the rest of the image.

To use the healing brush tool:

1. Select the healing brush tool.
2. Click the brush sample in the options bar and set brush options in the pop-up palette:
3. If you're using a pressure-sensitive digitizing tablet, choose an option from the Size menu to vary the size of the healing brush over the course of a stroke. Choose Pen Pressure to base the variation on the pen pressure. Choose Stylus Wheel to base the variation on the position of the pen thumbwheel. Choose Off to not vary the size.
4. Choose a blending mode from the Mode pop-up menu in the options bar:
5. Choose Replace to preserve noise, film grain, and texture at the edges of the brush stroke.

Determine how you want to align the sampled pixels:

1. If you select Aligned in the options bar, you can release the mouse button without losing the current sampling point. As a result, the sampled pixels are applied continuously, no matter how many times you stop and resume painting.
2. If you deselect Aligned in the options bar, the sampled pixels are applied from the initial sampling point each time you stop and resume painting.

For the healing brush tool in sampling mode, set the sampling point by positioning the pointer in any open image and Alt-clicking.

Drag in the image.

The sampled pixels are melded with the existing pixels each time you release the mouse button. Look in the status bar to view the status of the melding process. If there is a strong contrast at the edges of the area you want to heal, make a selection before you use the healing brush tool. The selection should be bigger than the area you want to heal but precisely follow the boundary of contrasting pixels. When you paint with the healing brush tool, the selection will prevent colors from bleeding in from the outside.

4.16 Importing Files

The import command lets you import files which are supported by Photoshop. It uses TWAIN interface for the same.

Photoshop opens and saves to the following file formats:

AVI	BMP	DCS 1.0 and 2.0	EPS PICT Preview
EPS TIFF Preview	Generic EPS	Filmstrip	GIF
JPEG	Kodak Photo CD	PCX	Photoshop PDF
Generic PDF	Photoshop 2.0	PICT	PICT Resource
PIXAR	PNG	PSD	Raw
ScitexCT	.TGA	TIFF	WBMP

4.17 Image Handling

There will be times when you need to make an object bigger or smaller as you copy it from one picture to another. You may need to straighten a titled horizon, or even stand something upright. You may even need to make someone face left instead of him facing right.

4.17.1 Resizing an Image

For this we use the Image Size dialog box, as shown here. You can see the pixel dimensions in pixels or percentages. You can also see the image print size in inches, centimeters, points, picas, or columns; percentage can also be found using the pop-up menus. When the dialog box is first opened, all the settings are to the 100% of the image. You can change this percentage to enlarge or reduce the image. But, the easiest way to do it to take the help of Constrain Properties.

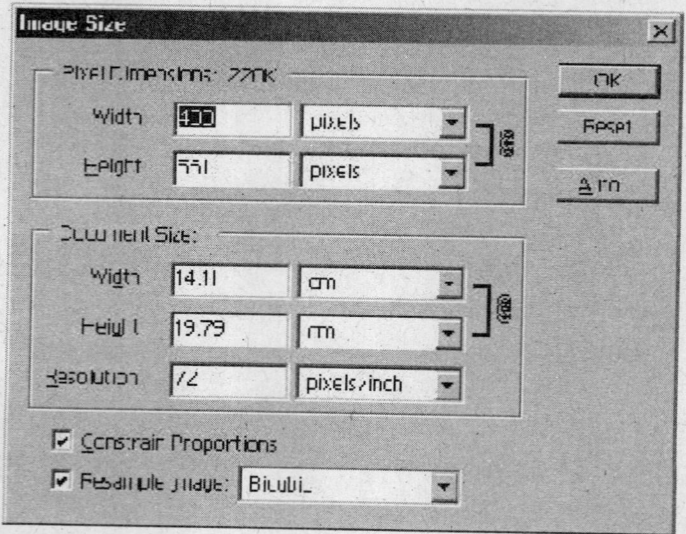

4.17.2 Resizing a Canvas

Resizing the canvas larger gives you extra work space around the image, instead of changing the size of the image. It is so because resizing uses the current background colour to fill in the space, be sure it is a colour you want. To resize the canvas, open the Image, Canvas Size dialog box, as shown on the next, to specify the height and width you want the canvas to be. You can specify any of the measurement systems you prefer on the pop-up menu. The new file size is calculated immediately and displayed.

The anchor at the bottom is used to determine where the image will be placed within the canvas. Click in the middle, to center the image on the enlarged canvas, or in any of the other boxes to place it relative to the increased canvas area.

4.17.3 Resizing a Selection

You can also resize a selected object. To do so, first select the object or a piece of an image to be resized. Use whichever Selection tool is most convenient. With the Selection Marquee active, choose Edit, Transform, Scale. This places a window that looks like the cropping window around your selected object. Drag on any of the corner handles on the box to change the size of the image while holding down the Shift key to maintain its proportions. If you drag on the side handles of the box, you will stretch the selection's height or width accordingly. The various steps are shown here and on the next few pages.

4.17.4 Rotating

There are many reasons why you might want to need to rate an image. If you have a scanned picture or a digital camera image that should be vertical but opens as a horizontally-oriented picture, rotating it at 90 degrees corrects the problem.

If the above picture of Zebra is rotated at 180 degrees, it will give you the picture as shown on the next page.

Under the Image menu and Rotate Canvas submenu, you have options like 90 degrees clockwise, 180 degrees or Counterclockwise (CCW).

If you are however, keen to rotate the picture according to the degrees of your choice, you can do so by choosing the Arbitrary dialog box, also available under the same submenu.

Result of this 30 degrees rotation can be seen here.

4.17.4.1 File size

The file size of an image is the digital size of the image file, measured in kilobytes (K), megabytes (MB), or gigabytes (GB). File size is proportional to the pixel dimensions of the image. Images with more pixels may produce more detail at a given printed size, but they require more disk space to store and may be slower to edit and print. Image resolution thus becomes a compromise between image quality (capturing all the data you need) and file size.

Another factor that affects file size is file format. Because of the varying compression methods used by GIF, JPEG, and PNG file formats, file sizes can vary considerably for the same pixel dimensions. Similarly, color bit-depth and the number of layers and channels in an image affect file size.

Photoshop supports a maximum pixel dimension of 300,000 by 300,000 pixels per image. This restriction places limits on the print size and resolution available to an image.

4.17.4.2 Resampling

Resampling is changing the amount of image data as you change either the pixel dimensions or the resolution of an image. When you downsample (decrease the number of pixels), information is deleted from the image. When you resample up (increase the number of pixels, or upsample), new pixels are added. You specify an interpolation method to determine how pixels are added or deleted.

Keep in mind that resampling can result in poorer image quality. For example, when you resample an image to larger pixel dimensions, the image loses some detail and sharpness. Applying the Unsharp Mask filter to a resampled image can help refocus the image details.

You can avoid the need for resampling by scanning or creating the image at a sufficiently high resolution.

If you want to preview the effects of changing pixel dimensions on screen or to print proofs at different resolutions, resample a duplicate of your file.

Photoshop resamples images using an interpolation method to assign color values to any new pixels based on the color values of existing pixels. You can choose which method to use in the Image Size dialog box.

Nearest Neighbor: A fast but less precise method that replicates the pixels in an image. This method is for use with illustrations containing edges that are not anti-aliased, to preserve hard edges and produce a smaller file. However, this method can produce jagged effects, which become apparent when you distort or scale an image or perform multiple manipulations on a selection.

Bilinear: A method that adds pixels by averaging the color values of surrounding pixels. It produces medium-quality results.

Bicubic: A slower but more precise method based on an examination of the values of surrounding pixels. Using more complex calculations, Bicubic produces smoother tonal gradations than Nearest Neighbor or Bilinear.

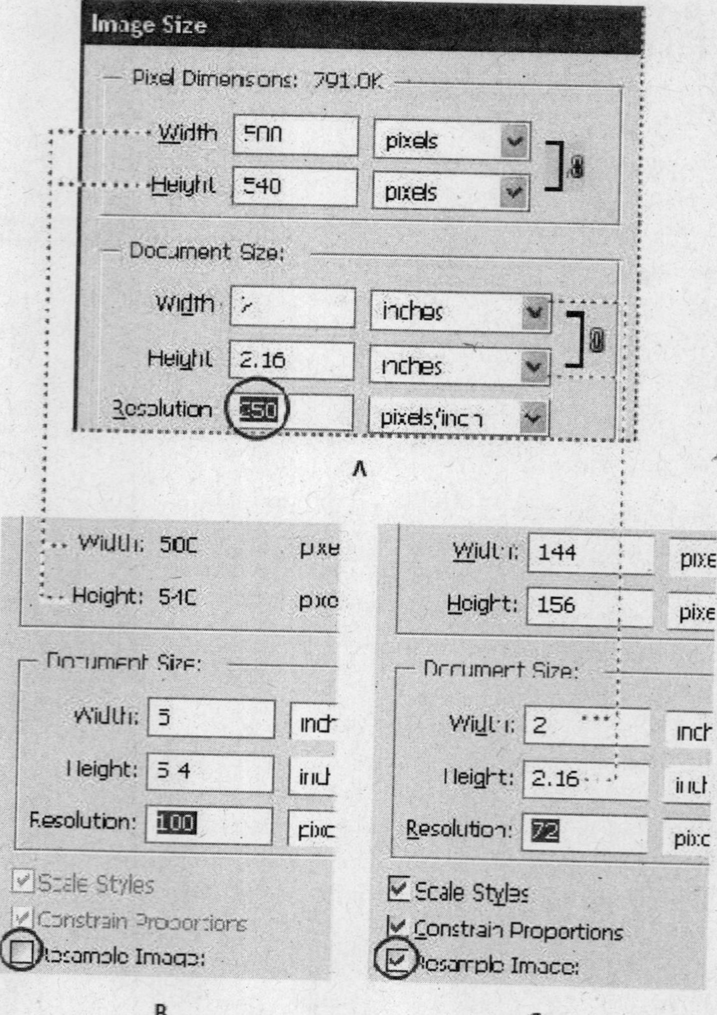

Pixel dimensions equal document (output) size times resolution.

A. Original dimensions and resolution ***B.*** *Decreasing the resolution without changing pixel dimensions (no resampling)* ***C.*** *Decreasing the resolution at same document size decreases pixel dimensions (resampling)*

Bicubic Smoother: A good method for enlarging images based on Bicubic interpolation but designed to produce smoother results.

Bicubic Sharper: A good method for reducing the size of an image based on Bicubic interpolation with enhanced sharpening. This method maintains the detail in a resampled image. If Bicubic Sharper oversharpens some areas of an image, try using Bicubic.

You can specify a default interpolation method to use whenever Photoshop resamples image data. Choose Edit > Preferences > General (Windows) or Photoshop > Preferences > General (Mac OS), and then choose a method from the Image Interpolation Methods menu.

4.17.5 Change pixel dimensions of an image

Changing an image's pixel dimensions affects not only its on screen size but also its image quality and its printed characteristics—either its printed dimensions or its image resolution.

1. Choose Image > Image Size.
2. To maintain the current ratio of pixel width to pixel height, select Constrain Proportions. This option automatically updates the width as you change the height, and vice versa.
3. Under Pixel Dimensions, enter values for Width and Height. To enter values as percentages of the current dimensions, choose Percent as the unit of measurement. The new file size for the image appears at the top of the Image Size dialog box, with the old file size in parentheses.
4. Make sure that Resample Image is selected, and choose an interpolation method.
5. If your image has layers with styles applied to them, select Scale Styles to scale the effects in the resized image. This option is available only if you selected Constrain Proportions.
6. When you finish setting options, click OK.

4.17.6 Change the print dimensions and resolution

When creating an image for print media, it's useful to specify image size in terms of the printed dimensions and the image resolution. These two measurements, referred to as the document size, determine the total pixel count and therefore the file size of the image; document size also determines the base size at which an image is placed into another application. You can further manipulate the scale of the printed image using the Print command; however, changes you make using the Print command affect only the printed image, not the document size of the image file.

If you turn on resampling for the image, you can change print dimensions and resolution independently (and change the total number of pixels in the image). If you turn off resampling, you can change either the dimensions or the resolution—Photoshop adjusts the other value automatically to preserve the total pixel count. For the highest print quality, it's generally best to change the dimensions and resolution first, without resampling. Then resample only as necessary.

1. Choose Image > Image Size.
2. Change the print dimensions, image resolution, or both:
   - To change only the print dimensions or only the resolution and adjust the total number of pixels in the image proportionately, select Resample Image and then choose an interpolation method.
   - To change the print dimensions and resolution without changing the total number of pixels in the image, deselect Resample Image.
3. To maintain the current ratio of image width to image height, select Constrain Proportions. This option automatically changes the width as you change the height, and vice versa.
4. Under Document Size, enter new values for the height and width. If desired, choose a new unit of measurement. Note that for Width, the Columns option uses the width and gutter sizes specified in the Units & Rulers preferences.
5. For Resolution, enter a new value. If desired, choose a new unit of measurement.

4.17.7 Cropping images

Cropping is the process of removing portions of an image to create focus or strengthen the composition.

You can crop an image using the Crop tool and the Crop command. You can also trim pixels using the Crop And Straighten and the Trim commands.

4.17.7.1 Crop an image using the Crop tool

1. Select the Crop tool
2. (Optional) Set resample options in the options bar.

- To crop the image without resampling (default), make sure that the Resolution text box in the options bar is empty. You can click the Clear button to quickly clear all text boxes.
- To resample the image during cropping, enter values for the height, width, and resolution in the options bar. The Crop tool won't resample the image unless the width and/or height, and resolution are provided. If you've entered height and width dimensions and want the values quickly exchanged, click the Swaps Height And Width icon .

Using the Crop tool

3. You can click the triangle next to the Crop tool icon in the options bar to open the Tool Preset Picker and select a resampling preset. As with all Photoshop tools, you can create your own Crop tool preset.

- To resample an image based on the dimensions and resolution of another image, open the other image, select the Crop tool, and click Front Image in the options bar. Then make the image you want to crop active.

4. Resampling while cropping uses the default interpolation method set in the General preferences.
5. Drag over the part of the image you want to keep to create a marquee. The marquee doesn't have to be precise—you can adjust it later.
6. If necessary, adjust the cropping marquee:

- To move the marquee to another position, place the pointer inside the bounding box and drag.
- To scale the marquee, drag a handle. To constrain the proportions, hold down Shift as you drag a corner handle.
- To rotate the marquee, position the pointer outside the bounding box (the pointer turns into a curved arrow), and drag. To move the center point around which the marquee rotates, drag the circle at the center of the bounding box. The marquee can't be rotated in Bitmap mode.

7. Set options to hide or shield the cropped portions:

- Specify whether you want to use a cropping shield to shade the area of the image that will be deleted or hidden. When Shield is selected, you can specify a color and opacity for the cropping shield. When Shield is deselected, the area outside the cropping marquee is revealed.
- Specify whether you want to hide or delete the cropped area. Select Hide to preserve the

cropped area in the image file. You can make the hidden area visible by moving the image with the Move tool. Select Delete to discard the cropped area.

8. The Hide option is not available for images that contain only a background layer. If you want to crop a background by hiding, convert the background to a regular layer first.
9. Do one of the following:

- To complete the crop, press Enter (Windows) or Return (Mac OS), click the Commit button in the options bar, or double-click inside the cropping marquee.
- To cancel the cropping operation, press Esc or click the Cancel button in the options bar.

4.18 Working with Selection

A selection isolates one or more parts of your image. By selecting specific areas, you can edit and apply effects and filters to portions of your image while leaving the unselected areas untouched.

Photoshop provides separate sets of tools to make selections of raster and vector data. For example, to select pixels, you can use the marquee tools or the lasso tools. You can use commands in the Select menu to select all pixels, to deselect, or to reselect.

To select vector data, you can use the pen or shape tools, which produce precise outlines called paths. You can convert paths to selections or convert selections to paths.

Selections can be copied, moved, and pasted, or saved and stored in an alpha channel. Alpha channels store selections as grayscale images called masks. A mask is like the inverse of a selection: it covers the unselected part of the image and protects it from any editing or manipulations you apply. You can convert a stored mask back into a selection by loading the alpha channel into an image.

4.18.1 Select, Deselect, and Reselect pixels

You can select all visible pixels on a layer or deselect any selected pixels.

If a tool is not working as expected, you may have a hidden selection. Use the Deselect command and try the tool again.

4.18.1.1 Select all pixels on a layer within the Canvas Boundaries

1. Select the layer in the Layers palette.
2. Choose Select > All.

4.18.1.2 Deselect Selections

Do one of the following:

- Choose Select > Deselect.
- If you are using the Rectangle Marquee tool, the Elliptical Marquee tool, or the Lasso tool, click anywhere in the image outside the selected area.

4.18.1.3 Reselect the Most Recent Selection

1. Choose Select > Reselect.

4.18.2 Select with the Marquee Tools

The marquee tools let you select rectangles, ellipses, and 1 pixel rows and columns.

1. Select a marquee tool:

Rectangular Marquee : Makes a rectangular selection (or a square, when used with the Shift key).

Elliptical Marquee: Makes an elliptical selection (or a circle, when used with the Shift key).

Single Row or Single Column Marquee: Defines the border as a 1 pixel wide row or column.

2. Specify one of the selection options in the options bar.

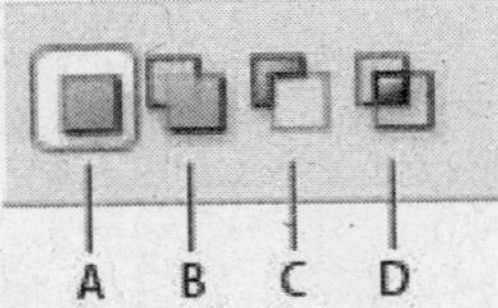

Selection options
***A.** New **B.** Add To **C.** Subtract From **D.** Intersect With*

3. Specify a feathering setting in the options bar. Turn anti-aliasing on or off for the Elliptical Marquee tool. See Soften the edges of selections.
4. For the Rectangle Marquee tool or the Elliptical Marquee tool, choose a style in the options bar:

   Normal: Determines marquee proportions by dragging.

   Fixed Aspect Ratio: Sets a height-to-width ratio. Enter values (decimal values are valid) for the aspect ratio. For example, to draw a marquee twice as wide as it is high, enter 2 for the width and 1 for the height.

   Fixed Size: Specifies set values for the marquee's height and width. Enter pixel values in whole numbers.

   In addition to pixels (px) you can also use specific units such as inches (in) or centimeters (cm) in height and width values.
5. For aligning your selection to guides, a grid, slices, or document bounds, do one of the following to snap your selection:
   - Choose View > Snap, or choose View > Snap To and choose a command from the submenu. The marquee selection can snap to a document boundary or to a variety of Photoshop Extras, controlled in the Snap To submenu.

Dragging a marquee from the corner of an image (left), and from the center of an image (right) by pressing Alt/Option as you drag

6. Do one of the following to make a selection:
   - With the Rectangle Marquee tool or the Elliptical Marquee tool, drag over the area you want to select.
   - Hold down Shift as you drag to constrain the marquee to a square or circle (release the mouse button before you release Shift to keep the selection shape constrained).
   - To drag a marquee from its center, hold down Alt (Windows) or Option (Mac OS) after you begin dragging.
   - With the Single Row or Single Column Marquee tool, click near the area you want to select, and then drag the marquee to the exact location. If no marquee is visible, increase the magnification of your image view.

4.18.3 Select with the Lasso tool

The Lasso tool is useful for drawing freeform segments of a selection border.

1. Select the Lasso tool , and select options.

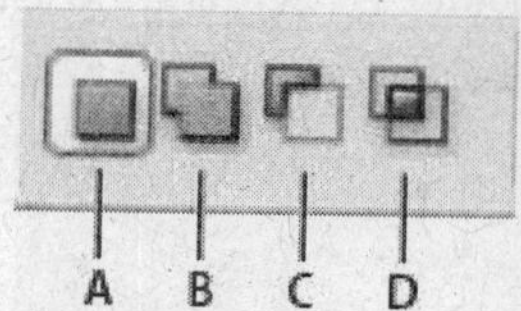

Selection options
A. *New* **B.** *Add To* **C.** *Subtract From* **D.** *Intersect With*

2. Drag to draw a freehand selection border.
3. Specify one of the selection options in the options bar.
4. (Optional) set feathering and anti-aliasing in the options bar.
5. To draw a straight-edged selection border when no other pixels are selected, press Alt (Windows) or Option (Mac OS), and click where segments should begin and end. You can switch between drawing freehand and straight-edged segments.
6. To erase recently drawn segments, hold down the Delete key until you've erased the fastening points for the desired segment.
7. To close the selection border, release the mouse without holding down Alt (Windows) or Option (Mac OS).
8. (Optional) Click Refine Edge to further adjust the selection boundary or view the selection against different backgrounds or as a mask.

4.18.4 Select with the Polygonal Lasso tool

The Polygonal Lasso tool is useful for drawing straight-edged segments of a selection border.

1. Select the Polygonal Lasso tool , and select options.
2. Specify one of the selection options in the options bar.
3. (Optional) Set feathering and anti-aliasing in the options bar.

4. Click in the image to set the starting point.
5. Do one or more of the following:

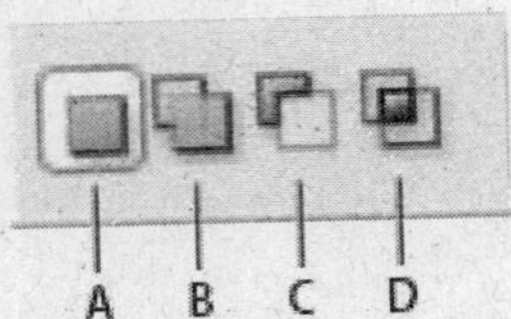

Selection options
***A.** New **B.** Add To **C.** Subtract From **D.** Intersect With*

- To draw a straight segment, position the pointer where you want the first straight segment to end, and click. Continue clicking to set endpoints for subsequent segments.
- To draw a straight line at a multiple of 45°, hold down Shift as you move to click the next segment.
- To draw a freehand segment, hold down Alt (Windows) or Option (Mac OS), and drag. When you finish, release Alt or Option and the mouse button.
- To erase recently drawn straight segments, press the Delete key.

6. Close the selection border:
   - Position the Polygonal Lasso tool pointer over the starting point (a closed circle appears next to the pointer), and click.
   - If the pointer is not over the starting point, double-click the Polygonal Lasso tool pointer, or Ctrl-click (Windows) or Command-click (Mac OS).
7. (Optional) Click Refine Edge to further adjust the selection boundary or view the selection against different backgrounds or as a mask.

4.18.5 Select with the Quick Selection tool

You can use the Quick Selection tool to quickly "paint" a selection using an adjustable round brush tip. As you drag, the selection expands outward and automatically finds and follows defined edges in the image.

1. Select the Quick Selection tool.
2. Specify one of the selection options in the options bar: New, Add to, Subtract from.
3. New is the default option if nothing is selected. After making the initial selection, the option changes automatically to Add to.
4. To change the Quick Selection tool brush tip size, click the Brush menu in the options bar and type in a pixel size or move the Diameter slider. Use the Size pop up menu options to make the brush tip size sensitive to pen pressure or a stylus wheel.
5. When creating a selection, press the right bracket (]) to increase the Quick Selection tool brush tip size; press the left bracket ([) to decrease the brush tip size.
6. Choose Quick Selection options.

   Sample All Layers: Creates a selection based on all layers instead of just the currently selected layer.

Auto-Enhance: Reduces roughness and blockiness in the selection boundary. Auto-Enhance automatically flows the selection further towards image edges and applies some of the edge refinement you can apply manually in the Refine Edge dialog with the Smooth, Contrast and Radius options.

7. Paint inside the part of the image you want to select.

   The selection grows as you paint. If updating is slow, continue to drag to allow time to complete work on the selection. As you paint near the edges of a shape, the selection area extends to follow the contours of the shape edge.

8. If you stop dragging and then click or drag in a nearby area, the selection will grow to include the new area.

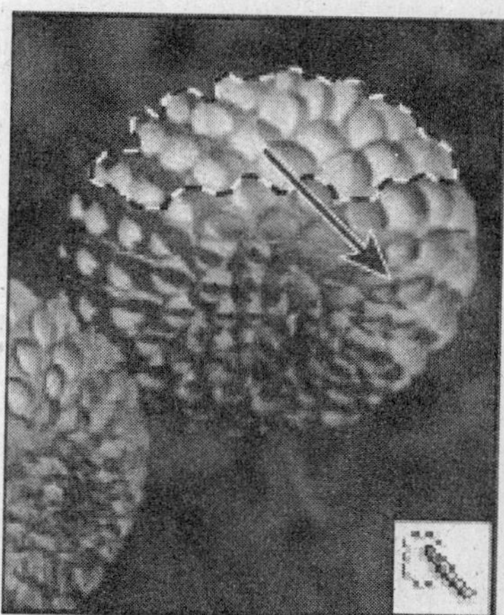

Painting with the Quick Selection tool to extend the selection

- To subtract from a selection, click the Subtract from option in the options bar, then drag over the existing selection.
- To temporarily switch between add and subtract modes, hold down the Alt (Windows) or Option (Mac) key.
- To change the tool cursor, choose Edit > Preferences > Cursors > Painting Cursors (Windows) or Photoshop > Preferences > Cursors > Painting Cursors (Mac OS). Normal Brush Tip displays the standard Quick Selection cursor with a plus or minus sign to show the selection mode.

9. (Optional) Click Refine Edge to further adjust the selection boundary or view the selection against different backgrounds or as a mask.

4.18.6 Select with the Magic Wand tool

The Magic Wand tool lets you select a consistently colored area (for example, a red flower) without having to trace its outline. You specify the color range, or tolerance, for the Magic Wand tool's selection, based on similarity to the pixel you click.

1. You cannot use the Magic Wand tool on an image in bitmap mode or on 32 bits-per-channel images.

2. Select the Magic Wand tool .
3. Specify one of the selection options in the options bar. The Magic Wand tool's pointer changes depending on which option is selected.
4. In the options bar, specify any of the following:

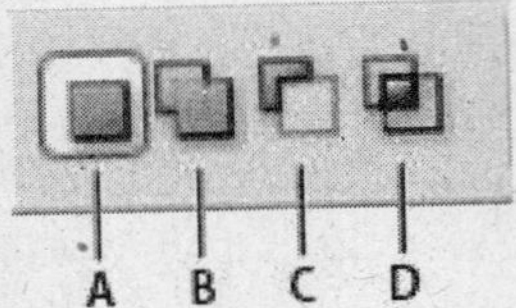

Selection options
***A.** New **B.** Add To **C.** Subtract From **D.** Intersect With*

Tolerance: Determines the similarity or difference of the pixels selected. Enter a value in pixels, ranging from 0 to 255. A low value selects the few colors very similar to the pixel you click. A higher value selects a broader range of colors.

Anti-aliased: Creates a smoother-edged selection.

Contiguous: Selects only adjacent areas using the same colors. Otherwise, all pixels in the entire image using the same colors are selected.

Sample All Layers: Selects colors using data from all the visible layers. Otherwise, the Magic Wand tool selects colors from the active layer only.

5. In the image, click the color you want to select. If Contiguous is selected, all adjacent pixels within the tolerance range are selected. Otherwise, all pixels in the tolerance range are selected.
6. (Optional) Click Refine Edge to further adjust the selection boundary or view the selection against different backgrounds or as a mask.

4.18.7 Select a Color Range

The Color Range command selects a specified color or color range within an existing selection or an entire image. If you want to replace a selection, be sure to deselect everything before applying this command. The Color Range command is not available for 32 bits-per-channel images.

To refine an existing selection, use the Color Range command repeatedly to select a subset of colors. For example, to select the green areas in a cyan selection, select Cyans in the Color Range dialog box, and click OK. Then reopen the Color Range dialog box, and select Greens. (The results are subtle because this technique selects parts of colors within a color mix.)

1. Choose Select > Color Range.
2. Choose the Sampled Colors tool from the Select menu.
3. You can also choose a color or tonal range from the Select menu, but you won't be able to adjust the selection. The Out Of Gamut option works only on RGB and Lab images. (An out of gamut color is an RGB or Lab color that cannot be printed using process color printing.)
4. Select one of the display options:

   Selection: Previews the selection that will result from the colors you sample in the image. White areas are selected pixels, black areas unselected, and gray areas partially selected.

Image: Previews the entire image. For example, you might want to sample from a part of the image that isn't on screen.

5. To toggle between the Image and Selection previews in the Color Range dialog box, press Ctrl (Windows) or Command (Mac OS).
6. Position the eyedropper pointer over the image or preview area, and click to sample the colors you want included.

Sampling color: Adjust the range of colors selected using the Fuzziness slider or by entering a value. The Fuzziness setting controls how wide a range of colors is in the selection, and increases or decreases the amount of partially selected pixels (gray areas in the selection preview). Set a low Fuzziness value to restrict the color range, a higher value to increase the range.

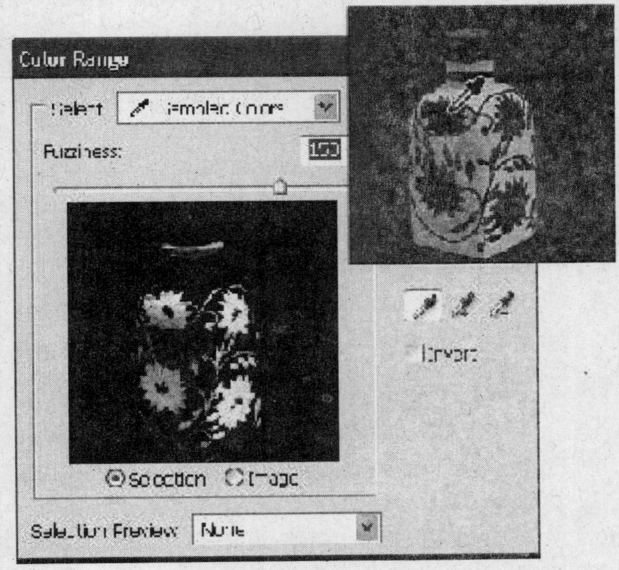

Sampling color

7. Adjust the selection:
   - To add colors, select the plus eyedropper, and click in the preview area or image.
   - To remove colors, select the minus eyedropper, and click in the preview area or image.
8. To activate the plus eyedropper temporarily, hold down Shift. Hold down Alt (Windows) or Option (Mac OS) to activate the minus eyedropper.
9. To preview the selection in the image window, choose an option for Selection Preview.
10. To revert to the original selection, hold down Alt (Windows) or Option (Mac OS), and click Reset.
11. To save and load color range settings, use the Save and Load buttons in the Color Range dialog box to save and reuse the current settings.

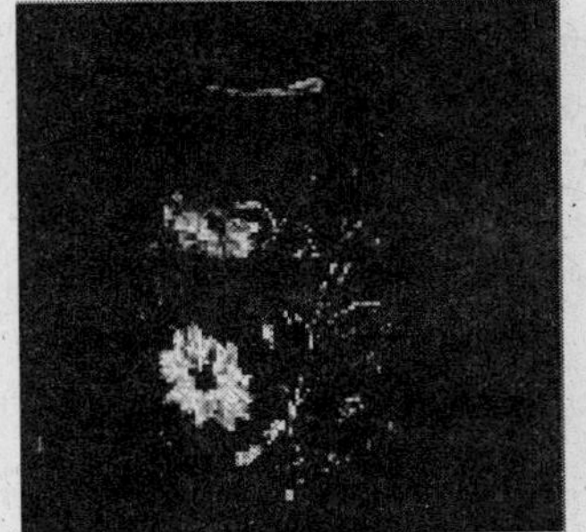

Increasing fuzziness expands selection

4.19 Brush Palette

In the Brushes palette, you can select preset brushes, like in the Brush Preset Picker, but you can also modify existing brushes and design new custom brushes. The Brushes palette contains the brush tip options that determine how paint is applied to an image.

The brush stroke preview at the bottom of the palette shows how paint strokes look with the current brush options.

4.19.1 Create a brush tip from an image

1. Use any selection tool to select a part of an image to use as a custom brush. Feather should be set to 0 pixels if you want to create a brush with a sharp edge. The brush shape can be up to 2500 pixels by 2500 pixels in size.
2. If you select color image, the brush tip image is converted to grayscale. Any layer mask applied to the image doesn't affect the definition of the brush tip.
3. If you want to define a brush with soft edges, select pixels with gray values. (Colored brush shapes appear as gray values.)
4. Choose Edit > Define Brush Preset.
5. Name the brush, and click OK.

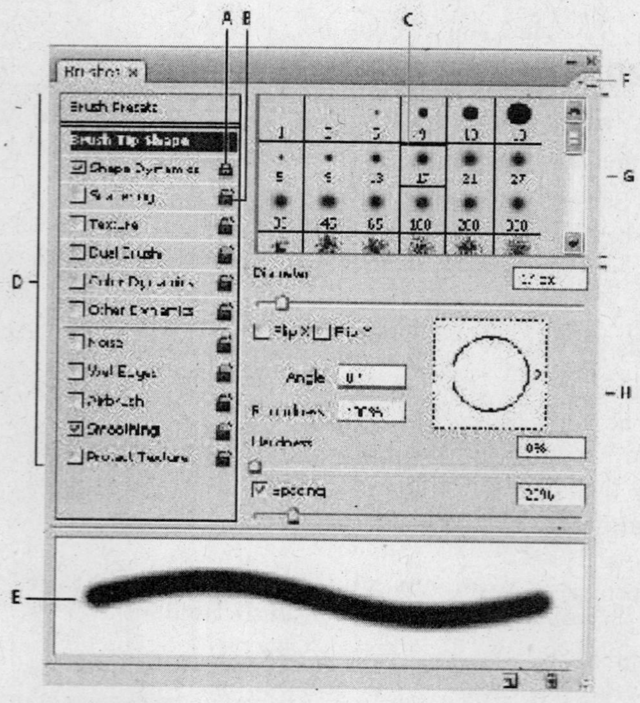

Brushes palette with Brush Tip Shape options displayed
A. Locked B. Unlocked C. Selected brush tip D. Brush settings E. Brush stroke preview F. pop-up menu G. Brush tip shapes (available when Brush Tip Shape option is selected) H. Brush options

4.19.2 Create a Brush and set Painting options

1. Open the Brushes palette by clicking the brushes palette button in the options bar. Make sure the Brush tool is selected to see the button.
2. In the Brushes palette, choose an existing brush preset to modify or select a brush shape from the Brush Tip Shape panel of the Brushes palette. You can also create a new brush tip from an image.
3. Select Brush Tip Shape on the left side of the Brushes palette, and set options.
4. Set other options for the brush as needed. See the following sections for information about the options.

- Brush shape dynamics
- Brush scattering
- Textured brush options
- Dual brushes
- Color dynamics Brush options
- Other dynamics brush options
- Other Brush options

5. To lock brush tip shape attributes, click the unlock icon . To unlock the tip, click the lock icon.
6. To save the brush for use later, choose New Brush Preset from the Brushes palette menu. To save your new brush permanently or distribute it to other users, you must save the brush as part of a set of brushes. Choose Save Brushes from the Brushes palette menu, and then save to a new set or overwrite an existing set. If you reset or replace the brushes in the Brushes palette without saving it in a set, you could lose your new brush.

4.20 Brush Shapes

You can set the following brush tip shape options in the Brushes palette:

Diameter: Controls the size of the brush. Enter a value in pixels or drag the slider.

Use Sample Size: Resets the brush to its original diameter. This option is available only if the brush tip shape was created by sampling pixels in an image.

Flip X: Changes the direction of a brush tip on its x axis.

Flip Y: Changes the direction of a brush tip on its y axis.

Angle: Specifies the angle by which an elliptical or sampled brush's long axis is rotated from horizontal. Type a value in degrees, or drag the horizontal axis in the preview box.

Roundness: Specifies the ratio between the brush's short and long axes. Enter a percentage value, or drag the points in the preview box. A value of 100% indicates a circular brush, a value of 0% indicates a linear brush, and intermediate values indicate elliptical brushes.

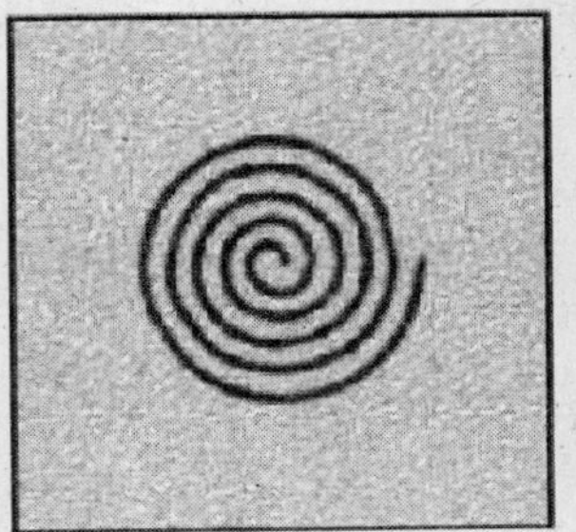
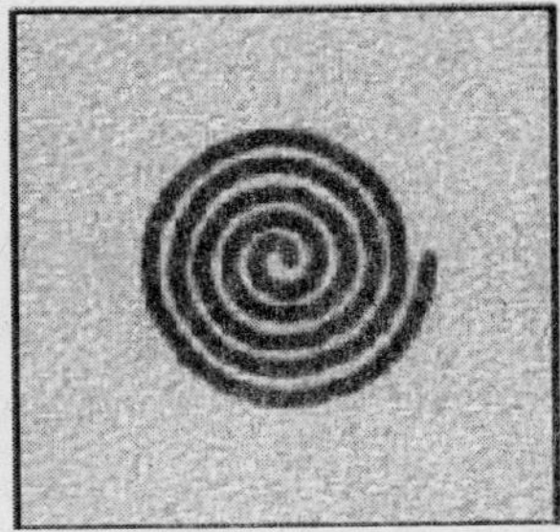

Brush strokes with different diameter values

Hardness: Controls the size of the brush's hard center. Type a number, or use the slider to enter a value that is a percentage of the brush diameter. You can't change the hardness of sampled brushes.

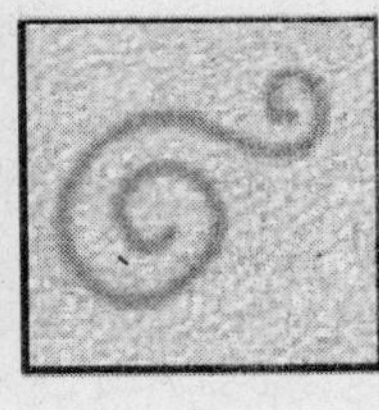

Flipping a brush tip on its x axis.
A. Brush tip in its default position B. Flip X selected C. Flip X and Flip Y selected

Spacing: Controls the distance between the brush marks in a stroke. To change the spacing, type a number, or use the slider to enter a value that is a percentage of the brush diameter. When this option is deselected, the speed of the cursor determines the spacing.

Flipping a brush tip on its y axis.
A. Brush tip in its default position B. Flip Y selected C. Flip Y and Flip X selected

4.21 Options Bar

This bar is used to find options related to the currently selected tool. It can be undocked from its position at the top of the screen and placed at the bottom of the screen. Most tools have options that are displayed in the tool options bar. The options bar is changed as different tools are selected. Some settings in the options bar are common to several tools but some are specific to one tool.

4.22 Layers

Layers are the various layers that you can create of the image or picture for the editing purposes and putting them one over the another for the final result.

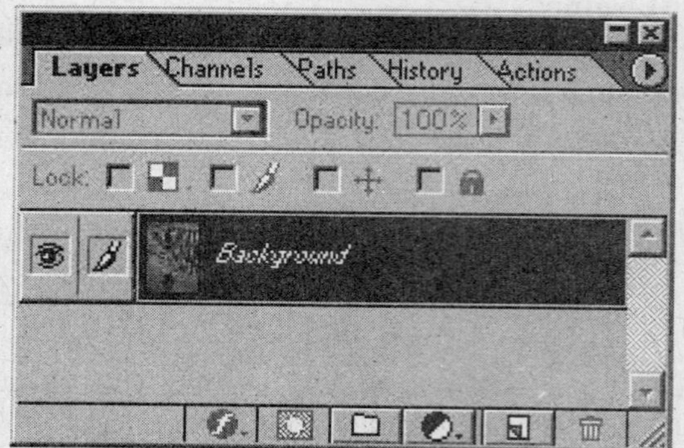

Masking is the method by which you can select a portion of the image or picture for editing and doing changes.

4.22.1 Layers

The Layers palette is where you control your layer. Be it be for creating, adding, deleting, hiding, and showing. The small versions of your images on the left of the palette are called thumbnails. Each of these small rectangles represent a separate layer.

If thumbnails are small for your liking, select the Palette Options to see more thumbnails.

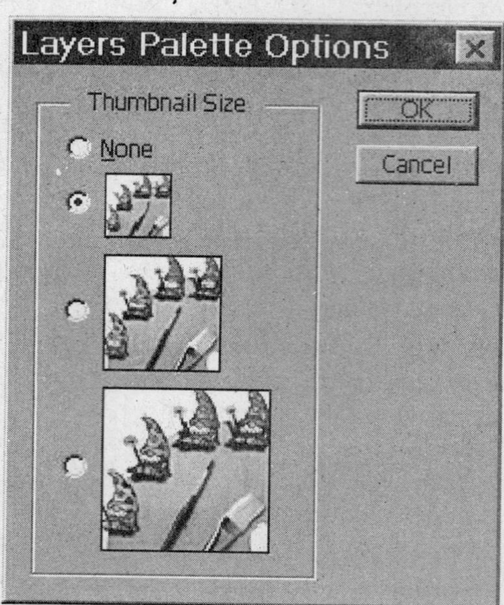

4.22.2 Creating a New Layer

1. Using the Airbrush and your biggest brush shape, choose any light to medium colour and spray paint a large patch of colour on the canvas.
2. Look at the thumbnail called Background.
3. Click the small page icon at the bottom of the Layer palette. You have just added a layer.

Another way of adding a new layer is by opening the menu on the right hand side of the dialog box and click at New Layer.

A new layer like above is added.

4.22.3 Hiding and Showing of Layers

To the left of the thumbnails, you will notice small icons that resemble eyes. These indicate that a layer is visible. If you see the eye, you can see the layer. If you click the eye, however, the eye disappears and the layer becomes hidden.

In the following figure Layer 1 is hidden and the other one is shown.

4.22.4 Working with Multiple Layers

Whenever you are combining two or more images the elements you paste over the background image are added on separate layers. You can use the Layer palette to control precisely how these elements are combined. You can also control the Blending modes that affect how one layer appears on top of another, just as you could when painting over an image or background.

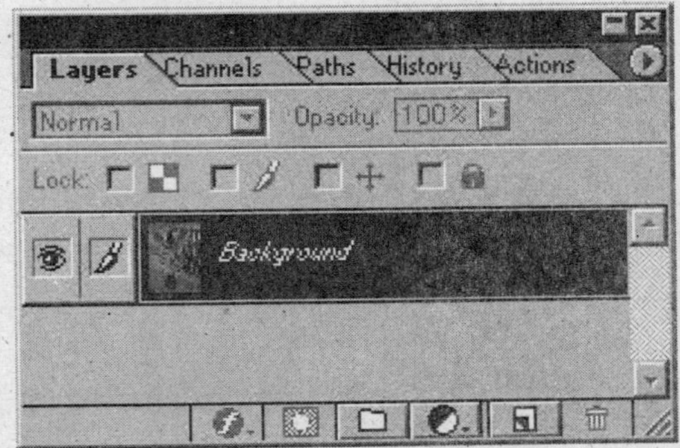

4.22.4.1 Merging Layers

The more layers you add to an image, and more effect that you add to those layers, the larger your image file will become. There are two main factors here:

Merging: Merging groups of layers without flattening the entire image conserves memory space but still allows you to work on the layers that you have not yet finished. Merging Down merges a layer with the one directly below it. You also can merge just the visible layers choosing the appropriate Layer, Merge command.

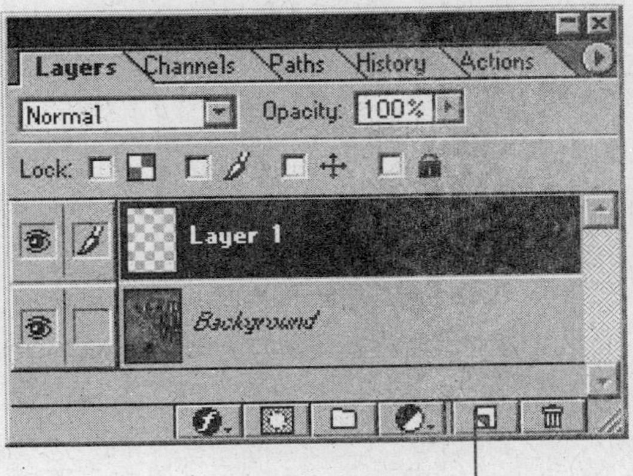

Create a New Layer

Flattening: Flattening, on the other hand, compresses all visible layers down to one layer. Any layers that you have made invisible at the time of flattening are lost. To flatten an image, simple choose Layer, Flatten Image, but make sure that you are done. At this point all the layers are reduced to one.

4.22.4.2 Layer Effects

A number of automated effects that you can apply to layers, shown on the next page, are available under Layer menu and Layer Style submenu. They include drop shadows, glows, beveling, and embossing, etc.

You can apply these and see the effects.

4.22.5 Change the stack order of layers and groups

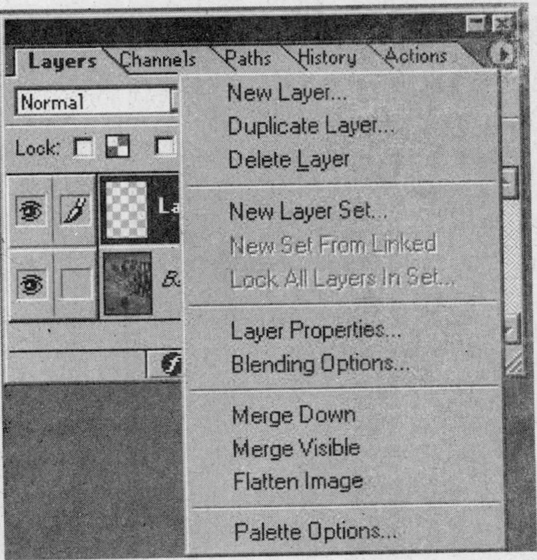

1. Do one of the following:
   - Drag the layer or group up or down in the Layers palette. Release the mouse button when the highlighted line appears where you want to place the layer or group.
   - To move a layer into a group, drag a layer to the group folder . If the group is closed, the layer is placed at the bottom of the group.

     If a group is expanded so that you can see all the layers within it, adding a layer beneath the expanded group automatically adds the layer to that group. To avoid this, collapse the group before adding the new layer.

- Select a layer or group, choose Layer > Arrange, and choose a command from the submenu. If the selected item is in a group, the command applies to the stacking order within the group. If the selected item is not in a group, the command applies to the stacking order within the Layers palette.
- To reverse the order of selected layers, choose Layer > Arrange > Reverse. These options appear dimmed if you do not have at least two layers selected.

  By definition, the background layer is always at the bottom of the stacking order. Therefore, the Send To Back command places the selected item directly above the background layer.

4.22.6 Show layer edges and handles

Showing the boundary or edges of the content in a layer can help you move and align the content. You can also display the transform handles for selected layers and groups so that you can resize or rotate them.

4.22.6.1 Display the edges of content in a selected layer

1. Choose View > Show > Layer Edges.

4.22.6.2 Display transform handles in a selected layer

1. Select the Move tool.
2. From the options bar, select Show Transform Controls.
3. You can resize and rotate layer content using the transform handles.

4.22.6.3 Move the content of layers

1. From the Layers palette, select the layers containing the objects you want to move.
2. Select the Move tool.
3. You can select the layers that you want to move directly in the document window. In the Move tool's options bar, select Auto Select, the choose Layer from the drop-down menu. Shift-click to select multiple layers. Select Auto Select, then choose Group, to select the entire group when you select one layer in the group.

Layer content with edges showing (left) and with transform mode selected (right)

4. Do one of the following:

- In the document window, drag any object onto one of the selected layers. (All objects on the layer will move together.)
- Press an arrow key on the keyboard to nudge the objects by 1 pixel.
- Hold down Shift and press an arrow key on the keyboard to nudge the objects by 10 pixels.

4.22.7 Align objects on different layers

You can align the content of layers and groups using the Move tool.

1. Do one of the following:
   - To align multiple layers, select the layers with the Move tool or in the Layers palette, or select a group.
   - To align the content of one or more layers to a selection border, make a selection in the image, and then select the layers in the Layers palette. Use this method to align to any specified point in the image.
2. Choose Layer > Align or Layer > Align Layers To Selection, and choose a command from the submenu. These same commands are available as Alignment buttons in the Move tool options bar.

   Top Edges: Aligns the top pixel on the selected layers to the topmost pixel on all selected layers, or to the top edge of the selection border.

   Vertical Centers: Aligns the vertical center pixel on each selected layers to the vertical center pixel of all the selected layers, or to the vertical center of the selection border.

   Bottom Edges: Aligns the bottom pixel on the selected layers to the bottommost pixel on selected layers, or to the bottom edge of the selection border.

   Left Edges: Aligns the left pixel on the selected layers to the left pixel on the leftmost layer, or to the left edge of the selection border.

   Horizontal Centers: Aligns the horizontal center pixel on the selected layers to the horizontal center pixel of all the selected layers, or to the horizontal center of the selection border.

   Right Edges: Aligns the right pixel on the linked layers to the rightmost pixel on all selected layers, or to the right edge of the selection border.

4.22.8 Automatically align image layers

The Auto-Align Layers command can automatically align layers based on similar content in different layers, such as corners and edges. You assign one layer as a reference layer, or let Photoshop automatically choose the reference layer. Other layers are aligned to the reference layer so that matching content overlays itself.

Using the Auto-Align Layers command, you can combine images in several ways:

- Replace or delete parts of images that have the same background. After aligning the images, use masking or blending effects to combine parts of each image into one image.
- Stitch images together that share overlapping content.
- For video frames shot against a static background, you can convert frames into layers, then add or delete content across multiple frames.

1. Copy or place the images you want to align into the same document. Each image will be in a separate layer.

   You can load multiple images into layers using a script. Choose File > Scripts > Load Files into Stack.

2. (Optional) In the Layers palette, create a reference layer by locking it. If you do not set a reference layer, Photoshop will analyze all the layers and select the one at the center of the final composition as the reference.

3. Select the remaining layers you want to align.

   To select multiple adjacent layers from the palette, Shift-click; To select noncontiguous layers, Ctrl-Click (Windows) or Option-click (Mac OS).

   Do not select adjustment layers, vector layers, or Smart Objects which do not contain information needed for alignment.

4. Choose Edit > Auto-Align Layers, and choose an alignment option. For stitching together multiple images that share overlapping areas—for example, to create a panorama—use the Auto, Perspective, or Cylindrical options. To align scanned images with offset content, use the Reposition Only option.

   Auto: Photoshop analyzes the source images and applies either a Perspective or Cylindrical layout, depending on which produces a better composite.

   Perspective: Creates a consistent composition by designating one of the source images (by default, the middle image) as the reference image. The other images are then transformed (repositioned, stretched, or skewed, as necessary) so that overlapping content across layers is matched.

   Cylindrical: Reduces the "bow tie" distortion that can occur with the Perspective layout by displaying individual images as on an unfolded cylinder. Overlapping content across layers is still matched. The reference image is placed at the center. Best suited for creating wide panoramas.

   Reposition Only: Aligns the layers and matches overlapping content, but does not transform (stretch or skew) any of the source layers.

5. After auto-aligning, you can use Edit > Free Transform to fine tune the alignment or make tonal adjustments to even out exposure differences between layers, then combine the layers into one composite image.

4.22.9 Auto blend layers

When stitching or combining images to create a composite image, exposure differences between the source images may create seams or inconsistencies in the combined image. Use the Auto-Blend Layers command to create the appearance of smooth transitions in the final images. Auto-Blend Layers is only available for RGB or grayscale images.

1. Copy or place the images you want to combine into the same document.

   Each image will be in a separate layer.

2. Align the layers so that common areas overlap.

   You can do this manually or using the Auto-Align Layers command.

3. With the layers still selected, choose Edit > Auto-Blend Layers.

Auto-Blend Layers applies layer masks as needed to each layer to mask out over or underexposed areas or content differences and create a seamless composite.

4.22.10 Rotate a layer

From the Layers palette, select the layer you want to rotate.

1. If anything is currently selected in the image, choose Select > Deselect.
2. Choose Edit > Transform > Rotate. A box defining the boundaries of the layer (called a bounding box) appears.
3. Move the pointer outside of the bounding box (the pointer becomes a curved, two-sided arrow), and then drag. Press Shift to constrain the rotation to 15° increments.
4. When you're satisfied with the results, press Enter (Windows) or Return (Mac OS), or click the check mark in the options bar. To cancel the rotation, press Esc, or click the Cancel Transform icon on the options bar.

4.23 Rotating Selections

The Rotate Canvas commands let you rotate or flip an entire image. The commands do not work on individual layers or parts of layers, paths, or selection borders. If you want to rotate a selection or layer, use the Transform or Free Transform commands.

1. Choose Image > Rotate Canvas, and choose one of the following commands from the submenu:

   180°: Rotates the image by a half-turn.

   90° CW: Rotates the image clockwise by a quarter-turn.

   90° CCW: Rotates the image counterclockwise by a quarter-turn.

   Arbitrary: Rotates the image by the angle you specify. If you choose this option, enter an angle between 359.99 and 359.99 in the angle text box. (In Photoshop, you can select CW or CCW to rotate clockwise or counterclockwise.) Then click OK.

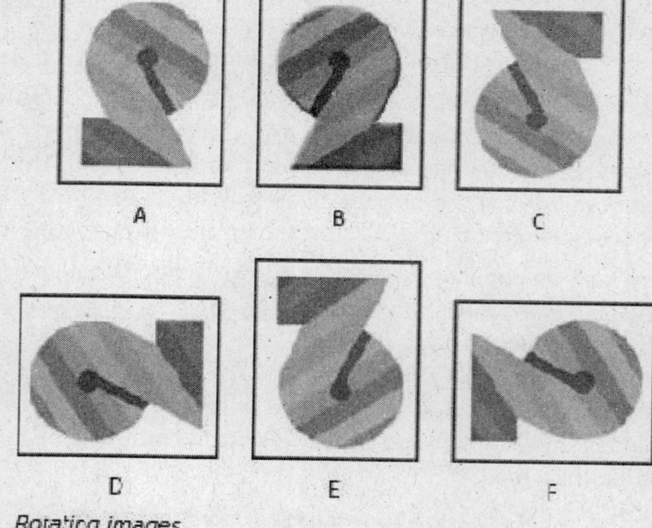

Rotating images

A. *Flip Horizontal* *B.* *Original image* *C.* *Flip Vertical* *D.* *Rotate 90⁰ CCW* *E.* *Rotate 180⁰* *F.* *Rotate 90⁰ CW*

4.24 Channels and Masks

Channels are grayscale images that store different types of information:

- Color information channels are created automatically when you open a new image. The image's color mode determines the number of color channels created. For example, an RGB image has a channel for each color (red, green, and blue) plus a composite channel used for editing the image.

- Alpha channels store selections as grayscale images. You can add alpha channels to create and store masks, which let you manipulate or protect parts of an image.
- Spot color channels specify additional plates for printing with spot color inks.

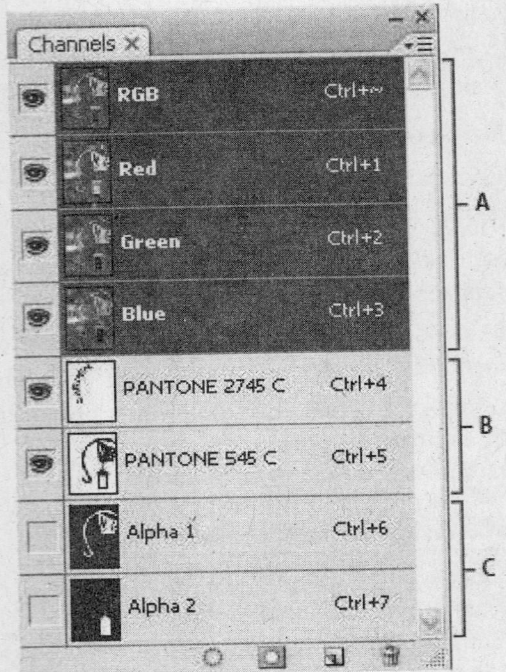

Channel types
***A.** Color channels **B.** Spot channels **C.** Alpha channels*

An image can have up to 56 channels. All new channels have the same dimensions and number of pixels as the original image.

The file size required for a channel depends on the pixel information in the channel. Certain file formats, including TIFF and Photoshop formats, compress channel information and can save space.

The size of an uncompressed file, including alpha channels and layers, appears as the rightmost value in the status bar at the bottom of the window when you choose Document Sizes from the pop up menu.

As long as you save a file in a format supporting the image's color mode, the color channels are preserved. Alpha channels are preserved only when you save a file in Photoshop, PDF, PICT, Pixar, TIFF, PSB, or raw formats. DCS 2.0 format preserves only spot channels. Saving in other formats may cause channel information to be discarded.

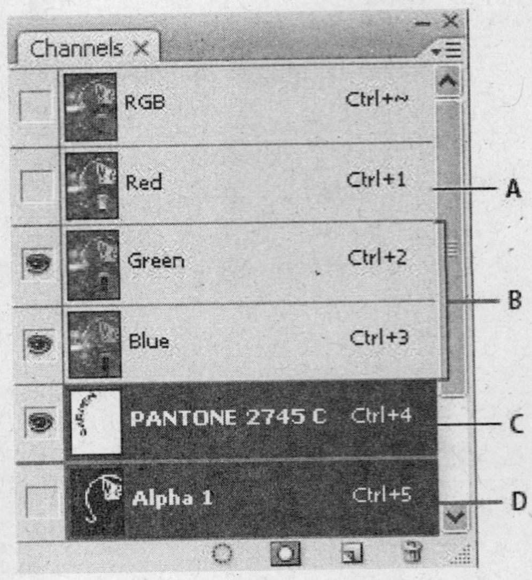

Selecting multiple channels
***A.** Not visible or editable **B.** Visible but not selected for editing **C.** Selected for viewing and editing **D.** Selected for editing but not viewing*

4.24.1 Channels palette overview

The Channels palette lists all channels in the image—composite channel first (for RGB, CMYK, and Lab images). A thumbnail of the channel's contents appears to the left of the channel name; the thumbnail is automatically updated as you edit the channel.

4.24.1.1 Display the Channels palette

1. Choose Windows > Channels.

4.25 Working with Channels

4.25.1.1 Resize or hide channel thumbnails

1. Choose Palette Options from the Channels palette menu. Click a thumbnail size or click None to turn off the display of thumbnails.
2. Viewing thumbnails is a convenient way of tracking channel contents; however, turning off the display of thumbnails can improve performance

4.25.1.2 Show or hide a channel

You can use the Channels palette to view any combination of channels in the document window. For example, you can view an alpha channel and the composite channel together to see how changes made in the alpha channel relate to the entire image.

Click in the eye column next to the channel to show or hide that channel. (Click the composite channel to view all default color channels. The composite channel is displayed whenever all the color channels are visible.)

4.25.1.3 Show color channels in color

Individual channels are displayed in grayscale. In RGB, CMYK, or Lab images, you can view the individual channels in color. (In Lab images, only the a and b channels appear in color.) If more than one channel is active, the channels always appear in color.

You can change the default to show the individual color channels in color. When a channel is visible in the image, an eye icon appears to its left in the palette.

1. Do one of the following:
   - In Windows, choose Edit > Preferences > Interface.
   - In Mac OS, choose Photoshop > Preferences > Interface.
2. Select Show Channels in Color, and click OK.

4.25.1.4 Select and edit channels

You can select one or more channels in the Channels palette. The names of all selected, or active, channels are highlighted.

- To select a channel, click the channel name. Shift-click to select (or deselect) multiple channels.
- To edit a channel, select it and then use a painting or editing tool to paint in the image. You can paint on only one channel at a time. Paint with white to add the selected channel's color at 100% intensity. Paint with a value of gray to add the channel's color at a lower intensity. Paint with black to fully remove the channel's color.

4.26 Creating Quick Mask

When you select part of an image, the area that is not selected is "masked" or protected from editing. So, when you create a mask, you isolate and protect areas of an image as you apply color changes, filters, or other effects to the rest of the image. You can also use masks for complex image editing such as gradually applying color or filter effects to an image.

Masks are stored in alpha channels. Masks and channels are grayscale images, so you can edit them like any other image with painting tools, editing tools and filters. Areas painted black on a mask are protected, and areas painted white are editable.

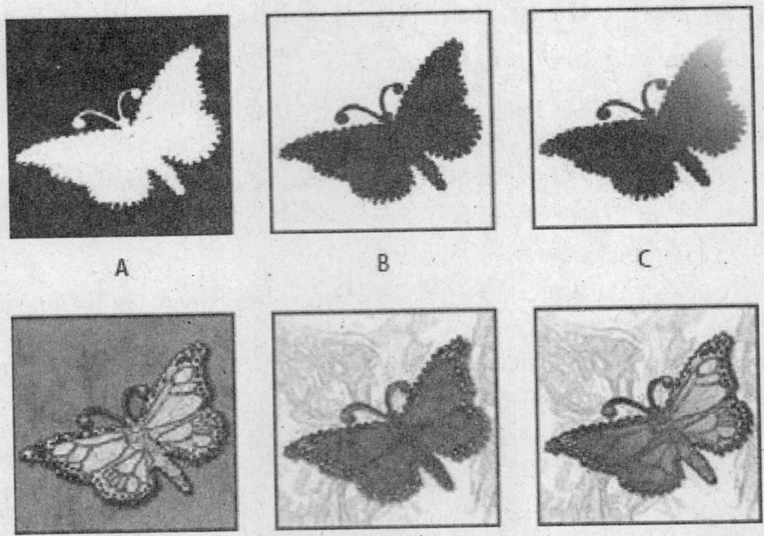

Examples of masks

A. Opaque mask used to protect the background and edit the butterfly B. Opaque mask used to protect the butterfly and colour the background C. Semitransparent mask used to color the background and part of the butterfly

Use Quick Mask mode to convert a selection to a temporary mask for easier editing. The Quick Mask appears as a colored overlay with adjustable opacity. You can edit the Quick Mask using any painting tool or modify it with a filter. Once you exit Quick Mask mode the mask is converted back to a selection on the image.

To save a selection more permanently, you can store it as an alpha channel. The alpha channel stores the selection as an editable grayscale mask in the Channels palette. Once stored as an alpha channel, you can reload the selection at any time or even load it into another image.

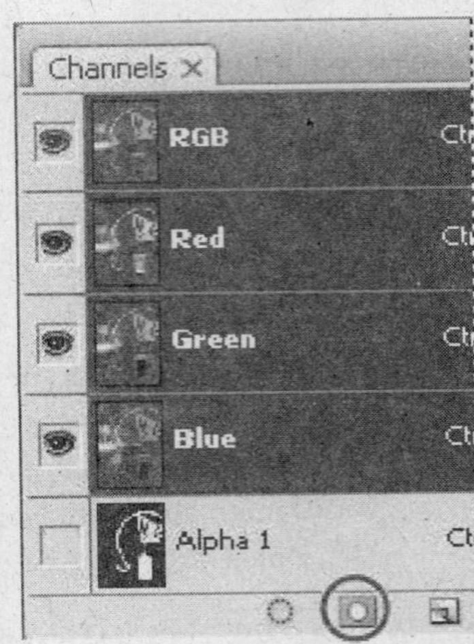

Selection saved as an alpha channel in Channels palette

You can mask or hide parts of a layer using a layer mask.

4.26.1.1 Create a temporary quick mask

To use Quick Mask mode, start with a selection and then add to or subtract from it to make the mask. You can also create the mask entirely in Quick Mask mode. Color differentiates the protected and unprotected areas. When you leave Quick Mask mode, the unprotected areas become a selection.

1. A temporary Quick Mask channel appears in the Channels palette while you work in Quick Mask mode. However, you do all mask editing in the image window.
2. Using any selection tool, select the part of the image you want to change.

   Click the Quick Mask mode button in the toolbox.

   A color overlay (similar to a rubylith) covers and protects the area outside the selection. Selected areas are left unprotected by this mask. By default, Quick Mask mode colors the protected area using a red, 50% opaque overlay.

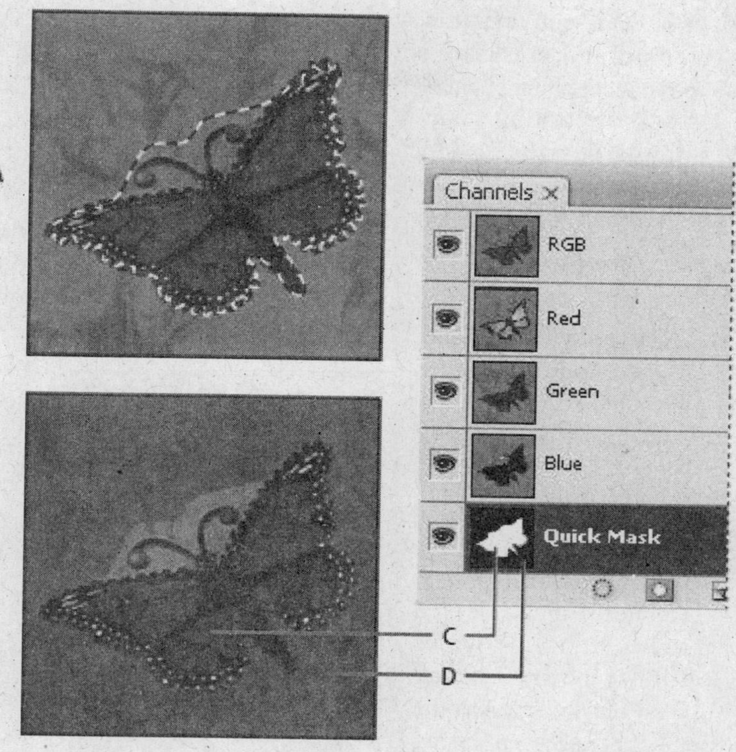

Selecting in Standard mode and Quick Mask mode

A. Standard mode B. Quick Mask mode C. Selected pixels appear as white in channel thumbnail D. Rubylith overlay protects area outside selection, and unselected pixels appear as black in channel thumbnail

3. To edit the mask, select a painting tool from the toolbox. The swatches in the toolbox automatically become black and white.
4. Paint with white to select more of an image (the color overlay is removed from areas painted with white). To deselect areas, paint over them with black (the color overlay covers areas painted with black). Painting with gray or another color creates a semitransparent area, useful for feathering or anti-aliased effects. (Semitransparent areas may not appear to be selected when you exit Quick Mask Mode, but they are.)
5. Click the Standard Mode button in the toolbox to turn off the quick mask and return to your original image. A selection border now surrounds the unprotected area of the quick mask.
6. If a feathered mask is converted to a selection, the boundary line runs halfway between the black pixels and the white pixels of the mask gradient. The selection boundary indicates the transition between pixels that are less than 50% selected and those that are more than 50% selected.
7. Apply the desired changes to the image. Changes affect only the selected area.
8. Choose Select > Deselect to deselect the selection, or save the selection by choosing Select > Save Selection.

9. You can convert this temporary mask to a permanent alpha channel by switching to standard mode and choosing Select > Save Selection.

4.26.1.2 *Change Quick Mask options*

1. Double-click the Quick Mask Mode button in the toolbox.
2. Choose from the following display options:

   Masked Areas: Sets masked areas to black (opaque) and selected areas to white (transparent). Painting with black increases the masked area; painting with white increases the selected area. When this option is selected, the Quick Mask button in the toolbox becomes a white circle on a gray background

   Selected Areas: Sets masked areas to white (transparent) and selected areas to black (opaque). Painting with white increases the masked area; painting with black increases the selected area. When this option is selected, the Quick Mask button in the toolbox becomes a gray circle on a white background

A

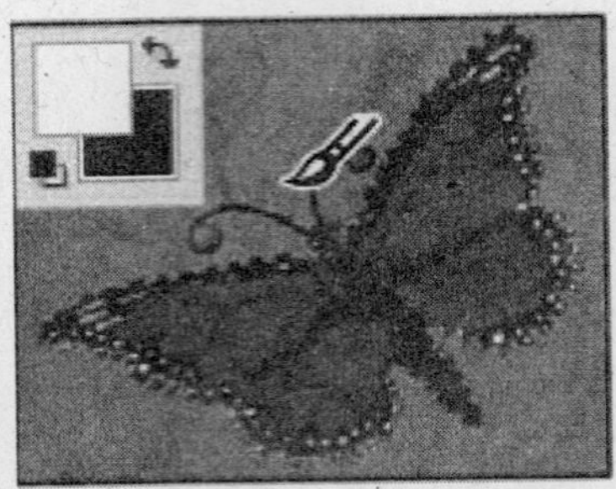

B

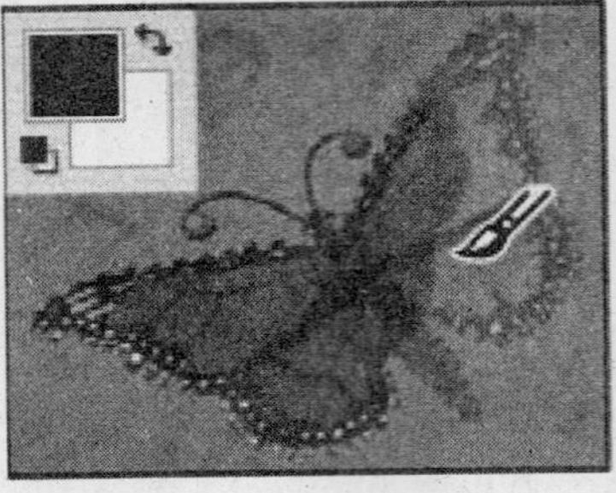

C

Painting in Quick Mask mode

A. *Original selection and Quick Mask mode with green chosen as mask color* ***B.*** *Painting with white in Quick Mask mode adds to the selection* ***C.*** *Painting with black in Quick Mask mode subtracts from the selection.*

3. To toggle between the Masked Areas and Selected Areas options for quick masks, Alt-click (Windows) or Option-click (Mac OS) the Quick Mask Mode button.
4. To choose a new mask color, click the color box, and choose a new color.
5. To change the opacity, enter a value between 0% and 100%.

6. Both the color and opacity settings affect only the appearance of the mask and have no effect on how underlying areas are protected. Changing these settings may make the mask more easily visible against the colors in the image.

4.27 Use of image editing software

Raster images are stored in a computer in the form of a grid of picture elements, or pixels. These pixels contain the image's color and brightness information. Image editors can change the pixels to enhance the image in many ways. The pixels can be changed as a group, or individually, by the sophisticated algorithms within the image editors. The domain of this article primarily refers to bitmap graphics editors, which are often used to alter photographs and other raster graphics. However, vector graphics software, such as Adobe Illustrator or Inkscape, are used to create and modify vector images, which are stored as descriptions of lines, Bézier splines, and text instead of pixels. It is easier to rasterize a vector image than to vectorize a raster image- how to go about vectorizing a raster image is the focus of much research in the field of computer vision.

People like vector images because they are easy to modify, containing descriptions of the shapes in them for easy rearrangement, as well as scalable, being rasterizable at any resolution- to rasterize a vector image is simply to render it, while scaling a raster image up involves guessing at data that isn't there (see aliasing and other articles on information theory for more),

4.28 White balance correction

This is a process in which you remove unrealistic colour casts so that objects which appear white in person are rendered white in your photo. Proper camera white balance has to take into account the 'colour temperature' of a light source., which refers to the relative warmth or coolness of white light. Setting white balance incorrectly may cause a colour shift in the image. For example, suppose the camera is told to use a colour temperature of sunlight to take an image of an indoor environment illuminated mainly by incadescent lights. The camera will expect excessive blue ligh and less red light, and set its algorithm to be more sensitive to the blue light. However, in an environment illuminated with incadescent lights, colour temperature is low with, excessive red light rather than the blue one. As a result, we shall see a reddish or yellowish image.

4.29 Dynamic Range Correction

It is a term used frequently in numerous fields to desscribe the ratio between the smallest and largest possible values of a changeable quantity, such as in sound and light. A human eyes take time to adjust to different light levels and the dynamic range of the human eye in a given scene is actually quite limited due to optical galare. The instanteneous dynamic range of human audio perception is similarly subject to masking, so that, for example, a whisper cannot be heard in loud surroundings. Nevertheless, a good quality audio reproduction system should be able to reproduce accurately both the quiet sounds and the loud; and a good quality visual display system should be able to capture both shadow details in nighttime scenes and bright areas of sunny scenes.

4.30 Photo Retouching

Several common problems can occur in old photographs and the particular problems in a photograph will determine the best strategy for its reconstruction. Here is a list of problems you are likely to encounter.

All or part of the photo is faded This problem results from the deterioration of the emulsion on an image, caused by exposure to ultraviolet light, air or fluctuating temperatures. (It could also result from an image that was overexposed to begin with.) sometimes the photograph may be perfect on one side and fade gradually to the other.

The photo has a color cast. A color photograph may have washed out colors or a yellow or red cast over its entire surface. This may be the result of the emulsion's chemical reation with air or paper.

The image is wrinkled, torn, scratched or covered with spots. Wrinkles and scratches are often a result of mistreatment of the photograph. Spot will develop from exposure to dust. Images stored in a damp environment can collect mold that appears as large or small splotches.

The surface is textured. Many old photographs were printed on textured paper. The removal of this surface can present problems during the retouching process.

Part of the photograph is missing. A vital portion of the image like a hand or a face may have a severe scratch on it or may be missing entirely. A corner may be missing or an area of the photograph may have peeled or faded away.

Bad photography The image may have superfluous elements like phone lines or portions that are out of focus. The image may have been shot at the wrong moment, the composition may be unbalanced or the image may be underexposed or overexposed.

Photo restoration can be extremely labor-intensive. Some images are simply beyond repair. Experience will show you which images are worth restoring and with ones.

Let us Revise

1. 3D computer graphics became possible in the late 1980s with the powerful SGI computers, which were later used to create some of the first fully computer-generated short films at Pixar.
2. Modern computer systems, dating from the 1980s and onwards, often use a graphical user interface (GUI) to present data and information with symbols, icons and pictures, rather than text.
3. 2D computer graphics are the computer-based generation of digital images—mostly from two-dimensional models, such as 2D geometric models, text, and digital images, and by techniques specific to them.
4. Vector graphics formats are complementary to raster graphics, which is the representation of images as an array of pixels, as it is typically used for the representation of photographic images.
5. Computer animation is the art of creating moving images via the use of computers.
6. The Bitmap mode uses only two colour values to display images—black and white, while the Grayscale mode offers 256 shades of gray that range from white to black.
7. Indexed Colour is a palette or rather a collection of palettes—256 to be exact.
8. Photoshop uses the foreground color to paint, fill, and stroke selections and the background color to make gradient fills and fill in the erased areas of an image.
9. Dithering is a technique used in computer graphics to create the illusion of varying shades of gray on a monochrome display or printer, or additional colors on a color display or printer.
10. It is possible to compress many types of digital data in a way which reduces the size of a computer file needed to store it or the bandwidth needed to stream it, with no loss of the full information contained in the original file.
11. GIF stands for Graphics Interchange Format. It is another format that is widely used for picture displayed on the World Wide Web.

12. Tagged Image File Format – Widely-used raster graphics file format developed by Aldus and Microsoft that handles monochrome, gray scale, 8-and 24-bit color.
13. A richly formatted document which may contain graphics as well as text that can be transferred to another type of computer system without losing the rich formatting.
14. Photoshop has lots of tools to work with. These tools are available on the left side of the screen in the form of a toolbar.
15. The move tool lets you drag a selection or layer to a new location in the image.
16. Lasso tools are used when you have to select irregular shapes.
17. Cropping tool helps you in getting rid of unwanted parts of the picture.
18. You can create user-slices with the slice tool, from a layer, from a selection (ImageReady), or from guides (ImageReady).
19. The airbrush tool applies gradual tones (including sprays of color) to an image, simulating traditional airbrush techniques.
20. The clone stamp tool takes a sample of an image, which you can then apply over another image or part of the same image.
21. The history brush tool lets you paint a copy of one state or snapshot of an image into the current image window.
22. The paint bucket tool fills adjacent pixels that are similar in color value to the pixels you click.
23. The marquee tools let you select rectangles, ellipses, rounded rectangles, and 1-pixel rows and columns.
24. You can view the color of a single area using the eyedropper tool, or you can use up to four color samplers to display color information for one or more locations in the image.
25. Resampling is changing the amount of image data as you change either the pixel dimensions or the resolution of an image.
26. Changing an image's pixel dimensions affects not only its on screen size but also its image quality and its printed characteristics.
27. Cropping is the process of removing portions of an image to create focus or strengthen the composition.
28. Layers are the various layers that you can create of the image or picture for the editing purposes and putting them one over the another for the final result.
29. Masking is the method by which you can select a portion of the image or picture for editing and doing changes.
30. The Auto-Align Layers command can automatically align layers based on similar content in different layers, such as corners and edges.

Multiple Choice Questions

1. Which of the following is not a colour specification format?
   (a) RGB (b) HSB (c) GIF
   (d) CMYK.
2. Which file format can be used when the picture is a photograph or has lots of colours?
   (a) .jpeg (b) .tif (c) .bmp
   (d) .pic.
3. TIFF stands for:
   (a) Temporary Instruction File Format
   (b) Total Inclusion File Format

(c) Tagged Interchange File Format
(d) Table Index File Format.

4. Which image file type is best for photo-realistic images?
(a) Laser (b) Bitmap. (c) Vector
(d) All of the above.

5. Which menu contains a command to adjust the colurs and the brightness of the picture?
(a) Layer (b) Select (c) Filter
(d) Image.

6. Graphic editing has to be performed:
(a) To improve the attributes of an existing image.
(b) To remove unwanted portions of the image.
(c) To add special effects, not possible with actual photography.
(d) all of the above.

7. Vector drawn objects are used for all the following except:
(a) Circles (b) Photographs (c) Boxes
(d) Lines

True/False Questions

1. 2D computer graphics are the computer-based generation of digital images—mostly from two-dimensional models, such as 2D geometric models, text, and digital images, and by techniques specific to them.
2. The Bitmap mode uses only two colour values to display images—black and white, while the Grayscale mode offers 300 shades of gray that range from white to black.
3. Dithering is a technique used in computer graphics to create the illusion of varying shades of gray on a monochrome display or printer, or additional colors on a color display or printer.
4. Tagged Image File Format – Widely-used raster graphics file format developed by Aldus and Microsoft that handles monochrome, gray scale, 8-and 24-bit color.
5. The move tool does not let you drag a selection or layer to a new location in the image.
6. You can create user-slices with the slice tool, from a layer, from a selection (ImageReady), or from guides (ImageReady).
7. The history brush tool does not let you paint a copy of one state or snapshot of an image into the current image window..
8. You can view the color of a single area using the eyedropper tool, or you can use up to four color samplers to display color information for one or more locations in the image.
9. Cropping is the process of removing portions of an image to create focus or strengthen the composition.
10. The Auto-Align Layers command can automatically align layers based on similar content in different layers, such as corners and edges.

Matching Columns

In the following case, commands are given in the left hand columns and their actions in the right hand column. Match them.

Column A	Column B	
A. RGB	1. A rectangular array of points	D

B.	Saturation	2.	2 colours
C.	A vector	3.	16 colours
D.	A bitmap	4.	Colour wavelength
E.	1 bit per pixel	5.	Colour of your monitor
F.	Hue	6.	The line described by location of its two end points
G	4 bits per pixel	7.	Intensity or purity of colour

Fill in the Blanks with appropriate words

a. zoom	b. .psd	c. patch	d. toolbox
e. Resolution	f. video controller card	g. vector	h. TWAIN

1. Images that are stored as lines, arces and curves are called _________ images.
2. _________ is the total number of a logical pixels, in terms of rows and columns, supported by the display system.
3. The total number of colours that could be handled by the monitor depends upon the memory capacity of the ____________.
4. The _________ tool used for repair a selected area with pixels from another area or a pattern.
5. _________ is a interface for obtaining images captured by certain scanner and digital cameras.
6. Hand tool is useful after the ________ tool to work on a part of a picture.
7. _________ holds tools for creating and editing images.
8. ________ is the extension of Photoshop file.

Descriptive Type Questions

1. Describe the various image types.
2. Describe the various colour modes.
3. What is Dithering?
4. Describe the various types of image compression and file formats.
5. Describe the following:

GIF	JPEG
JPEG 2000	PNG
TIFF	EXIF
PS	PDF

6. How would you start Photoshop?
7. How would you:

Install the software	Uninstall the software
Activate software	Register software

8. Descibe the various tools of Photoshop.
9. How would you resize an image?
10. Describe the various methods of selection.
11. Which are the types of brushes used in Photoshop?
12. What is the use of Options Bar?

13. What do you understand by Layers?
14. How would you rotate selections?
15. What are Channels?
16. Describe Masks.
17. What do you understand by 'White balance correction'?
18. Describe what type of photos can be retouched.

Answers to Objective Type Questions

Multiple Choice Questions

1. c	2. a	3. c	4. b
5. d	6. d	7. b	

True False Questions

1. T	2. F	3. T	4. T
5. F	6. T	7. F	8. T
9. T	10. T		

Matching Columns

A. 5	B. 7	C. 6	D. 1
E. 2	F. 4	G. 3	

Fill in the Blanks

1. g	2. e	3. f	4. c
5. h	6. a	7. d	8. b

Video and Animation 5

5.1 Video Basics

Once my cousin brought a video cassette of film Star Wars from USA. We were very happy at the prospect of seeing it on TV before it was officially released in India. But, our joy was really shortlived. The cassette was on NTSC and would not run on our Video Cassette Recorder. It could handle only the PAL cassettes. It was indeed a very bad experience since he had to take the cassette back with him. At that time there was nobody who could convert it from NTSC to PAL.

Similarly while creating multimedia project we have to take care of the fact, where the video is going to run. Though now-a-days most of the software run videos created for other software but still we must understand the various standard formats and the type of files they make.

Carefully planned, well-executed video clips can make a dramatic difference in a multimedia project. A clip of John F. Kennedy proclaiming, "Ich bin ein Berliner" in video and sound, is more compelling than a scrolling text field containing that same speech. Before deciding whether to add video to your project, however, it is essential to have an understanding of the medium, its limitations, and its costs.

Video standards and formats are still being refined as transport, storage, compression and display technologies take shape in laboratories and in the market place.

5.2 How Video Works?

If your project is to include video, consider whether you should shoot new footage or acquire pre-existing content for your video clips. There are many sources for film and video clips: a friend's home movies may suffice or you can go to a "stock" footage house or a television station or movie studio. But acquiring footage that do not own outright can be a nightmare – it is expensive and licensing rights and permissions may be difficult, if not impossible, to obtain. Each second of video could cost Rs.500 to Rs.1000 or more to license.

Even a "public domain clip" from the National Archives will cost a minimum of Rs.1250 to copy the footage and the turnaround time can take up to six weeks. Many companies sell royalty-free stock CDs specifically for multimedia production, but these are lower resolution than broadcast quality and less than full-frame video. On some projects, you will have no choice but to pay the price for required footage. If it is absolutely essential that your project should include a clip of Elvis Presley crooning "You Ain't Nothing but a Hound Dog," and an Elvis impersonator just won't do, you will have to negotiate for rights to use the real thing. If your budget can't cover the cost of licensing a particular video clip, you may have to consider using other alternatives: locating a less expensive archival video source, using a series of still images rather than video, or shooting your own video.

If you shoot your own video for a project, make sure you have releases from all persons who appear or speak and permission to use the audio effects and music you wave into it. Before you head out to the field with your camrecorder in hand, it is important to understand at least the basics of video recording and editing as well as the constraints of using video in a multimedia project.

Video formats and indivual clips are typically described in terms of the resolution of the individual frames, and the frame rate at which they are played. Frate rate is video playback speed or capture rate as determined in frame per second. On the video-capture adapter card, an analog-todigital converter (ADC) chip converts the wavering analog video and audio signals to a pattern of 0s and 1s, the binary language that describes all computer data.

5.2.1 Video in Multimedia Projects

Video is incorporated into multimedia projects, for many reasons:

- The project has certain relevant sequences/material that can be videographed.
- The project has certain sequences/material that cannot be produced with the help of animation.
- The project has to be made attractive with video.
- The project has live lectures or demonstration or other pre-recorded material to be incorporated.

5.3 Broadcast Video Standards

Four broadcast and video standards and recording formats commonly in use around the world are: NTSC, PAL, SECAM and HDTV. Because these standards and formats are not easily interchangeable, it is important to know where your multimedia project will be used.

A video cassette recorded in the United States will not play on a television set in any European country, even though the recording method and style of the cassette is "VHS." Likewise, tapes recorded in European PAL or SECAM formats will not playback on an NTSC video cassette recorder. Each system is based on a different standard that defines the way information is encoded to produce the electronic signal that ultimately creates a television picture.

Multiformat VCRs can playback all three standards but typically cannot dub from one standard to another. Dubbing between standards still requires high-end, specialized equipment.

5.3.1.1 NTSC

The United States, Japan and many other countries use a system for broadcasting and displaying video that is based upon the specifications set forth by the 1952 National Television Standards Committee. These standards define a method for encoding information into the electronic signal that ultimately creates a television picture.

As specified by the NTSC standard, a single frame of video is made up of 525 horizontal scan lines drawn onto the inside face of a phosphor-coated picture tube every 1/30th of a second by a fast-moving electron beam. The drawing occurs so fast that your eye perceives the image as stable. The electron beam actually makes two passes as it draws a single video frame, first laying down all the odd-numbered lines, then all the even-numbered lines.

Each of these passes (which happen at a rate of 60 per second, or 60 Hz) paints a field. The process of building a single frame from two fields is called interlacing, a technique that helps to prevent flicker on television screens. Remember that computer monitors use progressive-scan technology and draw the lines of an entire fame in a single pass, without interlacing them.

5.3.1.2 PAL

The Phase Alternate Line (PAL) system is used in the United Kingdom, Europe, Australia and South Africa and most of Asia. PAL is an integrated method of adding colour to a black-and-white television signal that paints 625 lines at a frame rate of 25 frames per second. Like NTSC, the even and odd lines are interlaced, each field taking 1/50th of a second to draw (50 Hz).

5.3.1.3 SECAM

The Sequential Colour and Memory (SECAM) system is used in France, Russia and few other countries. Although SECAM is a 625-line, 50 Hz system, it differs greatly from both the NTSC and the PAL colour systems in its basic technology and broadcast method. Often, however, TV sets sold in Europe utilize dual components and can handle both PAL and SECAM systems.

5.3.1.4 HDTV

There are six video formats in the ATSCDTV standard that are "High Definition Television." These are the 1080-line by 1920-pixels formats at all picture rates (24, 40 and 60 pictures per second) and the 720-line by 1280-pixel formats at the same picture rates. All of these formats have a 16:9 aspect ratio. High Definition Television (HDTV) provides high resolution in a 16:9 aspect ratio. This aspect ratio allows the viewing of Cinemascope and Panavision movies. There is contention between the broadcast and computer industries about whether to use interlacing or progressive-scan technologies.

The broadcast industry has promulgated an ultra-high-resolution, 1920 x 1080 interlaced format to become the cornerstone of a new generation of high-end entertainment centers, but the computer industry would like to settle on a 1280 x 720 progressive-scan system for HDTV. While the 1920 x 1080 format provides more pixels than the 1280 x 720 standard, the refresh rates are quite different. The higher-resolution interlaced format delivers only half the picture every 1/60 of a second and because of the interlacing, on highly detailed images there is a great deal of screen flicker at 30 Hz.

The computer people argue that the picture quality at 1280 x 720 is superior and steady. Both formats have been included in the HDTV standard by the Advanced Television Systems Committee. Today's multimedia monitors typically use a screen pixel ratio of 4:3 (640 x 480), but the new HDTV standard specifies a ratio of 16:9 (1280 x 720), much wider than tall. There is no easy way to stretch and shrink existing graphics material to fit this new aspect ratio, so new multimedia design and interface principles will be needed to be developed for HDTV presentations.

5.4 Analog video

It is the type of video in which all the information representing images is in a continuous scale electrical signal for both amplitude and time. Analog signals are continuous in nature whereas digital signals are discontinuous. Broadcast of an image larger than will fit on a standard TV screen so that the 'edge' of the image seen by a viewer is always bounded by the TV's physical frame or bezel is called overscan.

5.5 Digital video

Video where all the information representing images in in some kind of computer data form, which can be imanipulated and displayed by a computer is called digital video. A digital viceo architecture is made up of a format for encoding and playing back video files by a computer and includes a player that can recognize and play files created for that format. The major diital video archiecture are Apple's Quick Time, Microsoft's Windows Media Format and Real Network's Real Media.

5.5.1.1 Analog Vs Digital

Digital video has supplanted analog video as the method of choice for making video for multimedia use. While broadcast stations and professional production and post-production houses still use analog video hardware, digital video gear produces excellent finished products at a fraction of the cost of analog.

5.6 Video Recording and Tape formats

There are various video recording formats available, mostly by the comapnies which deal with them. Each one of them has its own to support its hardware. Some of them are listed below.

5.6.1 Ampex

A format owned by Ampex Corporation. In 1950s, it was the most popular one for recording audio and video. In 1970, Ampex introduced the first robotic library system which enabled TV stations to re-sequence TV commercials instantaneously. It is obsolete now.

5.6.2 VERA

In 1952 it was introduce by BBC. It used very high tape speed of about 200 inches/second to record the high frequencies recorded by video signals. It has also become obsolete now.

5.6.3 U-matic

It was introduced by Sony Corporation of Japan. It was among the first video formats to contain the videotape inside a cassette, as apposed to the various open-reel formats of the time. In 1990's, it was made absolute by Sony betacam-SP. U-matic is no longer used in mainstream production but would be remembered asa cheap and robust facility processed by almost all TV stations in the world.

5.6.4 Betamax

This format was used in the hand held video recorder. The cassettes contain half inch wide videotape ina design similar to the arlier, professional 3/4 inch U-matic format. The former is generally considered obsolete, though it is stell used in specialist applications by a small minority of people.

5.6.5 Betacam

It was developed in 1982 by Sony Corporation. It belongs to the family of half-inch professional videotape products. The cassettes come in two sizes S and L. Betacam cameras can only load S tapes, while VTRs can play both S and L tapes. The cassette is coloured differently depending on the format, allowing for easy visual identification.

5.6.6 Video 2000

This was introduced in the year 1979 and stopped in 1988. It uses double sided cassettes. The cassette was slightly largerthan VHS and could record four hours of video on each side.

5.6.7 Compact Video Cassette (CVC)

It was the one of the first videocassete formats to use a tape smaller than its earlier predecessors of VHS and Betamax. The system, which included the VCR and a handheld camera, was very small and lightweight for its time. This format used a cassette slightly larger than an audio cassette and was loaded with 1/4 inch videotape.

5.6.8 Camcoder

This one became very popular in early 2000's. In order to differentiate a camcorder from othe devices that are capable of recording video, like cell phones and compact digital cameras, a camcorder is generally identified as a portable device having video capture and recording as its primary function. All tape-based camcorders use removable media in form of video cassettes. Camcorders that permit using more than one type of media, like built-in hard disk drive and memory, are often called hybrid camcoders.

5.6.9 Video 8

It is a video cassette recorder system used with video cameras. The tapes were 8 mm thick and recorded video in analog format. The tapes were the size of audio cassettes making them portable and popular for use with cameras. The video quality is better than VHS and is one of the mominant formats for video cameras.

5.7 Shooting and Editing Video

5.7.1 Capturing, digitizing, and importing

To bring media files (assets) into an Adobe Premiere Pro project, you can capture, digitize, or import them, depending on the type of source material:

Capture: You capture digital video files from tape. That is, you transfer them from the source videotape to the hard drive. All digital camcorders and decks record video in digital formats, but it must be captured (transferred to disk) before Adobe Premiere Pro can use it in a project. Adobe Premiere Pro's capture function, in conjunction with a digital port or capture card (for example, IEEE 1394 or SDI), can capture digital video from tape and save it to disk as files that you can then add to your project.

Digitize: You digitize analog video. Analog video is recorded by analog camcorders and decks. The data must be digitized (converted to digital form) before a computer can store and process it. Adobe Premiere Pro's capture function, in conjunction with a digitizer card—or a device that can convert analog video to digital—can convert analog video to digital files readable by Adobe Premiere Pro.

Import: Use the Import command to bring files—for example, still images or audio you've downloaded—that are already on your hard drive into your Adobe Premiere Pro project. Adobe Premiere Pro lets you import numerous types of digital files.

5.7.1.1 To Set the Capture Format

1. With a project open, choose Project > Project Settings > Capture.
2. From the Capture Format menu, choose the settings that match your source material.

5.7.1.2 To Set Capture Preferences

1. Choose Edit > Preferences > Capture.
2. Specify whether you want to cancel capture on dropped frames, report dropped frames, or generate a batch log file.
3. Select whether to use device control timecode. If a device controller is in use (for example, for RS-422/232 or LANC-controlled devices), the last selection enables Adobe Premiere Pro to record the timecode supplied by the controller instead of attempting to record any timecode that might be written to the source tape.

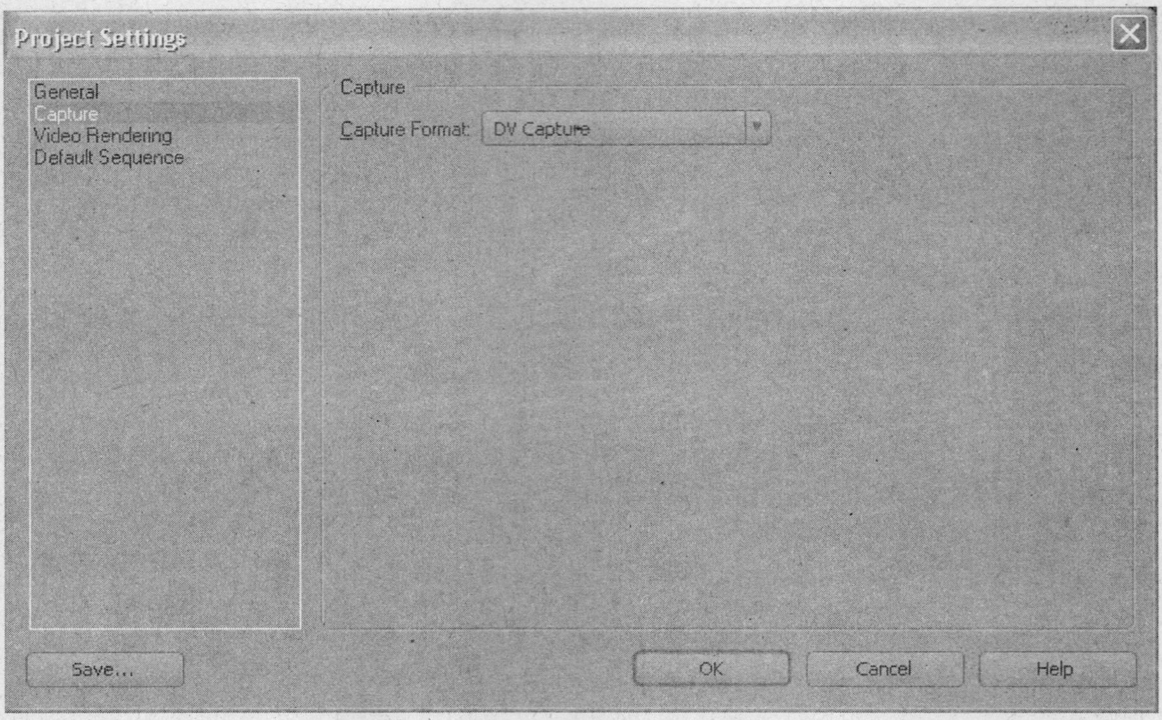

5.7.2 Digitizing Analog Video

In order to edit video shot in an analog format, you must first digitize it. You can digitize it by routing the video signal through either a digital camcorder that can digitize on the fly or a digitizing device installed in your computer. Alternatively, you can dub the analog footage to a digital format, and then capture the video from a digital device through a capture card as any other digital source. Depending on your equipment, you may be able to digitize analog video from any of several signal types, including component video, composite video, and S-video. Some digitizers provide device control. They connect to your source device through RS-232, RS-422, LANC, or Control-M jacks, enabling you to control the device through Adobe Premiere Pro's Capture panel and to perform batch capturing. Refer to the instructions included with your camcorder and digitizer/capture card.

5.7.2.1 About Capture Card Settings

Some of the capture settings you see in Adobe Premiere Pro may be from the plug-in software that came with your digitizer/capture card. Because of the differences among brands of cards, specific options and supported formats can vary. This complex relationship between video-capture cards and Adobe Premiere Pro can make it difficult to identify which part of

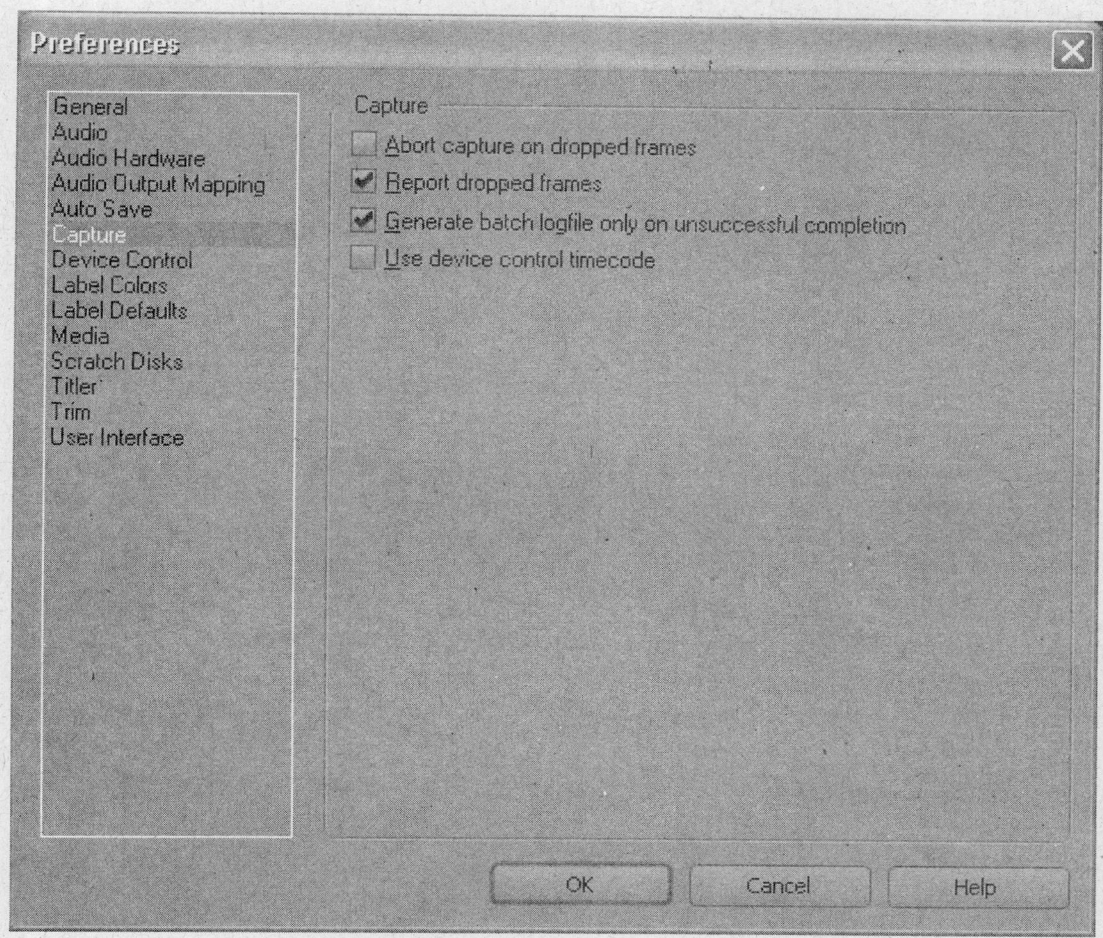

the system is responsible for a particular option or problem. Adobe, as well as most capture card manufacturers, provides troubleshooting documents online that can help you determine whether an option or problem is related to the video-capture card and its software or to Adobe Premiere Pro. Check the Adobe Premiere Pro website and the capture card manufacturer's website for troubleshooting resources.

Most of the supported capture cards install a settings file (preset) that you can select in the Adobe Premiere Pro New Project dialog box, in the Load Preset pane. This preset automatically sets all capture settings for optimal support of your capture card. For best results, use your capture card's preset, if provided, and don't change the capture settings in the Custom Settings pane.

5.7.2.2 To Digitize Analog Video

1. Quit Adobe Premiere Pro.
2. Connect your analog device's video and audio outputs to your digital device's (digitizer, digital camcorder or digital deck) analog inputs.
3. If the digital device is an external digitizer, deck, or camcorder, connect its digital output (IEEE 1394 or SDI) to the computer's digital port of the same type.

4. If the digital device is a digitizer with device controls, connect its device control port (RS-232, RS-422, LANC, or Control-M) with the analog device's port.
5. Turn on both devices.
6. If the digital device is a camcorder, put it into VTR or VCR (not Camera) mode.
7. Set the input selection control on the digital device to the correct analog input.
8. Start Adobe Premiere Pro.
9. When the Welcome screen appears, do one of the following:
   - Click New Project, select the capture card's preset (if available) from the Load Preset pane, and click OK.
   - Select an existing project that was set up with the capture card's preset.
10. Select File > Capture.
11. In the Capture panel, carefully check the settings on the Settings pane. If you need to change them, click Edit. (The settings in this dialog box are provided by the card manufacturer's plug-in software, not by Adobe Premiere Pro, and vary according to the analog capture card's brand and model. See the documentation for the software driver provided by the manufacturer of the capture card.)
12. Do one of the following:
    - If the digital device offers no device control, cue up your source using the analog device's own controls. Press Play on the analog device and click the Record button in the Capture panel.
    - If the digital device offers device control, capture or log footage using the Capture panel's controls, as you would with a digital source.

5.7.2.3 Digitizing Analog Audio

If you want to use audio that is not yet in digital form (for example, from an analog cassette or a live microphone), you need to digitize it through an audio or audio/video digitizer/capture card.

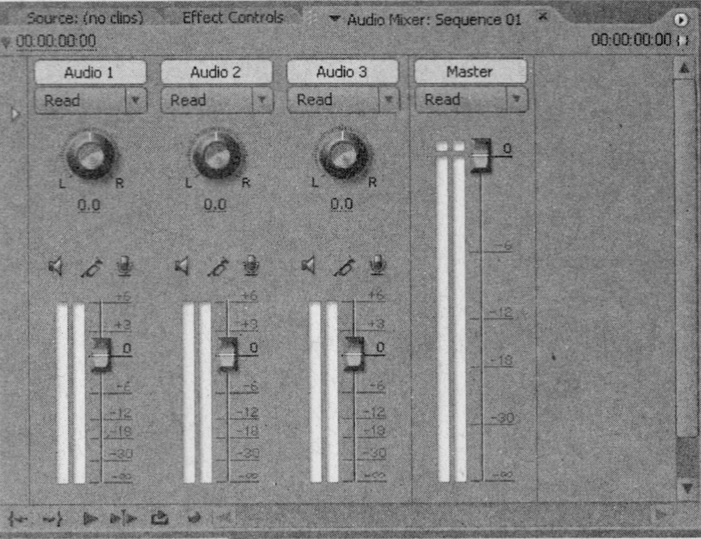

The quality of digitized audio and the size of the audio file depend on the sample rate (the number of samples per second) and bit depth (the number of bits per sample) of the digitized audio. Also, stereo audio requires twice as much disk space as mono audio. These parameters, controlled in the Capture Settings section of the Project Settings dialog box, determine how precisely the analog audio signal is represented in digital form. Higher sample rates and bit depths reproduce sound at higher levels of quality, but with correspondingly larger file sizes. Capture audio at the highest quality settings your computer can handle, even if those settings are higher than the settings you'll specify for final export or playback. This provides headroom, or extra data, that helps preserve quality when you adjust audio gain or apply audio effects such as equalization or dynamic range compression/expansion. Although the DV format can record two independent stereo audio pairs, Adobe Premiere Pro can capture only one stereo pair. It may be possible to select either stereo pair 1, stereo pair 2, or a mix of both stereo pairs, depending on the DV hardware you are using. Consult your DV equipment guide.

5.7.2.4 To Set the Location for Captured Audio

1. Choose Edit > Preferences > Scratch Disks.
2. For Captured Audio, select a location and click OK.

5.7.2.5 To record a voice-over

1. Connect the microphone to the mic-level input jack on your computer or sound card. If necessary, choose Edit > Preferences > Audio Hardware to configure the input device.
2. If you want to preview the Timeline panel as you record, position the current-time indicator in the Timeline panel a few seconds before the time when you want the voice-over to begin.
3. In the Audio Mixer, click the Record Enable button for any tracks on which you want to record audio.
4. In the Audio Mixer, click the Record button for the sequence. Adobe Premiere Pro prepares the sequence for recording but moves the playhead only when you press the Play button.
5. Select Meter Input(s) Only in the Audio Mixer menu to meter only your sound card's inputs.
6. Test the input levels by speaking into the microphone.
7. When you finish testing, deselect Meter Input(s) Only to meter the project's audio tracks also.
8. Speak into the microphone again. Watch the Audio Mixer level meters to ensure that the input levels for record-enabled tracks are high but not clipping.
9. Click the Play button in the Audio Mixer, and then start speaking your voice-over.

5.7.2.6 To Record an Analog Source

You can record audio from an analog source device, such as a cassette deck or turntable.

1. Connect the analog source to the appropriate input jack on your computer or sound card. If necessary, choose Edit > Preferences > Audio Hardware to configure the input device.
2. If you want to preview the Timeline panel as you record, position the current-time indicator in the Timeline panel a few seconds before the time when you want the recording to begin.
3. In the Audio Mixer, click the Record Enable button for any tracks on which you want to record audio.
4. In the Audio Mixer, click the Record button for the sequence. Adobe Premiere Pro prepares the sequence for recording but moves the playhead only when you press the Play button.
5. Select Meter Input(s) Only in the Audio Mixer panel menu to meter only your sound card's inputs.
6. Test the input levels by playing a selection from the analog source.
7. When you finish testing, deselect Meter Input(s) Only in the Audio Mixer panel menu to meter the project's audio tracks also.

8. Play a selection from the analog source again. Watch the Audio Mixer level meters to ensure that the input levels for record-enabled tracks are high but not clipping.
9. Click the Play button in the Audio Mixer, and then press Play on the source device.

5.7.2.7 *About Timecode*

Many camcorders and high-end video decks record timecode, which marks specific frames with unique addresses. Timecode is important whenever you want to capture exactly the same frames that were identified or captured previously, as in the following tasks:

- You want to log clips before you capture them.
- You plan to capture clips using batch (automated) capture.
- You want to recapture clips because the original files became corrupted or were deleted.
- You plan to export sequences to another system by using AAF or EDL.
- You're using a system in which you edit quickly with low-resolution captures, and later recapture the clips at full resolution and quality for the final version.
- You plan to synchronize captured video with audio recorded separately.

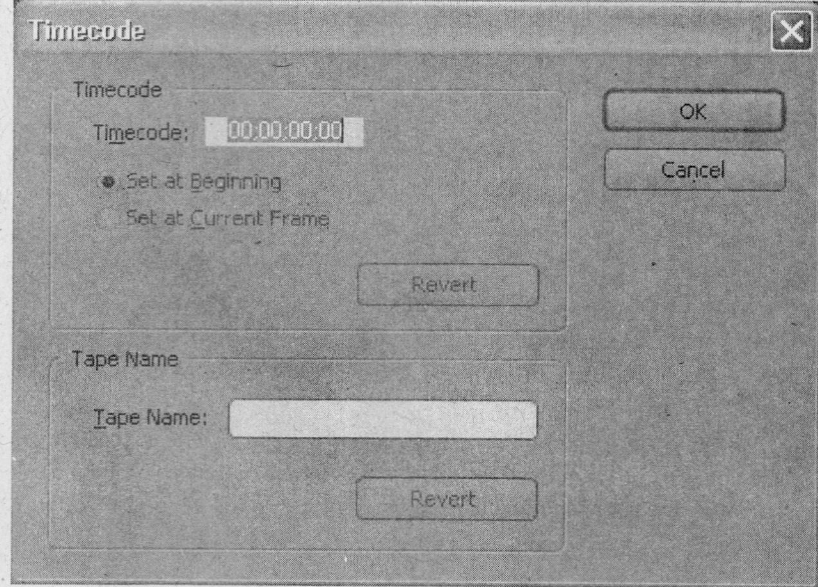

Unlike the numbers on time counters found in home VCRs, timecode is recorded onto videotape as part of the video signal. If footage lacks timecode, you can add it by copying it with a camera or deck that writes timecode. You can then log or capture the video from that device.

For best results, timecode should run continuously from the beginning to the end of the tape; it shouldn't restart from zero anywhere in the middle. In editing, if you log a capture In point such as 00:00:01:09 but that number occurs on the tape two or three times because of timecode restarts, Adobe Premiere Pro can't be certain which 00:00:01:09 is the place to start its capture. It can easily capture the wrong clips from tapes with discontinuous timecode. To ensure unbroken timecode, you need to either shoot it continuously or stripe your tape with it before shooting.

5.7.2.8 *Striping or Replacing Timecode*

You can ensure continuous timecode by recording timecode onto the tape before you use it. This process is called striping the tape. Striping is not necessary if you follow recommended shooting practices, but it can protect you from accidentally breaking timecode by miscuing a tape in your camera.

5.7.2.9 To Stripe a Tape with Timecode

1. Put an unused tape in the camera. It should have no timecode.
2. If you're using a camera for striping, attach the lens cap and disable audio recording.
3. Ensure that all camera settings (particularly the audio sample rate) are exactly the same as the settings you will use when you shoot. Use all these same settings whenever shooting on that tape.
4. Begin recording. Let the camera or deck run until the entire tape has been recorded.
5. Before you record video on a striped tape, play about 30 seconds of it from the beginning. Verify that the camcorder is reading the timecode you striped before you start shooting. The 30-second empty lead on the tape also helps in batch capturing.

5.7.2.10 To Replace DV Timecode

If your source footage is in DV format and its timecode isn't continuous, you can replace its timecode by making a DV copy, or dub, of the tape. The DV device making the copy records new timecode that is continuous, so you can then log and capture video, with the new timecode, from the copy.

1. Load the tape you shot into a camcorder or deck, and fully rewind it.
2. Load a new tape into a second camcorder or deck, which you will use to record the copy.
3. If the recording device includes an option to record video with the timecode from your original tape, be sure that this option is disabled. See the operating instructions for the device for information on this option.
4. If both devices are digital, connect them using a digital connection, such as IEEE 1394 or SDI. This will make a full-quality copy.
5. Connect the recording device to a television monitor.
6. Set both devices to VTR mode.
7. Make sure that the recording device is set to record from the digital port.
8. Begin recording the new tape and then start your original tape playing. Let the camcorders or decks run until the entire original tape has been copied.

5.7.2.11 Capturing Timecode

The timecode of source video is captured when you use device control. Timecode capture with controllable analog devices depends on the precision of your tape deck. If your tape deck cannot read the timecode accurately, you may have to calibrate your system or manually assign the timecode to your movie by matching frames.

5.7.2.12 To Set Timecode Manually for a Clip

At times you may want to change the timecode from that recorded by Adobe Premiere Pro. For example, you captured footage from a DV copy of a Hi8 tape originally recorded with RCTC (Rewritable Consumer Time Code). The DV copy, and the video files on your computer copied from it, carry the DV timecode, not the original RCTC. For convenience in referencing shot logs made for the original Hi8 tape, you want to reset the timecode to the original RCTC numbers.

1. Select the clip in the Project panel.
2. Choose File > Timecode, specify options as needed, and click OK.

5.7.2.13 *To Enter Timecode*

As you capture and edit video, you enter timecode values many times. For example, you enter timecode values to set In and Out points for clips and to navigate the Timeline panel. Adobe Premiere Pro provides many ways to enter timecode.

In Adobe Premiere Pro, the duration between the In and Out points includes the frames indicated by the timecode. For example, if you enter the same timecode for the In and Out points of a clip, the duration of the clip is one frame. When entering timecode, you can substitute periods for colons or type numbers without punctuation. Adobe Premiere Pro interprets the numbers you type as hours, minutes, seconds, and frames.

- To set a specific timecode, select the timecode, type a new timecode, and then press Enter.
- To adjust the current timecode by dragging, drag the timecode horizontally. For example, to set an earlier timecode, drag to the left.
- To adjust the current timecode by using a relative value, type the plus sign (+) or minus sign (–) and the number of frames to add or subtract. For example, to subtract five frames from the current timecode, select the entire timecode, type –5, and then press Enter.

5.7.3 Creating DVDs

You can burn a sequence to DVD directly from Adobe Premiere Pro, or save encoded files to a folder or as an ISO image that you can burn later with other DVD-burning software. You can create auto-play DVDs or menu-based DVDs. Adobe Premiere Pro provides several DVD menu templates that you can use as designed, or customize them to create a DVD. Adobe Premiere Pro creates DVDs that conform to DVD-video format. It doesn't create data or audio DVDs.

If you are creating a DVD using Adobe Encore DVD, you can export a sequence as an AVI or MPEG-2. You can export a sequence containing sequence markers, which are recognized by Adobe Encore DVD as chapter points.

5.7.3.1 *Types of DVDs*

In Adobe Premiere Pro, you can create auto-play DVDs with no menus, or menu-based DVDs that provide navigation options for your viewers.

Auto-play DVD: Begins playing when the disc is inserted into a DVD player. Auto-play DVDs work best for short movies, or movies that you want to play continuously in a loop playback mode. Auto-play DVDs contain no menus. You can add DVD markers to auto-play DVDs that allow your viewers to skip forward or back through the movie using the Next and Previous buttons on a DVD player's remote control.

Menu-based DVD with scene selection submenu: Displays a submenu of scenes that you specify with markers. These DVDs are best for long movies that play from start to finish, but that also contain scenes that the viewer might want to access from a submenu. On the main menu, the viewer can choose to play the movie or go to a scene selection submenu.

Menu-based DVD with movie selections: Divides a sequence into separate movies that viewers can access from the main menu. Using DVD main menu and stop markers, you can divide a sequence into individual movies. When you build the DVD, each movie corresponds to either the Play Movie or movie buttons on the main menu. You can also include scene markers that provide viewers with a scene selection submenu. The scene selection menu is for the entire sequence—you can't divide individual movies in your sequence into separate scene menus.

5.7.3.2 *DVD Creation Workflow*

Adobe Premiere Pro can burn a single sequence to DVD, but each sequence in your project can be burned to a separate DVD. Add all the content you want to include on DVD into a sequence. After you prepare the sequence, perform the following basic tasks:

1. Add scene, main menu, and stop markers.

   Adobe Premiere Pro creates DVD menus dynamically based on DVD markers you place in the sequence. DVD markers are separate from sequence markers, but you apply them from the Timeline panel in a similar way.

   If you are creating an auto-play DVD you can add scene markers so that the viewer can use a DVD player's remote control to move from scene to scene.

2. Choose a menu template.

   Adobe Premiere Pro templates are predesigned menus that come in several styles. Buttons on the templates automatically link to DVD markers placed in the sequence. Adobe Premiere Pro creates additional submenus as necessary to accommodate all the DVD markers in a sequence. You choose a template from the DVD Layout panel.

   Auto-play DVDs don't have menus, so you don't need to choose a template.

3. Customize the menu template.

   Edit titles, change graphics, or add video for backgrounds. You can also use video in button thumbnails by specifying a section of a clip to play in the button.

4. Preview the DVD.

   Check the functionality and the look of your DVD menus in the Preview DVD window.

5. Burn the DVD.

   Attach a write-capable DVD drive to your computer and burn your DVD content to disc. You can save the compressed files to a folder for playback from a computer hard drive. You can also save a DVD ISO image and distribute it or burn it later using other DVD-burning software.

5.7.3.3 *Preparing Content for DVD*

DVD content is compressed according to DVD specifications so that it will play reliably on a wide range of players. When preparing content for a DVD project pay attention to frame size and frame rate, so that content retains its quality in the transition to DVD.

For best results, make sure that you capture or record following these specifications:

Frame size NTSC standard 720 x 480 or PAL standard 720 x 576. If your project uses a different frame size, Adobe Premiere Pro scales it automatically.

Frame rate 29.97 fps (NTSC) or 25 fps (PAL). All footage in a single project must be of the same frame rate.

Aspect ratio 4:3 or 16:9 (widescreen).

Audio bit depth 16 bits.

Audio sample rate 48 kHz.

5.8 Video Compression

An HDTV camera generates a raw video stream of 149,299,200 bytes per second for 24fps video.

This stream must be compressed if digital TV is to fit in the bandwidth of available TV channels and if movies are to fit on DVDs. Fortunately, video compression is practical because the data in pictures is often redundant in space and time. For example, the sky can be blue across the top of a picture and that blue sky can persist for frame after frame. Also, because of the way the eye works, it is possible to delete some data from video pictures with almost no noticeable degradation in image quality.

TV cameras used in broadcasting usually generate 25 pictures a second (in Europe) or 29.97 pictures a second (in North America). Digital television requires that these pictures be digitized so that they can be processed by computer hardware. Each picture element (a pixel) is then represented by one luma number and two chrominance numbers. These describe the brightness and the color of the pixel (see YCbCr). Thus, each digitized picture is initially represented by three rectangular arrays of numbers.

A common (and old) trick to reduce the amount of data is to separate each picture into two fields upon broadcast/encoding: the "top field," which is the odd numbered horizontal lines, and the "bottom field," which is the even numbered lines. Upon reception/decoding, the two fields are displayed alternately with the lines of one field interleaving between the lines of the previous field. This format is called interlaced video; two successive fields are called a frame. The typical field rate is then 50 (Europe/PAL) or 59.94 (US/NTSC) fields per second. If the video is not interlaced, then it is called progressive video and each picture is a frame. MPEG-2 supports both options.

Another common practice to reduce the data rate is to "thin out" or subsample the two chrominance planes. In effect, the remaining chrominance values represent the nearby values that are deleted. Thinning works because the eye better resolves brightness details than chrominance details. The 4:2:2 chrominance format indicates that half the chrominance values have been deleted. The 4:2:0 chrominance format indicates that three quarters of the chrominance values have been deleted. If no chrominance values have been deleted, the chrominance format is 4:4:4. MPEG-2 allows all three options.

MPEG-2 specifies that the raw frames be compressed into three kinds of frames: intra-coded frames (I-frame), predictive-coded frames (P-frames), and bidirectionally-predictive-coded frames (B-frames).

5.9 Video Compression based on Motion Compensation

An I-frame is a compressed version of a single uncompressed (raw) frame. It takes advantage of spatial redundancy and of the inability of the eye to detect certain changes in the image. Unlike P-frames and B-frames, I-frames do not depend on data in the preceding or the following frames. Briefly, the raw frame is divided into 8 pixel by 8 pixel blocks. The data in each block is transformed by a discrete cosine transform. The result is an 8 by 8 matrix of coefficients. The transform converts spatial variations into frequency variations, but it does not change the information in the block; the original block can be recreated exactly by applying the inverse cosine transform. The advantage of doing this is that the image can now be simplified by quantizing the coefficients. Many of the coefficients, usually the higher frequency components, will then be zero. The penalty of this step is the loss of some subtle distinctions in brightness and color. If one applies the inverse transform to the matrix after it is quantized, one gets an image that looks very similar to the original image but that is not quite as nuanced.

Next, the quantized coefficient matrix is itself compressed. Typically, one corner of the quantized matrix is filled with zeros. By starting in the opposite corner of the matrix, then zigzagging through the matrix to combine the coefficients into a string, then substituting run-length codes for consecutive zeros in that string, and then applying Huffman coding to that result, one reduces the matrix to a smaller array of numbers. It is this array that is broadcast or that is put on DVDs. In the receiver or the player, the whole process is reversed, enabling the receiver to reconstruct, to a close approximation, the original frame.

Typically, every 15th frame or so is made into an I-frame. P-frames and B-frames might follow an I-frame like this, IBBPBBPBBPBB(I), to form a Group Of Pictures (GOP); however, the standard is flexible about this.

5.10 MPEG-1

MPEG-1 is a standard for lossy compression of video and audio. It is designed to compress VHS-quality raw digital video and CD audio down to 1.5 Mbit/s (26:1 and 6:1 compression ratios respectively) without excessive quality loss, making video CDs, digital cable/satellite TV and digital audio broadcasting (DAB) possible.

Today, MPEG-1 has become the most widely compatible lossy audio/video format in the world, and is used in a large number of products and technologies. Perhaps the best-known part of the MPEG-1 standard is the MP3 audio format it introduced.

The MPEG-1 standard is published as ISO/IEC 11172 - Information technology—Coding of moving pictures and associated audio for digital storage media at up to about 1.5 Mbit/s. The standard consists of the following five Parts:

- Systems (storage and synchronization of video, audio, and other data together)
- Video (compressed video content)
- Audio (compressed audio content)
- Conformance testing (testing the correctness of implementations of the standard)
- Reference software (example software showing how to encode and decode according to the standard)

5.10.1 Applications

- Most popular computer software for video playback includes MPEG-1 decoding, in addition to any other supported formats.
- The popularity of MP3 audio has established a massive installed base of hardware that can play back MPEG-1 Audio (all three layers).
- "Virtually all digital audio devices" can play back MPEG-1 Audio. Many millions have been sold to-date.
- Before MPEG-2 became widespread, many digital satellite/cable TV services used MPEG-1 exclusively.
- The widespread popularity of MPEG-2 with broadcasters means MPEG-1 is playable by most digital cable and satellite set-top boxes, and digital disc and tape players, due to backwards compatibility.
- MPEG-1 is the exclusive video and audio format used on Video CD (VCD), the first consumer digital video format, and still a very popular format around the world.
- The Super Video CD standard, based on VCD, uses MPEG-1 audio exclusively, as well as MPEG-2 video.
- The DVD-Video format uses MPEG-2 video primarily, but MPEG-1 support is explicitly defined in the standard.

- The DVD-Video standard originally required MPEG-1 Layer II audio for PAL countries, but was changed to allow AC-3/Dolby Digital-only discs. MPEG-1 Layer II audio is still allowed on DVDs, although newer extensions to the format, like MPEG Multichannel, are rarely supported.
- Most DVD players also support Video CD and MP3 CD playback, which use MPEG-1.
- The international Digital Video Broadcasting (DVB) standard primarily uses MPEG-1 Layer II audio, and MPEG-2 video.
- The international Digital Audio Broadcasting (DAB) standard uses MPEG-1 Layer II audio exclusively, due to MP2's especially high quality, modest decoder performance requirements, and tolerance of errors.

MPEG-1 Video exploits perceptual compression methods to significantly reduce the data rate required by a video stream. It reduces or completely discards information in certain frequencies and areas of the picture that the human eye has limited ability to fully perceive. It also exploits temporal (over time) and spatial (across a picture) redundancy common in video to achieve better data compression than would be possible otherwise. (See: Video compression)

5.10.2 Color space

Before encoding video to MPEG-1, the color-space is transformed to Y'CbCr (Y'=Luma, Cb=Chroma Blue, Cr=Chroma Red). Luma (brightness, resolution) is stored separately from chroma (color, hue, phase) and even further separated into red and blue components. The chroma is also subsampled to 4:2:0, meaning it is reduced by one half vertically and one half horizontally, to just one quarter the resolution of the video. This software algorithm also has analogies in hardware, such as the output from a Bayer pattern filter, common in digital colour cameras.

Because the human eye is much less sensitive to small changes in color than in brightness, chroma subsampling is a very effective way to reduce the amount of video data that needs to be compressed. On videos with fine detail (high spatial complexity) this can manifest as chroma aliasing artifacts. Compared to other digital compression artifacts, this issue seems to be very rarely a source of annoyance.

Because of subsampling, Y'CbCr video must always be stored using even dimensions (divisible by 2), otherwise chroma mismatch ("ghosts") will occur, and it will appear as if the color is ahead of, or behind the rest of the video, much like a shadow.

Y'CbCr is often inaccurately called YUV which is only used in the domain of analog video signals. Similarly, the terms luminance and chrominance are often used instead of the (more accurate) terms luma and chroma.

5.10.3 Resolution/Bitrate

MPEG-1 supports resolutions up to 4095×4095 (12-bits), and bitrates up to 100 Mbit/s.

MPEG-1 videos are most commonly seen using Source Input Format (SIF) resolution: 352x240, 352x288, or 320x240. These low resolutions, combined with a bitrate less than 1.5 Mbit/s, make up what is known as a constrained parameters bitstream (CPB), later renamed the "Low Level" (LL) profile in MPEG-2. This is the minimum video specifications any decoder should be able to handle, to be considered MPEG-1 compliant. This was selected to provide a good balance between quality and performance, allowing the use of reasonably inexpensive hardware of the time.

5.10.4 Frame/picture/block types

MPEG-1 has several frame/picture types that serve different purposes. The most important, yet simplest, are I-frames.

5.10.4.1 I-frames

I-frame is an abbreviation for Intra-frame, so-called because they can be decoded independently of any other frames. They may also be known as I-pictures, or keyframes due to their somewhat similar function to the key frames used in animation. I-frames can be considered effectively identical to baseline JPEG images.

High-speed seeking through an MPEG-1 video is only possible to the nearest I-frame. When cutting a video it is not possible to start playback of a segment of video before the first I-frame in the segment (at least not without computationally-intensive re-encoding). For this reason, I-frame-only MPEG videos are used in editing applications.

I-frame only compression is very fast, but produces very large file sizes: a factor of 3× (or more) larger than normally encoded MPEG-1 video, depending on how temporally complex a specific video is I-frame only MPEG-1 video is very similar to MJPEG video. So much so that very high-speed and theoretically lossless (in reality, there are rounding errors) conversion can be made from one format to the other, provided a couple of restrictions (color space and quantization matrix) are followed in the creation of the bitstream.

The length between I-frames is known as the group of pictures (GOP) size. MPEG-1 most commonly uses a GOP size of 15-18. i.e. 1 I-frame for every 14-17 non-I-frames (some combination of P- and B- frames). With more intelligent encoders, GOP size is dynamically chosen, up to some pre-selected maximum limit.

Limits are placed on the maximum number of frames between I-frames due to decoding complexing, decoder buffer size, recovery time after data errors, seeking ability, and accumulation of IDCT errors in low-precision implementations most common in hardware decoders

5.10.4.2 P-frames

P-frame is an abbreviation for Predicted-frame. They may also be called forward-predicted frames, or inter-frames (B-frames are also inter-frames).

P-frames exist to improve compression by exploiting the temporal (over time) redundancy in a video. P-frames store only the difference in image from the frame (either an I-frame or P-frame) immediately preceding it (this reference frame is also called the anchor frame).

The difference between a P-frame and its anchor frame is calculated using motion vectors on each macroblock of the frame. Such motion vector data will be embedded in the P-frame for use by the decoder.

A P-frame can contain any number of intra-coded blocks, in addition to any forward-predicted blocks.

If a video drastically changes from one frame to the next (such as a cut), it is more efficient to encode it as an I-frame.

5.10.4.3 B-frames

B-frame stands for bidirectional-frame. They may also be known as backwards-predicted frames or B-pictures. B-frames are quite similar to P-frames, except they can make predictions using both the previous and future frames (i.e. two anchor frames).

It is therefore necessary for the player to first decode the next I- or P- anchor frame sequentially after the B-frame, before the B-frame can be decoded and displayed.

This makes B-frames very computationally complex, requires larger data buffers, and causes an increased delay on both decoding and during encoding. This also necessitates the display time stamps (DTS) feature in the container/system stream. As such, B-frames have long been subject of much controversy, they are often avoided in videos, and are sometimes not fully supported by hardware decoders.

No other frames are predicted from a B-frame. Because of this, a very low bitrate B-frame can be inserted, where needed, to help control the bitrate. If this was done with a P-frame, future P-frames would be predicted from it and would lower the quality of the entire sequence. However, similarly, the future P-frame must still encode all the changes between it and the previous I- or P- anchor frame (a second time) in addition to much of the changes being coded in the B-frame. B-frames can also be beneficial in videos where the background behind an object is being revealed over several frames, or in fading transitions, such as scene changes.

A B-frame can contain any number of intra-coded blocks and forward-predicted blocks, in addition to backwards-predicted, or bidirectionally predicted blocks.

5.10.4.4 D-frames

MPEG-1 has a unique frame type not found in later video standards. D-frames or DC-pictures are independent images (intra-frames) that have been encoded DC-only (AC coefficients are removed) and hence are very low quality. D-frames are never referenced by I-, P- or B- frames. D-frames are only used for fast previews of video, for instance when seeking through a video at high speed.

Given moderately higher-performance decoding equipment, this feature can be approximated by decoding I-frames instead. This provides higher quality previews, and without the need for D-frames taking up space in the stream, yet not improving video quality.

5.11 MPEG-2

MPEG-2 is a standard for "the generic coding of moving pictures and associated audio information". It describes a combination of lossy video compression and lossy audio data compression methods which permit storage and transmission of movies using currently available storage media and transmission bandwidth.

5.11.1 Systems

MPEG-2 includes a Systems section, part 1, that defines two distinct, but related, container formats. One is the MPEG transport stream, designed to carry digital video and audio over possibly lossy media, where the beginning and the end of the stream may not be identified, such as broadcasting or magnetic tape, examples of which include ATSC, DVB, SBTVD and HDV. MPEG-2 Systems also defines the MPEG program stream, a container format designed for file-based media such as hard disk drives, optical discs and flash memory.

MPEG-2/System is formally known as ISO/IEC 13818-1 and as ITU-T Rec. H.222.0. ISO authorized the "SMPTE Registration Authority, LLC" as the registration authority for MPEG-2 format identifiers. The registration descriptor of MPEG-2 transport is provided by ISO 13818-1 in order to enable users of the standard to unambiguously carry data when its format is not necessarily a recognized international standard.

This provision will permit the MPEG-2 transport standard to carry all types of data while providing for a method of unambiguous identification of the characteristics of the underlying private data.

5.11.2 Video

The Video section, part 2 of MPEG-2, is similar to the previous MPEG-1 standard, but also provides support for interlaced video, the format used by analog broadcast TV systems. MPEG-2 video is not optimized for low bit-rates, especially less than 1 Mbit/s at standard definition resolutions. All standards-compliant MPEG-2 Video decoders are fully capable of playing back MPEG-1 Video streams conforming to the Constrained Parameters Bitstream syntax. MPEG-2/Video is formally known as ISO/IEC 13818-2 and as ITU-T Rec. H.262.

With some enhancements, MPEG-2 Video and Systems are also used in some HDTV transmission systems.

5.11.3 Video Profiles and Levels

MPEG-2 video supports a wide range of applications from mobile to high quality HD editing. For many applications, it's unrealistic and too expensive to support the entire standard. To allow such applications to support only subsets of it, the standard defines profile and level.

The profile defines the subset of features such as compression algorithm, chroma format, etc. The level defines the subset of quantitative capabilities such as maximum bit rate, maximum frame size, etc.

A MPEG application then specifies the capabilities in terms of profile and level. For example, a DVD player may say it supports up to main profile and main level (often written as MP@ML). It means the player can play back any MPEG stream encoded as MP@ML or less.

The tables below summarizes the limitations of each profile and level. There are many other constraints not listed here.

MPEG-2 Profiles

Abbr.	Name	Picture Coding Types	Chroma Format	Aspect Ratios	Scalable modes
SP	Simple profile	I, P	4:2:0	square pixels, 4:3, or 16:9	none
MP	Main profile	I, P, B	4:2:0	square pixels, 4:3, or 16:9	none
SNR	SNR Scalable profile	I, P, B	4:2:0	square pixels, 4:3, or 16:9	SNR (signal-to-noise ratio) scalable
Spatial	Spatially Scalable profile	I, P, B	4:2:0	square pixels, 4:3, or 16:9	SNR- or spatial-scalable
HP	High profile	I, P, B	4:2:2 or 4:2:0	square pixels, 4:3, or 16:9	SNR- or spatial-scalable

Exempting scalability (a rarely used feature where one MPEG-2 stream augments another), the following are some of the constraints on levels:

MPEG-2 Levels

Abbr.	Name	Frame rates (Hz)	Max horizontal resolution	Max vertical resolution	Max luminance samples per second (approximately height x width x framerate)	Max bit rate in Main profile (Mbit/s)
LL	Low Level	23.976, 24, 25, 29.97, 30	352	288	3,041,280	4
ML	Main Level	23.976, 24, 25, 29.97, 30	720	576	10,368,000, except in High profile, where constraint is 14,475,600 for 4:2:0 and 11,059,200 for 4:2:2	15
H-14	High 1440	23.976, 24, 25, 29.97, 30, 50, 59.94, 60	1440	1152	47,001,600, except that in High profile with 4:2:0, constraint is 62,668,800	60
HL	High Level	23.976, 24, 25, 29.97, 30, 50, 59.94, 60	1920	1152	62,668,800, except that in High profile with 4:2:0, constraint is 83,558,400	80

5.11.4 Applications

5.11.4.1 DVD-Video

The DVD-Video standard uses MPEG-2 video, but imposes some restrictions:

- Allowed Dimensions

  720 × 480, 704 × 480, 352 × 480, 352 × 240 pixel (NTSC)

  720 × 576, 704 × 576, 352 × 576, 352 × 288 pixel (PAL)
- Allowed Aspect ratios (Display AR)

  4:3

  16:9 (1.85:1 and 2.35:1, among others, are often listed as valid DVD aspect ratios, but are actually a "letterboxed" 16:9 image)
- Allowed Frame rates

  29.97 frame/s (NTSC)

  25 frame/s (PAL)

By using a pattern of REPEAT_FIRST_FIELD flags on the headers of encoded pictures, pictures can be displayed for either two or three fields and almost any picture display rate (minimum T! of the frame rate) can be achieved. This is most often used to display 23.976 (approximately film rate) video on NTSC.

- Audio+video bitrate

  Video peak 9.8 Mbit/s

  Total peak 10.08 Mbit/s

  Minimum 300 kbit/s
- YUV 4:2:0

  Additional subtitles possible

  Closed captioning (NTSC only)

- Audio

  Linear Pulse Code Modulation (LPCM): 48 kHz or 96 kHz; 16- or 24-bit; up to six channels (not all combinations possible due to bitrate constraints)

  MPEG Layer 2 (MP2): 48 kHz, up to 5.1 channels (required in PAL players only)

  Dolby Digital (DD, also known as AC-3): 48 kHz, 32–448 kbit/s, up to 5.1 channels

  Digital Theater Systems (DTS): 754 kbit/s or 1510 kbit/s (not required for DVD player compliance)

  NTSC DVDs must contain at least one LPCM or Dolby Digital audio track.

  PAL DVDs must contain at least one MPEG Layer 2, LPCM, or Dolby Digital audio track.

  Players are not required to play back audio with more than two channels, but must be able to downmix multichannel audio to two channels.

- GOP structure (Group Of Pictures)

  Sequence header must be present at the beginning of every GOP

  Maximum frames per GOP: 18 (NTSC) / 15 (PAL), i.e. 0.6 seconds both

  Closed GOP required for multi-angle DVDs

5.11.4.2 HDV

HDV is a format for recording and playback of high-definition MPEG-2 video on a DV cassette tape.

5.11.4.3 MOD and TOD

MOD and TOD are recording formats for use in consumer digital file-based camcorders.

5.11.4.4 XDCAM

XDCAM is a professional file-based video recording format.

5.11.4.5 DVB

Application-specific restrictions on MPEG-2 video in the DVB standard:

- Allowed resolutions for SDTV:

  720, 640, 544, 528, 480 or 352 × 480 pixel, 24/1.001, 24, 30/1.001 or 30 frame/s

  352 × 240 pixel, 24/1.001, 24, 30/1.001 or 30 frame/s

  720, 704, 544, 528, 480 or 352 × 576 pixel, 25 frame/s

  352 × 288 pixel, 25 frame/s

- For HDTV:

  720 x 576 x 50 frame/s progressive (576p50)

  1280 x 720 x 25 or 50 frame/s progressive (720p50)

  1440 or 1920 x 1080 x 25 frame/s progressive (1080p25 – film mode)

  1440 or 1920 x 1080 x 25 frame/s interlace (1080i50)

  1920 x 1080 x 50 frame/s progressive (1080p50) possible future H.264/AVC format

5.11.4.6 ATSC

The ATSC A/53 standard, used in the United States, uses MPEG-2 video at the Main Profile @ High Level, with additional restrictions:

- The maximum bitrate of the MPEG-2 video stream is exactly 19.4 Mbit/s for broadcast television, and exactly 38.8 Mbit/s for the "high-data-rate" mode (e.g., cable television). (The practical limit is somewhat lower, since the MPEG-2 video stream must fit inside a transport stream, with overhead, sent out at 19.3927... Mbit/s for broadcast.)
- The amount of MPEG-2 stream buffer required at the decoder (the vbv_buffer_size_value) must be less than or equal to 999,424 bytes.
- In most cases, the transmitter can't start sending a coded image until within a half-second of when it's to be decoded (vbv_delay less than or equal to 45000 90-kHz clock increments).
- The stream must include colorimetry information (gamma curve, the precise RGB colors used, and the relationship between RGB and the coded YCbCr).
- The video must be 4:2:0 (chrominance resolution must be 1/2 of luma horizontal resolution and 1/2 of luma vertical resolution).

Allowed video resolutions, aspect ratios, and frame/field rates:

- 1920 × 1080 pixel (16:9, with square pixels), at 30p, 29.97p, 24p, 23.976p, 60i, or 59.94i
- 1280 × 720 pixel (16:9, with square pixels), at 60p, 59.94p, 30p, 29.97p, 24p, or 23.976p
- 704 × 480 pixel (either 4:3 or 16:9 – either way, with non-square pixels), at 60p, 59.94p, 30p, 29.97p, 24p, 23.976p, 60i, or 59.94i
- 640 × 480 pixel (4:3, with square pixels), at 60p, 59.94p, 30p, 29.97p, 24p, 23.976p, 60i, or 59.94i

Note that although the ATSC A/53 standard limits transmission to these 18 formats (and their 1000/1001-rate slowed-down versions), the U.S. Federal Communications Commission declined to mandate that television stations obey this part of the ATSC's standard. In theory, television stations in the U.S. are free to choose any resolution, aspect ratio, and frame/field rate, within the limits of Main Profile @ High Level. Many stations do go outside the bounds of the ATSC specification by using other resolutions – for example, 720 × 480.

Also note that the ATSC specification and MPEG-2 allow the use of progressive frames, even within an interlaced video sequence. For example, NBC stations transmit a 1080i60 video sequence – meaning the formal output of the MPEG-2 decoding process is sixty 540-line fields per second. But for prime-time television shows, those 60 fields can be coded with 24 progressive frames. Some NBC stations do this, meaning they actually transmit an 1080p24 video stream (a sequence of 24 progressive frames per second) with metadata instructing the decoder to interlace them (and repeat them in 3:2 pulldown) before display.

Thus, it would be incorrect to say that the ATSC standard doesn't contain 1080p video, or that broadcast HDTV doesn't use 1080p video. The ATSC specification allows 1080p30 and 1080p24 sequences – just not 1080p60 sequences. They aren't used in practice, because broadcasters want to be able to switch between 60 Hz (news, soap operas) and 24 Hz (prime-time) content without ending the MPEG-2 sequence. However, the ATSC specification also allows broadcasters to transmit progressive frames within an interlaced sequence, and some broadcasters actually do this in practice. Their transmissions could fairly be described as 1080p24, since they contain 24 progressively-coded frames per second. (This is the same mechanism used by HD-DVD to code 1080p24 content – progressive frames within an interlaced sequence.)

The 1080-line formats are encoded with 1920 × 1088 pixel luma matrices and 960 × 540 chroma matrices, but the last 8 lines are discarded by the MPEG-2 decoding and display process. MPEG-2 audio was a contender for the ATSC standard during the DTV "Grand Alliance" shootout, but lost out to Dolby AC-3. The Grand Alliance issued a statement finding the MP2 system to be "essentially equivalent" to Dolby, but only after the Dolby selection had been made. Later, a story emerged that MIT had entered into an agreement with Dolby whereupon the university would be awarded a large sum if the MP2 system was rejected. Dolby also offered an incentive for Zenith to switch their vote (which they did), however it is unknown whether they accepted the offer.

5.11.4.7 ISDB-T

All the text about MPEG-2 in ATSC is also valid for ISDB-T, except that in the main TS is aggregated a second program for mobile devices compressed in MPEG-4 H.264 AVC for video and AAC-LC for audio, mainly known as 1Seg.

5.12 MPEG-4

MPEG-4 is a patented collection of methods defining compression of audio and visual (AV) digital data. It was introduced in late 1998 and designated a standard for a group of audio and video coding formats and related technology agreed upon by the ISO/IEC Moving Picture Experts Group (MPEG) (ISO/IEC JTC1/SC29/WG11) under the formal standard ISO/IEC 14496 - Coding of audio-visual objects. Uses of MPEG-4 include compression of AV data for web (streaming media) and CD distribution, voice (telephone, videophone) and broadcast television applications.

MPEG-4 absorbs many of the features of MPEG-1 and MPEG-2 and other related standards, adding new features such as (extended) VRML support for 3D rendering, object-oriented composite files (including audio, video and VRML objects), support for externally-specified Digital Rights Management and various types of interactivity. AAC (Advanced Audio Coding) was standardized as an adjunct to MPEG-2 (as Part 7) before MPEG-4 was issued.

MPEG-4 is still a developing standard and is divided into a number of parts. Companies promoting MPEG-4 compatibility do not always clearly state which "part" level compatibility they are referring to. The key parts to be aware of are MPEG-4 part 2 (including Advanced Simple Profile, used by codecs such as DivX, Xvid, Nero Digital and 3ivx and by Quicktime 6) and MPEG-4 part 10 (MPEG-4 AVC/H.264 or Advanced Video Coding, used by the x264 encoder, by Nero Digital AVC, by Quicktime 7, and by high-definition video media like Blu-ray Disc).

Most of the features included in MPEG-4 are left to individual developers to decide whether to implement them. This means that there are probably no complete implementations of the entire MPEG-4 set of standards. To deal with this, the standard includes the concept of "profiles" and "levels", allowing a specific set of capabilities to be defined in a manner appropriate for a subset of applications.

Initially, MPEG-4 was aimed primarily at low bit-rate video communications; however, its scope as a multimedia coding standard was later expanded. MPEG-4 is efficient across a variety of bit-rates ranging from a few kilobits per second to tens of megabits per second. MPEG-4 provides the following functionalities:

- Improved coding efficiency
- Ability to encode mixed media data
- Error resilience to enable robust transmission
- Ability to interact with the audio-visual scene generated at the receiver

MPEG-4 provides a series of technologies for developers, for various service-providers and for end users:

- MPEG-4 enables different software and hardware developers to create multimedia objects possessing better abilities of adaptability and flexibility to improve the quality of such services and technologies as digital television, animation graphics, the World Wide Web and their extensions.
- Data network providers can use MPEG-4 for data transparency. With the help of standard procedures, MPEG-4 data can be interpreted and transformed into other signal types compatible with any available network.
- The MPEG-4 format provides end users with a wide range of interaction with various animated objects.
- Standardized Digital Rights Management signaling, otherwise known in the MPEG community as Intellectual Property Management and Protection (IPMP).

The MPEG-4 format can perform various functions, among which might be the following:

- Multiplexes and synchronizes data, associated with media objects, in such a way that they can be efficiently transported further via network channels.
- Interaction with the audio-visual scene, which is formed on the side of the receiver.

5.13 MPEG-7

MPEG-7 is a multimedia content description standard. It was standardized in ISO/IEC 15938 (Multimedia content description interface). This description will be associated with the content itself, to allow fast and efficient searching for material that is of interest to the user. MPEG-7 is formally called Multimedia Content Description Interface. Thus, it is not a standard which deals with the actual encoding of moving pictures and audio, like MPEG-1, MPEG-2 and MPEG-4. It uses XML to store metadata, and can be attached to timecode in order to tag particular events, or synchronise lyrics to a song, for example.

It was designed to standardize:

- a set of Description Schemes (short DS in the standard) and Descriptors (short D in the standard)
- a language to specify these schemes, called the · Description Definition Language (short DDL in the standard)
- a scheme for coding the description

5.13.1 MPEG-7 objectives

- Provide a fast and efficient searching, filtering and content identification method.
- Describe main issues about the content (low-level characteristics, structure, models, collections, etc.).
- Index a big range of applications.
- Audiovisual information that MPEG-7 deals with are : Audio, voice, video, images, graphs and 3D models
- Inform about how objects are combined in a scene.
- Independence between description and the information itself.

5.13.2 Parts

The MPEG-7 (ISO/IEC 15938) consists of different Parts. Each part covers a certain aspect of the whole specification.

MPEG-7 Parts

Part	Number	First public release date (First edition)	Latest public release date (edition)	Latest amendment	Title	Description
Part 1	ISO/IEC 15938-1	2002	2002	2006	Systems	the architectural framework of MPEG-7, the carriage of MPEG-7 content and the binary format for MPEG-7 descriptions (BiM)
Part 2	ISO/IEC 15938-2	2002	2002		Description definition language	
Part 3	ISO/IEC 15938-3	2002	2002	2009	Visual	
Part 4	ISO/IEC 15938-4	2002	2002	2006	Audio	
Part 5	ISO/IEC 15938-5	2003	2003	2008	Multimedia description schemes	
Part 6	ISO/IEC 15938-6	2003	2003	2007	Reference software	
Part 7	ISO/IEC 15938-7	2003	2003	2008	Conformance testing	
Part 8	ISO/IEC 15938-8	2002	2002	2007	Extraction and use of MPEG-7 descriptions	
Part 9	ISO/IEC 15938-9	2005	2005		Profiles and levels	
Part 10	ISO/IEC 15938-10	2005	2005		Schema definition	
Part 11	ISO/IEC TR 15938-11	2005	2005		MPEG-7 profile schemas	
Part 12	ISO/IEC 15938-12	2008	2008		Query format	

5.14 MPEG-21

The MPEG-21 standard, from the Moving Picture Experts Group, aims at defining an open framework for multimedia applications. MPEG-21 is ratified in the standards ISO/IEC 21000 - Multimedia framework.

Specifically, MPEG-21 defines a "Rights Expression Language" standard as means of sharing digital rights/permissions/restrictions for digital content from content creator to content consumer. As an XML-based standard, MPEG-21 is designed to communicate machine-readable license information and do so in a "ubiquitous, unambiguous and secure" manner.

Among the aspirations for this standard that the industry hopes will put an end to illicit file sharing is that it will constitute: "A normative open framework for multimedia delivery and consumption for use by all the players in the delivery and consumption chain. This open framework will provide content creators, producers, distributors and service providers with equal opportunities in the MPEG-21 enabled open market."

MPEG-21 is based on two essential concepts: the definition of a fundamental unit of distribution and transaction, which is the Digital Item, and the concept of users interacting with them. Digital Items can be considered the kernel of the Multimedia Framework and the users can be considered as who interacts with them inside the Multimedia Framework.

At its most basic level, MPEG-21 provides a framework in which one user interacts with another one, and the object of that interaction is a Digital Item. Due to that, we could say that the main objective of the MPEG-21 is to define the technology needed to support users to exchange, access, consume, trade or manipulate Digital Items in an efficient and transparent way.

5.15 Animation

Animation is the process of making an object appear to move by rapidly displaying a series of pictures of it, each one in it is slightly in different position; a techniques used in producing Computer-generated movies. An animation is created by recording a series of still images of drawings, objects, people, etc., in various positions of incremental movement. It may not be necessary to move the objects to create the illusion of movement — colours and the background can be changed from frame to frame so that there is a perception of a moving object. Before we go further into animation, we must understand the two main topics of animation, viz., Keyframes and Tweening.

5.15.1 Keyframes and Tweening

Frankly speaking, keyframes are the first and the last frames of an action. Tweening, is the process of generating intermediate frames between two images to give the appearance that the first image evolves smoothly into the second image. Tweening is a key process in all types of animation, including computer animation. For example, for showing the motion of the square moving from lower left corner to the upper right corner of the frames, the initial and final positions provide the keyframes, while the middle frames are intermediate frames. There are many ways of creating an animation, depending on the materials used. The material can be one of the following two types:

1. Flat, such as drawings or cut-out pieces of paper.
2. Dimensional, such as clay, puppets, household objects, or even people.

5.16 Cel Animation

Cel animation is a traditional form of animation used in the production of cartoons or animated movies where each frame of the scene is drawn by hand. In a cel or frame animation, the entire animation sequence is split into different frames. The traditional cel animation process became obsolete by the beginning of the 21st century.

Today, animator's drawings and the backgrounds are either scanned into or drawn directly into a computer system. Various software programs are used to colour the drawings and simulate camera movement and effects. The final animated piece is output toone of several delivery media, including traditional 35 mm film and newer media such as digital video.

5.17 Computer Animation

The term 'Computer Animation' categories 2D (two dimensional) and 3D (three dimensional) animation.

It is also called 'Vector Animation' and is typically created using programs like Adobe Flash and Macromedia Director, both are covered in the next chapter.

We had read earlier that 2D animation was all cartoons in the form of drawings, which are shown one after the another to give the effect of walking cartcons. 2D animation, is rendered in a two-dimensional space, 3D animation, however, is rendered ina virtual three-dimensional space, using polygons captured by various virtual cameras to film the animation.

For 3D animations, all frames must be rendered after modelng is complete. For 2D vector animations, the rendering process is the keyframe illustration process, while tweened frames are rendered as needed.

For pre-recorded presentations, the redered frames are transferred to a different format or medium such as film or digital video. The frames may also be endered in real time as they are presented to the end-user audience. Low bandwidth animations transmitted via the internet (e.g., 2D Flash, X3D) often use softwareon the end-users computer to render in real time as an alternative to streaming or pre-loaded high bandwidth animations.

5.18 Morphing

Short for metamorphosing; a revolutionary animation technique used to "fill in the blanks" between dissimilar figures so that one seems to melt into another, such as changing a man to a warewolf, a bat to a vampire or a rock singer to a panther.

Morphing, a common film industry specials effects technique is related closely to another, more prosaic animation technique called tweening (short for in-betweening) which refers to the computer's capability to calculate and draw frames that are intermediate between the "key" frames hand-down by the artist.

Morphing is the process of tweening to a different object. It has the following applications:

1. Development (of any object) can be simulated (shown artifically) by first obtaining still images at successive stages and then morphing into a child can be shown as a movie using he technique of morphing.
2. Similarly, movement of objects (of animals, humans or cartoon characters) can be simulated. For example, if you take still images at different stages of movement and then apply tweening (using a multimedia software), you can create motion in the object.
3. Morphing can be used to illustrate evolution in interesting ways. For example, a morph can showhow early simple arthopods developed into the diverse insects that exists today.
4. Many interesting effects can be created using morphing technique. It is increasingly being used as a special effect on TV and in motion pictures.

Let us Revise

1. Video standards and formats are still being refined as transport, storage, compression and display technologies take shape in laboratories and in the market place.
2. If you shoot your own video for a project, make sure you have releases from all persons who appear or speak and permission to use the audio effects and music you wave into it.
3. Four broadcast and video standards and recording formats commonly in use around the world are: NTSC, PAL, SECAM and HDTV.

4. As specified by the NTSC standard, a single frame of video is made up of 525 horizontal scan lines drawn onto the inside face of a phosphor-coated picture tube every 1/30th of a second by a fast-moving electron beam.
5. PAL is an integrated method of adding colour to a black-and-white television signal that paints 625 lines at a frame rate of 25 frames per second.
6. Although SECAM is a 625-line, 50 Hz system, it differs greatly from both the NTSC and the PAL colour systems in its basic technology and broadcast method.
7. There are six video formats in the ATSCDTV standard that are "High Definition Television." These are the 1080-line by 1920-pixels formats at all picture rates (24, 40 and 60 pictures per second) and the 720-line by 1280-pixel formats at the same picture rates.
8. Analog signals are continuous in nature whereas digital signals are discontinuous.
9. A digital video architecture is made up of a format for encoding and playing back video files by a computer and includes a player that can recognize and play files created for that format.
10. You capture digital video files from tape. That is, you transfer them from the source videotape to the hard drive.
11. You digitize analog video. Analog video is recorded by analog camcorders and decks.
12. Use the Import command to bring files—for example, still images or audio you've downloaded—that are already on your hard drive into your Adobe Premiere Pro project.
13. The quality of digitized audio and the size of the audio file depend on the sample rate (the number of samples per second) and bit depth (the number of bits per sample) of the digitized audio.
14. Many camcorders and high-end video decks record timecode, which marks specific frames with unique addresses.
15. Auto-play DVDs work best for short movies, or movies that you want to play continuously in a loop playback mode.
16. Using DVD main menu and stop markers, you can divide a sequence into individual movies.
17. An I-frame is a compressed version of a single uncompressed (raw) frame.
18. MPEG-1 is a standard for lossy compression of video and audio.
19. MPEG-1 supports resolutions up to 4095×4095 (12-bits), and bitrates up to 100 Mbit/s.
20. P-frame is an abbreviation for Predicted-frame. They may also be called forward-predicted frames, or inter-frames (B-frames are also inter-frames).
21. B-frame stands for bidirectional-frame. They may also be known as backwards-predicted frames or B-pictures.
22. D-frames or DC-pictures are independent images (intra-frames) that have been encoded DC-only (AC coefficients are removed) and hence are very low quality.
23. MPEG-2 is a standard for "the generic coding of moving pictures and associated audio information".
24. MPEG-4 is a patented collection of methods defining compression of audio and visual (AV) digital data.
25. MPEG-7 is a multimedia content description standard.
26. The MPEG-21 standard, from the Moving Picture Experts Group, aims at defining an open framework for multimedia applications.
27. Animation is the process of making an object appear to move by rapidly displaying a series of pictures of it, each one in it is slightly in different position; a techniques used in producing Computer-generated movies.

28. Keyframes are the first and the last frames of an action.
29. Tweening, is the process of generating intermediate frames between two images to give the appearance that the first image evolves smoothly into the second image.
30. The term 'Computer Animation' categories 2D (two dimensional) and 3D (three dimensional) animation.

Multiple Choice Questions

1. Full form of PAL is:
   (a) project active line (b) program alternating line (c) phase alternating line
   (d) none of the above.
2. S-video uses:
   (a) Two wires (b) Three wires (c) One wire
   (d) None of the above
3. Which of the following is not a television signal format?
   (a) SECAM (b) HDTV (c) MPEG
   (d) PAL.
4. Which image file type is best for photo-realistic images?
   (a) Laser (b) Bitmap. (c) Vector
   (d) All of the above.
5. AVI stands for:
   (a) Audio Video Interface (b) Audio Visual Interface (c) Audio Video Interleave
   (d) None of the above.
6. MPEG stands for:
   (a) motion picture environment group.
   (b) multipurpose element grid.
   (c) moving picture experts group.
   (d) None of the above.
7. In a video camera, CCD stands for:
   (a) colour coding data (b) charge coupled device (c) carbon crystal digitizer
   (d) none of the above.
8. Which format is used in digital cameras?
   (a) MPEG2 (b) MPEG4 (c) MPEG1
   (d) SWF.

True/False Questions

1. Four broadcast and video standards and recording formats commonly in use around the world are: NTSC, PAL, SECAM and HDTV.
2. Although SECAM is a 625-line, 50 Hz system, it differs greatly from both the NTSC and the PAL colour systems in its basic technology and broadcast method.

3. A digital video architecture is made up of a format for encoding and playing back video files by a computer and includes a player that can recognize and play files created for that format.
4. Use the Export command to bring files—for example, still images or audio you've downloaded—that are already on your hard drive into your Adobe Premiere Pro project.
5. Auto-play DVDs work best for short movies, or movies that you want to play continuously in a loop playback mode.
6. MPEG-1 is a standard for lossy compression of video and not audio.
7. B-frame stands for bidirectional-frame. They may also be known as backwards-predicted frames or B-pictures.
8. MPEG-4 is a patented collection of methods defining compression of audio and visual (AV) digital data.
9. Animation is the process of making an object appear to move by rapidly displaying a series of pictures of it, each one in it is slightly in different position; a techniques used in producing Computer-generated movies.
10. The term 'Computer Animation' categories only 2D (two dimensional) animation.

Matching Columns

In the following case, commands are given in the left hand columns and their actions in the right hand column. Match them.

Column A	Column B
A. MPEG-4	1. The process of smoothly interpolating between two different images
B. MPEG-1	2. phase alternating line
C. MPEG-2	3. TV broadcasting standard
D. MPEG	4. efficient method of object oriented content based storage and retrieval of multimedia content
E. Morphing	5. designed for DVD applications
F. PAL	6. compressed format
G NTSC	7. designed for CD-ROM based

Fill in the Blanks with appropriate words

a. .avi	b. MPEG-4	c. MPEG decoder	d. MPEG2
e. MPEG-1	f. optical	g. bit rate	h. MPEG-2

1. MPEG-1 uses fixed ____________.
2. __________ is the compression format used to create video CDs.
3. DVD is ____________ disc storage media format.
4. Viewing a MPEG video on a micro computer requires a ____________.

5. __________ uses variable bit rate encoding which means that different scenes can play back at different rates.
6. __________ is the standard movie/video format for windows.
7. __________ video compression is used to deliver high quality picture in DVD movies.
8. ________ is used for both straming and downloadable web content.

Descriptive Type Questions

1. Describe the basics of video.
2. How does video works?
3. Describe the following broadcasting video standards:

   NTSC
   PAL
   SECAM
   HDTV
   Digital video
   Analog video

4. Describe the following video recording and tape formats:

   Ampex
   VERA
   U-matic
   Betamax
   Betacam
   Video 2000
   Compact Video Cassette
   Camcoder
   Video 8

5. How would you capture, digitize and import the various video files?
6. How would you create DVDs?
7. What is video compression?
8. What is MPEG-1?
9. Describe the followings:

   I-frames
   P-frames
   B-frames
   D-frames

10. What do you know of the following:

    MPEG-2
    MPEG-4
    MPEG-7
    MPEG-21

11. What do you understand by animation? How are they created?
12. Describe the following:

    Keyframes
    Tweening

13. What is cel animation
14. What do you understand by Computer Animation?
15. Describe Morphing.

Answers to Objective Type Questions

Multiple Choice Questions

1. c	2. a	3. c	4. b
5. c	6. c	7. b	8. c

True False Questions

1. T	2. T	3. T	4. F
5. T	6. F	7. T	8. T
9. T	10. F		

Matching Columns

A. 4	B. 7	C. 5	D. 6
E. 1	F. 2	G. 3	

Fill in the Blanks

1. g	2. e	3. f	4. c
5. h	6. a	7. d	8. b

Multimedia Authoring 6

6.1 Multimedia Authoring Basics

For developing a multimedia project, you have to assemble few things. Among them the main is software, which is authoring tool. These tools are softwaree packages with standard user interface elements that are used to produce contents for web publishing. They provide an integrated environment for binding together content and functions of your project, and typically includes everything needed to create, edit and import specific types of data, assemble raw data into playback sequence and provide a structured method or language for responding to the user input.

6.2 Some Authoring Tools

Each of the software for building multimedia projects contains one or more authoring systems, the tools for creating and editing multimedia elements and the tools for housekeeping taks such as capturing images from the screen, translating file formats and moving files among computers.

The basic requirements for the authoring tools are:

- Tools for creating and editing
- Modeling and Animation tools
- Image and editing tools
- Optical character recognition software
- Sound editing programs
- Animation, video and digital movies

6.2.1 Tools for Creating and Editing

Tools are very important for creating crafted bitmap images. Software like CorelDRAW and Photoshop have such tools. Some software applications combine both drawing and painting capabilities, but many authoring systems import only bit mapped images.

6.2.2 Modeling and Animation Tools

Software for these are: Auto Desk's 3D Studio Max, Macromedia's Extreme 3D, etc. There are also specialized applications for creating and animating 3-D text like Fontographer, Type-Designer, Font Manager, Making Pretty Text, Font Chameleon.

6.2.3 Image and Editing Tools

Image editing applications are specialized and powerful tools for enhancing the existing bitmapped images. These applications also provide tools for painting and drawing that can be used to create images from scratch as well as images digitized from scanners, video frame grabbers, digital cameras, clip art files, or original artwork files created with a painting or a drawing package.

6.2.4 Optical Character Recognition Software

OCR is the software which turns bit-mapped characters into electronically recognizable ASCII text. The software breaks the bitmap image into chunks according to whether it contain text or graphics by examining the texture ,and density areas of the bitmap and by detecting edges.

6.2.5 Sound Editing Programs

Using editing software, you can make our own sound effects and install them as system beeps that indicate an error warning or special activity. Both MAC and Windows systems provide system sounds, which are available as soon as we install the operating system. For digital waveform sounds, Windows ships with the Sound Recorder program that provides some ruimentary features for sound editing; most soundboards for PC's include editing software such as Creative Lab's Wave Studio.

6.2.6 Animation, Video and Digital Movies

Most authoring tools adopt either frame or object oriented approach to animation, but rarely both. Movie-making tools such as Quick Time from MAC and Microsoft Video for Windows, also known as Audio Video Interleaved (AVI), technologycan be used to create, edit and present digitized motion video segments in a small window.

6.2.7 Types of Authoring Tools

Authoring software provides an integrated environment for ninding together the content and the functions in the multimedia project. Authoring systems should have the ability to create, edit, and import specific types of data, assemble raw data into playback sequence or a cue sheet; and should provide a structured meith or language for responding to user input. The various authoring tools are categorized into the followings:

6.2.7.1 Card or page based authoring tools

Here the multimedia elements are organized in the form of books having pages. Every page of the book may contain many media elements including sounds, video and animations. As the user or consumer proceeds with the project, the pages progress in sequence, as determined by the user interaction.

6.2.7.2 Icon based Authoring Tools

Here the multimedia elements are organized in the form of a structure or flow chart. These icons include menu choice, graphic images, sounds and computations. We can also edit the structure by rearranging and fine-tuning the icons and their properties. The authoring tools in this category are Authorware Professional, Icon Author and Quest, both from Windows.

6.2.7.3 Time based Authoring Tools

These tools arrange the project in a such a way that all the elements are active using a time line. This time line is defined by the user himself. The speed at which these transitions occur, can also be accurately controlled. These tools take the help ofa software time which is a typical clock that starts at the beginning of the project and graduates minute after minute.

6.2.7.4 Object Oriented Authoring Tools

Here the multimedia elements are arranged in a hierarchical order with parent and child relationships.

Objects take care of themselves, i.e., given a message they do their thing without external procedures and programming. Object oriented tools are particularly useful for games that contain many components with many characteristics and for simulating real life situations, events and constituenat properties.

6.3 Micromedia Director

The Director is a software used to create Movies. It is similar to Flash, about which you read in the last chapter. The Director's user interface is designed around a movie metaphor. Each project you create can be thought of as a movie, with a cast of characters, a score, a stage where the action takes place, and a director (you, the author). Each media element that appears in your movie (sound, video, images, text, buttons, and so on) can be thought of as a member of the movie's cast. In Director, the Cast window is where you view the list of media elements that appear in your movie.

As with a real movie, each Director movie has a score. However, the score of a Director movie contains more than just music. The Score window in Director contains information about when and where each of the cast members appears on the Stage. The Score describes the action that happens in the movie.

The action in a Director movie takes place in a window called the Stage. To create a Director movie, you add cast members (media elements) to the Cast window by creating them in Director or importing them. Next, you place them on the Stage as sprites. A sprite is simply a copy of a cast member that appears on the Stage. Then you refine the actions of the sprites by editing them on the Stage or in the Score.

6.3.1 Score Editor

Like the Stage, the Score provides a view of your movie. The Stage provides a graphical view, while the Score provides a view of the movie's timeline. The Stage displays the point in time that is selected within the Score. The Score organizes and controls a movie's content over time in rows called channels. The Score includes many Sprite channels for the movie's sprites. Sprite channels are numbered and control when sprites appear in the movie. Additionally, the Score includes effects channels that control the movie's tempo, sound, colour palettes, transitions, and scripted behaviours.

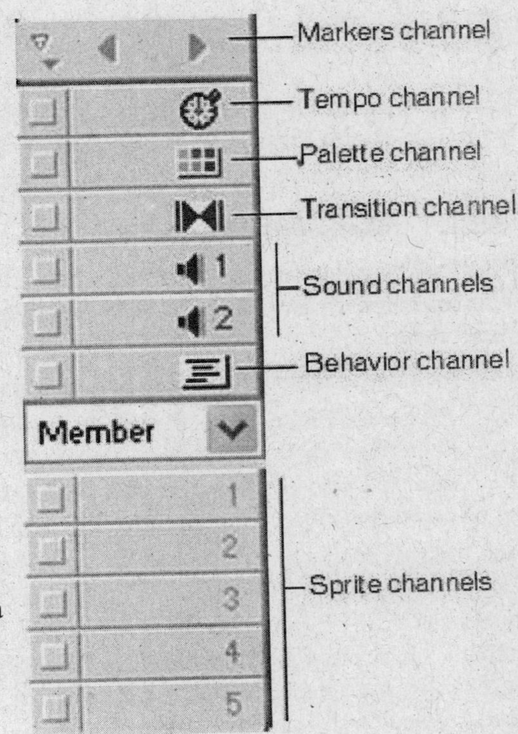

The Score displays channels in the order shown in the figure next. Only the Sprite channels are displayed by default.

6.3.1.1 Effects and sprite channels in the Score

While the rows of the Score contain channels, the columns of the Score contain frames. A frame in a movie represents a single point in time, which is similar in theory to a frame in a celluloid film. Frame numbers are listed above the columns in the Score.

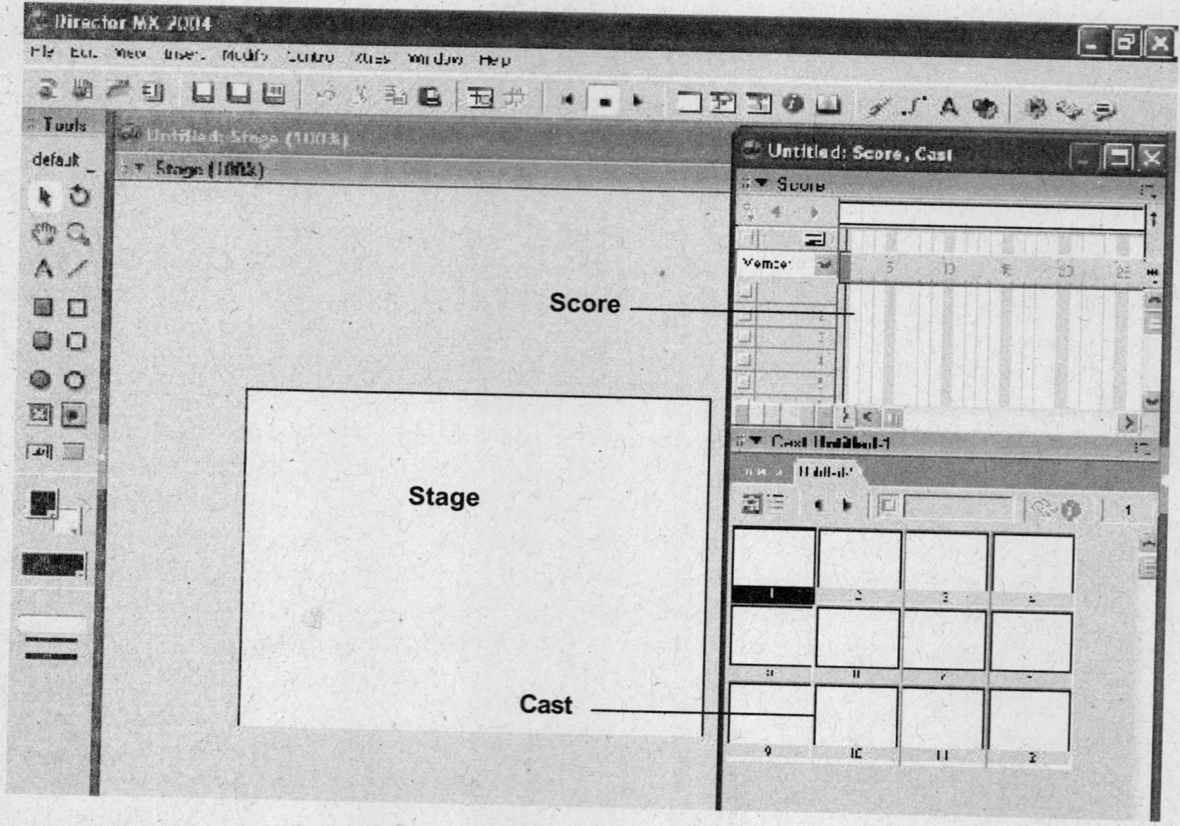

A red vertical line, called the playhead, moves across the frames in the Score to indicate which point in time is currently displayed on the Stage. You can also click any frame in the Score to move the playhead to that frame, and you can drag the playhead backward or forward through frames.

6.3.2 Cast Editor

The Cast window contains the cast members of your movie. You can use the Cast window to create or import new cast members, to view existing cast members, and to control the properties of each cast member.

As you work in Director, you can expect to use two types of cast members:

- Cast members can be the media elements of your movie, such as sounds, text, graphics, animation, and video. These cast members are placed on the Stage as sprites.
- Some cast members may appear in the Score but not on the Stage. These cast members include scripts, palettes, fonts, and transitions, which you can use in the effects channels on the Score.

In the Cast window, you can create or import new cast members to appear as sprites on the Stage. Creating a Director movie consists largely of defining sprites' properties, where they appear, when they appear in the movie, and how they behave. Different sprites can be created from a single cast member. Each sprite can have its own values for different properties, and most changes to these properties do not affect the cast member. Most changes to a cast member, however, will change the sprites created from that cast member. A typical cast window is shown here.

6.3.2.1 *The Cast window filled with cast members*

To create a new cast member:

1. If the Cast window is not already displayed, select Window > Cast.
2. On the Tool palette, select a text, drawing, or control button.
3. Click the Stage to place the new cast member.
4. The cast member now appears in the Cast window.

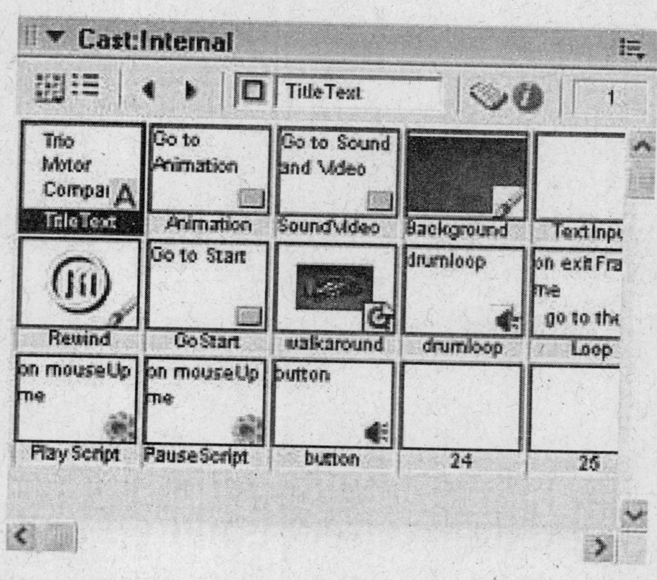

To import a cast member from an existing media file:

1. If the Cast window is not already in thumbnail view, click the Cast View Style button.
2. In thumbnail view in the Cast window, right-click an empty cast member, and select Import.
3. Navigate to a media file, select the file, and click the Import button.
4. The cast member now appears in the Cast window.

6.3.3 Toolbars

One of the more useful Director tools is the toolbar, which presents icon shortcuts to common functions and operations. The following table gives a quick summary of the icon shortcuts in the Director toolbar, as they appear from left to right.

Table of Director Toolbar

Icon	Tool	Function
	New Movie	Opens a new movie
	New Cast	Opens a new cast library
	Open	Opens an existing movie or cast library
	Import	Imports media
	Save	Saves the movie or cast library

	Save All	Saves the movie and all the Cast windows
	Publish	Saves the current movie as a Shockwave Movie and creates the HTML page
	Undo	Undoes the last action
	Cut	Cuts the selected object and places it on the Clipboard
	Copy	Copies the selected object and places it on the Clipboard
	Paste	Pastes the object on the Clipboard into the selected space
	Find Cast Member	Lets you locate a specific cast member quickly
	Exchange Cast Members	Swaps the cast member on the Stage for the selected one.
	Rewind	Moves to the first frame of the movie
	Stop	Stops the movie if it is currently playing
	Play	Plays the movie if it is currently stopped
	Stage	Opens the Stage
	Cast Window	Opens the Cast window
	Score Window	Opens the Score window
	Property inspector	Opens the Property inspector window
	Library palette	Opens the Library palette
	Paint Window	Opens the Paint window
	Vector Shape	Opens the vector shape window

A	Text window	Opens the text window
	Shockwave 3D	Opens the Shockwave 3D window
	Behaviour inspector	Opens the Behaviour inspector
	Script window	Opens the currently selected script, or opens a new script if one is not selected
	Message window	Opens the Message window

6.3.4 Library palette

A library palette is a palette which contains Director's built-in behaviours. A Library palette can also store custom cast libraries. You can add anything to the Library palette that can be contained in Cast window. This can be very useful for any commonly used artwork, as well as for behaviours that you do not want to be edited accidentally.

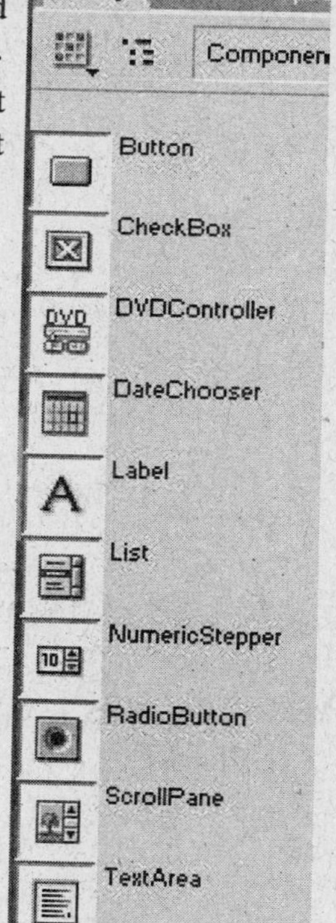

To add your own elements to the Library palette, create a new, unlinked Cast window that contains behaviours and graphics, save it, and then drag the Cast file into the folder called LIBS, which is found in the Director application folder.

6.3.5 Inspector

You use inspectors to view and modify the attributes of text cast members, sprites, and behaviours (scripts). There are four types of inspectors in Director, each performs a specific task:

6.3.5.1 Property Inspector

Use the Property inspector to display the current properties of any selected element, including the Stage, as well as the active movie. You can adjust any available properties of nearly every element in your movie by using this window.

6.3.5.2 Behaviour Inspector

Use the Behaviour inspector to create new behaviours (scripts) and modify existing ones.

6.3.5.3 Text Inspector

Use the Test Inspector to format text and add hypertext links.

6.3.5.4 Memory Inspector

The Memory Inspector displays the amount of memory (RAM) that is being used by the Director application and the element contained in the movie.

6.3.6 Menu Bar

Director uses a fairly complicated set of menus, submenus, and related dialog boxes, in an arrangement that is consistent with Macromedia's user-interface guidelines across the product line. The idea, of course, is that someone familiar with other Macromedia products, like Flash, can adapt to Director fairly quickly.

Menu name	Functions handled
File	Opening, saving and printing of files. Creating projectors (run-time versions of your movies), Shockwave movies and Java applets, Setting preferences, previewing in a browser, and terminating the program.
Edit	Clipboard operations (cut, copy, paste) and various kinds of selection. Searching and replacing text. Launching external resource editors.
View	Offers various ways of looking at the Score (the window that controls where animation sprites are placed). Also controls onion-skinning in the Paint window.
Insert	Insertion and deletion of keyframes and animation frames into the Score. Serves as an alternate way of inserting media cast members into the Cast window (the library of resources that Director uses).
Modify	Changing properties for the movie, individual cast members (resources), sprites, and the Score. Also provides a means of editing text in a text field, modifying scripts (interpreted code that is attached to sprites or other interface elements and that executes when designated events occur), rearranging the order of cast members on the Stage, and converting cast members to different bit depths.
Control	Playback of Director, moving from frame to frame, setting volume, handling sprite recording, debugging features, and recompiling scripts.
Xtras	Gives information and access to Xtras (Director plug-ins) and graphic filter Xtras. Protecting and updating older versions of Director movies, and importing PowerPoint files.
Window	Calls up any control windows used in Director, such as the Score, the Cast window, the Bitmap editor, the Library palette, Text Inspectors, and others.
Help	Accesses Director Help, which provides a detailed help and indexing system for all sorts of Director and scripting problems. Also calls up Help tutorials. Accesses registration information and links to Macromedia's Web site.

6.3.7 Cast Libraries

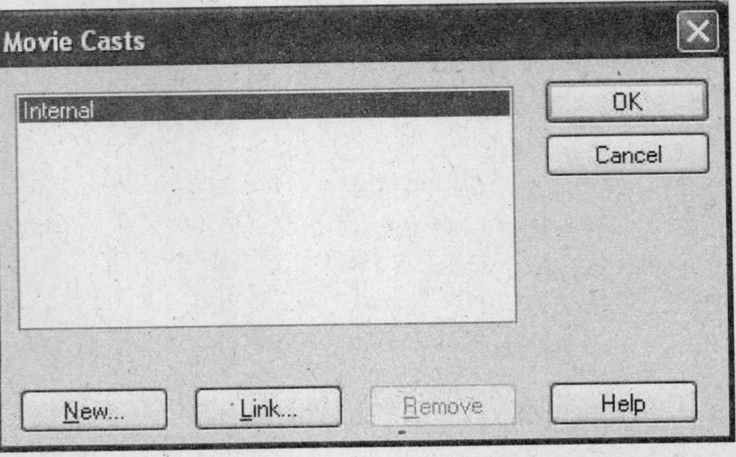

Represents a single cast library within a movie. A movie can consist of one or more cast libraries. A cast library can consist of one or more cast members, which represent media in a movie, such as sounds, text, graphics, and other movies.

You can link cast libraries to a movie by choosing Modify, Movie and then Casts. Having a linked file of any sort means that the information about that file is kept in a separate file rather than within the Director movie itself. For example, if you linked a bitmap image, every time Director started up it would load that image from the disk, rather than from its own internal resources. This approach has the advantage of making it easier to work with dynamic files, or pictures that change on a regular basis. The disadvantage comes from the location of the file; the picture (or other resource) is not already contained in the movie, so it has to be processed into a Director cast member. Depending on the size and type of the image, this process can involve an appreciable wait.

6.3.8 Painting Techniques

Director uses its graphics editor, the Paint window, for most of its painting requirements. Creating successive frames of an animation is relatively easy to do with the Paint window and it offers several unique tools, such as onion skinning and registration points, to help you.

You can open the Paint window at any time within Director by choosing Window, Paint. If no cast member was selected, then the Paint window automatically creates a fresh canvas on which to paint. If you dis-select a cast member before opening the Paint window, it will open with that cast member at the ready. Unless your images use an external editor, you can also double-click a bitmap cast member to open it up in the Paint window.

The various brushes and other tools used in the Paint window are likely to be familiar to anyone who has used another paint program. They are represented by the double vertical column of buttons in the Tools palette located on the left side of the Paint window.

The following table shows all the Paint Window Tools.

Icon	*Tool name*	*Paint Operations*
	Lasso	Free-form selection tool. Used to select irregularly shaped areas. Also can be set to Shrink in order to exclude background colours.
	Marquee	Rectangular selection tool. This is the required selection mode for most special effects. Can be set to Shrink, in order to exclude background colours.
	Registration Point	Determines the registration point of the graphic when drawn on the Stage. Double-click this button to set the registration point to the center of the graphic.
	Eraser	Paints the graphic with the selected background colour. Double clicking the button erases the whole screen.
	Hand	Used to move the graphic around. Especially useful with the Magnifying Glass tool.
	Magnifying Glass	Doubles the current magnification of the image, up to eight times. If the shift key is held down, clicking the image while this tool is active zooms back out, in increments of 50 percent, to the original size of the image.

	Eyedropper	Sets the foreground colour to the colour under the Eyedropper's tip.
	Paint Bucket	Fills all contignous pixels of the same colour and pattern with the foreground colour and pattern.
	Text	Places text into the graphic. This text can only be edited while the insertion point is active; after that, it becomes part of the graphic.
	Pencil	Draws a line 1 pixel wide. If any colour but the foreground colour is selected, the line is drawn in the foreground colour; otherwise, the background colour is used.
	Air Brush	Creates a random pattern of dots of varying sizes. Can be used for texturing effects, but does not work as well as airbrushes in other programs.
	Paint Brush	Paints the graphic with the foreground colour, using the selected ink. By clicking and holding down the mouse button, you can select an alternate brush.
	Arc	Draws an arc, using the currently selected line width to draw the curve. Click and drag to establish the starting tangent, and then drag to the end point.
	Line	Draws a line. Click to establish the line, and then drag to pull it to its full length. Constrain the line horizontally, vertically, or to a 45-degree angle by pressing the Shift key while drawing the line.
	Filled Rectangle	Paints a filled rectangle, using the current foreground colour and pattern. If a non-zero line width is selected, the rectangle will have a border of that width.
	Rectangle	Paints a hollow rectangle, using the current foreground colour and line width.
	Filled Ellipse	Paints a filled oval, using the current foreground colour. If a non-zero line width is selected, the oval will have a border of that width.
	Ellipse	Paints a hollow oval, using the current foreground colour and line width.

	Tool	Description
	Filled polygon	Paints a filled polygon, using the current foreground colour, pattern, and line-width. Click once at each vertex of the polygon, and then double-click to complete the shape.
	Polygon	Paints a hollow polygon, using the current foreground colour and line width. Click at each vertex of the polygon, and then double click to complete the shape.
	Foreground/	Allows selection of the foreground and background colours. The foreground is the top-left colour chip; the background is the bottom-right colour chip. Clicking either colour chip opens the Colour palette of colour choices.
	Gradient Colours	Sets the start and destination colours of a gradient.
	Pattern	Selects the pattern fill to be used with the Tool palette's filled shapes. Foreground and background colours of the pattern are selected in the Foreground/ Background Colour Selector.
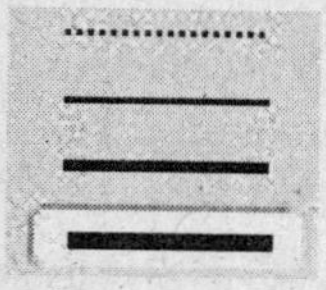	Line Weight Selector	Selects the line weight to be used by the Tool palette's various drawing tools. Choose from No Line, One Pixel Line, Two Pixel Line and Three Pixel Line.

6.3.9 Importing Images

Importing lets you create cast members from external media. You can either import data into a Director movie file or create a link to the external file and re-import the file each time the movie opens. Linked files let you display dynamic media from the Internet, such as sports scores, sounds, and weather pictures, which makes downloading movies faster.

Director can import cast members from almost every popular media file format.

You can import files by using the Import dialog box, dragging files from the desktop to a Cast window, or by using Lingo or JavaScript syntax.

6.3.9.1 To import cast members and specify import options:

1. In Thumbnail view, select an empty position in a cast.

   If no cast position is selected, Director places the new cast member in the first available position in the current cast in Thumbnail view. In List view, Director places the new cast member at the end of the list.
2. Select File > Import.
3. To import a file from the Internet, click Internet and enter a URL in the Find URL text box.

4. To import local files, select the type of media to import from the Files of Type (Windows) or the Show (Macintosh) pop-up menu.

   All the files in the current directory appear unless you make a selection.

5. To select a file or files to import, do one of the following:

   · Double-click a file.

   · Select one or more files, and click Add.

   · Click Add All.

   · You can switch folders and import files from different folders at the same time.

6. From the Media pop-up menu at the bottom of the dialog box, select an option to specify how to treat imported media:

   Standard Import imports all selected files, storing them inside the movie file but not updating them when changes are made to the source material. If you select the option to import from the Internet in step 3, Director retrieves the file immediately from the Internet if a connection is available.

   All digital video files like DVD, Windows Media, QuickTime, RealMedia, and so on, are linked automatically to the original external file (see the next option, Link to External File), even if you select Standard Import.

   Link to External File creates a link to the selected files and imports the data each time the movie runs. If you choose to import from a URL via the Internet, the media is dynamically updated. For more information, see About linking to files.

   Text and RTF files are always imported and stored inside the movie file (see the previous option, Standard Import), even if you select Link to External File.

   Include Original Data for Editing preserves the original data in the movie file for use with an external editor.

   When this option is selected, Director keeps a copy of the original cast member data and sends the original to the external editor when you edit the cast member. This option preserves all the editor's capabilities. For example, if you specify Photoshop to edit PICT images, Director maintains all the Photoshop object data.

   · Import PICT File as PICT prevents PICT files from being converted to bitmaps.

7. When you finish selecting the files, click Import.

   If you've imported a bitmap with a colour depth or colour palette that differs from the current movie, the Image Options dialog box appears, so you can enter additional information.

6.3.9.2 To import files by dragging:

1. In the Explorer (Windows) or on the system desktop (Macintosh), select a file or files to import.

2. Drag the files from the desktop to the desired position in the Cast window Thumbnail view or to the Cast window List view.

   If you drag the files to List view, the imported files are added at the bottom of the list.

6.3.9.3 To import files with Lingo or JavaScript syntax:

· Use the ImportFileInto method to import a file. Set the file Name cast member property to assign a new file to a linked cast member. For more information about this property, see the Scripting Reference topics in the Director Help Panel.

6.3.10 Working with Stage

The Stage is the part of a movie that your users will see. You use the Stage to determine where media elements, or cast members, should appear onscreen. When you determine where you want the cast member to appear, you place a copy of that cast member, called a sprite, on the Stage.

During authoring, you can define the properties of the Stage, such as its size and colour. For example, as you work on your movie, you can make the Stage either larger or smaller than its original size. You can also scale the coordinates for the sprites on the Stage, so that they continue to fill the entire screen. Guides, grids, and Align and Tweak windows are available to align sprites on the Stage.

6.3.10.1 Placing Flash content on the Stage

Lingo or JavaScript syntax can set whether Flash content appears at the front of the Stage and whether specific areas of Flash content and the Stage overlap.

- To determine whether Flash content plays in front of all other layers on the Stage and whether ink effects work, set the directToStage property.
- To determine which Stage coordinate coincides with a specified coordinate in Flash content, use the flashToStage method.
- To determine which Flash content coordinate coincides with a specified coordinate on the Director Stage, use the stageToFlash method.
- To improve performance for a Director movie that uses static (not animated) Flash content, set the static property.
- To control whether the Flash content graphics are visible, set the imageEnabled property.
- To control whether the Flash content plays sounds, set the sound property.
- To control whether Director uses anti-aliasing to render Flash content, set the quality property.

6.3.11 Sprites and Score

A sprite is an object that controls when, where, and how cast members appear in a Macromedia Director MX 2004 movie. Multiple sprites can use the same cast member. You can also switch cast members assigned to a sprite as the movie plays. You use the Stage to control where a sprite appears, and you use the Score to control when it appears in your movie.

Sprites appear on the Stage layered according to the channel in which they are assigned in the Score. Sprites in higher-numbered channels appear in front of sprites in lower-numbered channels. A movie can include as many as 1000 sprite channels. Use the Movie tab of the Property inspector to control the number of channels.

Sprite properties include the sprite's size and location, the cast member assigned to the sprite, the sprite's name, and the frames in which the sprite occurs. Different properties can alter the appearance of a sprite. You can rotate, skew, flip, and change the colour of sprites without affecting cast members. You can change sprite properties with the Property inspector or Lingo or JavaScript syntax.

You can also give each sprite a unique name. You can assign a name by using the Property inspector, and then view the sprite by name in the Score and on the Stage. Assigning a name lets you refer to the sprite by that name in Lingo or JavaScript syntax and not just by the channel number that it occupies.

You can move a sprite to a different channel and not worry about changing scripts. Editing scores and code scripts is much easier when you refer to a sprite by its name.

In Lingo or JavaScript syntax, some properties are available only for certain types of sprites. Such properties typically are characteristics that are related to the specific sprite type. For example, Lingo or JavaScript syntax has several digital video properties that determine the contents of tracks in digital video sprites.

6.3.11.1 Changing when a sprite appears on the Stage

A sprite controls where and when media appears on the Stage. You can change when a sprite appears on the Stage by moving the sprite to different frames in the Score and by changing the number of frames the sprite spans. You can either drag sprites to new frames or copy and paste them. Copying and pasting is easier when moving sprites more than one screen width in the Score. You can also copy and paste to move sprites from one movie to another.

When you copy a sprite from one movie to another, save the source movie first.

6.3.11.2 Moving a sprite in the Score

To change when a sprite appears on the Stage:

1. Select Window > Score to display the Score.
2. Select a sprite or sprites.
3. Drag the sprite to a different frame.

To move a sprite without spreading it over additional frames, hold down the Spacebar and drag. This technique is also useful for moving any sprite that consists mostly (or entirely) of keyframes.

To copy or move sprites between frames:

1. Select a sprite or sprites.
2. Select Edit > Cut Sprites or Edit > Copy Sprites.
3. Position the pointer where you want to paste the sprite, and select Edit > Paste Sprites.

   If the pasting will overwrite existing sprites, select one of the following Paste options in the Paste Options dialog box:

   Overwrite Existing Sprites replaces the sprites with the content of the Clipboard.

   Truncate Sprites Being Pasted pastes the Clipboard contents in the space available without replacing existing sprites.

   Insert Blank Frames to Make Room adds new frames for the contents of the Clipboard.

6.3.12 Using Text

You have several options for creating Text cast members. Each method of adding text to your movie has advantages that recommend it for a specific application. You can:

1. Add text directly to the Stage.
2. Enter text in the Text window.
3. Import text created in other applications.

The Text tool in Director's Tool palette enables you to add text directly on the Stage, in the location you choose. The Text-tool method of creating text is ideal when you need small amounts of text, such as a title that is precisely positioned on the Stage. When you create text using this method, you must edit the text attributes by using the Text inspector.

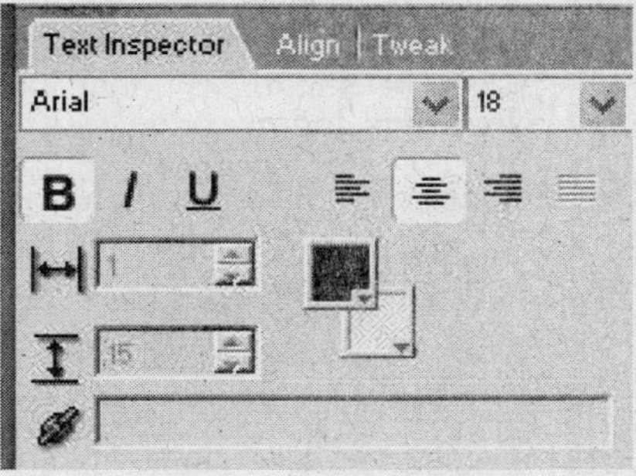

When you need larger blocks of text, importing the text or using the Text window is a better choice. The Text window, like most word processors, enables you to format text as you create it, including applying size, style, and alignment attributes to the text. Text created in the Text window can be edited any time to change the attributes, the formatting, or the text itself. You can edit text either on the Stage or in the Text editing window.

6.3.12.1 Using Text Window

The Text window enables you to create and format blocks of text. It contains features for formatting text as well as for applying text attributes. Although not suitable for large, multipage documents such as books, the Text window works well for creating blocks of text to use in your movies. You might require a couple of paragraphs, for example, to describe your product or services. You can edit a Text cast member at any time during the development of your movie, even while it is running. In addition to the format of the text itself, you can specify text properties that tell Director how you want to display your text. Creating a Text cast member in the Text window is a simple matter of opening the Text window and entering the text you want to use.

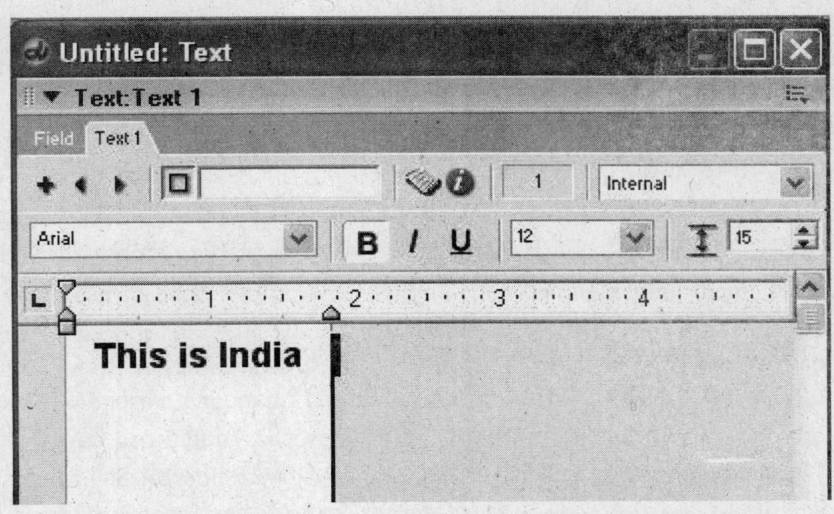

6.3.13 Using Sound

Sounds can take a movie from the mundane to the spectacular. They can inform, guide, and stimulate the interest of the user. Understanding the basics of Director's use of sound provides the foundation you need for using sounds creatively and efficiently in your movies.

Two key issues should be behind every audio decision you make when working with Director and sounds:

- The needs of your audience: A sound should enhance the movie while balancing the needs and resources of the user.
- File size: Sound files can be huge, requiring significant resources to store and play them. Therefore, the idea is to choose and edit sounds carefully, to balance creativity and file size.

6.3.13.1 *Importing internal and linked sounds*

Director handles sounds as either internal or linked. You can determine whether a sound is internal or linked when you import it. Each type of sound has advantages for different situations.

Director stores all the sound data for an internal sound cast member in a movie or cast file and loads the sound completely into RAM before playing it. After an internal sound is loaded, it plays very quickly. This makes internal sound best for short sounds, such as beeps or clicks, that recur frequently in your movie. For the same reason, making a large sound file an internal sound is not a good choice because the sound might use too much memory.

Director does not store sound data in a linked sound cast member. Instead, it keeps a reference to a sound file's location and imports the sound data each time the sound begins playing. Because the sound is never entirely loaded into RAM, the movie uses memory more efficiently.

Also, Director streams many sounds, which means it begins playing the sound while the rest of the sound continues to load from its source, whether on disk or over the Internet. This can dramatically improve the downloading performance of large sounds. Linked sounds are best for longer sounds such as voice-overs or non-repeating music.

Director can stream the following sounds:

- QuickTime, Shockwave Audio, and MP3 sounds that are linked from a URL.
- QuickTime, Shockwave Audio, MP3, AIFF, and WAV sounds that are linked to a local file.

Director imports AIFF and WAV sounds (both compressed and uncompressed), AU, Shockwave Audio, and MP3. For best results, use sounds that have 8- or 16-bit depth and a sampling rate of 44.1, 22.050, or 11.025 kHz.

6.3.13.2 *To import a sound:*

1. Select File > Import.
2. Select sound files to import.
3. To determine whether the imported sounds are internal or linked, select a Media option:

   Standard Import makes all the selected sounds internal sound cast members.

   Link to External File makes all the selected sounds linked.

   Include Original Data for Editing lets you edit original sound files in Director.
4. Click Import dialog box.

6.3.14 Using Digital Video

Digital video is simply the result of capturing, storing, transmitting, and displaying a rapid succession of digitized images on a computer. The why of digital video is perhaps as important as the what. Digital video provides a superior means of transmitting images and sounds of real-world events and animations in your Director movies. The result, of course, is that the impact of your movies on your audience increases.

Director uses several video formats, AVI (Video for Windows), Windows Media, DVD content, RealMedia, and QuickTime. AVI and Windows Media movies can be imported into Director only from the Windows platform.

6.3.14.1 *Playing digital video direct-to-Stage*

Director can play digital video using a feature called direct-to-Stage. Direct-to-stage lets video drivers installed on the computer completely control the video playback.

The direct-to-Stage feature cannot be used with DVD or RealMedia digital video because DVD is always direct-to-stage and RealMedia is always non-direct-to-stage.

Direct-to-stage often provides the best performance from a digital video, but it has two disadvantages:

- The digital video always appears in front of all other sprites on the Stage, no matter which channel contains the sprite.
- Ink effects do not work, so it is difficult to conceal the video's bounding rectangle with Background Transparent ink.

When direct-to-Stage is off, Director layers a digital video on the Stage exactly the same as other sprites, and Background Transparent ink works normally. (Matte ink does not work for digital video sprites.)

6.3.14.2 *To set direct-to-Stage options:*

1. Select a digital video cast member or sprite.
2. Click the QuickTime or Windows Media tab in the Property inspector.
3. Select or deselect Direct-to-Stage (DTS).
4. If the cast member or sprite is a QuickTime video, select one of the following Playback options:

   Sync to Soundtrack makes the digital video skip frames (if necessary) to keep up with its soundtrack. The digital video might also take less time to play.

   Play Every Frame makes every frame of the digital video appear but does not play the soundtrack because the video cannot play the soundtrack asynchronously while the video portion plays frame by frame. Depending on the data rate of the digital video, the sprite might play more smoothly with this option selected, but this is not a certainty. In addition, playing every frame might cause the digital video to take more time to play.
5. If the sprite or cast member is a QuickTime video, select Controls to display a controller bar below the movie to let the user to start, stop, and step through the movie.

6.3.15 Creating Behaviour

Without any scripting or programming experience, you can use the Behaviour inspector to create and modify Behaviours to perform basic actions. To create Behaviours with more complex structures, you must understand scripting in Lingo or JavaScript syntax. Using the Behaviour inspector is a good way to learn Lingo or JavaScript syntax. You can examine the scripts created by the Behaviour inspector to see how basic functions are assembled. To view the associated script, select any Behaviour and click the Script button.

Most Behaviours detect an event and then perform one or more actions in response. The Behaviour inspector lists the most common events and actions used in Behaviours. For experienced programmers, the Behaviour inspector also provides a shortcut for writing simple scripts.

To always edit Behaviours in the Script window instead of the Behaviour inspector, select Edit > Preferences > Editors. In the Editors Preferences dialog box, select Behaviours from the list and then click Edit. In the Select Editor box, select Script Window. (If you are using a Macintosh OS X operating system, select the Director menu, instead of the Edit menu, to access Preferences.)

To create or modify a Behaviour:

Do one of the following:

- To create a new Behaviour, click the Behaviours pop-up menu, select New Behaviour, and enter a name for the new Behaviour.

  The Behaviour appears in the currently selected Cast window in the first empty position. Select an empty cast position first if you want the Behaviour to appear in a different place.
- To modify a Behaviour, select it in the Behaviour inspector.

  Click the arrow in the lower left of the Behaviour inspector to expand the editing pane.

The editing pane shows the events and actions in the current Behaviour. If you are creating a new Behaviour, no events or actions appear.

- To add a new event or action group to the Behaviour, select an event from the Events pop-up menu and then select actions for the event from the Actions pop-up menu.

  You can choose as many actions as you need for a single event.
- To change an existing event or action group, select an event from the list and then add or remove actions in the Actions list.
- To delete an event or action group, select the event and press Delete.
- To change the sequence of actions in an event or action group, select an event from the Events list, select an action from the Actions list, and then click the up and down arrows above the Actions list to change the order of actions.
- To lock the current selection so that nothing changes in the Behaviour inspector when new sprites are selected, click the Lock Selection button in the lower left of the expanded Behaviour inspector.

If you are familiar with Lingo or JavaScript syntax, you can also edit a Behaviour's script directly.

6.3.16 Using Behaviour Inspector

The Behaviour Inspector provides a means for you to view and edit existing predefined Behaviours and to create new ones in a cast. You cannot modify or delete Behaviours in the Library palette, but you can view, edit, delete, or create a Behaviour in the Cast window.

The Behaviour Inspector, provides easy access to information about the Behaviour, including Behaviour's name, type, script, description, the names and values of any parameters (properties) associated with the Behaviour, and the span of frames to which the Behaviour is applied. You can open the Behaviour Inspector by choosing Window, Behaviour Inspector.

The Behaviour Inspector is built on a series of panes that can be collapsed or expaned as needed. In its default state, these panes are hidden. You click the two triangles on the left side of the Inspector to expand or collapse the panes.

6.3.17 Basics of Lingo

Both Lingo and JavaScript syntax use some terms that are specific to each language, in addition to some terms that are shared between each language.

Important scripting terms are listed here in alphabetical order. These terms are used throughout the *Director Scripting Reference*, so it will help to understand these terms before moving forward.

- Constants are elements whose values do not change. For example, in Lingo, constants such as TAB, EMPTY, and RETURN always have the same values, and cannot be modified. In JavaScript syntax, constants such as Math.PI and Number.MAX_VALUE always have the same values, and cannot be modified. You can also create your own custom constants in JavaScript syntax by using the keyword const.
- Events are actions that occur while a movie is playing. Events occur when a movie stops, a sprite starts, the playhead enters a frame, the user types at the keyboard, and so on. All events in Director are predefined, and always have the same meaning.
- Expressions are any part of a statement that produces a value. For example, 2 + 2 is an expression.
- Functions refer to either top-level functions or specific types of JavaScript syntax code.

  A top-level function instructs a movie to do something while the movie is playing or returns a value, but it is not called from any specific object. For example, you would call the top-level list() function by using the syntax list(). Like a function, a method also instructs a movie to do something while the movie is playing or returns a value, but it is always called from an object.

  A function is used in JavaScript syntax to represent an event handler, a custom object, a custom method, and so on. The use of JavaScript functions in these cases is described in the applicable topics later in this reference.
- Handlers, or event handlers, are sets of statements within a script that run in response to a specific event and subsequent message. When an event occurs, Director generates and sends a corresponding message to scripts, and a corresponding handler runs in response to the message. The names of handlers are always the same as the events and messages they respond to.

  Although in JavaScript syntax an event is actually handled by a function, the term *handler* is used generically throughout this reference to refer to both Lingo handlers and JavaScript syntax functions that handle events.
- Keywords are reserved words that have a special meaning. For example, in Lingo, the keyword end indicates the end of a handler. In JavaScript syntax, the keyword var indicates that the term following it is a variable.
- Lists (Lingo) or Arrays (JavaScript syntax) are ordered sets of values used to track and update an array of data, such as a series of names or the values assigned to a set of variables. A simple example is a list of numbers such as [1, 4, 2].
- Messages are notices that Director sends to scripts when specific events occur in a movie. For example, when the playhead enters a specific frame, the enterFrame event occurs and Director sends an enterFrame message. If a script contains an enterFrame handler, the statements within that handler will run, because the handler received the enterFrame message. If no scripts contain a handler for a message, the message is ignored in script.
- Methods are terms that either instruct a movie to do something while the movie is playing or return a value, and are called from an object. For example, you would call the insertFrame() method from the Movie object, using the syntax _movie.insertFrame(). Although similar in

functionality to top-level functions, methods are always called from an object, and top-level functions are not.

- Operators are terms that calculate a new value from one or more values. For example, the addition (+) operator adds two or more values together to produce a new value.
- Parameters are placeholders that let you pass values to scripts. Parameters only apply to methods and event handlers, and not to properties. They are required by some methods and optional for others.

  For example, the Movie object's go() method sends the playhead to specific frame, and optionally specifies the name of the movie that frame is in. To perform this task, the go() method requires at least one parameter, and allows for a second parameter. The first required parameter specifies what frame to send the playhead to, and the second optional parameter specifies what movie the frame is in. Because the first parameter is required, a script error will result if it is not present when the go() method is called. Because the second parameter is optional, the method will perform its task even if the parameter is not present.
- Properties are attributes that define an object. For example, a sprite in a movie has specific attributes, such as how wide it is, how tall it is, its background colour, and so on. To access the values of these three specific attributes, you would use the Sprite object's width, height, and backColour properties.
- Statements are valid instructions that Director can execute. All scripts are made up of sets of statements. The following Lingo is a single complete statement.

  _movie.go("Author")
- Variables are elements used to store and update values. Variables must start with a letter, an underscore (_), or the dollar sign ($). Subsequent characters in a variable name can also be digits (0-9). To assign values to variables or change the values of many properties, you use the equals (=) operator.

6.4 Flash

Flash is the most popular program for creating animations not only for Windows based programs but for Internet. Lots of web sites are using Flash tools to create animations to enhance the looks of the site. It is a vector graphics file format (extension .swf) developed by Macromedia to enable designers to add animation and interactivity to multimedia Web pages. Flash files can be played back with a downloadable Shockwave plug-in or a Java program. The file format has been released by Macromedia as an open standard for the Internet.

6.4.1 Starting Flash CS3

Since Flash CS3 is a windows based program, it can be started by using the Start button and then clicking at the Programs and Adobe Design Premium CS3 submenu. This leads to the submenu of Adobe Design Premium CS3. From here you click at Adobe Flash CS3 Professional to start the program.

Once the software starts, it gives rise to an opening screen which is shown next. It asks you what step you want to perform. Click at that to start. Clicking at New Document will give rise to a blank page, which is shown on next to next page.

Primarly there is Timeline window. The items on this window can be described as next.

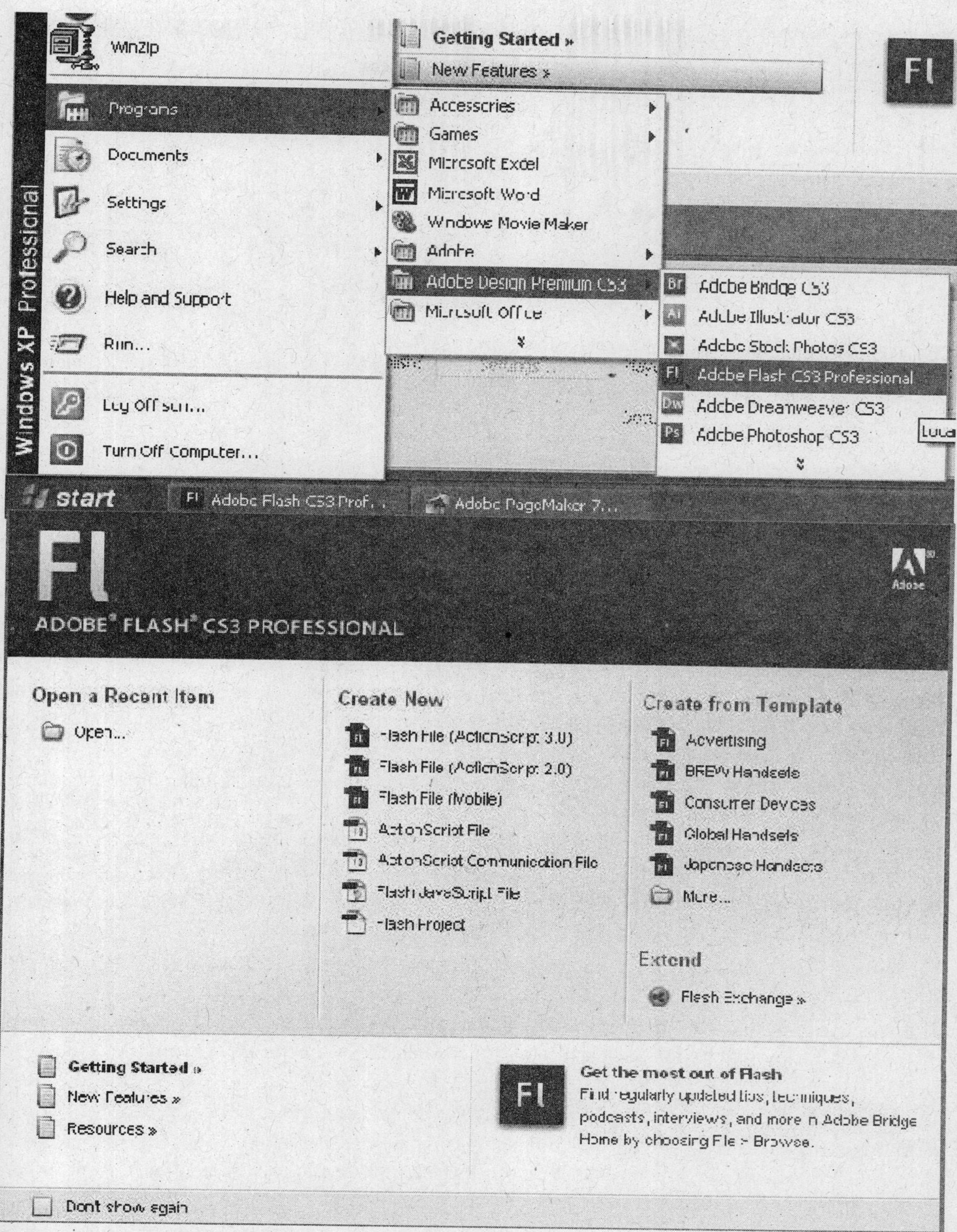
WinZip
Programs
Documents
Settings
Search
Help and Support
Run...
Log Off
Turn Off Computer...
Windows XP Professional
start
Adobe Flash CS3 Prof...
Adobe PageMaker 7...
Getting Started »
New Features »
Accessories
Games
Microsoft Excel
Microsoft Word
Windows Movie Maker
Adobe
Adobe Design Premium CS3
Microsoft Office
Adobe Bridge CS3
Adobe Illustrator CS3
Adobe Stock Photos CS3
Adobe Flash CS3 Professional
Adobe Dreamweaver CS3
Adobe Photoshop CS3
Fl
ADOBE® FLASH® CS3 PROFESSIONAL
Adobe
Open a Recent Item
Open...
Create New
Flash File (ActionScript 3.0)
Flash File (ActionScript 2.0)
Flash File (Mobile)
ActionScript File
ActionScript Communication File
Flash JavaScript File
Flash Project
Create from Template
Advertising
BREW Handsets
Consumer Devices
Global Handsets
Japanese Handsets
More...
Extend
Flash Exchange »
Getting Started »
New Features »
Resources »
Get the most out of Flash
Find regularly updated tips, techniques, podcasts, interviews, and more in Adobe Bridge Home by choosing File > Browse.
Don't show again

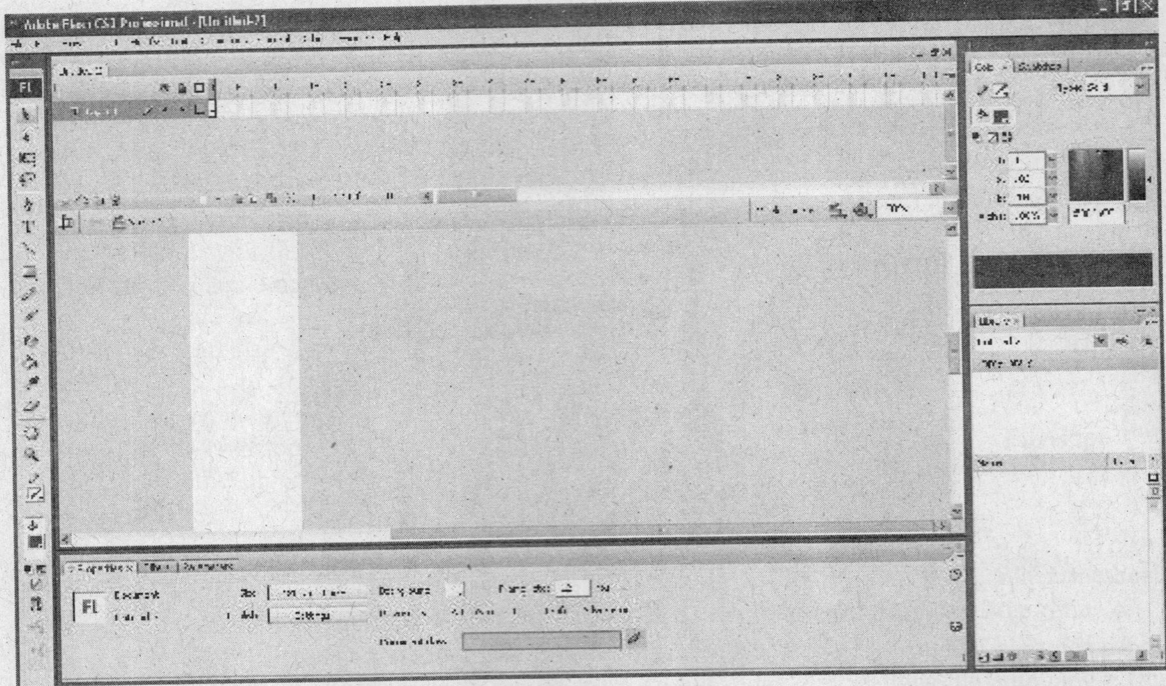

Title bar: This bar has the title.

Active Layer Toggle: To make a layer active, either click the layerbar, or select a frame or group of frames.

Show/Hide Layer Toggle: Click the dot beneath the eyeball icon to hide the contents of this layer from view on the stage. When the layer is hidden, a red X appears over the dot. To return the layer to visibility, click the X.

Lock/Unlock Layer Toggle: This toggle locks or unlocks the layer to either prevent or enable further editing.

Layer Colour Toggle: This toggles the coloured layer outlines on or off. When on, the dot changes into a small square outline of the same colour as the outlines for the layer.

Playhead or Current Frame Indicator: The Playhead indicates the current Frame. Drag it along the Timeline to move from one area of the Timeline to another.

Timeline Header: The Timeline Header is the ruler that measures the time of the timeline: each tick is one frame.

Frame View Options Button: This button accesses the Frame View Options opp-up menu that affords many options for the manner in which both the Timeline Header and the Frames are displayed.

Insert Layer: This is used to insert a new layer above the currently active layer.

Add Motion Guide: Motion guide layers let you draw paths along which tweened instances, groups, or text blocks can be animated. You can link multiple layers to a motion guide layer to have multiple objects follow the same path. A normal layer that is linked to a motion guide layer becomes a guided layer.

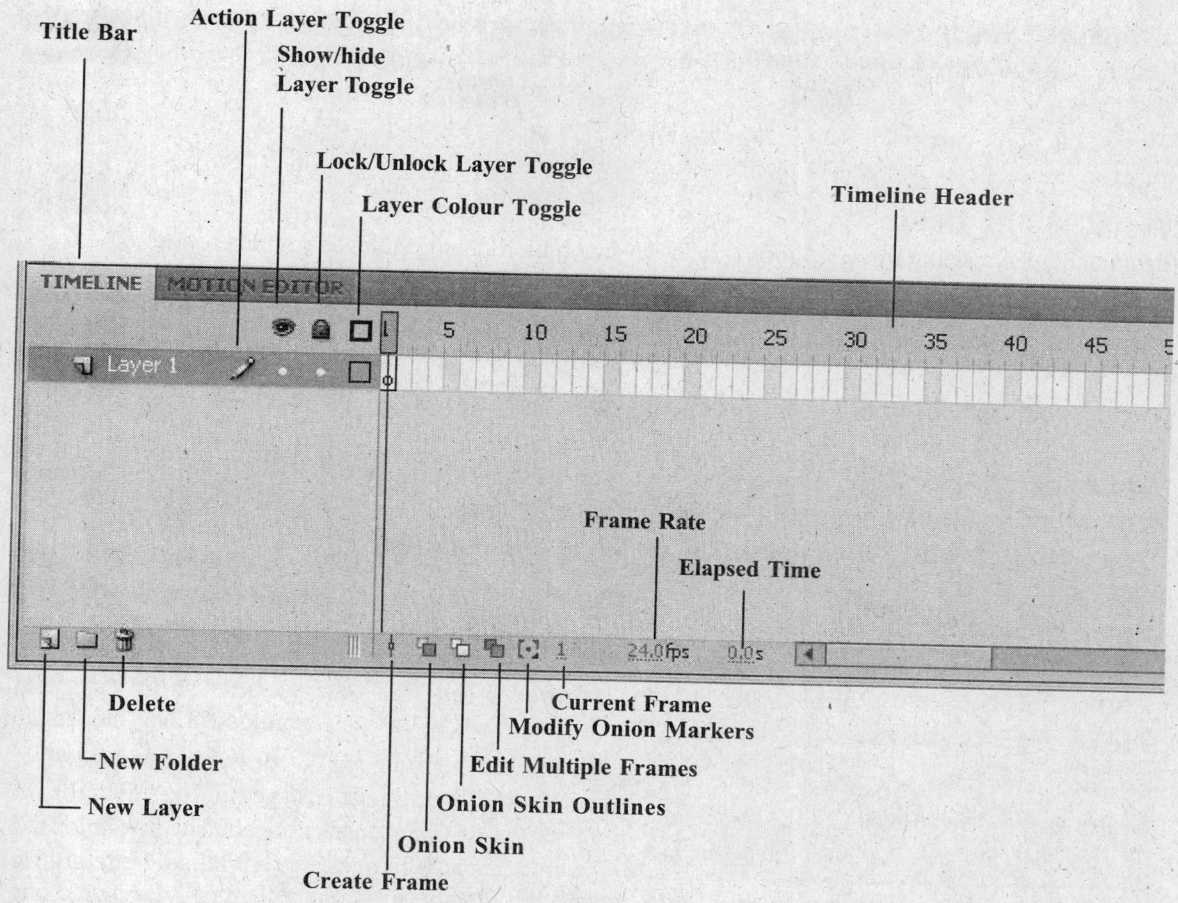

Insert Layer Folder: Adds a new folder in the layers.

Delete Layer: This button deletes the currently active layer.

Centre Frame: It is used to shift the Timeline so that the current frame is centered in the visible area of the Timeline.

Onion Skin: This feature enables you to see several frames of animation simultaneously.

Onion Skin Outlines: This enables you to see only the outlines of several frames of animation simultaneously.

Edit Multiple Frames: Click this button to make each frame between the Onion skin Markers editable.

Modify Onion Markers: Click the button to evoke the Modify Onion Markers pop-up. In addition to manual adjustments, these options are used to control the behaviour and range of Onion Skinning.

Current Frame: This indicates the number of the current Frame. It is very useful when working with small Frame sizes, which can be specified from the Frame View Options.

Frame Rate Indicator: This displays the Frame Rate of the Movie as it plays.

Elapsed Time: This indicates the total movie time, measured in seconds, that would elapse from frame 1 to the current frame—provided that the movie is played back at the specified frames per second.

Before we going any further and see what is there on the screen of Flash CS3, let us first understand what is there under the various menu bars, starting with File menu.

6.4.2 File menu

Various options of the menu are:

New: This command generates a new document.

Open: Use this command to open an existing Flash compatible file from the Open dialog box which it opens. The various files which can be opened are: .fla (flash movie), .spa (futuresplash movie), .ssk (smart sketch drawing), and .swf (flash player movie).

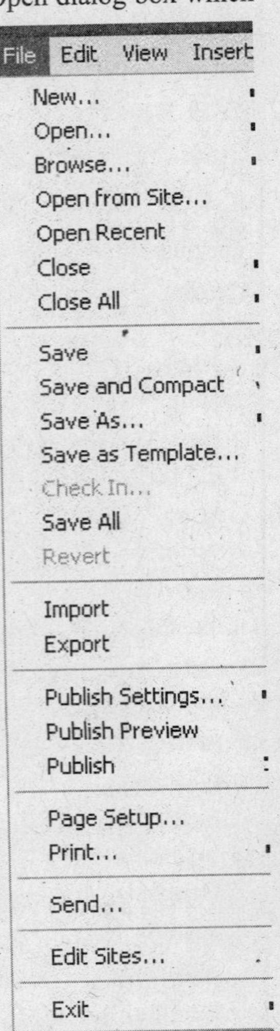

Browse: This command allows you to browse through the various files and then select the one you want to open.

Open from Site: This command allows you to select file from the web site.

Open recent: This command allows you to select one of the recently opened files.

Close: This command would close any open movie.

Close All: This command would close all the open movies.

Save: This command will save the current movie.

Save and Compact: This command would not only save the file for you but also make it compact for better handling.

Save As: This command will allow you to save the current movie under a new name.

Save As Template: This command will allows you to save your animation in the form of a template.

Save All: This command would save all the open files.

Revert: This command will lead you to the previously saved version of the file.

Import: This command allows you to import files of various other formats. Among the accepted format are: .emf (Enhanced Metafile), .wmf (Windows Metafile), .wav (Sound files), .eps or .ai (Adobe Illustrator), .swf or .spl (Flash Player), .dxf (AutoCAD DXF), .bmp or .dib (Bitmap), .jpg (JPEG Image), .gif (GIF Image), .png (PNG Image). Among the various options under this are: Import to Stage, Import to Library, and Open External Library.

Export: This command will allow the current movie to a new file with a new format. The formats in which it can be saved are: .swf (Flash Player), .swt (Geneartor Template), .spl (FutureSplash Player), .avi (Windows AVI), .mov (Quick/Time), .gif (Animated GIF), .wav (WAV audio), .emf (EMF Sequence), .wmf (WMF sequence), .eps (EPS 3.0 Sequence), .ai(Adobe Illustrator

Sequence), .dxf(AutoCAD DXF), .bmp(Bitmap), .jpg(JPEG Sequence) and .png (PNG Sequence). Among the various options under this command are: Emport Image and Export Movie.

Publish Setting: This command allows you to publish the settings of the current file.

Publish Preview: This command lists all the file types currently available which include HTML, Flash, GIF, etc.

Publish: This command will allow Flash to create the new files whereeyer the Flash movie was last saved.

Page Setup: This command will allow you to set margins, paper size, and different options of the layout.

Print: Use this command to print the current movie frame on the printer.

Send: This command allows you to send e-mail messages from Flash CS3.

Edit Sites: This allows you to edit the files from the site.

Exit: This allows you to exit from Flash CS3.

6.4.3 Edit menu

Various options of the menu are:

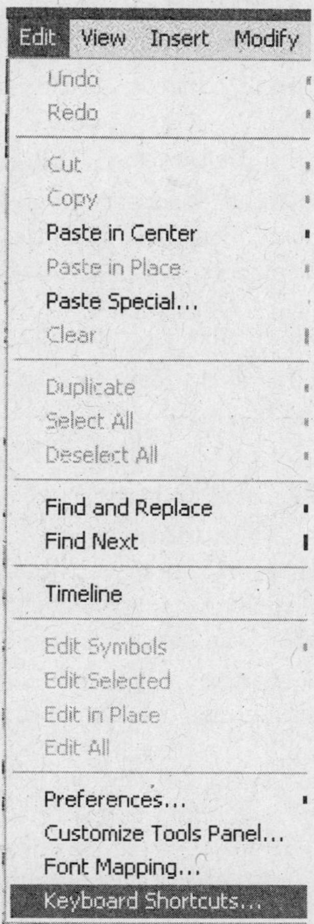

Undo: This command allows you to undo the last command given by you.

Redo: If you suddenly realize that the command which you have undone, you can redo it.

Cut: This command allows the selected item to be cut and made available at clipboard for later use.

Copy: This command allows the selected item to be copied and made available at clipboard for later use.

Paste in Center: This command allows the item from clipboard to be pasted in the center of the frame.

Paste in Place: This command is very similar to Paste, except that it pastes item precisely in the same place from which it was copied.

Paste Special: This command pastes from the clipboard in a required format specified by you. The dialog box has the following options:

Source: This is readout displays the local path to the source of the item that is on the clipboard.

Paste: Click button.

Paste link: Another click button.

As: This field may have several choices depending upon the nature of the item and also on which button has been activated above.

Result: It indicates the result of the selected combination of the Paste/Paste Link and As options.

Display as Icon: This check box is enabled when any combination of these options permits the selected item to be pasted as icon.

Change Icon: This button is evoked when Display as Icon is enabled. Click to open the Change Icon dialog box.

Clear: This command clears the clipboard of all its contents.

Duplicate: This command is used to duplicate a selected item.

Select All: It selects all the selectable items on the desktop.

Deselect All: This command does the reverse of the above.

Find and Replace: This command finds the required text and allows it to be replaced with other.

Find Next: This command finds the next occurrence of the required text.

Timeline: It is a set of commands which are shown here.

Cut Frames: Cuts the frame and keeps it in memory for pasting it somewhere else.

Copy Frames: Copies the frame but keeps the original intact.

Paste Frames: Pastes the frames from the memory.

Clear Frames: Clears the frame..

Remove Frames: Removes the selected frames.

Select All Frames: Selects all the frames.

Edit Symbols: Select an instance of a symbol and choose this command to edit in symbol-editing mode.

Edit Selected: This command is only enabled if a group or symbol is selected on the stage.

Edit in Place: When you edit a symbol, Flash updates all the instances of that symbol in the movie. Flash provides three ways for you to edit symbols. You can edit the symbol in context with the other objects on the Stage using the Edit in Place command. Other objects are dimmed to distinguish them from the symbol you are editing. The name of the symbol you are editing is displayed in an information bar at the top of the Stage, to the right of to the current scene name.

Edit All: When editing a group, Edit All is used to go back to editing the normal Flash scene.

Preference: As you can see from the dialog box on the next page, there are 5 panels. Let us see what each one of them has.

General: This has the following options.

On launch: For On Launch options, select an option to specify which document Flash opens when you start the application. Select Show Start Page to display the Start Page. Select New Document to open a new, blank document. Select Last Documents Open to open the documents that were open when you last quit Flash. Select No Document to start Flash without opening a document.

Undo: For Undo, enter a value from 2 to 300 to set the number of undo/redo levels. Undo levels require memory; the more undo levels you use, the more system memory is consumed. The default is 100. Next select Document- or Object-level undo. Document-level undo maintains a single list of all your actions for the entire Flash document. Object-level undo maintains separate lists of your actions for each object in your Flash document. Object-level undo gives you greater flexibility, since you can undo an action on one object without having to also undo actions on other objects that may have been modified more recently than the target object.

Printing: For Printing Options, select Disable PostScript if you want to disable PostScript output when printing to a PostScript printer. By default, this option is deselected. Select this option if you have problems printing to a PostScript printer, but keep in mind that this will slow down printing.

Test Movie: For Test Movie Options, select Open Test Movie in Tabs to have Flash open a new document tab in the application window when you select Control > Test Movie. The default is to open the test movie in its own window.

Selection: For Selection Options, select or deselect Shift Select to control how Flash handles selection of multiple elements. When Shift Select is off, clicking additional elements adds them to the current selection. When Shift Select is on, clicking additional elements deselects other elements unless you hold down Shift. Select Show Tooltips to display tooltips when the pointer pauses over a control. Deselect this option if you don't want to see the tooltips. Select Contact Sensitive to have objects become selected when any part of them is included in the marquee rectangle when dragging with the Selection or Lasso tools. The default is that objects are only selected when the tool's marquee rectangle completely surrounds the object.

Timeline: For Timeline Options, select Span Based Selection to use span-based selection in the Timeline, rather than the default frame-based selection. Select Named Anchor on Scenes to have Flash make the first frame of each scene in a document a named anchor. Named anchors let you use the Forward and Back buttons in a browser to jump from scene to scene in a Flash application.

Highlight Color: For Highlight Color, select a color from the panel, or select Use Layer Color to use the current layer's outline color. For Project, select Close Files with Project to have all files in a project close when the project file is closed. Select Save Files on Test or Publish Project to have each file in a project saved whenever the project is tested or published.

ActionScript: This has the following options.

Editing Options: Choose whether you want automatic indentation, code hints, etc., from here.

Automatic indentation: When automatic indentation is turned on, the text you type after an opening parenthesis [(] or opening curly brace ({) is automatically indented according to the Tab Size setting in ActionScript preferences. For more information, see Formatting code.

Tab Size: It specifies the number of characters a new line is offset by when automatic indentation is turned on.

Code hints: It enables code hinting in the Script pane. For more information about using code hinting, see About code hinting in Flash.

Delay: It specifies the delay (in seconds) before code hints are displayed.

Font: It specifies the font used in the Script pane.

Use dynamic font mapping: It checks to ensure that the selected font family has the necessary glyphs to render each character. If not, Flash substitutes a font family that contains the necessary characters.

Encoding: It specifies the character encoding used when opening, saving, importing, and exporting ActionScript files.

Reload modified files: It lets you select when to see warnings about whether a script file is modified, moved, or deleted. Select between Always, Never, or Prompt.

• **Always** No warning is displayed when a change is detected, and the file is automatically reloaded.

• **Never** No warning is displayed when a change is detected, and the file remains in the current state.

• **Prompt (Default)** Warning is displayed when a change is detected, and you can choose whether or not to reload the file.

When building applications that involve external script files, this feature helps you avoid overwriting a script that a team member has modified since you opened the application, or publishing the application with older versions of scripts. The warnings let you automatically close a script, and reopen the newer, modified version.

Syntax colors: It specifies the colors for code coloring in your scripts. With code coloring enabled, you can select the colors to be displayed in the Script pane.

Language: It opens the ActionScript Settings dialog box.

AutoFormat: This has the options shown above and can be tried by clicking at each one one of them to see the result in the preview.

Clipboard: This has the following options.

Colour Depth: Choose none if you are only pasting back into Flash. If you want to copy bitmaps to the clipboard, choose a bitmap format.

Resolution: Choose the resolution at which you want to capture bitmaps.

Size Limit: If your computer has limited memory, choose None, else use this box to limit the use of RAM that will be gobbled up by bitmaps on the clipboard.

Smooth: It is antialiasing, which means that the edges of shapes and lines will be dithered to look smooth on the screen.

Gradients: This drop-down menu controls the quality of gradient fills that are created when copying to the Windows clipboard.

FreeHand Text: Select and maintain text as blocks to keep text editable in a pasted FreeHand file.

Drawing: This has the following options.

Pen Tool: Choose the options for tool from here.

Other options are:

Connect curves, **Smooth curves**, **Recognize lines**, **Recognize shapes** and **Click accuracy**.

Text: This has the following options.

Font Mapping Default: To select a font to use when substituting missing fonts in documents you open in Flash.

Vertical text: For Vertical Text options, select Default Text Orientation to make the default orientation of text vertical, which is useful for some Asian language fonts. By default, this option is deselected. Select Right to Left Text Flow to reverse the default text display direction. This option is deselected by default. Select No Kerning to turn off kerning for vertical text. This option is deselected by default but is useful to improve spacing for some fonts that use kerning tables.

Input Method: For Input Method, select the appropriate language.

Warnings: This has the following options, as shown in the figure below. You can choose them all to work normally in Flash CS3.

PSD File Importer: This has the following options, as shown in the figure below.

AI File Importer: This has the following options, as shown in the figure below.

Customize Tools Panel: Using this command you can customize your tools.

Font Mapping: This command is used for mapping the font which may be missing.

Keyboard Shortcuts: This command shows you the various keyboard shortcuts.

6.4.4 View menu

Various options of the menu are:

Go to: This command opens as submenu which has the options like First, Previous, Next and Last scenes. Select the one you want to see.

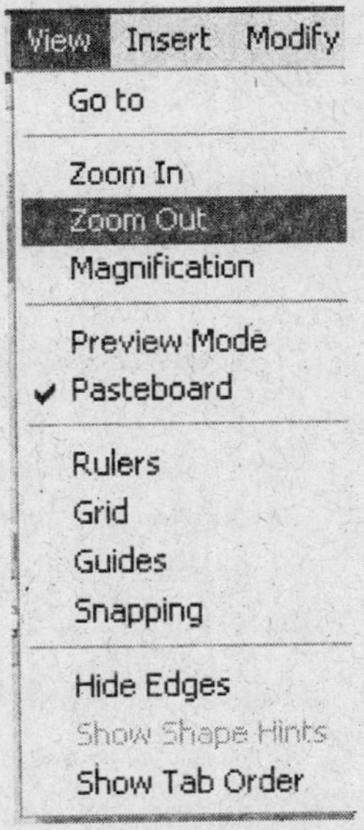

Zoom in: This command allows you to zoom in.

Zoom out: This command allows you to zoom out.

Magnification: This command allows you to choose the various options of magnification of your screen ranging from 25% to 800%, Show Frame and Show All.

Preview Mode: This command has the following options:

Outlines: This command allows user to see all the shapes as outlines, mainly used for reshaping graphics.

Fast: This command is used to speed up the display on the screen.

Anti-Alias: This command dithers the edges of the shapes and lines so that they look smoother on the screen. It also slows down the display.

Anti-Alias Text: This command also toggles with the Fast command. It smoothers the edges of text only and works best with large font sizes.

Full: This command is used to see the full preview on the screen.

Pasteboard: This command can make the light-grey area that surrounds the Stage visible.

Rulers: This command shows/hides the Rulers on or off the screen.

Grid: This command shows/hides the Drawing Grid on or off the screen. The option of Edit Grid is also there.

Guides: This command allows you to work on guides, like Show guides, Lock guides, Snap to guides and Edit guides.

Snapping: This command has the following options:

Snap Align: This command allows you to snap/unsnap the aligment of the object.

Snap to Grid: This command toggles to put Snap to Grid on or off.

Snap to Guides: This command toggles to put Snap to Guides on or off.

Snap to Pixels: This command toggles to put Snap to pixels on or off.

Snap to Objects: This command toggles between Snap to objects on or off.

Edit Snapping: This command allows you to edit the snap option of the object.

Hide Edges: This shows/hides edges on the screen.

Show Shape Hints: This command makes Shape hints visible/invisible from the screen.

Show Tab Order: This command makes Shape hints visible/invisible from the screen

6.4.5 Insert menu

Various options of the menu are:

New Symbol: This command is used to create a new symbol and work in Symbol editing mode.

Timeline: This command allows you to insert the following items:

Layer: This command creates a new layer directly above the active layer.

Layer Folder: This command adds a layer folder above the selected layer.

Motion Guide: This command adds a Motion Guide layer above the selected layer.

Frame: This command inserts a new frame at any selected point on the Timeline.

Keyframe: This command converts a selected frame into a Keyframe.

Blank Keyframe: This command inserts a new Keyframe at a selected point on the Timeline.

Create Motion Tween: This command is one step in the process of creating a tweened animation.

Timeline Effects: This command inserts various timeline effects as Assistants, Effects and Transform/Transition. Each one of them have options too.

Scene: This command inserts a new, empty Scene immediately following the currently active Scene.

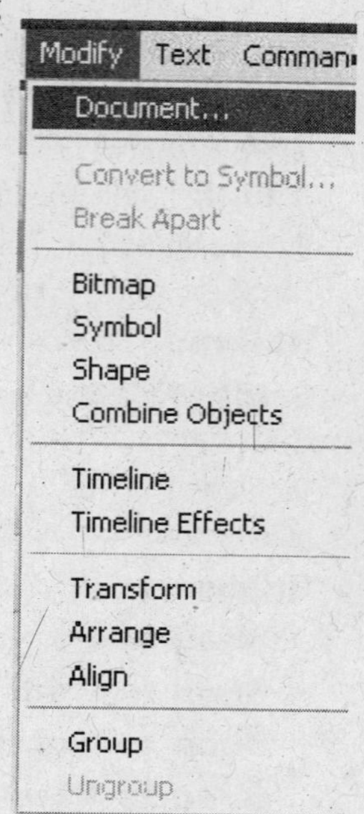

6.4.6 Modify menu

Various options of the menu are:

Document: It gives rise to Document Properties dialog box, which is used to change: Frame Rate, Frame Dimensions, Grid spacing and Colour.

Dimensions: This establishes the Dimensions of the Movie, in pixel units.

Match Printer: This matches the Movie Dimensions to the currently selected printer's maximum printable dimensions.

Match contents: This button adjusts the Movie Dimensions to include all active objects, from left-hand corner to the lower right-hand corner of the entire movie.

Background Colour: This is used to choose a new background colour.

Frame Rate: This is used to change the Frame rate.

Ruler Units: This pull down menu specifies units for the movie.

Make default: Click this button and your settings will become the default for all subsequent movies created.

Convert to Symbol: It converts a selected item on stage into a new symbol and evoke the Symbol Properties dialog box.

Break Apart: It works with merged and object drawings, movie clips, buttons, graphic symbols, and even imported bitmaps. Because you can ungroup graphics easily to make them editable, the Break Apart command is generally used only for text and bitmaps.

Bitmap: This command has two options:

Swap Bitmap: This command is used to swap an imported bitmap with another in the document.

Trace Bitmap: This command is used to convert an imported bitmap into a vector graphic with editable, discrete areas of colour.

Symbol: This command has two options:

Swap Symbol: You can assign a different symbol to an instance to display a different instance on the Stage and preserve all the original instance properties, such as color effects or button actions.

Duplicate Symbol: Duplicating a symbol lets you use an existing symbol as a starting point for creating a new symbol.

Shape: This command has following options:

Smooth: Using this you can smooth existing curved segments.

Straighten: Using this you can reshape lines and shape outlines by straightening them.

Optimize: Another way to smooth curves is to optimize them. This refines curved lines and fill outlines by reducing the number of curves used to define these elements. Optimizing curves also reduces the size of the Flash movie and the exported Flash Player movie.

Convert lines to fills: You can modify shapes by converting lines to fills, expanding the shape of a filled object, or softening the edges of a filled shape by modifying the curves of the shape.

Expand Fill/Soften: Expand Shape and Soften Edges work

Filled Edges: Best on small shapes that do not contain many small details. Applying Soften Edges to shapes with extensive detail can increase the file size of a Flash Player movie.

Add Shape Hint: Using this command you can add hints to the shape.

Remove All Hints: Using this command you can remove the hints added to the shape.

Combine Objects: You can use the Combine Object commands to create new shapes by combining or altering existing objects. In some cases, the stacking order of selected objects determines how the operation works. The Combine Objects commands are:

Union: The Union command lets you join to shapes two or more shapes into a single shape.

Intersect: The Intersect command lets you create an object from the intersection of two or more objects.

Punch: The Punch command lets you remove portions of a selected object as defined by the overlapping portions of another selected object arranged in front of it.

Crop: The Crop command lets you use the shape of one object to crop another object. The front or topmost object defines the shape of the cropped area.

Timeline: It has the following commands under it:

Distribute to Layers: To distribute objects to layers, you select the objects in one or more layers and choose this command.

Layer Properties: Using this command you can see the properties of various layers.

Reverse Frames: This is used to reverse the animation squence.

Synchronize Symbols: This command is used to recalculate the number of frames.

Convert to Keyframes: To distribute objects to layers, you select the objects in one or more layers and choose this command.

Clear Keyframe: This command changes a Keyframe back into a simple Frame, whereupon the contents of the former Keyframe will be replaced with copies of the Keyframe immediately previous in the Timeline.

Convert to Blank Keyframes: To distribute objects to layers, you select the objects in one or more layers and choose this command.

Timeline Effects: Flash includes prebuilt Timeline effects that let you create complex animations with a minimal number of steps. You can apply Timeline effects to the following objects: Text, Graphics, including shapes, groups, and graphic symbols, Bitmap images and Button symbols.

Transform: Use this to access the Transform pop-up, home to the following commands: Free Tranform, Distort, Envelope, Scale, Rotate and Skew, Rotate 90^0 CW, Rotate 90^0 CCW, Flip Vertical, Flip Horizontal and Remove Transform.

Arrange: Use this to open the arrange submenu. The various options are:

Bring to Front: This moves the symbol to the absolute front of the stack.

Bring Forward: This moves the symbol one step forward in the stack.

Send Backward: This moves the symbol one step backward in the stack.

Send to Back: This moves the symbol way back of the stack.

Lock: Use this to lock the symbol in its current position in the stack.

Unlock all: Use this to release the symbol from it's locked status in the stack.

Align: This command can be used to align objects in various positions like, Left, Horizontal Center, Right, Top, Vertical Center, Bottom, Distrubute Widths, Distribute Heights, Make Same Width, Make Same Height, and To Stage.

Group: This command groups the various selected items to one group.

Ungroup: This command is reverse of the above command, ungroups the grouped objects.

6.4.7 Text menu

Various options of the menu are:

Font: It shows all the fonts available in the windows directory which can be chosen according to your requirement.

Size: It shows the various sizes to choose from ranging from 8 to 120.

Style: Use this to set the style like Plain, Bold, Italics, Superscript or Subscript.

Align: You can set the alignment of the text in all possible 4 alignments like Left, Right, Centre or Justify.

Letter Spacing: You can set the space between the characters from here.

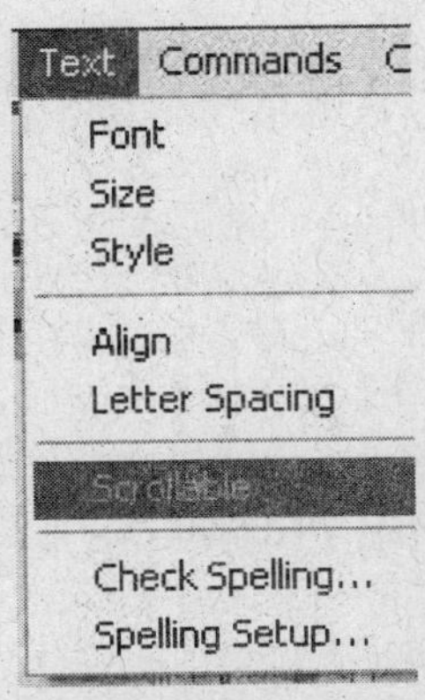

Scrollable: You can use the scroll and maxscroll properties of the TextField object to control vertical scrolling and the hscroll and maxhscroll properties to control horizontal scrolling in a text block. The scroll and hscroll properties contain a number that specifies the topmost visible line in a text block; you can read and write these properties.

Check Spelling: You can check the spelling of your text by using this command.

Spelling Setup: You can set the spelling options from here.

6.4.8 Commands menu

Various options of the menu are:

Manage Saved Commands: You can get the saved commands from here.

Get More Commands: You can get more commands from the Interenet using this command.

Run Commands: It allows you to run the commands.

Copy Motion as XML: You can copy the motion as XML.

Export Motion XML: You can export the motion as XML.

Import Motion XML: You can import the motion as XML.

6.4.9 Control menu

Various options of the menu are:

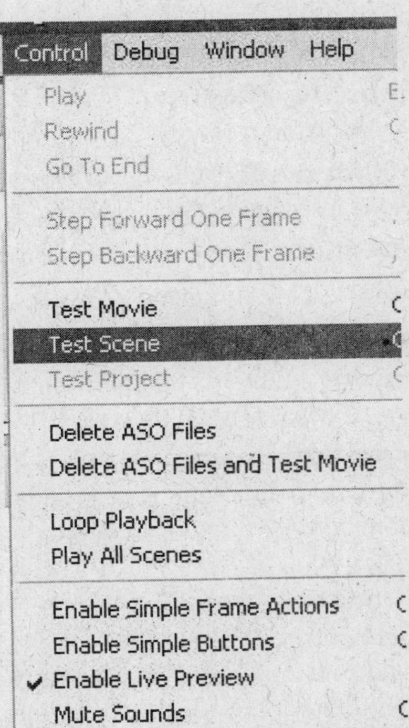

Play: It plays the movie.

Rewind: It returns the movie back to frame one.

Go To End: It takes you to the end of the movie.

Step Forward One Frame: It command is used to step the movie one frame forward.

Step Backward One Frame: This command is used to step the movie one frame backwards.

Test Movie: This command utilizes the settings established in the Publish Settings dialog box to export the current movie and instantly play it within a new Flash Player window.

Debug Movie: This command allows you to degub the faults in your movie.

Test Scene: This command tests the current scene only, whereas Test Movie runs the whole movie.

Test Project: This command tests the project.

Delete ASO Files: During compilation, Flash sometimes creates files with .aso extensions in the /aso subdirectory of the default global classpath directory. The .aso extension stands for

ActionScript object (ASO). For each ActionScript 2.0 file that is implicitly or explicitly imported and successfully compiled, Flash generates an ASO file. The file contains the bytecode that's produced from the associated ActionScript (AS) file. Therefore, these files contain the compiled form (the bytecode) of a class file. If you experience problems in which Flash appears to be compiling older versions of a file you have edited, delete the ASO files and then recompile. If you plan to delete ASO files, delete them when Flash is not performing other operations, such as checking syntax or exporting SWFs.

Delete ASO Files and Test Movie: This command deletes both aso and text movie files.

Loop Playback: It enables looping with all subsequent implementations of the Play, Test Movie, and Test Scene commands.

Play All Scenes: This command overrides the default single scene playback and enables all scenes to be played with subsequent implementations of the Play, Test Movie, and Test Scene commands.

Enable Simple Frame Actions: Use this only during tests and playback within Flash.

Enable Simple Buttons: This command toggles whether buttons are enabled.

Enable Live Preview: The Live Preview feature lets you view components on the Stage as they will appear in the published movie.

Mute Sounds: This command is a toggle that turns sound on or off.

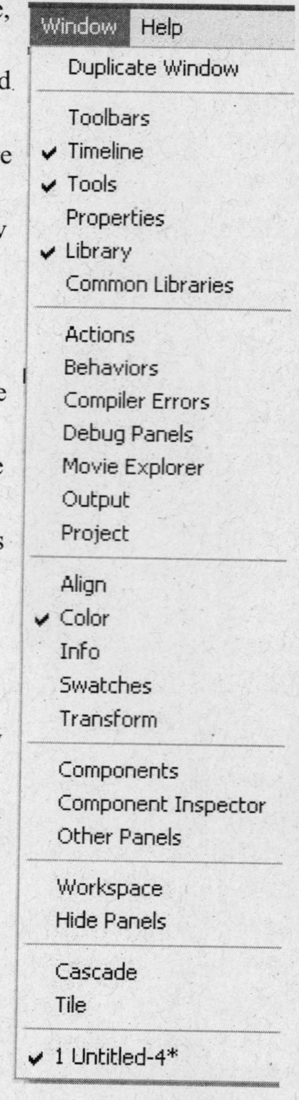

6.4.10 Windows menu

This menu has several commands that are used to control and arrange the display of multiple movies.

Duplicate Window: This command opens the currently active movie in a new window.

Toolbars: This command opens the options of selecting various toolbars like Main, Controller and Edit bar.

Timeline: This command opens the Timeline pallette.

Tools: This command opens the Tools pallette.

Properties: This command opens the Properties Option palette.

Library: Libraries opened from the Libraries menu function like the Library that's accessed with Windows, Library.

Common Library: You can use the sample common libraries included with Flash to add buttons or sounds to your documents. You can also create custom common libraries, which you can then use with any documents that you create.

Actions: You can assign an action to a button or a movie clip to make an action execute when the user clicks a button or rolls the pointer over it, or when the movie clip loads or reaches a certain frame. You assign the action to an instance of the button or movie clip; other instances of the symbol aren't affected.

Behaviours: It allows you to have the Behaviours pallette on the screen.

Debugger: It allows you to degbug your movie.

Movie Explorer: The Movie Explorer helps you arrange, locate, and edit media. With its hierarchical tree structure, the Movie Explorer provides information about the organization and flow of a document.

Output: This command opens the Output window, which shows precise file-size reports on every scene, symbol, text and so on.

Align: This command opens the Align option pallete.

Color Mixer: This command opens the Color Mixer palette.

Color Swatch: This command opens the Color Swatch palette.

Info: This command opens the Info palette on the screen.

Transform: This command opens the Transform palette.

Components: It opens the Components control panel on the screen.

Component Inspector: It opens the Component Inspector control panel on the screen.

Other Panels: This command has the following options:

Accessability: You can see the accessability of your document from here.

History: You can see the history of your document from here.

Scene: This command shows the scene dialog box.

Screens: This command shows the screens dialog box.

Strings: This opens the Strings pallette for you.

Workspace Layout: It has the options of setting it to Default, Save Current or Manage.

Hide Panels: It hides all the open panels.

Cascade: This command opens all windows so that they overlap in a cascade descending from the top left to the bottom right.

Tiles: You can open two tiles of the same document using this command.

6.4.11 Help menu

This menu has the various options shown here.

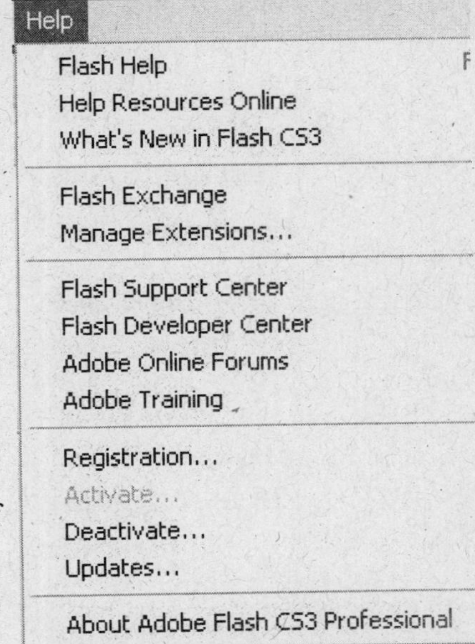

Flash Help: Opens the Help for you to ask the system what you want to know.

Getting Started with Flash: Helps you in working in Flash.

Flash LiveDocs: You can download live documents of Flash.

What's New in Flash CS3: Tells you what is new in the new version of Flash.

Flash Exchange: Clicking at this takes you to the web site of Adobe.

Flash Help: The following set of commands help you in reaching Adobe and getting the required information from the developer of the software. These commands are: Flash Support Center, Flash Developer Center, Flash Documentation Resource Center, Adobe Online Forums, and Adobe Training.

Try Flash Professional CS3: This command allows you to try the advanced version of the software known as Flash Professional CS3.

About Flash Basic: Displays the copyright page of the software.

6.5 Understanding Tools of Flash CS3

Like any other software, Flash CS3 has its own set of tools, which are very important to understand before you use them. The toolbar is shown here:

Most of these tools have multiple dimensions, i.e., some of them have more tools under them. Let us start with Arrow Tool.

6.5.1 Selection Tool

The Selection tool lets you select entire objects by clicking an object or dragging to enclose the object within a rectangular selection marquee.

To select a stroke, fill, group, instance, or text block:

Select the Arrow tool and click the object.

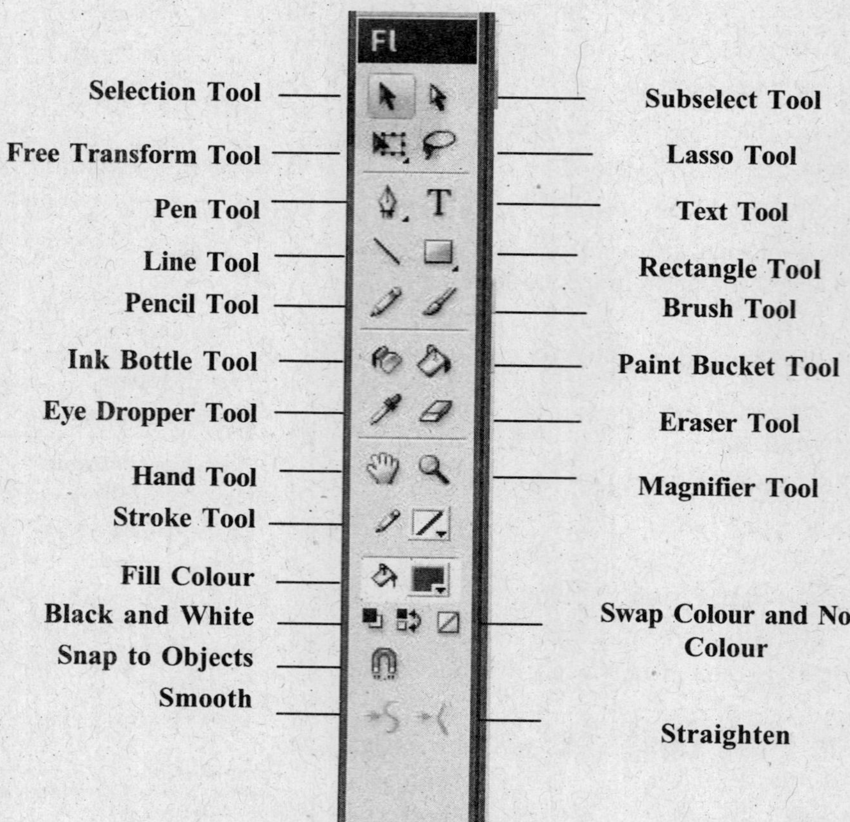

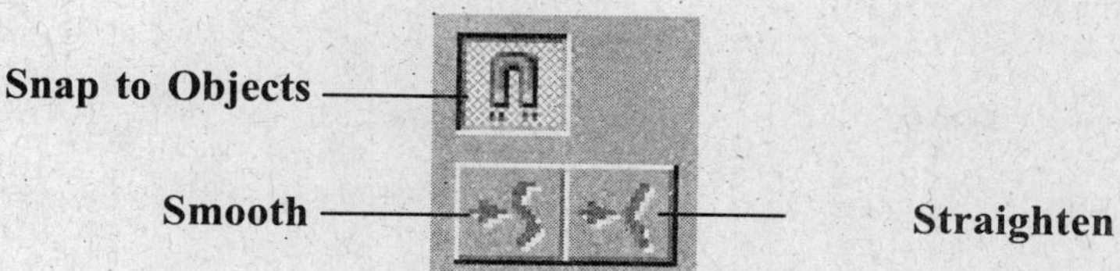

To select connected lines:

Select the Arrow tool and double-click one of the lines.

To select a filled shape and its stroked outline:

Select the Arrow tool and double-click the fill.

To select objects within a rectangular area:

Select the Arrow tool and drag a marquee around the object or objects that you want to select. Instances, groups, and type blocks must be completely enclosed to be selected.

6.5.2 The Subselection Tool

It is used to select more than one items.

6.5.3 The Free Transform Tool

You can use the Free Transform tool to freely transform objects, groups, instances, or text blocks. You can perform individual transformations or combine several transformations, such as moving, rotating, scaling, skewing, and distortion.

To transform freely:

1. Select a graphic object, instance, group, or text block on the Stage.
2. Click the Free Transform tool.

   Moving the pointer over and around the selection changes the pointer to indicate which transformation function is available.
3. Drag the handles to transform the selection, as follows:

   To move the selection, position the pointer over the object within the bounding box, and drag the object to a new position. Do not drag the transformation point. To set the center of rotation or scaling, drag the transformation point to a new location.

   To rotate the selection, position the pointer just outside a corner handle and drag. The selection rotates around the transformation point.

   Shift-drag to rotate in 45° increments.

   Alt-drag to rotate around the opposite corner.

   To scale the selection, drag a corner handle diagonally to scale in two dimensions. Drag a corner handle or a side handle horizontally or vertically to scale in the respective direction only. Shift-drag to resize proportionally.

   To skew the selection, position the pointer on the outline between the transformation handles and drag.

   To distort shapes, press Control and drag a corner handle or a side handle. Shift-Control-drag a corner handle to taper the object—to move the selected corner and the adjoining corner equal distances from their origins.

The Free Transform tool cannot transform symbols, bitmaps, video objects, sounds, gradients, object groups, or text. If a multiple selection contains any of these, only the shape objects are distorted. To transform text, first convert the characters to shape objects.

4. To end the transformation, click outside the selected object, instance, or text block.

This has the following options as shown.

Rotate and Skew: Rotating an object turns it around its transformation point. The transformation point is aligned with the registration point, which defaults to the center of the object, but you can move the point by dragging it. When you rotate an object by dragging, you can also skew and scale the object in the same operation. When you rotate an object using the Transform panel, you can scale the object in the same operation.

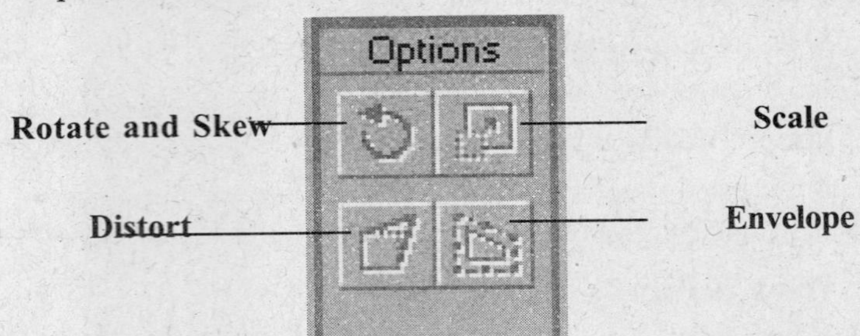

Scale: This button is used to initate scaling of a selected line, shape, group, symbol, button, object, or other item. When the Scale button is clicked, the item is put into scale mode, and handles appear for scaling of the time.

Distort: When you apply a Distort transformation to a selected object, dragging a corner handle or an edge handle on the bounding box moves the corner or edge and realigns the adjoining edges. Shift-dragging a corner point tapers the object—that is, it moves that corner and the adjoining corner an equal distance and opposite direction from each other. The adjoining corner is the corner opposite the direction you drag. Control-dragging a middle point on an edge moves the entire edge freely.

Envelope: The Envelope modifier lets you warp and distort objects. An envelope is a bounding box that contains one or more objects. Changes made to an envelope's shape affect the shape of the objects contained within the envelope. You edit the shape of an envelope by adjusting its points and tangent handles.

6.5.4 The Lasso Tool

It is used to group-select odd or irregular shaped areas of your drawing. After the areas are selected, they can be moved, scaled, rotated, or reshaped as a single unit. The Lasso tool can also be used to split shapes or select portions of a line or shape.

To select objects by drawing a straight-edged selection area:

1. Select the Lasso tool and select the Polygon Mode modifier in the Options section of the toolbox.
2. Click to set the starting point.
3. Position the pointer where you want the first line to end, and click. Continue setting end points for additional line segments.
4. To close the selection area, double-click.

To select objects by drawing both freehand and straight-edged selection areas:

1. Select the Lasso tool and deselect the Polygon Mode modifier.
2. To draw a freehand segment, drag on the Stage.

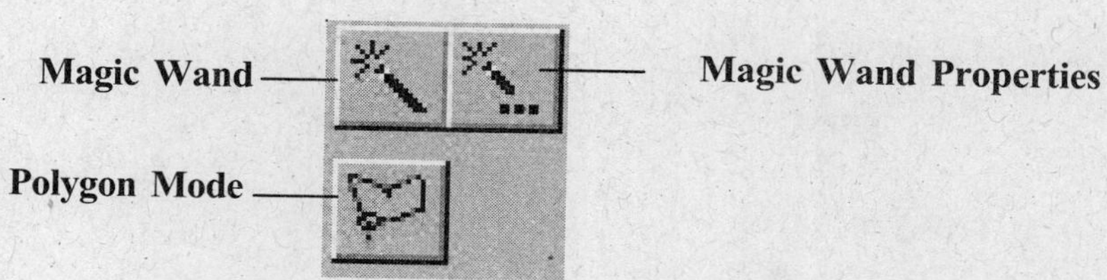

3. To draw a straight-edged segment, hold down Alt-click (Windows) or Option-click (Macintosh) to set start and end points. You can continue switching between drawing freehand and straight-edged segments.
4. To close the selection area, do one of the following:

   If you are drawing a freehand segment, release the mouse button.

   If you are drawing a straight-edged segment, double-click.

This tool has 3 options: Polygon Mode, Magic Wand and the Magic Wand properties.

Polygon Mode: Here selection points are created by a mouse click, causing a straight selection line to extend between mouse clicks. Double click to complete the selection.

Magic Wand Modifier: It is used to select ranges of a similar colour in a bitmap that has been broken apart. After you select areas of the bitmap, you can change their fill colour or delete them.

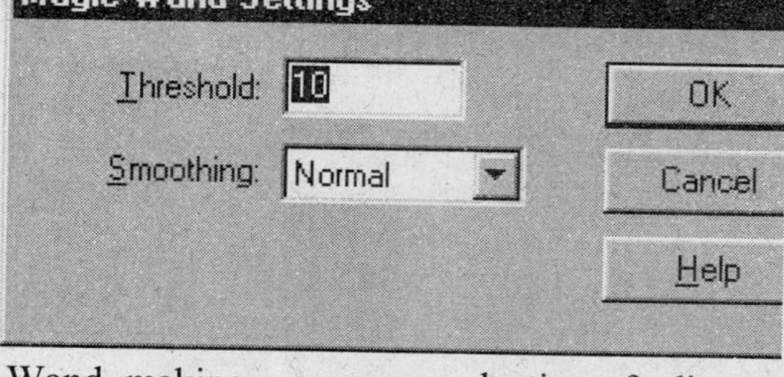

Magic Wand Properties: This has 2 settings: Threshold and Smoothing.

Threshold Setting: This defines the breadth of adjacent colour values that the Magic Wand Modifier will include in a selection. The higher the setting, the broader the selection of adjacent colours, and conversely, a smaller number results in the Magic Wand, making a narrower selection of adjacent colours.

Smoothing Setting: This determines to what degree the edge of the selection should be smoothed.

6.5.5 The Pen Tool

When you draw with the Pen tool, you click to create points on straight line segments, and click and drag to create points on curved line segments.

You can adjust straight and curved line segments by adjusting points on the line. You can convert curves to straight lines and the reverse.

You can also display points on lines that you create with other Flash drawing tools, such as the Pencil, Brush, Line, Oval, or Rectangle tool, to adjust those lines.

6.5.6 The Text Tool

To place text blocks on the Stage, you use the Text tool. You can place type on a single line that expands as you type or in a fixed-width block that wraps words automatically. Flash displays a round handle at the upper right corner of text blocks that extend, and a square handle for text blocks with a defined width.

6.5.7 The Line Tool

Drawing with the Line tool creates a perfectly straight line that extends from the starting point to the end point.

6.5.8 The Rectangle Tool

You can use the Rectangle tool to easily create a rectangle shape.

To draw a straight line, oval, or rectangle:

1. Select the Line, Oval, or Rectangle tool.
2. Select Window > Properties and select stroke and fill attributes in the Property inspector. You cannot set fill attributes for the Line tool.
3. For the Rectangle tool, specify rounded corners by clicking the Round Rectangle modifier and entering a corner radius value. A value of zero creates square corners.
4. Drag on the Stage. If you are using the Rectangle tool, press the Up and Down Arrow keys while dragging to adjust the radius of rounded corners.

   For the Oval and Rectangle tools, Shift-drag to constrain the shapes to circles and squares.

   For the Line tool, Shift-drag to constrain lines to multiples of 45°.

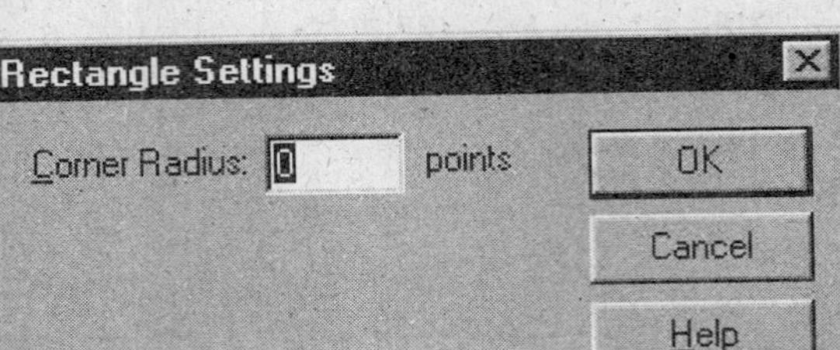

6.5.9 The Pencil Tool

It is used to draw lines and shapes. This tool has a option in the form of Pencil Mode.

Pencil Mode pop-up menu has 3 options as shown here. These help in processing of the lines as they are drawn. Two are Straighten and Smooth. The third one is freehand ink mode which turns off all other line processing.

Straighten: Drawing with this option processes your drawings while taking into account line and shape recognition.

Smooth: Drawing with this option reduces the zeal with which Flash automatically processes your drawings.

Ink: Drawing with this option turns off all Flash processing.

6.5.10 The Brush Tool

It is used to paint with brush-like strokes and to fill enclosed areas with colours. The fills can be solid colours, gradients, or fills derived from bitmaps.

This tool can have either 4 options depending upon the type of pressure sensitive tablet you are using. These are: Pressure Modifier, which only appears if your a pressure sensitive tablet attached to your computer; Brush size and Brush shapes.

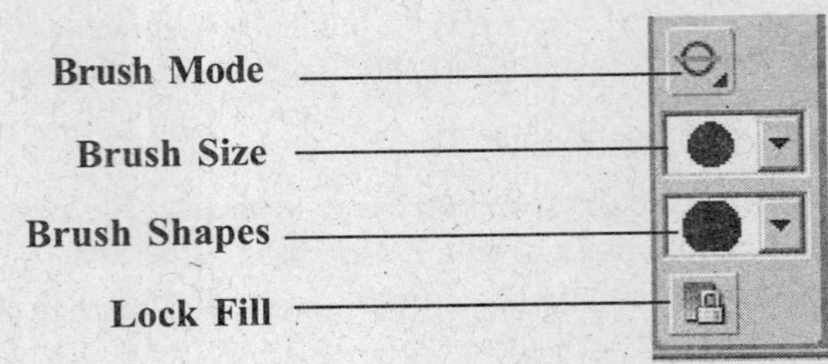

Brush Mode Modifier: This is a drop-down menu with 5 modes for applying strokes:

Paint Normal, Paint Fills, Paint Behind, Paint Selection, and Paint Inside. Let us see what each of them does.

Paint Normal: It applies brush strokes over the top of any lines or fills. In this mode, a black scrawl covers all elements: background, outline, fill, and drawn lines.

Paint Fills: This mode applies brush strokes to replace any fills, but leaves lines untouched. In Paint Fills mode, a similar black scrawl covers both the grey fill and the background.

Paint Behind: This mode applies brush strokes only to blank areas and leaves all fills, lines, and other items untouched. .

Paint Selection: This mode applies brush strokes only to selected fills.

Paint Inside: This mode applies brush strokes only to the fill area where the brush stroke was first initiated. It never paints over lines.

Brush Size Tool: This is a drop-down menu with a range of ten preset available brush sizes. Although the sizes are shown as circles, the diameter size applies to all brush shapes. In the case of an oblong brush, the diameter size refers to the broadest span of the brush. You can combine brush sizes and shapes for a wide variety of custom brush tips.

Brush Shape Tool: This is a simple pop-up menu with 9 possible brush shapes, based on circle, ellipse, square, rectangle, and line shapes. The oval, rectangle, and line shapes are available in several angles.

Brush Lock Fill Tool: This is a toggle button that controls how Flash handles areas filled with gradient colour. Once this button is pressed, all subsequent areas that are painted with the same gradient will appear to be part of a single, continuous filled shape. This modifier locks the angle, size, and point of origin of the current gradient so that it remains constant throughout the scene.

6.5.11 The Ink Bottle Tool

It is used to change the colour, style, and thickness of existing lines. It is most often used in conjunction with the Dropper tool.

6.5.12 The Paint Bucket Tool

It is used to fill enclosed areas with colour, gradients or bitmap fills. When the Paint Bucket tool is active, three modifier appear in the modifier tray. The button modifiers are the Lock Fill and Transform Fill. The pop-up menu is the Gap Size Modifiers.

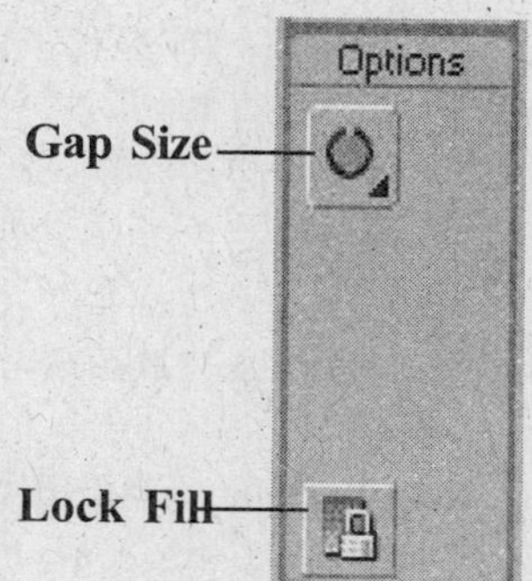

Paint Bucket Gap Size: This modifier pop-up offers four settings that control how the Paint Bucket tool will treat gaps when filling. These settings are Don't Close Gaps, Close Small Gaps, Close Medium Gaps and Close Large Gaps. If gaps are too large, you may have to close them manually.

Paint Bucket Lock Fill: It is the same button as the Brush Lock Fill Modifier. With this you can handle the fill gradient colours. It locks he angle, size, and point of origin of the current gradient so that it remains constant throughout.

6.5.13 The Eye Dropper Tool

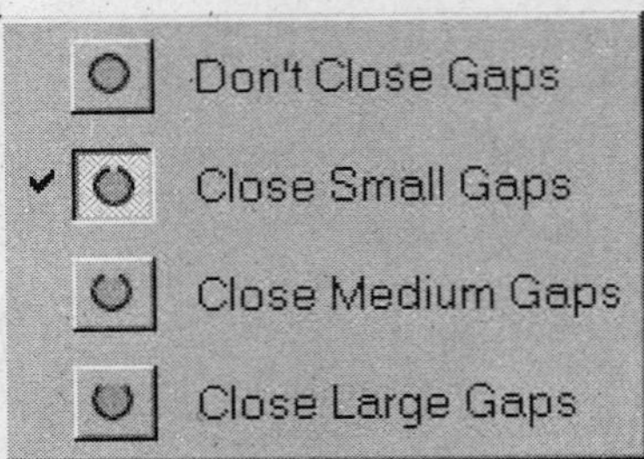

It is used to acquire the colour and style information from existing pencil lines, brush strokes, and fills. The Eye Dropper tool has no modifiers, but then it does not need modifiers.

With the shift key pressed when the Dropper tool is over a line, fill, or brush stroke, the cursor changes to an inverted U shape. In this mode, use of Dropper tool changes the attributes for all editing tools in Flash to match the attributes of the area clicked.

6.5.14 The Eraser Tool

Where there are drawing tools, can eraser be long behind. It must be there.

To quickly delete everything on the Stage:

Double-click the Eraser tool.

To remove stroke segments or filled areas:

1. Select the Eraser tool and then click the Faucet modifier.
2. Click the stroke segment or filled area that you want to delete.

To erase by dragging:

1. Select the Eraser tool.
2. Click the Eraser Mode modifier and choose an erasing mode:

   Erase Normal erases strokes and fills on the same layer.

   Erase Fills erases only fills; strokes are not affected.

   Erase Lines erases only strokes; fills are not affected.

   Erase Selected Fills erases only the currently selected fills and does not affect strokes, selected or not. (Select the fills you want to erase before using the Eraser tool in this mode.)

   Erase Inside erases only the fill on which you begin the eraser stroke. If you begin erasing from an empty point, nothing will be erased. Strokes are unaffected by the eraser in this mode.
3. Click the Eraser Shape modifier and choose an eraser shape and size. Make sure that the Faucet modifier is not selected.
4. Drag on the Stage.

When the eraser tool is active, 3 modifiers appear in the modifier tray. Two of these modifiers, the Eraser Mode Modifier and the Eraser Shape Modifier, are pop-ups. The third modifier, the Faucet button, is used to clear enclosed areas of fill.

Erase Mode Modifier: This modifier both controls and limits what and how the Eraser tool erases. The Erase Mode Modifier has 5 options:

Erase Normal: In this mode the Eraser tool functions like a normal eraser. It erases all lines and fills that it passes over, as long as they are on the active layer.

Erase Fills: In this mode the Eraser tool becomes a specialty eraser, erasing only fills and leaving lines only and leaving fills unaffected.

Erase Lines: In this mode the Eraser tool changes specialties, i.e., it works by erasing lines only and leaving fills unaffected.

Erase Selected Fills: In this mode the Eraser tool becomes even more specialized and only erases fills that are currently selected, leaving unselected fills and all lines unaffected.

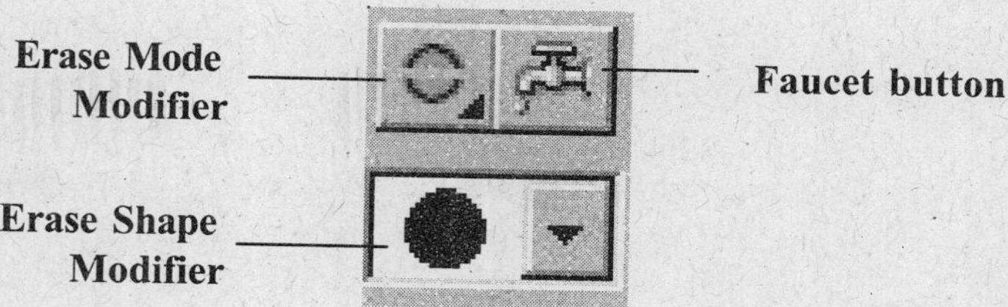

Erase Inside: In this mode the Eraser tool only erases the area of fill on which you initiate erasing. This is much like the erase Selected Fills mode, with the exception that the selection is accomplished with the initial erasure. In this mode, the eraser leaves all other fills and all lines unaffected.

Erase Normal
Erase Fills
Erase Lines
Erase Selected Fills
Erase Inside

Erase Shape Modifier: This modifier defines both the size and shape or the eraser. It is a simple drop-down menu with 10 brushes available in 2 shapes, circular and square. These are arrayed in two banks of 5 sizes each, ranging from small to large.

6.5.15 The Hand Tool

When you are zoomed in close on the screen, you can easily navigate the Flash workspace contents by using the Hand Tool. This tool is used by clicking and dragging, while holding the mouse, in the direction you want to move the screen.

6.5.16 The Magnifier Tool

This tool is similar to various zoom tools you see in other programs. It has two options: Zoom in and Zoom out. Zoom in brings you closer into the drawing so that you can view it at a greater level of magnification, while Zoom out pulls you away from the drawing by showing it at a lesser level of magnification. Each level of Zoom in brings you in twice as close while each level of Zoom out pulls you away in increments of one half.

To view the entire Stage on the screen, or to view just a particular area of your drawing at high magnification, you can change the magnification level. The maximum magnification depends on the resolution of your monitor and the document size.

To Magnify or Reduce your view of the Stage, do one of the following:

To zoom in on a certain element, select the Zoom tool and click the element. To switch the Zoom tool between zooming in or out, use the Enlarge or Reduce modifiers or Alt-click .

To zoom in on a specific area of your drawing, drag a rectangular selection marquee with the Zoom tool. Flash sets the magnification level so that the specified rectangle fills the window.

To zoom in on or out of the entire Stage, choose View > Zoom In or View > Zoom Out.

To zoom in or out by a specified percentage, choose View > Magnification and select a percentage from the submenu, or select a percentage from the Zoom control at the lower left corner of the application window.

To display the contents of the current frame, choose View > Magnification > Show All, or choose Show All from the Zoom control at the lower left corner of the application window. If the scene is empty, the entire Stage is displayed.

To display the entire Stage, choose View > Magnification > Show Frame or choose Show Frame from the Zoom control at the lower left corner of the application window.

To display the work area surrounding the Stage, choose View > Work Area. The work area is shown in light gray. Use the Work Area command to view elements in a scene that are partly or completely outside of the Stage. For example, to have a bird fly into a frame, you would initially position the bird outside of the Stage in the work area.

6.5.17 The Fill Tool

You can transform a gradient or bitmap fill by adjusting the size, direction, or center of the fill.

To adjust a gradient or bitmap fill with the Fill Transform tool:

1. Select the Fill Transform tool.
2. Click an area filled with a gradient or bitmap fill.

   When you select a gradient or bitmap fill for editing, its center point appears, and its bounding box is displayed with editing handles. When the pointer is over any one of these handles, it changes to indicate the function of the handle.

   Press Shift to constrain the direction of a linear gradient fill to multiples of 45°.
3. Reshape the gradient or fill in any of the following ways:

   To reposition the center point of the gradient or bitmap fill, drag the center point.

   To change the width of the gradient or bitmap fill, drag the square handle on the side of the bounding box. (This option resizes only the fill, not the object containing the fill.)

   To change the height of the gradient or bitmap fill, drag the square handle at the bottom of the bounding box.

   To rotate the gradient or bitmap fill, drag the circular rotation handle at the corner. You can also drag the lowest handle on the bounding circle of a circular gradient or fill.

   To scale a linear gradient or a fill, drag the square handle at the center of the bounding box.

   To change the radius of a circular gradient, drag the middle circular handle on the bounding circle.

   To skew or slant a fill within a shape, drag one of the circular handles on the top or right side of the bounding box.

   To tile a bitmap inside a shape, scale the fill.

   To see all of the handles when working with large fills or fills close to the edge of the Stage, choose View > Work Area.

6.6 Drawing Objects in Flash

Using the various drawing tools you can draw the various objects on the screen.

6.6.1 Drawing Lines

Line tool allows you to draw various lines on the screen.

Follow the following steps to draw line.

1. Click at line tool.

2. Move the mouse pointer over the Stage area until the pointer changes from Arrow to Plus.
3. Drag to draw a line of your desired length.
4. Release the mouse button.
5. The line appears as required by you.

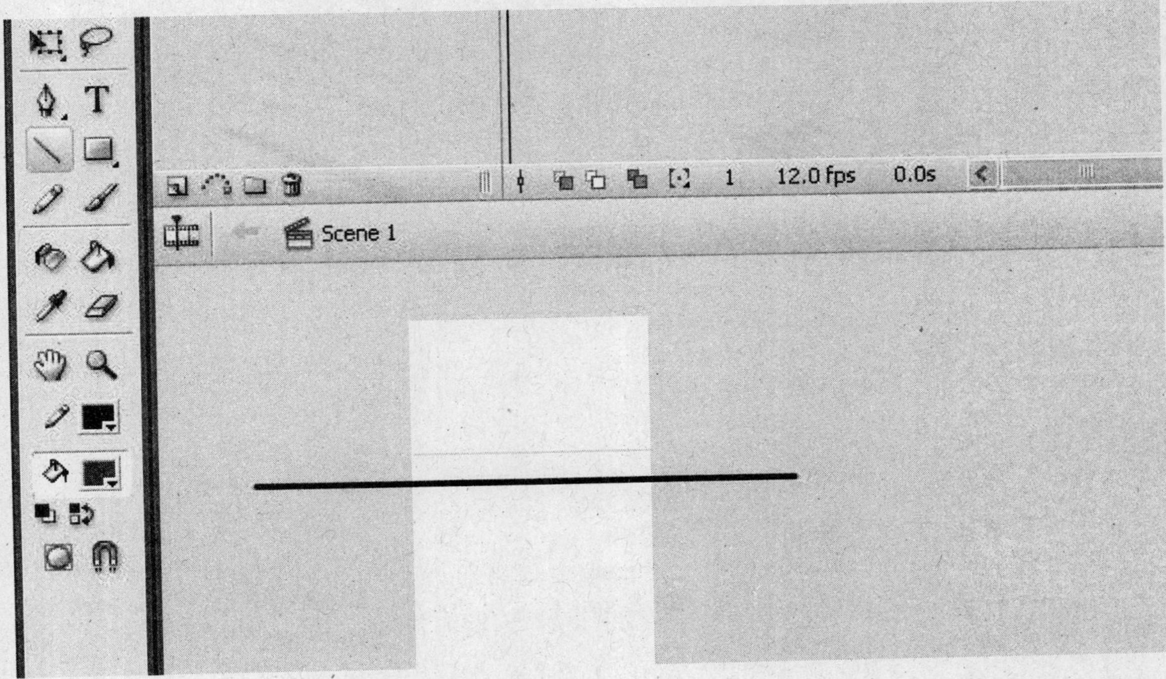

6.6.2 Drawing Free Form Line

Follow the following steps to draw a free form line.

1. Click at pencil tool.
2. Click at Pencil mode tool.
3. Select the freeform line from the options.
4. Drag your cursor on the Stage to draw the line.
5. Release the mouse button.
6. The line appears to your specifications, as shown next.

6.6.3 Formatting the line

Using the various readymade formats available in Flash you can change the shape of the line according to your needs.

Follow the following steps to format the line.

1. Click at Arrow tool.
2. Click the line segment you want to format.

3. Get the Properties dialog box on the screen.
4. From the dialog box, click the line sub-menu.
5. From the various lines visible, select the one which you want.
6. Click the weight of the line, a slider appears.
7. From the slider choose the thickness you want.
8. Change the colour of the line if needed.

6.6.4 Drawing a Custom Line

Using the various readymade readymade styles of lines available in the software you can draw a line of your needs.

Follow the following steps to create a line.

1. Click at Pencil or Line tool.
2. Click Windows menu.
3. Click Properties.
4. Click at Custom.
5. The stroke dialog box appears.
6. Click at the thickness of the line you want.
7. Click at Type of line you want.
8. With each type you get the option, like in this case of Dashed, you get the Dash spacing, which has been defined as 6.

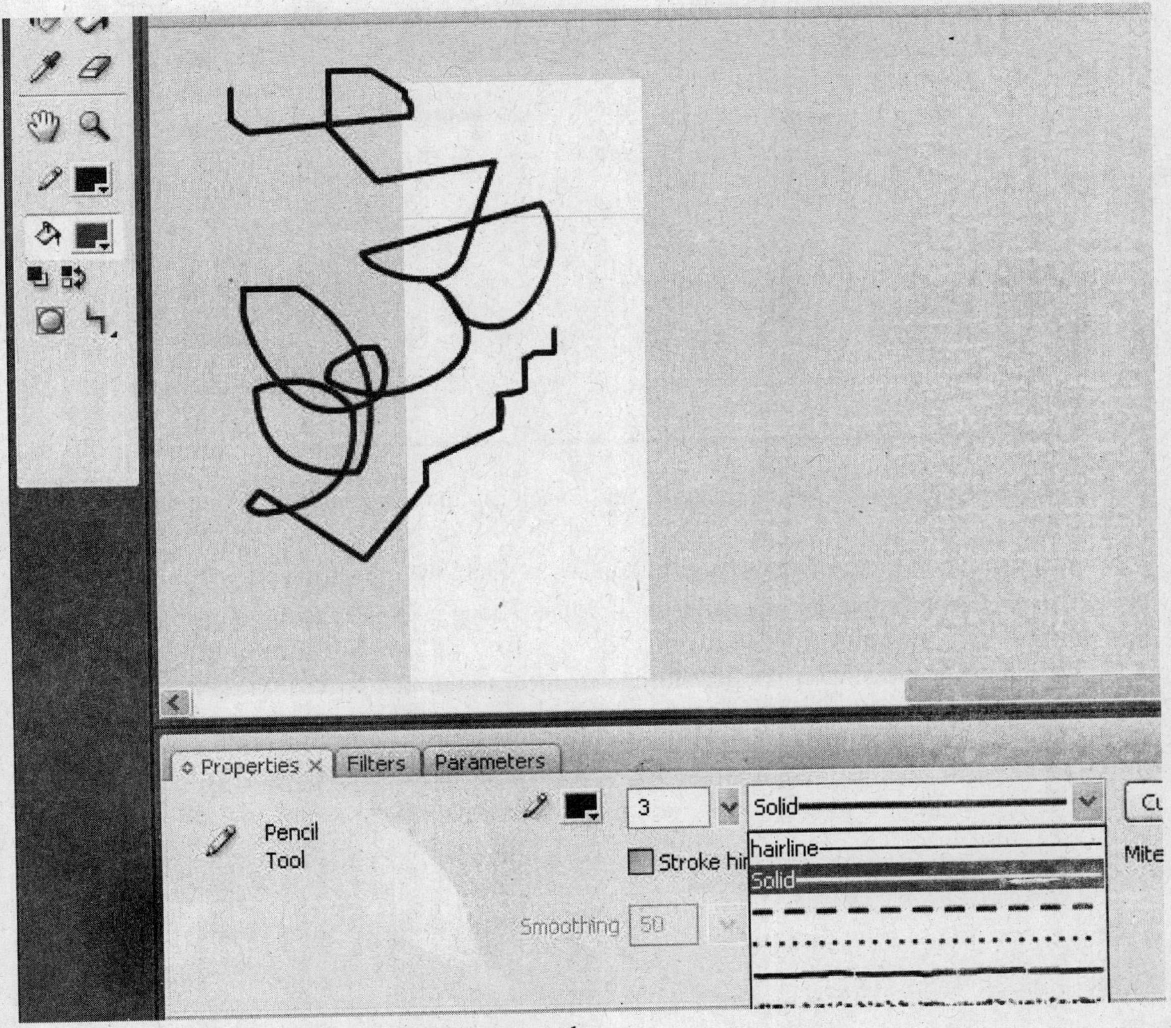

9. If you want you can make the corners sharp.
10. Click Ok.
11. Draw your custom line on Stage.
12. The line appears as per your needs, as shown next.

6.6.5 Drawing Curves with the Pen Tool

Using the pen tool too you can draw curves.

Follow the following steps to create curves.

1. Click at Pen tool.
2. Move the cursor pointer over the Stage area until the pointer changes from Arrow to Pen
3. Begin dragging to start the curve.
4. A curve bar appears.

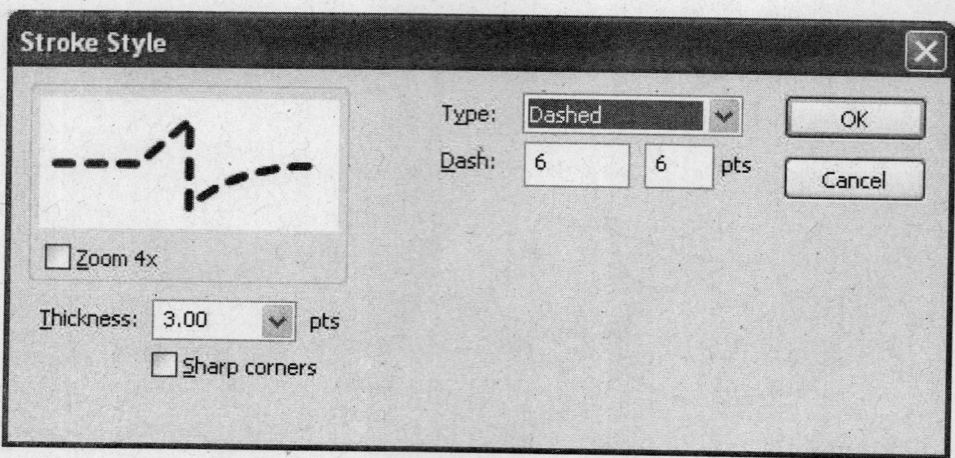

5. You can rotate the curve bar by dragging tool to achieve the bend and line length you want for the curve.
6. Start dragging and release the mouse button when you have drawn the curve you want.
7. You can add more curves to an existing curved line as long as the Pen tool is still active. Simply drag another line segment.
8. Flash automatically attaches the second line segment to the first curved line.

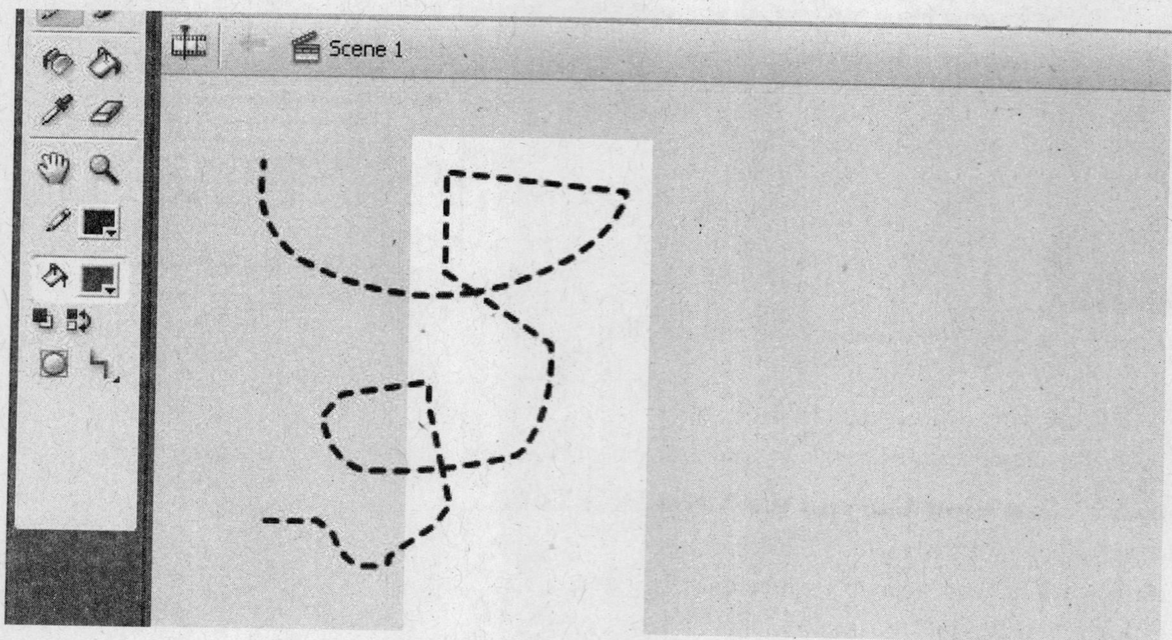

6.6.6 Drawing Oval Shape

Follow the following steps to draw an oval shape.

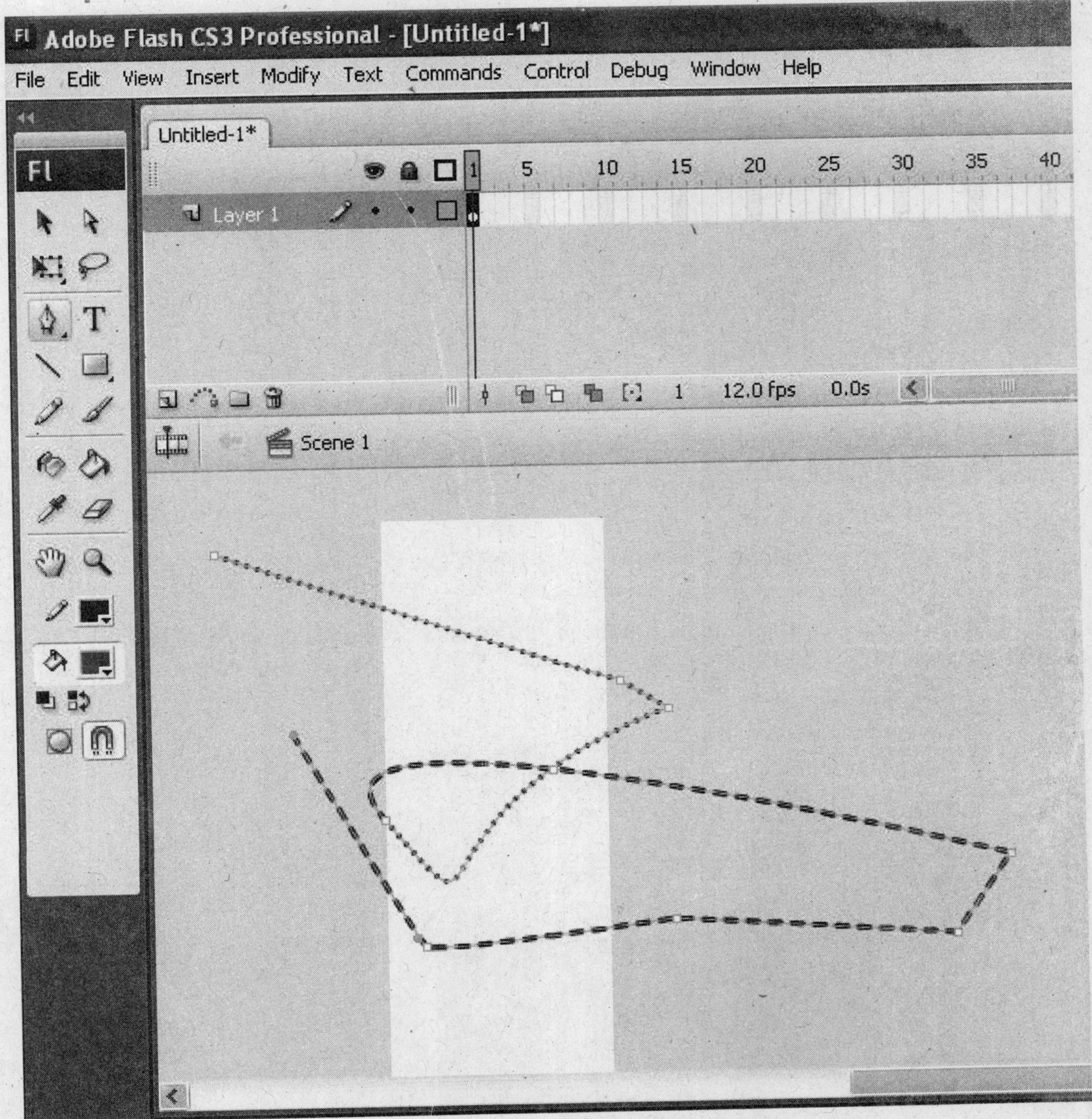

1. Click at Oval tool.
2. Move the cursor over the Stage area until Arrow changes to Plus.
3. You can draw a shape without a fill by changing the fill colour to white.
4. Drag to draw the shape you want.
5. Release the mouse button.
6. The shape appears as per your needs.

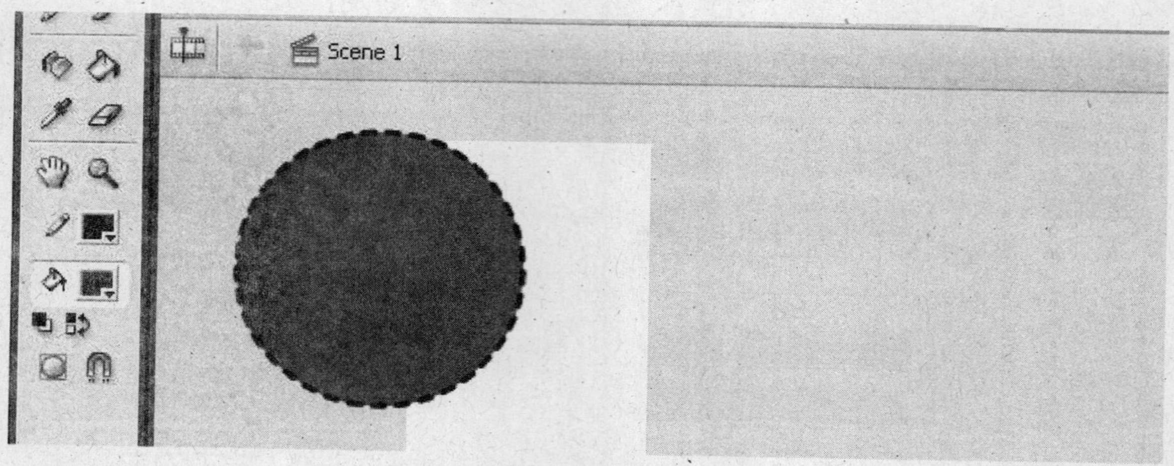

6.6.7 Drawing Rectangle Shape

Follow the following steps to draw an oval shape.

1. Click at Rectangle tool.
2. Click fill colour and hold down the mouse button.
3. The fill colour palette appears.
4. Move over a fill colour and release the mouse button or when the pointer changes from Arrow to Dropper.
5. Drag to draw the shape.
6. Release the mouse button.
7. The shape appears as per your needs.

6.6.8 Drawing Rectangle with Rounded Corners

Follow the following steps to drawing rectangle with rounded corners.

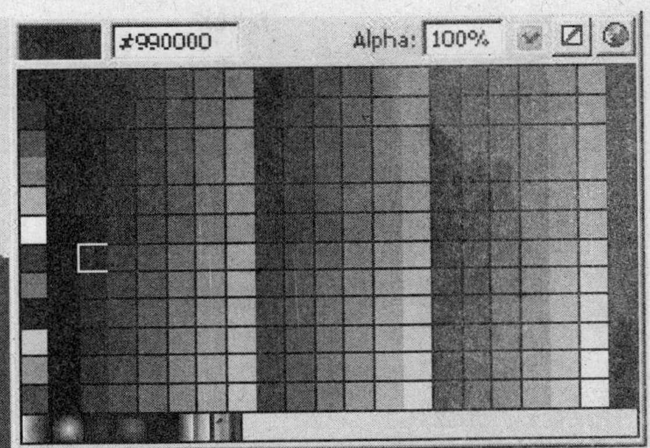

1. Click at Rectangle tool.
2. Click Rectangle setting button in the Options area of the toolbar.
3. The Rectangle Settings dialog box appears.
4. Type a corner radius setting.
5. Click Ok.
6. Draw a rectangle shape with rounded corners. To draw regular corners again, enter 0 as the radius setting.

6.6.9 Drawing with Brush Tool

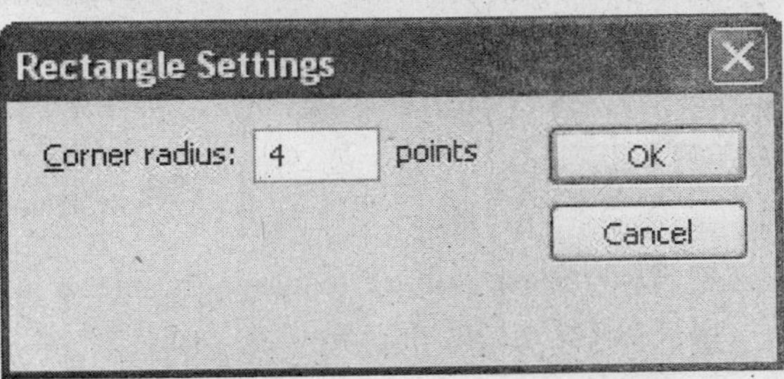

Follow the following steps to draw an object with Brush tool.

1. Click at Brush tool.
2. Click down arrow to select the brush size.
3. Now select the brush shape too.
4. After selecting a brush size and shape, move your cursor over the Stage.

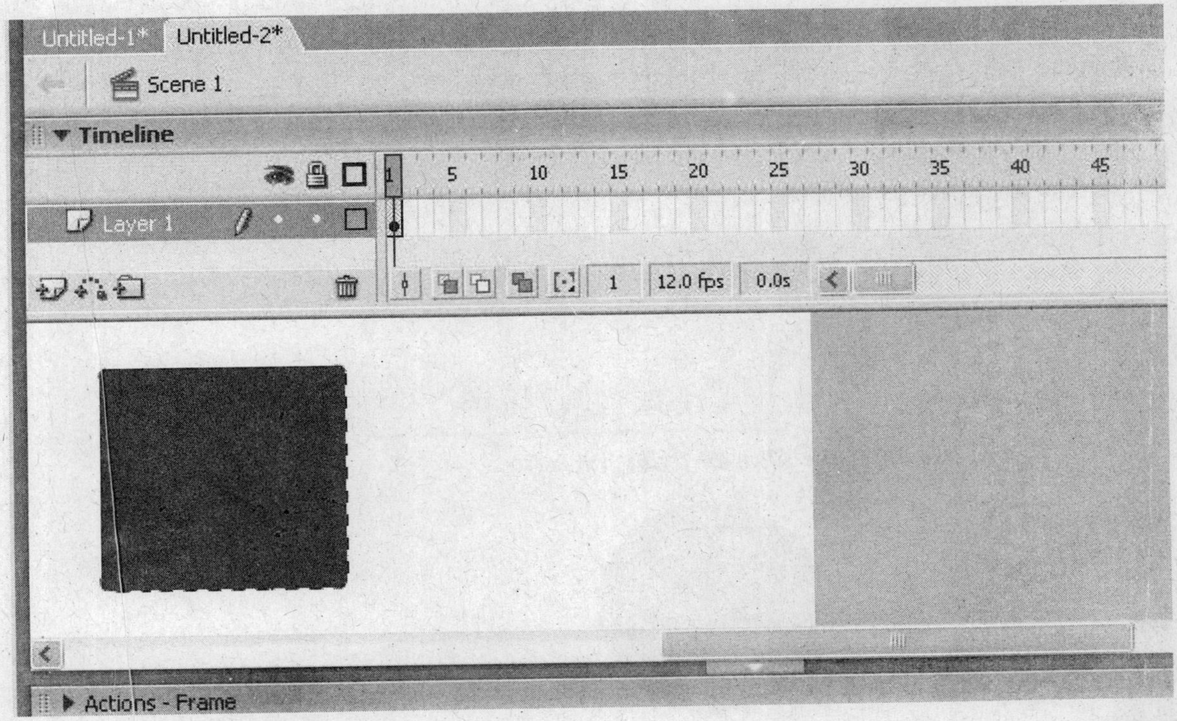

5. The mouse pointer displays the brush size and shape you selected.
6. Drag to begin drawing.
7. A shape appears according to your needs, as shown below.

6.6.10 Filling shapes with Paint Bucket Tool

Follow the following steps to fill the shape with pain bucket tool.

1. Click at Paint Bucket tool.
2. Click fill colour and hold down the mouse button.
3. The fill colour pallet opens.
4. Select a colour.
5. Click the shape you want to fill.
6. The colour fills the shape.

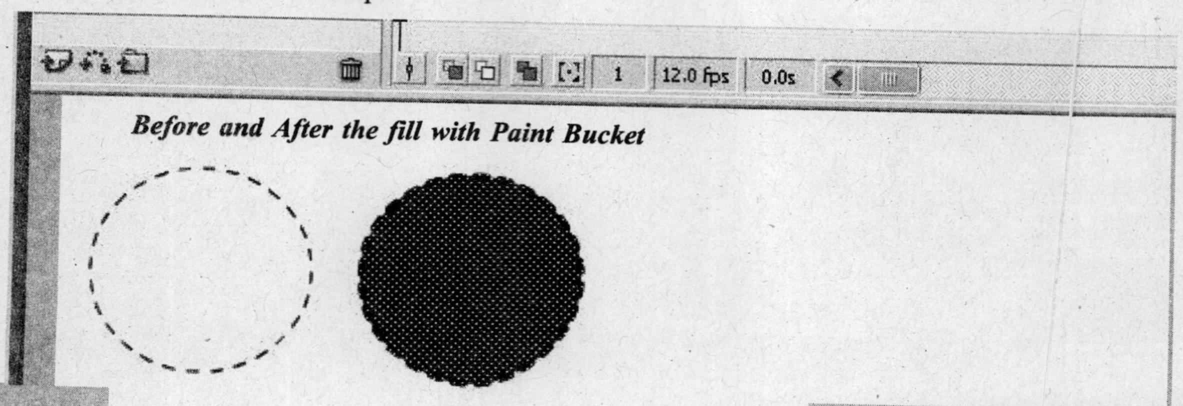

6.6.11 Filling shapes with Gradient Fill

Follow the following steps to fill the shape with gradient colour fill.

1. Click at Paint Bucket tool.
2. Click fill colour and hold down the mouse button.
3. The fill colour pallet opens.
4. Select a gradient colour given at the bottom of the colour pallet.
5. Click the shape you want to fill.
6. The gradient colour fills the shape.

There are various types of gradients available in Flash. There are fills which fill the colour from Left to Right, Top to Bottom, Middle to Outer Edges or even Outer edges to Middle. These are 2 colours or more than 2 colours. Two options are shown next.

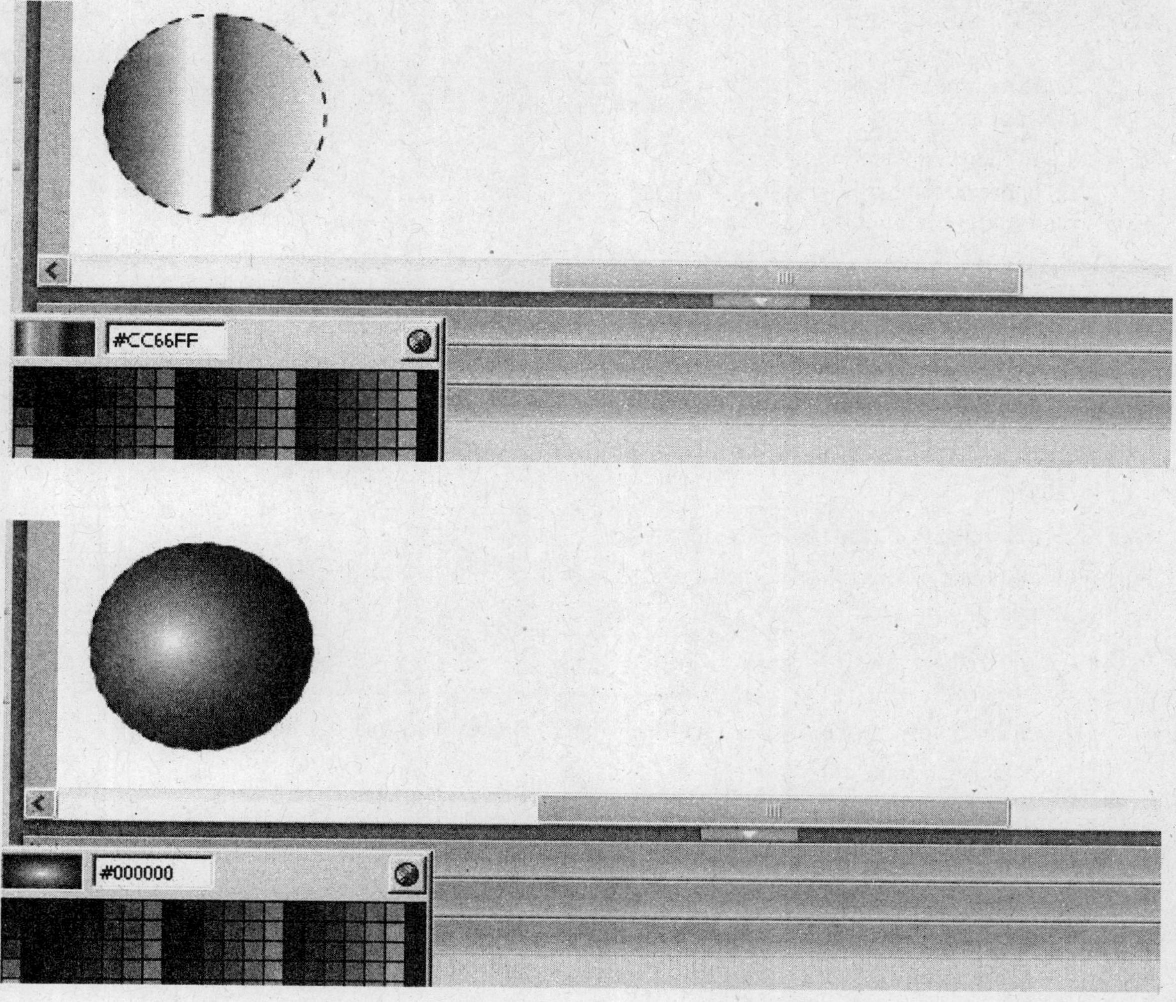

6.7 Creating Animations in Flash

Animation involves lots of steps. An animation in fact is running the various scenes together. So for running an animation, you must know how many scenes are there, how much time each has to take, and so. In this chapter, you will read about all this.

6.7.1 Setting Speed and Dimensions of the Document

Follow the following steps to set the properties of the movie.

1. Click at Modify.
2. Click Document.

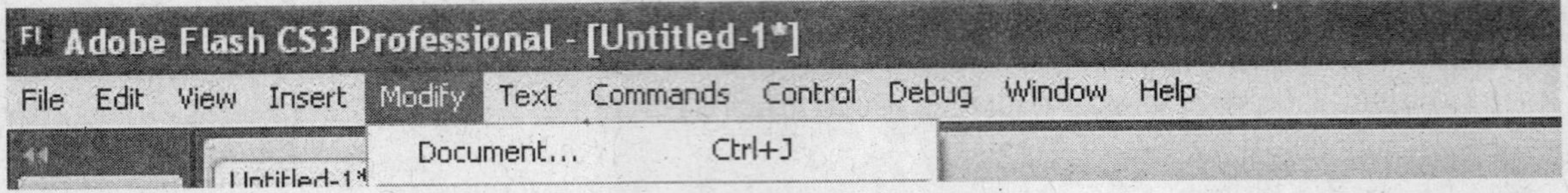

3. The Document Properties dialog box appears.
4. Type the number of frames per second you want the movie to play in the Frame Rate text box.
5. Type a width value in the Width text box.
6. Type a height value in the Height text box.
7. Click Ok.
8. The new dimensions are adjusted.

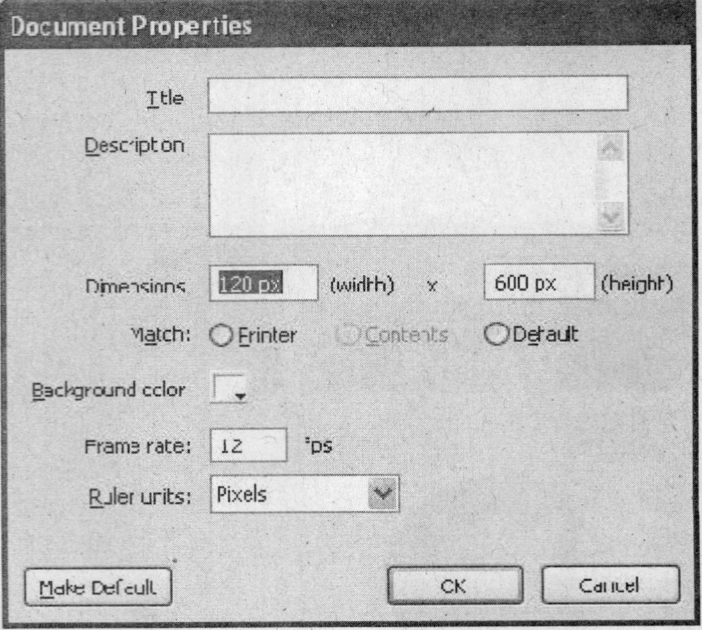

6.7.2 Adding Frames

Follow the following steps to set frames for the movie.

6.7.2.1 Adding A Regular Frame

1. Click an empty frame on the Timeline where you want to insert a new frame.
2. Click Insert menu.
3. Click at Timeline and then Frame.
4. A new frame is added.

6.7.2.2 Adding A Keyframe

1. Click an empty frame or a regular frame on the timeline where you want to place a new keyframe.
2. Click Insert menu.
3. Click at Timeline and then Keyframe.

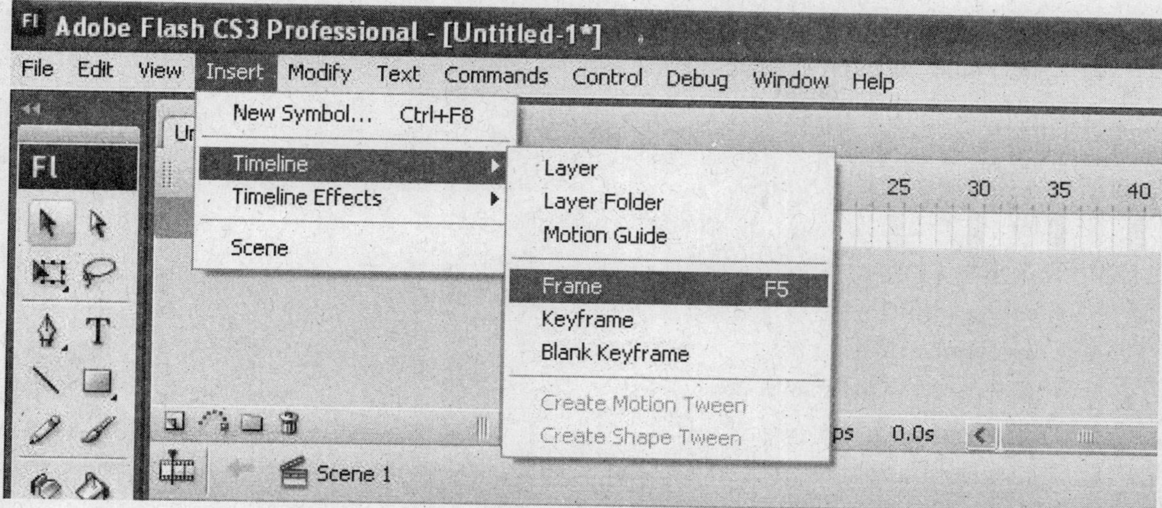

4. A new keyframe is added.

6.7.2.3 *Adding A Blank Keyframe*

1. Click a frame on the Timeline where you want to insert a blank keyframe.
2. Click Insert menu.
3. Click Timeline and then Blank Keyframe.
4. A new blank keyframe is added.

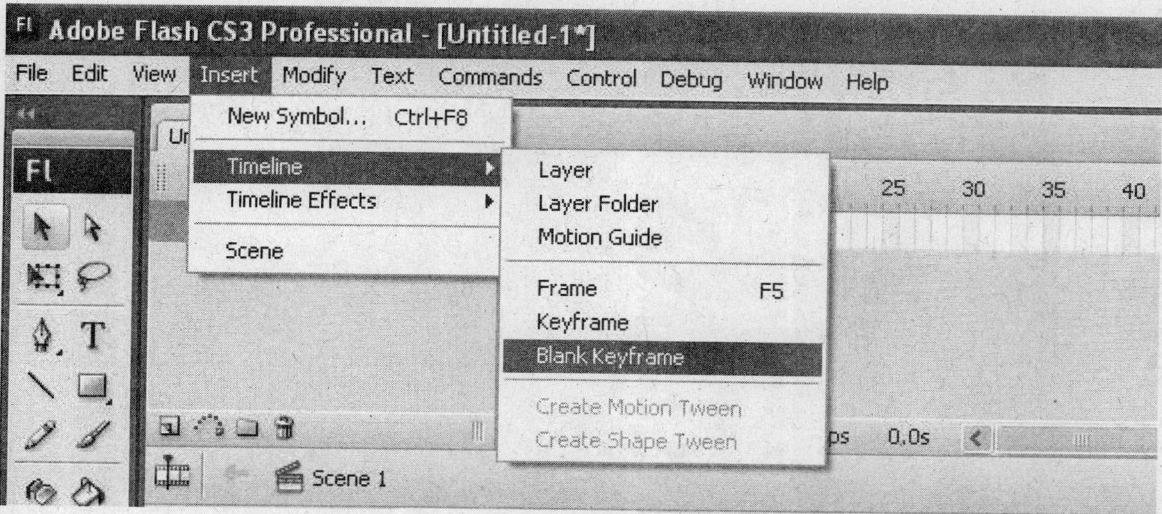

6.7.2.4 *Adding Multiple Frames*

1. Select two or more frames by clicking them.
2. To select multiple frames, click the first frame in the range, press the Shift key and click the last frame in the range.

3. Click Insert menu.
4. Click Frame to insert regular frames, or click Blank Keyframe to make the new frames all keyframes.
5. Flash inserts the same number of new frames and lengthens the movie.

6.7.2.5 *Deleting A Keyframe*

1. Click the frame, or range of frames, you want to delete.
2. To delete a range of frames, select the range first.
3. Click Insert menu.
4. Click Remove Frames.
5. The required frame/frames are deleted.

6.7.2.6 *Removing Keyframe Status*

1. To convert a keyframe to a regular frame, first click on the keyframe you want to change.
2. Click Insert menu.
3. Click Clear Keyframes.
4. The required frame/frames are converted.

6.7.3 Creating Animation Frame by Frame

Follow the following steps to create a movie frame by frame.

6.7.3.1 *Add Content to the First Frame*

1. Click the first frame in the layer you want to frame.
2. Place the object you want to animate or just insert an image from the clipart.
3. Click the next frame in the Timeline.
4. Add a keyframe. Flash inserts a keyframe that duplicates the previous frame's contents.

5. Change the object slightly. I have changed it to 90^0 to the right, as can be seen below.

6. Repeat the steps 4 and 5. This time the image will turn face down, as shown next.

7. Now again repeat the same steps, making the figure turn to 270^0 so that now it faces to the left, as shown on next page.

8. This way you can change the angle to a smaller degree and make more frames if you want to have real fun.
9. Click at first keyframe in the layer and press Enter.
10. You animation will be shown on the screen.

6.7.3.2 *Onion-skinning an Animation*

1. Click a frame.
2. Click Onion icon at the bottom of the Flash Timeline.
3. Flash displays dimmed images from the surrounding frames and places onion-skin markers at the top of the Timeline.
4. To turn off onion-skinning, you can click the onion icon again.

6.7.3.3 *Onion-skinning Outlines*

1. Click a frame.
2. Click Onion skin outline icon at the bottom of the Flash Timeline.
3. Flash displays outlines of the images from the surrounding frames and places onion-skin markers at the top of the Timeline.
4. To make the content of the onion-skin frames editable, click onion-skin outline marker.

6.7.3.4 *Changing the Marker Display*

1. To change how the onion-skin markers appear on the Timeline, click at Modify Onion Markers icon.
2. The Modify menu appears with options for changing the marker display.
3. Click the marker setting you want to apply.

6.7.3.5 *Previewing your Animation*

1. Click Control menu.
2. Click Test Movie.
3. Flash exports your movie to the Flash Player and plays the animation.

6.7.3.6 *Adjusting the Animation Speed*

1. Click the keyframe you want to add frames to.
2. Click Insert menu.
3. Click Frame. Flash adds a frame after the keyframe.
4. Because adding just one regular frame is not always enough, repeat steps 2 and 3 above to add a few more frames to the sequence.
5. To test the animation, click the first frame in the Timeline and press Enter.

6.7.4 Selecting Frames

You can select one or more frames for various purposes.

6.7.4.1 *Select a Single Frame*

1. Click the frame you want to select.
2. Flash highlights the frame in the Timeline.
3. If you have difficulty selecting a regular frame between two keyframes, press and hold Ctrl, then click the frame you want to select.

6.7.4.2 *Selecting Multiple Frames*

1. Click the first frame in the range of frames you want to select.
2. Press and hold Shift and click the last frame in the range.
3. Flash selects all the frames in-between.
4. To select multiple frames between two keyframes, click anywhere between the two keyframes.

6.7.4.3 *Modify Frame Properties*

1. Click the frame you want to modify.
2. Click Modify menu.
3. Click Frame.
4. The Frame panel opens.
5. You can type a label for the frame, if desired. The label appears in the Timeline.
6. You can use the other panel tabs to make changes to the frame object.
7. Click at X to close the panel.

6.7.4.4 *Move a Frame*

1. Click the frame to select it.
2. Flash highlights the frame in the Timeline.
3. Click and drag the frame to a new location in the Timeline. The pointer changes to Hand.
4. Drop the frame in place. The frame moves.

6.7.4.5 *Copy a Frame*

1. Click the frame to select it.
2. Flash highlights the frame in the Timeline.
3. Click Edit menu.
4. Click Copy Frames.
5. Click a frame where you want to place the copy.
6. Click Edit.
7. Click Paste Frames. The frame is pasted at the require location.

6.7.4.6 *Select a Single Frame*

1. Click the frame you want to select.
2. Flash highlights the frame in the Timeline.
3. If you have difficulty selecting a regular frame between two keyframes, press and hold Ctrl, then click the frame you want to select.

Let us Revise

1. Director is a software to create movies.
2. Stage is the window where all the action takes place.
3. Score provides the movie's timeline.
4. The Cast Window contains the cast members of your movie.
5. In the Cast window, you can create or import new cast members to appear as sprites on the Stage.
6. Toolbar presents icon shortcuts to common functions and operations.
7. A library palette is a palette which contains Director's built-in behaviours.
8. There are four types of inspectors in Director, each performs a specific task:.
9. The main menus in Director are: File, Edit, View, Insert, Modify, Control, Xtras, Window and Help.
10. A movie can consist of one or more cast libraries.
11. Director uses its graphics editor, the Paint window, for most of its painting requirements.
12. Importing lets you create cast members from external media
13. You use the Stage to determine where media elements, or cast members, should appear onscreen.
14. A sprite is an object that controls when, where, and how cast members appear in a Macromedia Director MX 2004 movie.
15. The Text tool in Director's Tool palette enables you to add text directly on the Stage.
16. The Text window, enables you to create and format blocks of text.
17. Sound can inform, guide, and stimulate the interest of the user.

18. Digital video is simply the result of capturing, storing, transmitting, and displaying a rapid succession of digitized images on a computer.
19. Director can play digital video using a feature called direct-to-Stage.
20. You can use the Behaviour inspector to create and modify behaviours to perform basic actions.
21. Flash is the most popular program for creating animations not only for Windows based programs but for Internet.
22. The Selection tool lets you select entire objects by clicking an object or dragging to enclose the object within a rectangular selection marquee.
23. You can use the Free Transform tool to freely transform objects, groups, instances, or text blocks.
24. The Lasso tool can also be used to split shapes or select portions of a line or shape.
25. When you draw with the Pen tool, you click to create points on straight line segments, and click and drag to create points on curved line segments.
26. To place text blocks on the Stage, you use the Text tool.
27. Drawing with the Line tool creates a perfectly straight line that extends from the starting point to the end point.
28. Pencil tool is used to draw lines and shapes.
29. The Brush Tool is used to paint with brush-like strokes and to fill enclosed areas with colours. The fills can be solid colours, gradients, or fills derived from bitmaps.
30. The Ink Bottle Tool is used to change the colour, style, and thickness of existing lines.
31. The Paint Bucket Tool is used to fill enclosed areas with colour, gradients or bitmap fills.
32. The eye dropper tool is used to acquire the colour and style information from existing pencil lines, brush strokes, and fills.
33. When you are zoomed in close on the screen, you can easily navigate the Flash workspace contents by using the Hand Tool.
34. Line tool allows you to draw various lines on the screen.
35. Using the pen tool too you can draw curves.
36. An animation in fact is running the various scenes together.

Multiple Choice Questions

1. Sound cannot be incorporated in the movie.
   (a) Yes **(b) No.**
2. Cast library of a movie can be changed.
   (a) True **(b) False.**
3. You can create Digital video using Director.
   (a) Yes **(b) No.**
4. Stage is the place where all the action takes place.
   (a) True (b) False.
5. Text window is used for typing small text.
   (a) True **(b) False.**
6. A scripting language is considered
   (a) a subset of HTML (b) a form of BASIC **(c) a very high** level language
   (d) a very low level language

7. How can you use text in a shape tweening
   (a) Text cannot be used in a shape tweening
   (b) make sure that text is broken tweening
   (c) make sure the text is broken apart
   (d) None of the above.
8. A media steam can be
   (a) On demand (b) live **(c) both** (a) and (b)
   (d) None of the above.
9. The biggest obstacles in the use of animation on the web
   (a) bandwidth limitations (b) difference in platforms (c) browser support
   (d) All of the above.
10. With multimedia authoring software you can make
    (a) video productions and animations
    (b) games and interactive web sites
    (c) demo disks and guided tours
    (d) all of the above.
11. Director software is used to create
    (a) animations
    (b) multimedia presentations
    (c) interactive multimedia applications
    (d) all of the above.
12. Elements are organized as pages of a book or a stack of cards in an ____________ authoring system.
    (a) Card based (b) Icon based (c) Time based
    (d) None of the above.
13. A broadcasting service transmitted via the Internet.
    (a) Web radio (b) Internet radio **(c) Web or Inter**net radio
    (d) None of these.
14. Page based authoring system contains media object(s)
    (a) buttons (b) text fields (c) graphic objects
    (d) all of the above
15. Streaming media is a media that is consumed ________ while it is being delivered.
    (a) read (b) heard (c) viewed
    (d) all of the above.

True/False Questions

1. Score provides the movie's timeline.
2. **Toolbar does not present** icon shortcuts to common functions and operations.
3. The main menus in Director are: File, Edit, View, Insert, Modify, Control, Xtras, Window and Help.
4. Importing lets you create cast members from external media
5. The Text tool in Director's Tool palette enables you to add text directly on the Stage.
6. Digital video is simply the result of capturing, storing, transmitting, and displaying a rapid succession of

digitized images on a computer.

7. Flash is the most popular program for creating animations not only for Windows based programs but for Internet.
8. **The Lasso tool cannot be use**d to split shapes or select portions of a line or shape.
9. Drawing with the Line tool creates a perfectly straight line that extends from the starting point to the end point.
10. **The Ink Bottle Tool is not use**d to change the colour, style, and thickness of existing lines.
11. When you are zoomed in close on the screen, you can easily navigate the Flash workspace contents by using the Hand Tool.
12. An animation in fact is running the various scenes together.

Matching Columns

In the following case, commands are given in the left hand columns and their actions in the right hand column. Match them.

Column A	Column B
A. Mask layer	1. .avi h
B. Program used to create full, multimedia productions, such as simulations and tutorials	2. The final stage of multimedia project production e
C. Tranporting real time voice and video over telecommunication services	3. script editor for debugging the user code f
D. A motion picture compression system	4. encapsulated postscript g
E. Multimedia authoring	5. GIF i
F. Lingo	6. two or more j
G. EPS	7. layer used to create an extra effect in Flash a
H. The standard movie/video format for windows	8. authoring software b
I. A compressed bitmap file tominimize the file size	9. video conferencing c
J. Frame necessary to create animation	10. MPEG d

Fill in the Blanks with appropriate words

a. timebased	b. timeline	c. icon based	d. object
e. JPEG	f. Shockwave format	g. virtual reality	h. viewed
i. Colour lookup table	j. cast	k. Lingo	l. end

1. The __________ is a multimedia database containing still images, sound files, text, palattes, quickdraw shapes, programming scripts, etc. j
2. In a multimedia authoring systems, multimedia elements and events are often treated as __________ that live ina hierarchical order of parent and child relationships. d
3. Elements and events are organized along a timeline in __________ authoring system. a
4. Multimedia elements and interaction events are organized as onjects in a structural framework or process in an ____________ authoring system. c
5. ________ is one of the file formats used by macromedia flash to save animation sequence. f
6. The GIF format uses a _________ to store the colour values of pixels. i

7. __________ is look and feel of virtual objects in virtual domain. g
8. For still pictures, the file format is _____________ and and for motion pictures the file format is MPEG. e
9. With time-based tools elements and events are organized along a ________. b
10. Card-based tools are best used with elements that can be _____________ individualy like the pages of a book. h
11. Time based tools are best to use when you have a message with a beginning and ___________. l
12. Director utilizes ___________ a full featured object oriented scripting language, to enable interactivity and programme control. k

Descriptive Type Questions

1. What is there on Director's interface?
2. What does the Score Editor do?
3. What is Cast Editor?
4. Describe the various tools available under Toolbar in Director.
5. What does Library palette contain?
6. What are Inspectors?
7. Describe the various commands available under the menu.
8. Which are the painting tools available in Director.
9. How would you import images to the Stage in Director?
10. What are Sprites?
11. How would you use the Text window?
12. What is Digital Video?
13. What are Behaviours?
14. Write a short note on Lingo.
15. What is the Cast window?
17. Describe what all is available under the following menus of Flash.

    File menu
    Edit menu
    View menu
    Insert menu
    Modify menu
    Text menu
    Control menu
    Windows menu
    Help menu
18. What does the following tools do?

    Arrow Tool
    The Subselection Tool
    The Line Tool
    The Lasso Tool
    The Pen Tool
    The Text Tool
    The Oval Tool
    The Rectangle Tool
    The Pencil Tool
    The Brush Tool
    The Free Transform Tool
    The Fill Transform Tool
    The Ink Bottle Tool
    The Paint Bucket Tool

The Dropper Tool — The Eraser Tool

The Hand Tool — The Magnifier Tool

19. How would you draw with various lines?
20. How would you customize a line?
21. How would you draw curves with the Pen tool?
22. How would you draw an oval shape?
23. How would you draw a rectangle shape?
24. How is brush tool used?
25. How is paint bucket tool used?
26. How would you set speed and dimensions of a movie?
27. How would you add various frames?
28. Describe the process of creating an animation frame by frame?
29. How would you select frames?
30. How would you modify frame properties?
31. How would you move, copy, select a frame?

Answers to Objective Type Questions

Multiple Choice Questions

1. b	2. b	3. b	4. a
5. b	6. c	7. b	8. c
9. d	10. d	11. d	12. a
13. c	14. d	15. d	

True False Questions

1. T	2. F	3. T	4. T
5. T	6. T	7. T	8. F
9. T	10. F	11. T	12. T

Matching Columns

A. 7	B. 8	C. 9	D. 10
E. 2	F. 3	G. 4	H. 1
I. 5	J. 6		

Fill in the Blanks

1. j	2. d	3. a	4. c
5. f	6. i	7. g	8. e
9. b	10. h	11. l	12. k

HTML Basics

7

7.1 Document Overview

HTML stands for Hypertext Markup Language. This is text oriented language used for writing programs to create web sites. There is no need for compiling or doing anything else as you would do in any other programming language. However, there are few things which you have to take care of as you do in your text related documents. You can have Headings, Paragraphs, Bulleted text, etc. You can even have tables too. However, there is no fix page layout as such. HTML does not support it. You can have the text in Bold, Italics, etc. But, each one of the above set of text, has to be tagged accordingly, e.g., Heading, for the text to be taken as headings. In fact Markup means this only. But, remember the file has to be text and not a word processing document. A simple ASCII text file.

As said earlier, HTML is used to create web sites. Since we now know that the text files are created using HTML but how are these so-called text files going to be used. These text files are used with programs called HTML browsers, take these HTML files and create web sites.

Follow the following steps to create a new web page:

1. Open a text editor or word processor.
2. Choose file> New to create a new, blank document.

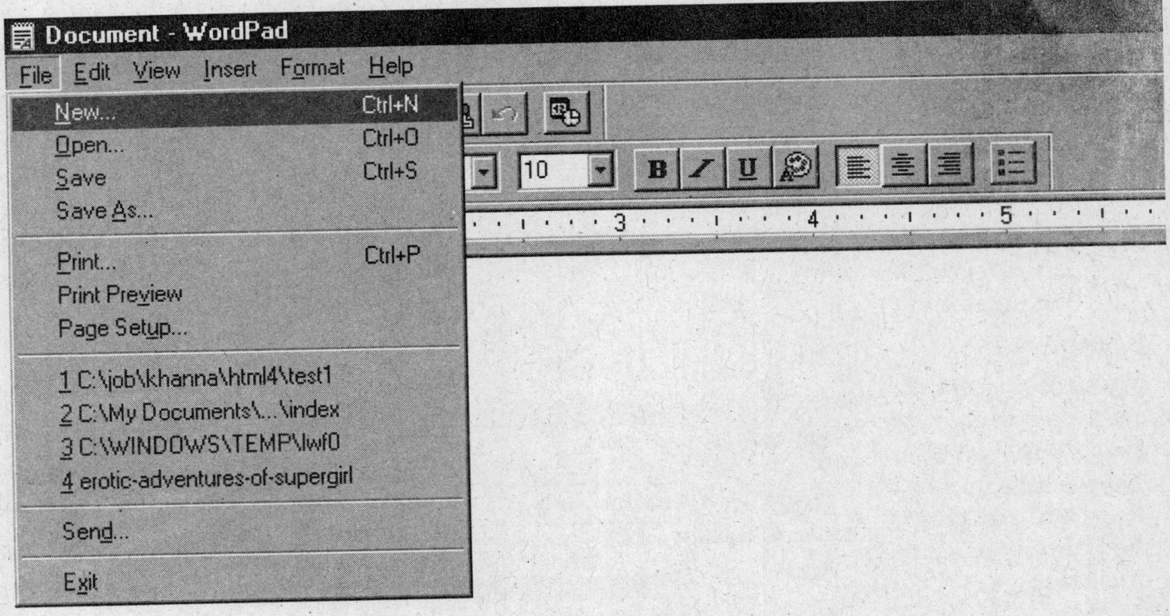

3. Type the following text to create the HTML content as shown next:
   Use
for line breaks

4. Choose File>Save As.
5. In the dialog box that appears, choose Text Document for the type.
6. Give the document the .htm or .html extension.
7. Choose the folder in which to save the Web page.
8. Click Save.

Remember

You must save the file in the Text Document format. Without this your file will have problem.

7.1.1 Looking at Your Page in a Browser

Once you have created a page, you'll want to see how it looks like in a browser. In fact, since you do not know which browser the actual user will be using, it's a good idea to look at the page in several browsers.

Follow the following steps to look at your page in a browser:

1. Open your browser software (Netscape Communicator, Microsoft Internet Explorer, etc.)
2. Choose File > Open, Open File, or Open Page (just not Open Location), depending on the browser.
3. In the dialog box that appears find the Web page that you want as it will appear when you actually publish it on the server.

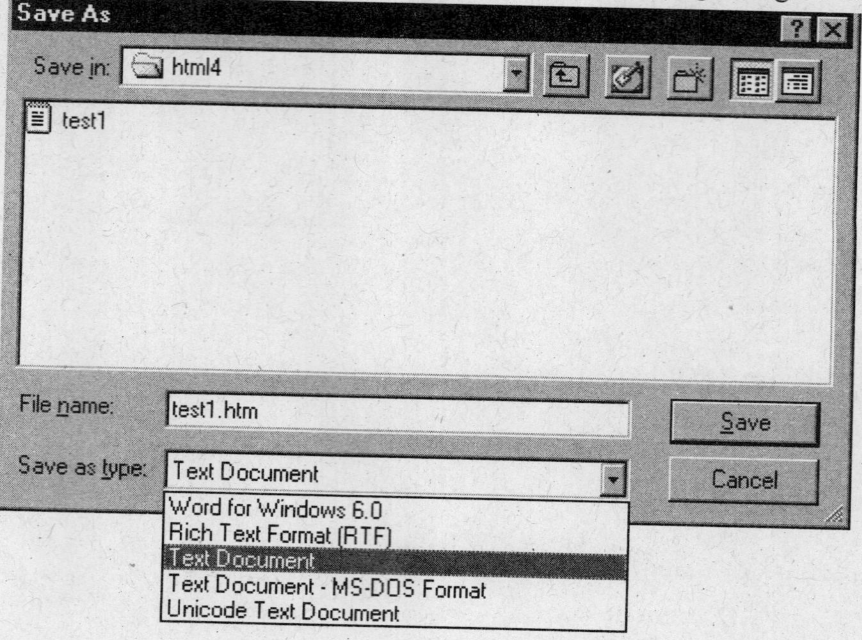

Remember

If your Web pages does not appear in the Open dialog box, make sure that you have saved it as Text Only and given it the .htm or html extension.

You don't have to close

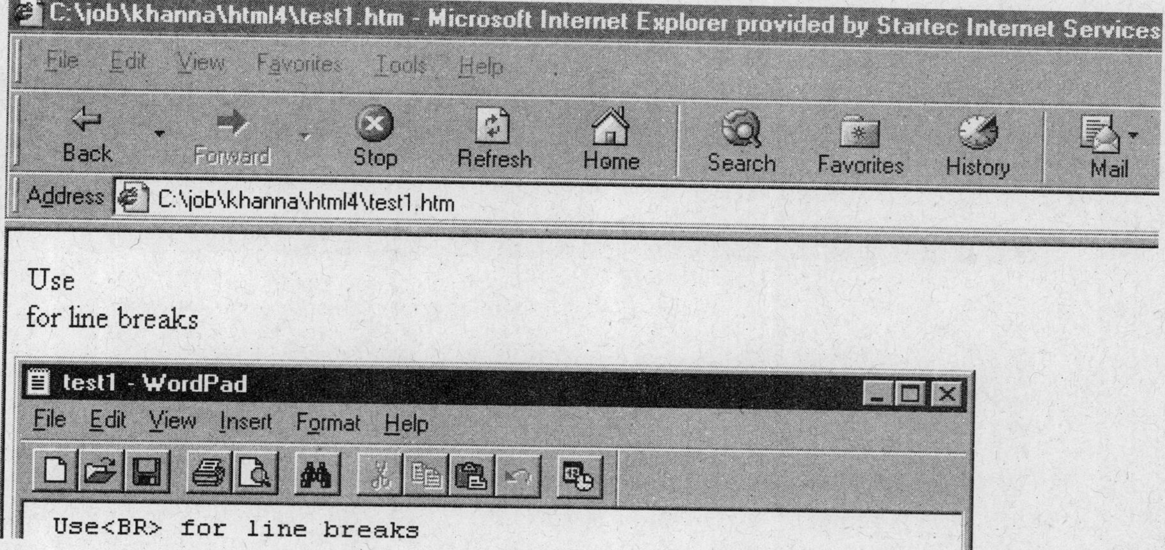

the document in the text editor before you view it with a browser. This makes editing much faster. You can switch to the editor, make your changes, and then back to the browser and click Reload to view the changes. It is not necessary to publish your pages on the sever before you view them. Publishing them on the server does not change them in any way (it only moves them to a new location).

7.1.2 Home Page Designating

Home page is the page which is shown on the screen, when the site is opened. The most common home page name is index.html but this varies from server to server.

To designate one page as the home page:

1. Create the home page as described above.
2. Name the file index.html (or whatever the default home page name is for your server).
3. Place the home page in the principal directory that contains your Web site.

Remember

Your home page should have links to all the other information available at your Web site. Your home page should be a table of contents to your site, not just the first page.

If you want your users to be able to reach the other pages in your site, make your home page clean, neat, and fast.

See the home page of Naukri.com, which is self explanatory.

7.1.3 Starting your Web page

When you want to see your page in the browser, the browser needs information right away about the kind of document it is, and how it should be displayed. You should begin every Web page with the !DOCTYPE and HTML tags.

Follow the following steps to start your Web page:

1. Type <!DOCTYPE HTML PUBLIC "-// W3C//DTD HTML at the top of your Web page, as shown on the next page.

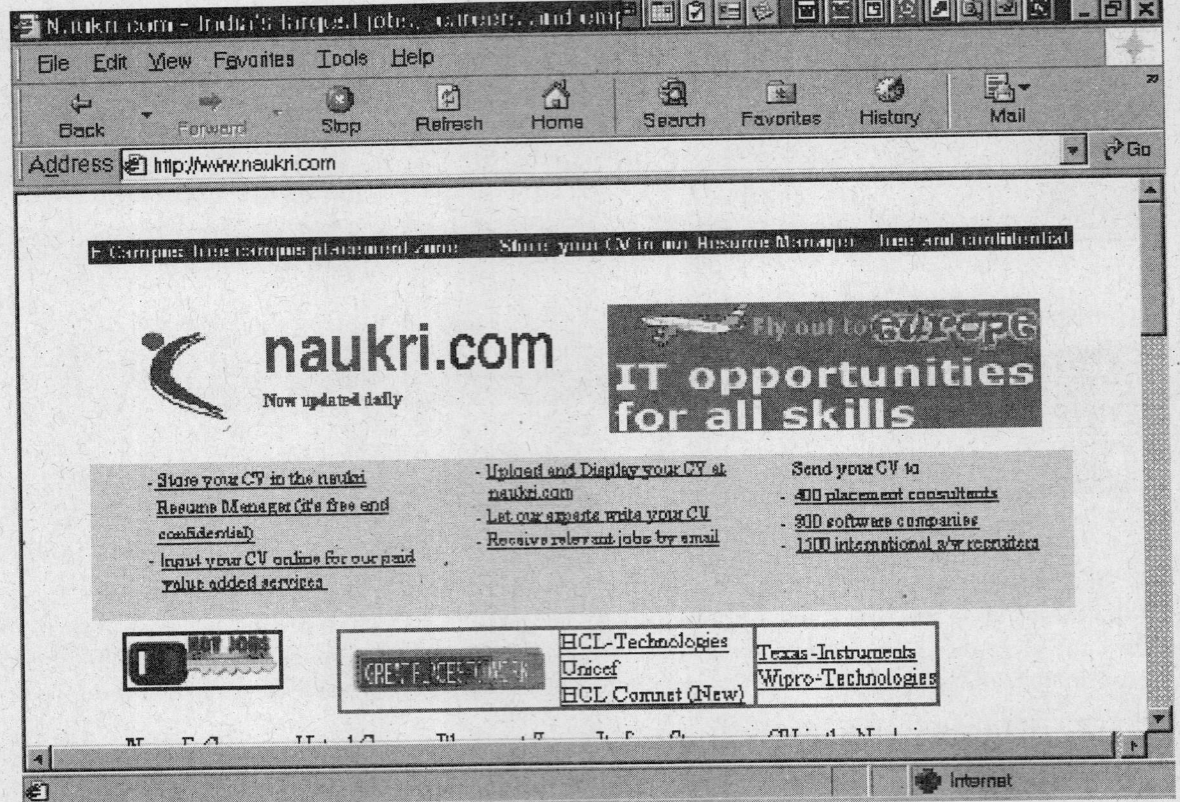

2. Type the version of HTML you're using, in this case 4.0. If you are using lots of fonts and colours, use the word Transitional with 4.0. If the pages have lots of frames, use HTML 4.0 Frameset.
3. Type //EN"> <HTML>.
4. Now your text file is ready. Save it under a name.
5. Start your browser and open this particular file.
6. See that there is a blank web page since you have not given any substance to your page. This is what we will do in the next step.

Remember

While you can get away without either the !DOCTYPE or HTML tags, you should always include both to ensure that your page is correctly recognized, regardless of the browser used.

Create a template with the !DOCTYPE and HTML tags already typed in as a starting point for all your pages.

7.2 Header Elements

Nothing is complete without a head and a body. Look at yourself and you know what I am talking about. Similarly in HTML too we have Head and Body as the two main sections. The Head section provides information about the URL of your Web page as well as its relationship with the other pages

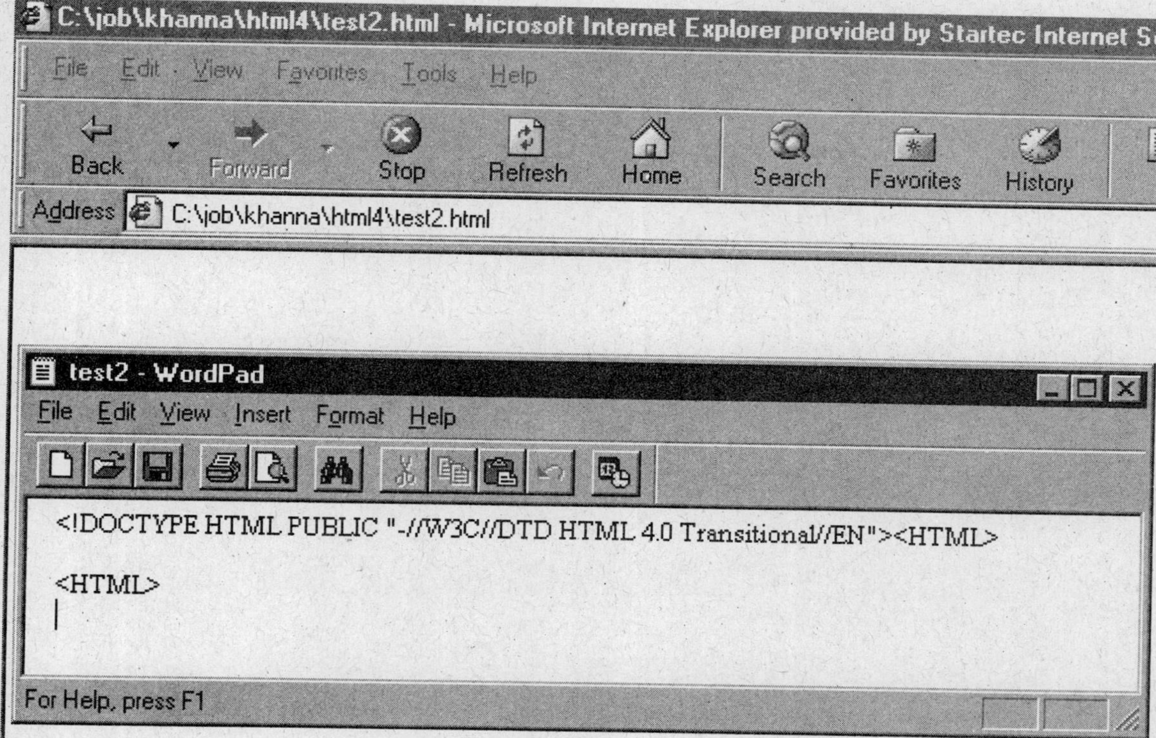

at your site. The only element in the HEAD section that is visible to the user is the title of the Web page. The BODY of your HTML document contains the bulk of your Web page, including all the text, graphics, and formatting.

Follow the following steps to create the Head section:

1. Directly after the initial !DOCTYPE and HTML type <HEAD>.
2. Create the HEAD section, including the TITLE.
3. Type </HEAD>.

Follow the following steps to create the BODY:

1. After the final </HEAD> tag and before anything else, type <BODY>.
2. Create the contents of your Web page.
3. Type </BODY>.

7.2.1 Creating a Title

Each page must have a title. A title should be short and descriptive. In some browsers, the title appears in the title bar of the window; in others, the title is centered at the top of the screen. The title is used in search indexes as well as in browsers' history lists and bookmarks.

Follow the following steps to create a title:

1. Place the cursor between the opening and closing HEAD tags, as shown on the next page.
2. Type <TITLE>.

3. Enter the title of your web page.
4. Type </TITLE>.

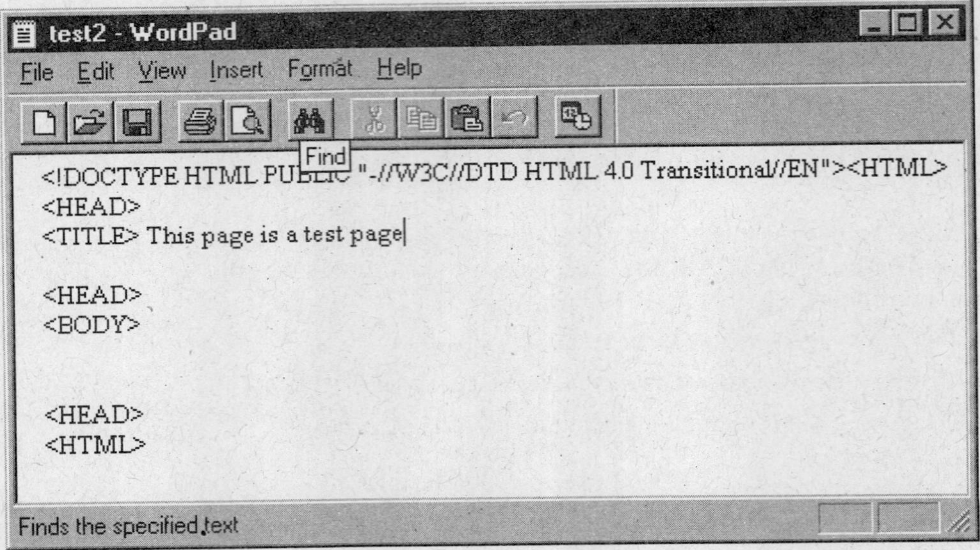

Remember

There must be only one TITLE tag in each HTML document. A title cannot contain any formatting, images, or links to other pages. Don't use colons or backslashes in your titles. These symbols cannot be used by some operating systems for file names. It's good idea to use a common element to begin each page's title.

For example, you could begin each page with My Page: followed by the specific area described on that page.

7.3 Section headings

Various type of headings can be placed in the text. Maximum of 6 headings are allowed. But, you can use only 3 at a time. Each one of the heading is numbered from 1 onward. Obviously you cannot repeat the numbers.

Let us try to create a heading.

1. In the BODY section of your HTML document, type (Hn where n is a number from 1 to 6, depending on the level of header that you want to create). Here I have used it as H1.
2. Type the contents of the header, in this case I have typed it as "Information Technology Class X.
3. Type </Hn> where n is the same number used in step 1, in this case H1.
4. The result of this typing and result in browser are both shown next.

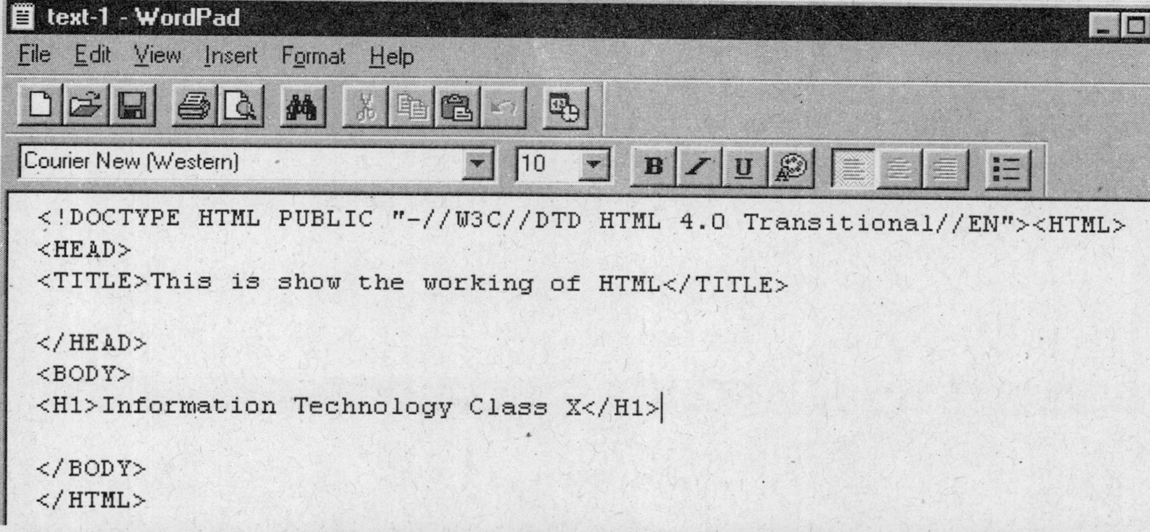

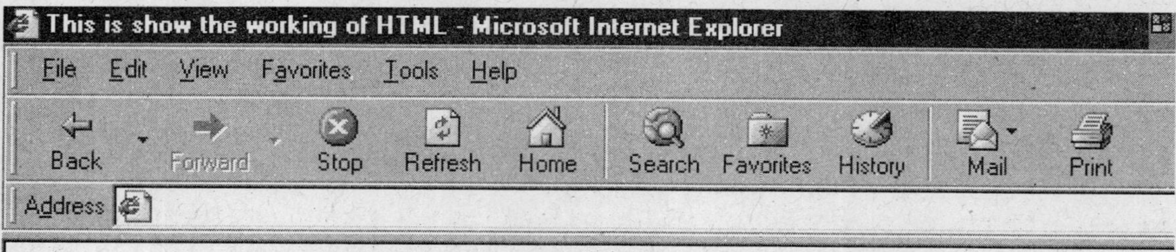

7.4 Block headings

For every new paragraph in HTML you must use the p tag, as was mentioned in the earlier paragraph. The following example shows how it is done.

1. After the heading line, press Enter to reach the next line in Word Pad.
2. Type <p> to start the new paragaph.

3. Type the text which you want to put in the paragraph. I have typed here KHANNA PUBLISHING PVT. LTD.
4. Close the paragraph by using the tag </p>.
5. The text in Word Pad and its effect in the browser are shown next.

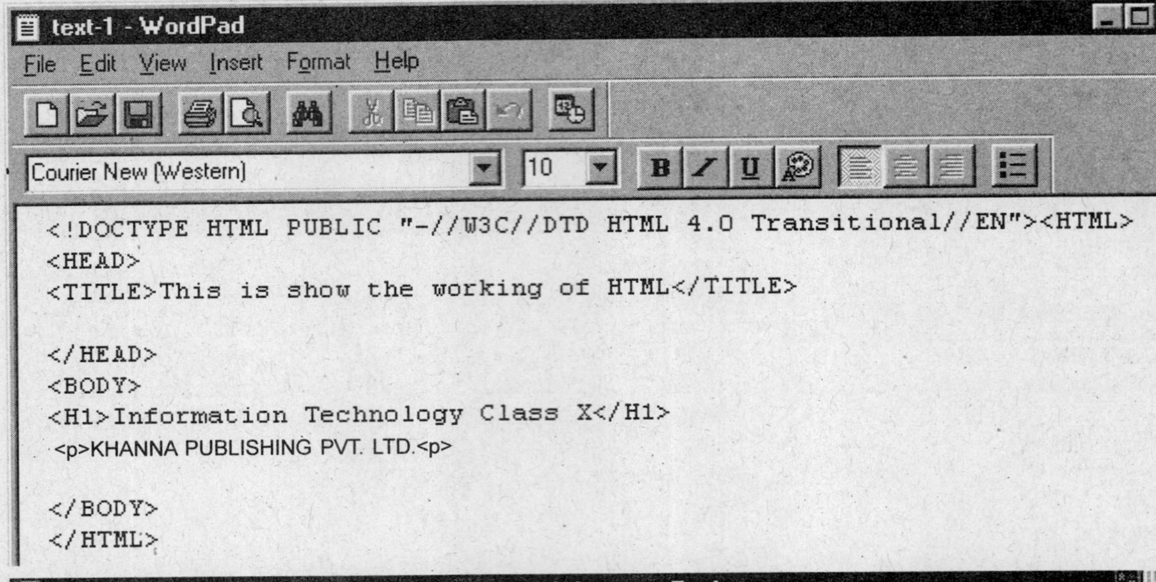

```
<!DOCTYPE HTML PUBLIC "-//W3C//DTD HTML 4.0 Transitional//EN"><HTML>
<HEAD>
<TITLE>This is show the working of HTML</TITLE>

</HEAD>
<BODY>
<H1>Information Technology Class X</H1>
<p>KHANNA PUBLISHING PVT. LTD.<p>

</BODY>
</HTML>
```

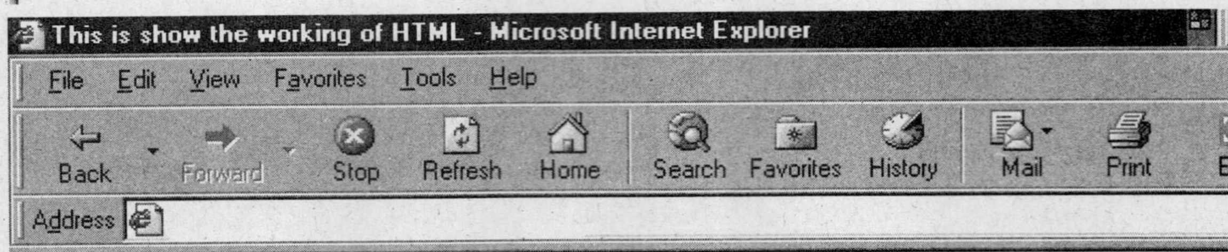

7.5 Lists

HTML support 3 type of lists: Unordered lists, Ordered lists and Definition lists. Ordered lists are numbered in some fashion, while Unordered lists are bulleted. Definition lists consist of a term followed by its definition.

Both ordered and unordered lists require start and end tags as well as the use of a special element to indicate where each list item begins (the <LI> tag). Unordered lists can be preceded by one of several bullet styles: a closed circle, an open circle, or a square.

The tags for an unordered list are <UL> and </UL>. Ordered lists can be preceded by Arabic numerals, uppercase or lowercase Roman numerals, or uppercase or lowercase alphanumeric characters. The tags for an ordered list are <OL> and </OL>. Definition lists require a start tag (<DL>) and end tag (</DL>) and two special elements: one for definition terms (the <DT> tag) and one for definitions (the <DD>) tag.

In addition to these three types of lists, HTML also allows two other types of lists that are much less commonly used: Directory lists (which use the <DIR> tag) and Menu lists (the <MENU> tag). However, these two types of lists are not very popular.

7.5.1 Unordered Lists

As said earlier, this list uses the <UL> and </UL> tags. The only element that can be contained inside the <UL> and </UL> tags is a list item, signified with the list item element. The list item element uses the <LI> tag (and optionally the </LI> tag) and contains the actual content of your lists. Both <UL> and <LI> have the same set of attributes:

```
TYPE="CIRCLE"
TYPE="DISC"
TYPE="SQUARE"
```

The CIRCLE attribute value is used for a hollow bullet, the DISC type creates a solid bullet, and the SQUARE value renderes a solid block. The default appearance for a list is with a disc. You can use an optional </LI> end tag at the end of each list item, however, the </UL> end tag is always required at the end of the unordered list.

Even though both the <UL> tag and the <LI> tag can take the TYPE attribute, it's much more common to use the attribute with the <UL> tag so that the entire list takes on the appearance you desire. For example, here is some HTML that generates two separate lists:

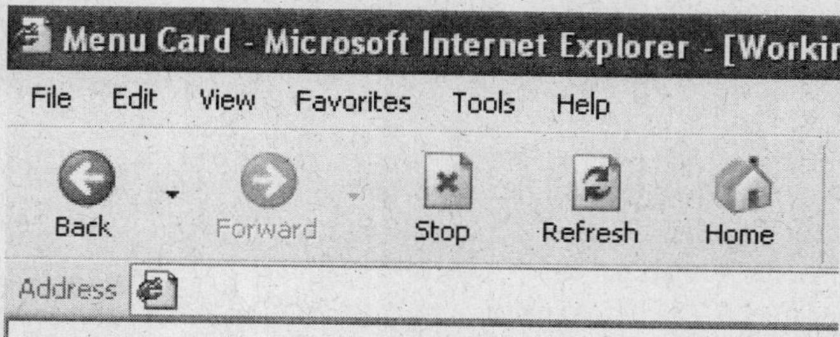


```
<TITLE>Menu Card</TITLE>
<BODY>
<p><Breakfast>
<UL>
<LI>Eggs
<LI>Milk
<LI>Apples
<LI>Coffee
</UL>
```

```
<p>Dinner
<UL TYPE="SQUARE">
<LI>Soup
<LI>Salad
<LI TYPE="CIRCLE"> Chicken
<LI TYPE="DISC">Rice
<LI TYPE="CIRCLE">Dessert
</UL>
```

See the result of this in the browser next.

One important aspect of lists is that you can nest one list inside another to create a sublist. The default appearance of the sublists will vary from the main list, with the first sublist using circle bullets and the next nested list, using squares. For example:

```
<UL>
<LI>Microsoft
    <UL>
    <LI>Windows
    <LI>Office
        <UL>
        <LI>Microsoft Word
        <LI>Microsoft Excel
        </UL>
    <LI>Internet Explorer
    </UL>
<LI>Adobe
    <UL>
    <LI>PageMaker
        <UL>
        <LI>Version 7.0
        </UL>
    </UL>

<LI>CorelDRAW
    <UL>
```

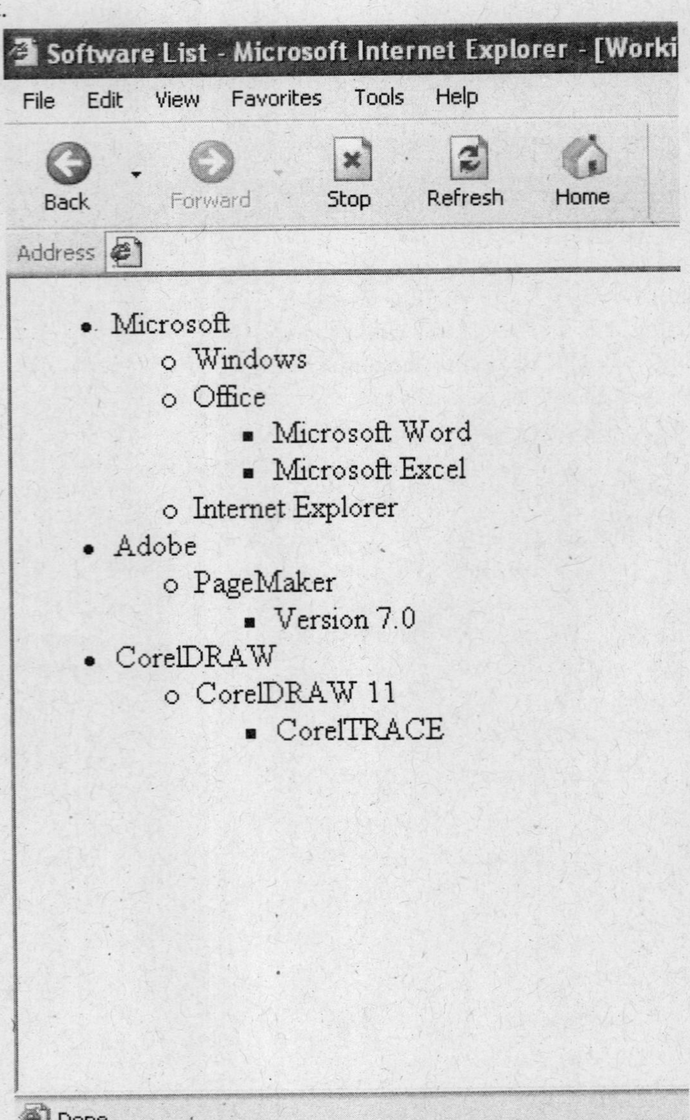

```
      <LI>CorelDRAW 11
         <UL>
         <LI>CorelTRACE
         </UL>
      </UL>
   </UL>
```

The list would be displayed with the sublists indented beneath the main list, much like we have shown in the source code for readability. There are a total of seven lists here. Each <UL> tag begins a new list. The main list (Microsoft, Adobe, and CorelDRAW) has six sublists - two per bulleted point. The above figure shows the same.

7.5.2 Creating Ordered Lists

The ordered list element's <OL> and </OL> tags are used to create ordered lists. Like unordered lists, ordered list must contain list item elements (with the <LI> tag) to contain your list's text. In fact, ordered lists are identical in behaviour to unordered lists, except they use numbers instead of bullets and you can use an attribute to start numbering at a number other than one.

Here are the attributes you can use with the <OL> tag:

```
TYPE="1"    (Arabic numbers)
TYPE="a"    (lowercase alphanumeric)
TYPE="A"    (uppercase alphanumeric)
TYPE="i"    (lowercase Roman numbers)
TYPE="I"    (uppercase Roman numbers)
START="X"   (Arabic numbers)
```

The Type attribute allows you to specify the numbering system you want to use. Arabic numbers are the default. In addition, when you are using ordered lists, the <LI> tag can use the VALUE attribute to make a particular list item have a certain number.

The value attribute is shown here:

```
<OL>
<LI>Milk
<LI>Bread
<LI>Ham
<LI VALUE="10">Coffee
<LI>Fruit
</OL>
```

In a browser the order of this list would appear as follows:

1. Milk
2. Bread
3. Ham

10. Dark Chocolate
11. Fruit

7.5.3 Definition Lists

The definition list element uses the <DL> start tag and the </DL> end tag to create a definition list. This list is rendered without bullets. The <DT> tag is used for definition terms (that is, the name or title of the item you are defining). The <DD> tag is used for the definitions themselves. For example,

```
<DL>
<DT>Microsoft Excel
<DD>A spreadsheet program
<DT>Microsoft Word
<DD>A word processing program
</DL>
```

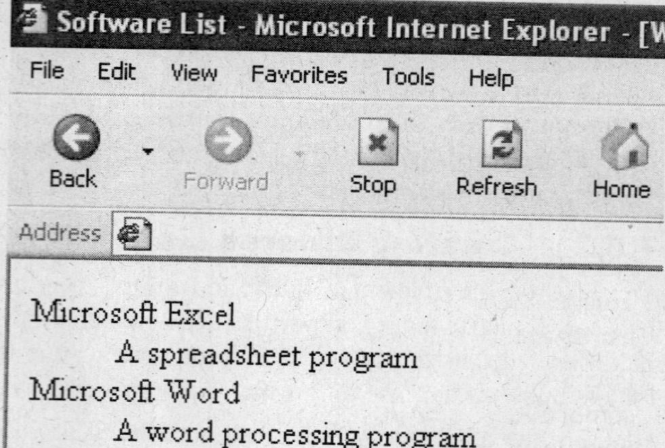

Here is how this would look in the browser.

7.5.4 Using Directory and Menu Lists

There are two other types of lists defined in HTML: Directory lists and Menus. However, these two types of lists are rarely used, and Navigator and Internet Explorer treat them identically to the way they treat unordered lists.

The directory list element is signified by the <DIR> and </DIR> tags. This element was intended to be used for directory lists of short items (some sources recommend 20 or fewer characters so they can be listed in columns 24 characters wide). Here is a quick example of a directory list:

```
<DIR>
<LI>Item 1
<LI>Item 2
<LI>Item 3
</DIR>
```

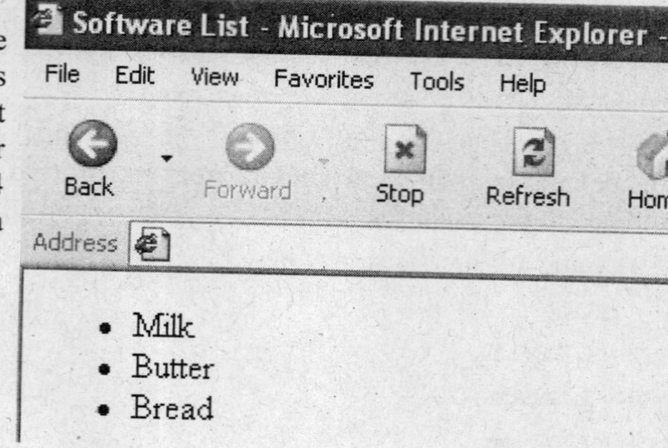

Similarly the <MENU> and </MENU> tags make up the menu element, which is used for the menu lists. Menus can appear with different spacing results in different browsers, but Navigator and Internet Explorer don't display menu lists any differently than unordered lists. Here is a quick sample menu:

```
<MENU>
<LI>Milk
<LI>Butter
```

```
<LI>Bread
</MENU>
```

For both directory and menu lists, the only item that should be contained is a list-item element (the <LI> tag).

7.6 Uniform Resource Locators

Full form of URL is Uniform Resource Locator. It is the location of a web site or called the domain name of the site. It is like the telephone number of the person. For better understanding, let us see what the domain name means.

7.6.1 Understanding Domain Names

As we know, there is nobody who controls the Internet. Then you might wonder as to who allots the name to the users. An addressing system was designed by the Internet Engineering Task Force (IETF). This addressing scheme assigns names and numbers to identify the computers on the Internet. These names are called domain names and numbers are called IP addresses.

Every computer system on the Internet has both a domain name and an IP address. This address contains four sets of numbers separated by periods or dots. Each set of numbers can have the values ranging from 1 to 255, The numbers between the dots is called an octet. An IP address is organized from left to right where the leftmost represents the largest network organization and the rightmost octet describes the actual network connection. These combined parts are always unique for the given host. This scheme has been proved good but the numbers become difficult to manage and to quite an extent impossible to remember. A method for recognition of computers by names was therefore devised. A smaller network making up the Internet, and having many computers or even smaller networks within it, is called a domain. This domain may represent either a type of organization or a geographical location. Smaller networks and computers forming part of the domain may be further split up into sub-domains.

For example, my network connection has the following codes:

```
nda.vsnl.net.in
```

These codes signify the following:

nda	A code given by VSNL, denoting their computer name.
vsnl	Organization code of the service provider, in this case VSNL.
net	Network provider
in	Country code, i.e., India.

Various other options for Network providers are:

com	A company or commercial organization Example, microsoft.com
net	Network resources or Internet Service provider Example, internic.net
mil	Available to United States Government agencies, including the US military Example, army.mil
org	Organization, like Non-profit Government Organizations (NGOs), Religious bodies, etc.

	Example, osho.org
gov	Government organizations. Example, pmo.gov
edu	Educational institutions, colleges, schools, etc. Example, du.edu
to	This is relatively new alternative to the .com extensions. It can be used for virtually any purpose. Example, toinfo.to

Some other options for Countries are (there are many more) :

au	Australia
uk	United Kingdom
usa	United States of America
fr	France
ca	Canada

7.7 Images

HTML supports all kind of graphic images. They can be logos or photographs. Graphics once inserted are displayed on the site page. Follow the following steps to insert an image on a page:

1. Place the cursor where you want the image to appear.
2. Type <IMG SRC=" image.ext" where image.ext indicates the location of the image file on the server.
3. In the example I have typed this after the <HEAD> line. Since I would be using GLOBE.JPG in the text, I have used its location.
4. If desired, type BRODER = n, where n is the thickness of the border in pixels. I have not used any.
5. Type the final >.
6. See the result, how it looks in the browser on the next page. Also note the text how it is typed in the word pad.

Remember

You can add graphics with extensions like, GIF, JPEG, PNG, or any other kind of images that the browser recognizes. Don't expect your visitors to he site to wait for more than 30 seconds to load and view your page.

So get the smaller images, create miniatures of large images and let visitors choose to view the larger images only if desired.

7.7.1 Specifying Size for Fast Viewing

As mentioned above your image should be small so that it can be loaded fast. If you specify the image's dimensions, the browser can fill in the text around the image as the image loads, so that your visitors can read the page without having to wait for the images. Follow the following steps to specify the size of your image:

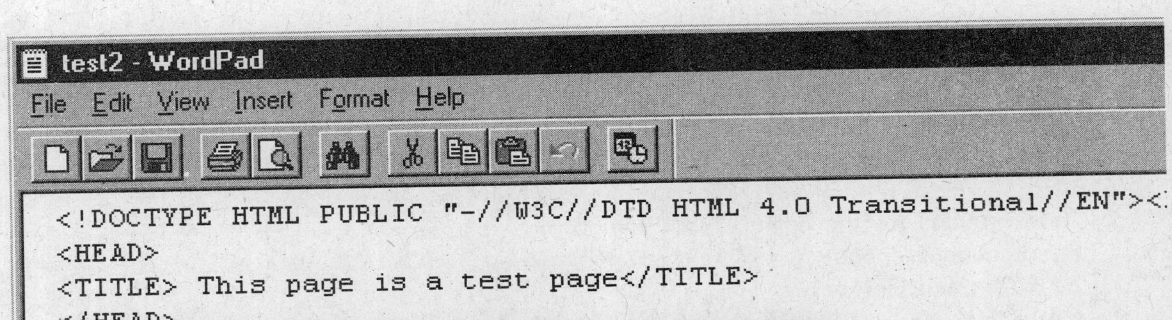

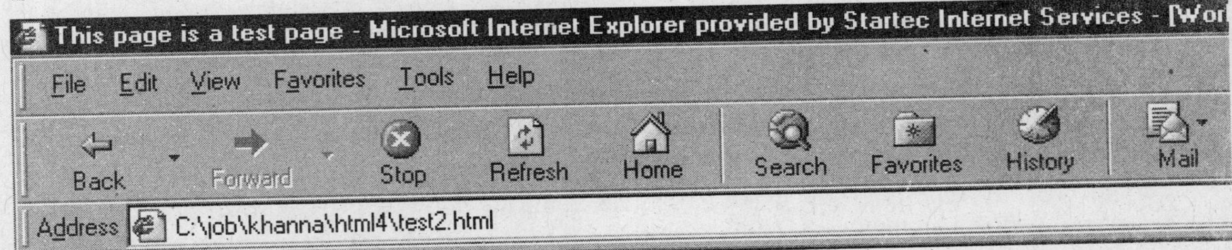

I am trying to learn HTML

After learning **HTML**, I will create my own Web page.

1. Open the image in Photoshop, or other image editing program.
2. Choose Image > Image Size.
3. Choose pixels for the unit of measure in both the Width and Height pop-up menus.
4. Write down the values shown in the Width and Height text boxes. In this case the width is 150 and height is 185 pixels.
5. In your HTML document where you wish the image to appear, type <IMG SRC = " image.location", where image.location is the location of the image on the server. This is done as was done in the previous case.

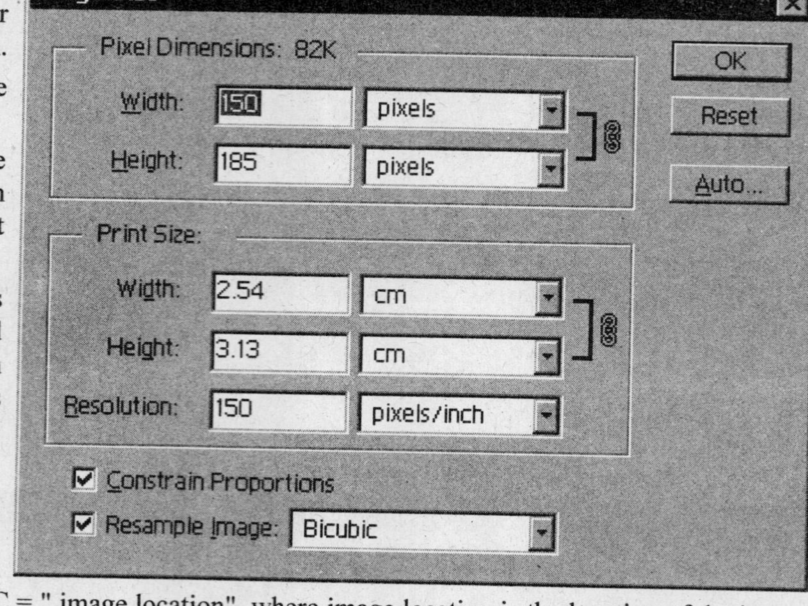

6. Type WIDTH=x HEIGHT=y, using the values you jotted down in step 4 to specify the values for x and y (the width and height of your image) in pixels. In this case width would be 150 and height to be 185.

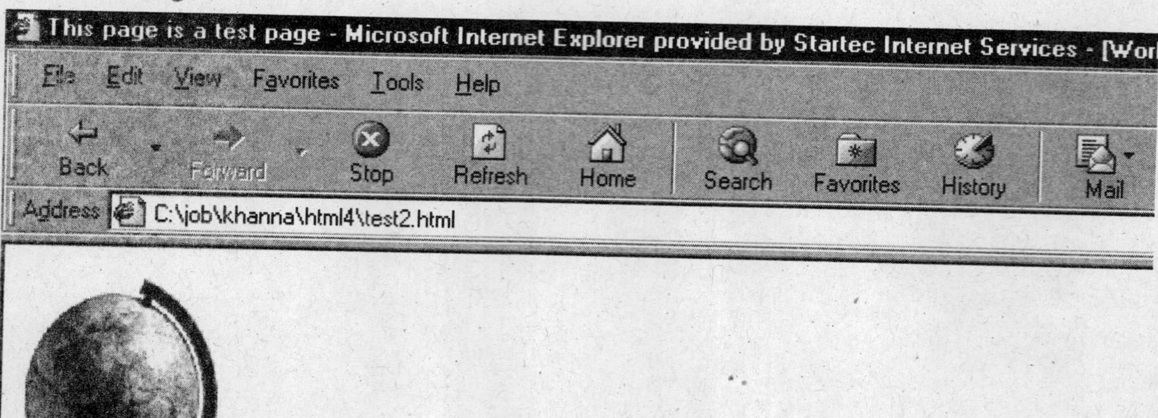

I am trying to learn HTML

7. Add other image attributes as described and then type the final >.
8. See how the figure looks like on the next page. I have deliberately used width as 100 and height as 145, since if I had used the same options, you would not have noticed the difference in the picture. Text is also given there.

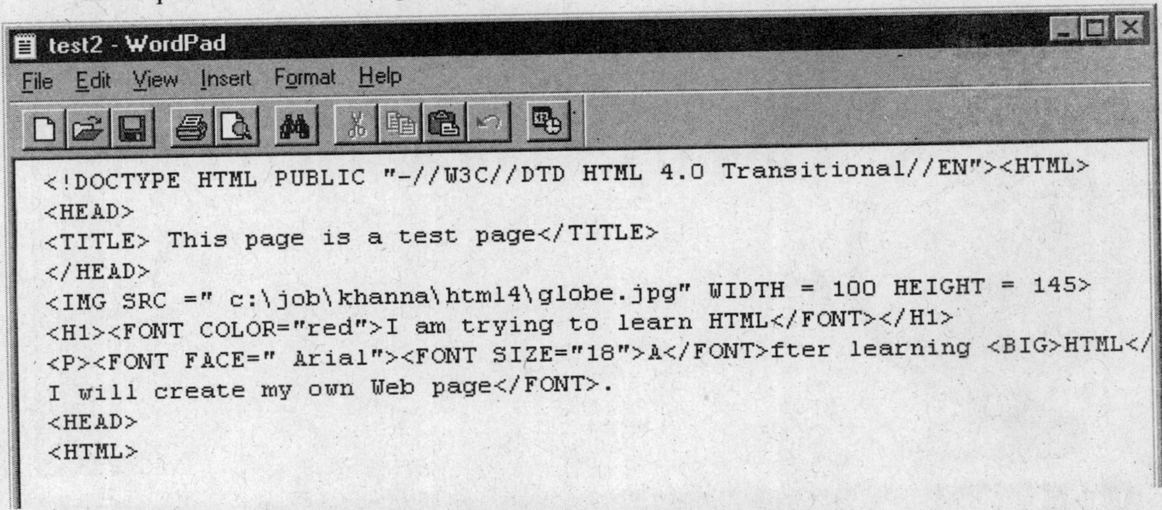


```
<!DOCTYPE HTML PUBLIC "-//W3C//DTD HTML 4.0 Transitional//EN"><HTML>
<HEAD>
<TITLE> This page is a test page</TITLE>
</HEAD>
<IMG SRC =" c:\job\khanna\html4\globe.jpg" WIDTH = 100 HEIGHT = 145>
<H1><FONT COLOR="red">I am trying to learn HTML</FONT></H1>
<P><FONT FACE=" Arial"><FONT SIZE="18">A</FONT>fter learning <BIG>HTML</
I will create my own Web page</FONT>.
<HEAD>
<HTML>
```

7.7.2 Wrapping Text around Images

It is not that you would always have the image covering the full width of the screen. You can use the ALIGN attribute (with the left and right variables only) to wrap text around an image.

1. Type <IMG SRC = "image.location" as was done earlier.
2. Either type ALIGN=left to align the image to the left of the screen while the text flows to the right or type ALIGN= right to align the image to the right edge of the screen while the text flows on the left side of the image.
3. Add other image attributes, as described in other parts of this chapter, if desired.
4. Type the final >.
5. See the result in the browser, as shown next alongwith the HTML text .

In this case I have used the option of aligning the image to the left and let the text flow on the right.

Remember

When you choose ALIGN=right, it's the image that goes to the right (while the text goes to the left). When you choose ALIGN=left, again the image will be on the left side with the text flowing around the right side.

7.7.3 Wrapping Text between Two Images

1. Type <IMG SRC=" right.image" ALIGN=right> where right.image indicates the location of the image that should appear on the right side of the screen. In this case I would be using the above Globe.JPG on the right.
2. Type the text that should flow around the first image.
3. Type <IMG SRC=" left.image". ALIGN=left> where left.image indicates the location of the

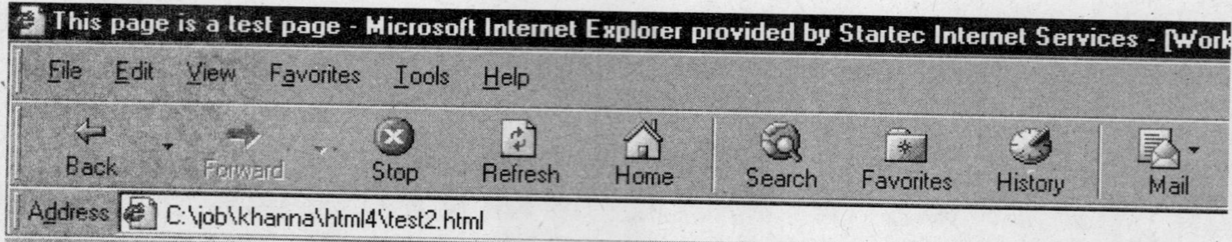

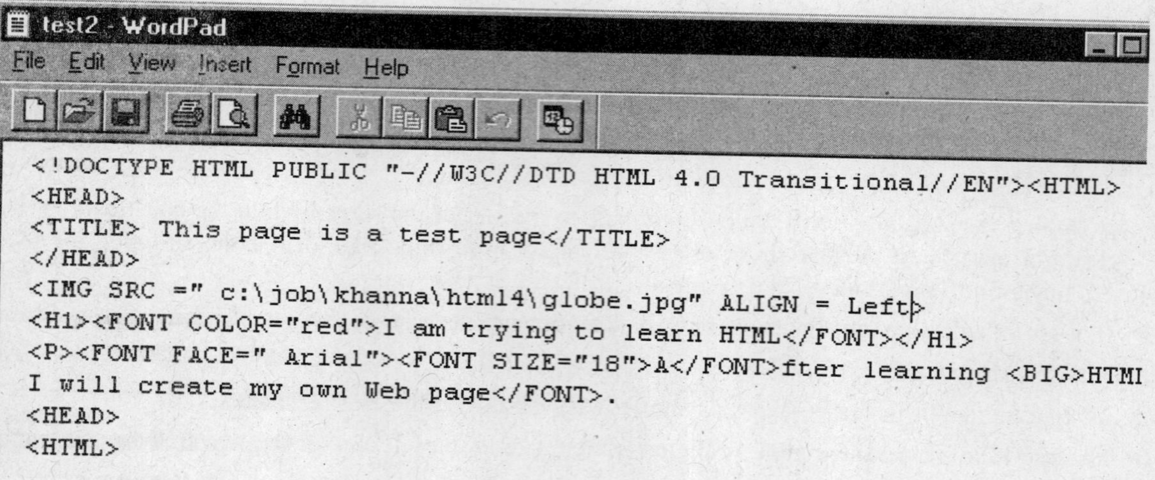


```
<!DOCTYPE HTML PUBLIC "-//W3C//DTD HTML 4.0 Transitional//EN"><HTML>
<HEAD>
<TITLE> This page is a test page</TITLE>
</HEAD>
<IMG SRC =" c:\job\khanna\html4\globe.jpg" ALIGN = Left>
<H1><FONT COLOR="red">I am trying to learn HTML</FONT></H1>
<P><FONT FACE=" Arial"><FONT SIZE="18">A</FONT>fter learning <BIG>HTMI
I will create my own Web page</FONT>.
<HEAD>
<HTML>
```

image that should appear on the left side of the screen. In this case I am using another picture of the same globe.

4. If desired, type <P> to begin a new paragraph. that will be aligned with the image placed in step 3.
5. Type the text that should flow around the second image.
6. See the result as it appears in the browser, below. Text is shown on the next page.

Remember

Each image will continue to push the text to on side until it either encounters a break or until there is no more text.

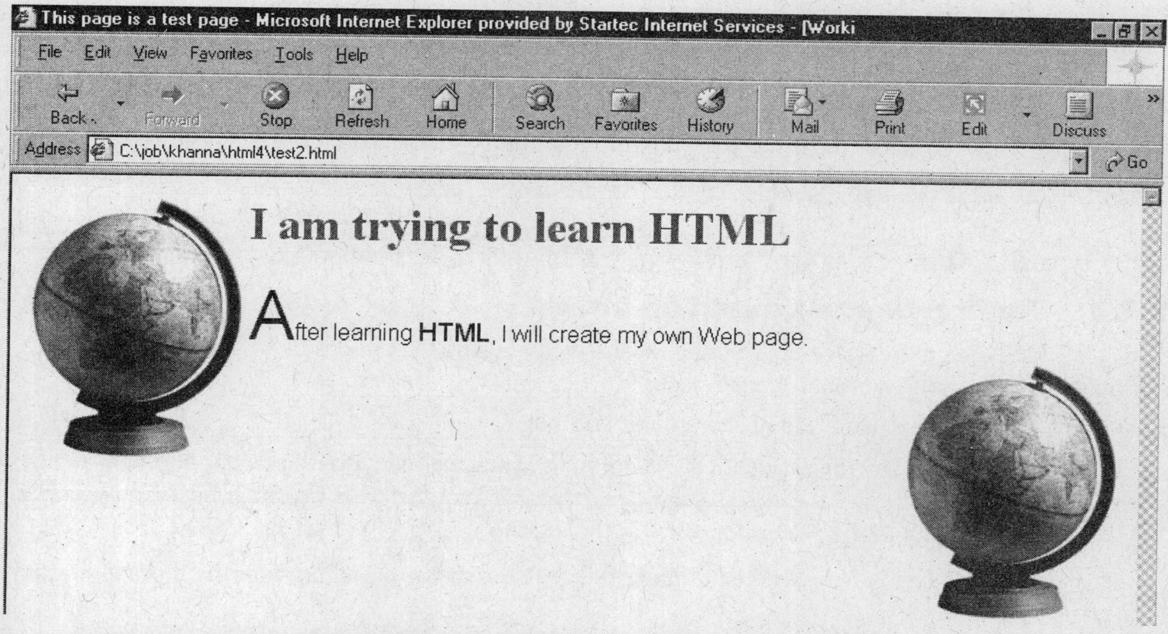

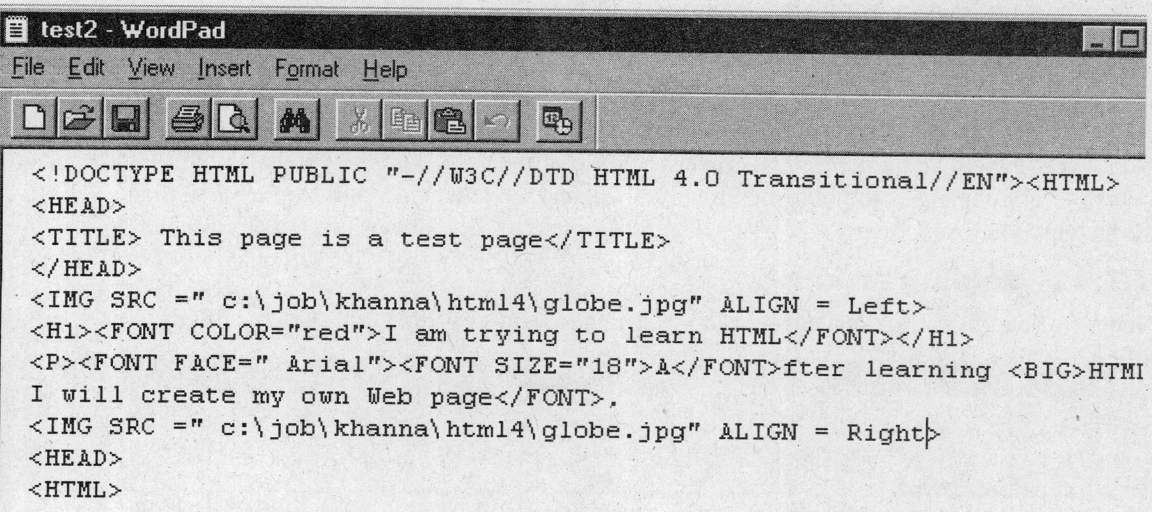

7.7.4 Stopping Text Wrap

A wrapped image affects all the text that follows it, unless you insert a special line break. The CLEAR attribute added to the regular BR tag indicates that the text should not begin until the specified margin is clear (that is, at the end of the image or images).

Follow the following steps to stop the text from wrapping:

1. Create your image and the text, as was done before.
2. Place the cursor where you want to stop wrapping text to the side of the image.

3. Either type <BR CLEAR= left> to stop flowing text until there are no more images aligned to the left margin.

   Or

   type <BR CLEAR = right> to stop flowing text until there are no more images aligned to the right margin.

   Or

   type <BR CLEAR = all> to stop flowing text until there are no more images on either margin.

7.7.5 Adding Space around an Image

You can actually put more space above or below the picture using the options of VSPACE and HSPACE attributes to add a buffer around your image.

Follow the following steps to add space around an image:

1. Type <IMG SRC =" image.location" where image.location indicates the location of your image.
2. Type HSPACE=x where x is the number of pixels of space to add on both the right and left sides of the image.
3. Type VSPACE=y where y is the number of pixels of space to add on both the top and bottom of the image.
4. Add other image attributes as desired and type the final >.

See, on the next page, how the spaced out image of the globe would look after giving the instructions as shown below.

Remember

You don't have to add both HSPACE and VSPACE at the same time. If you just want to add space to one side of the image, use Photoshop to add blank space to that side, and skip HSPACE and VSPACE altogether. Microsoft Internet Explorer leaves 4 pixels to the right of the image, by default.

7.7.6 Scaling an image

Supposing you want to change the size of an image, you can do it by just specifying a new height

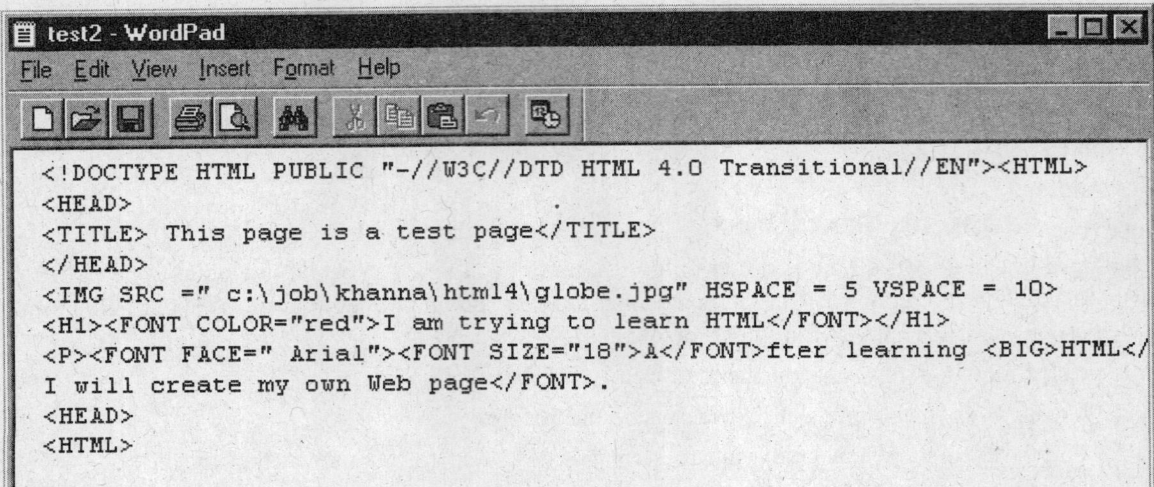


```
<!DOCTYPE HTML PUBLIC "-//W3C//DTD HTML 4.0 Transitional//EN"><HTML>
<HEAD>
<TITLE> This page is a test page</TITLE>
</HEAD>
<IMG SRC =" c:\job\khanna\html4\globe.jpg" HSPACE = 5 VSPACE = 10>
<H1><FONT COLOR="red">I am trying to learn HTML</FONT></H1>
<P><FONT FACE=" Arial"><FONT SIZE="18">A</FONT>fter learning <BIG>HTML</
I will create my own Web page</FONT>.
<HEAD>
<HTML>
```

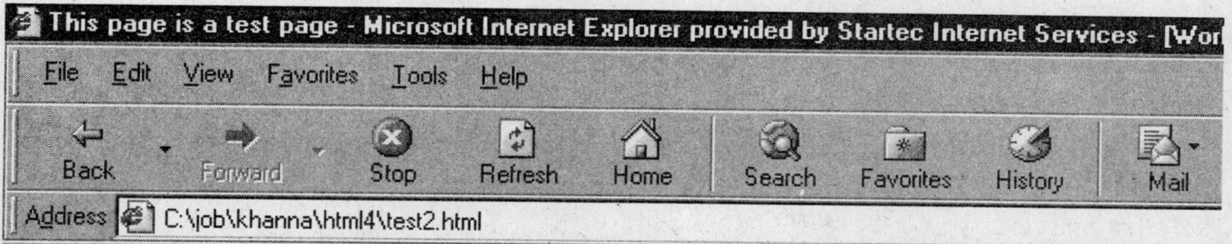

and width in pixels. This way you can have large images on your page without long loading times. Follow the following steps to scale an image:

1. Type <IMG SRC =" image.location where image.location is the location of the image.
2. Type WIDTH=x HEIGHT=y where x and y are the desired width and height, respectively, in pixels, of your image.
3. Add any other image attributes as discussed earlier and then type the final >.

Remember

Do not increase the size of the image too much, it will take more time to load and will make the image messy.

Don't use the WIDTH and HEIGHT extensions to reduce the image size. Instead, created a smaller image. It will load faster and look better..

7.7.7 Aligning Images

We had earlier wrapped the image to the left and right of the text. Now we will make use of the

ALIGN attributes for aligning images with text. You can align an image in various ways to a single line in a paragraph.

Follow the following steps to align an image with text:

1. Type <IMG SRC=" image.location” where image.location indicates the location of the image.
2. Type ALIGN= direction where direction is one of the attributes: texttop, top, middle, absmiddle, bottom, or absbottom.
3. Add other attributes as desired and then type the final >.
4. Type the text with which you wish to align the image.

In my example, I have taken the same globe and positioned it at various places with respect the text. See how it looks next. HTML text is also shown on the next page.

Remember

You may not align an image and wrap text around it at the same time. Internet Explorer has trouble with aligning more than one image on a line. The results are erratic. In addition, it treats texttop as top, absmiddle as middle and absbottom as Bottom.

7.7.8 Using a Banner

Banner is what you place at the top of the web site. It is reflected on all the pages of your site.

Follow the following steps to place a banner at the top of each page:

1. Create an image that measures approximately 450 x 100 pixels, as shown here. You can make it narrower and shorter, but you shouldn’t make it much wider, otherwise it won’t fit easily on most screens.
2. After converting it to indexed color, using the smallest bits/pixels ratio you can stand, save it as a GIF image.
3. Use this exact same image at the top of each of your Web pages, by typing <IMG SRC=" image.name">, where image.name is the location on the server of the banner.

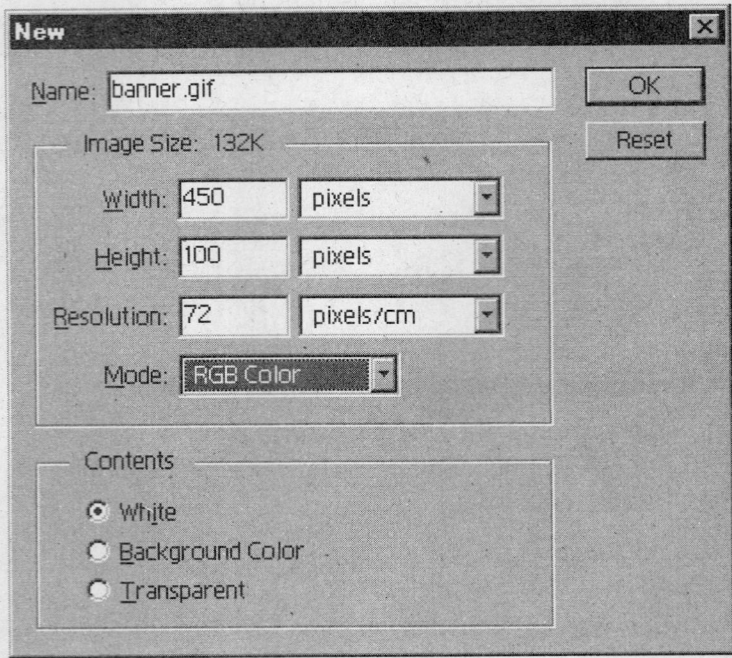

7.7.9 Adding Horizontal Rules

This graphic element is completely supported by the majority of the browsers is the horizontal rule. There are several attributes you can use to jazz up horizontal rules. Follow the following steps to insert a horizontal rule:

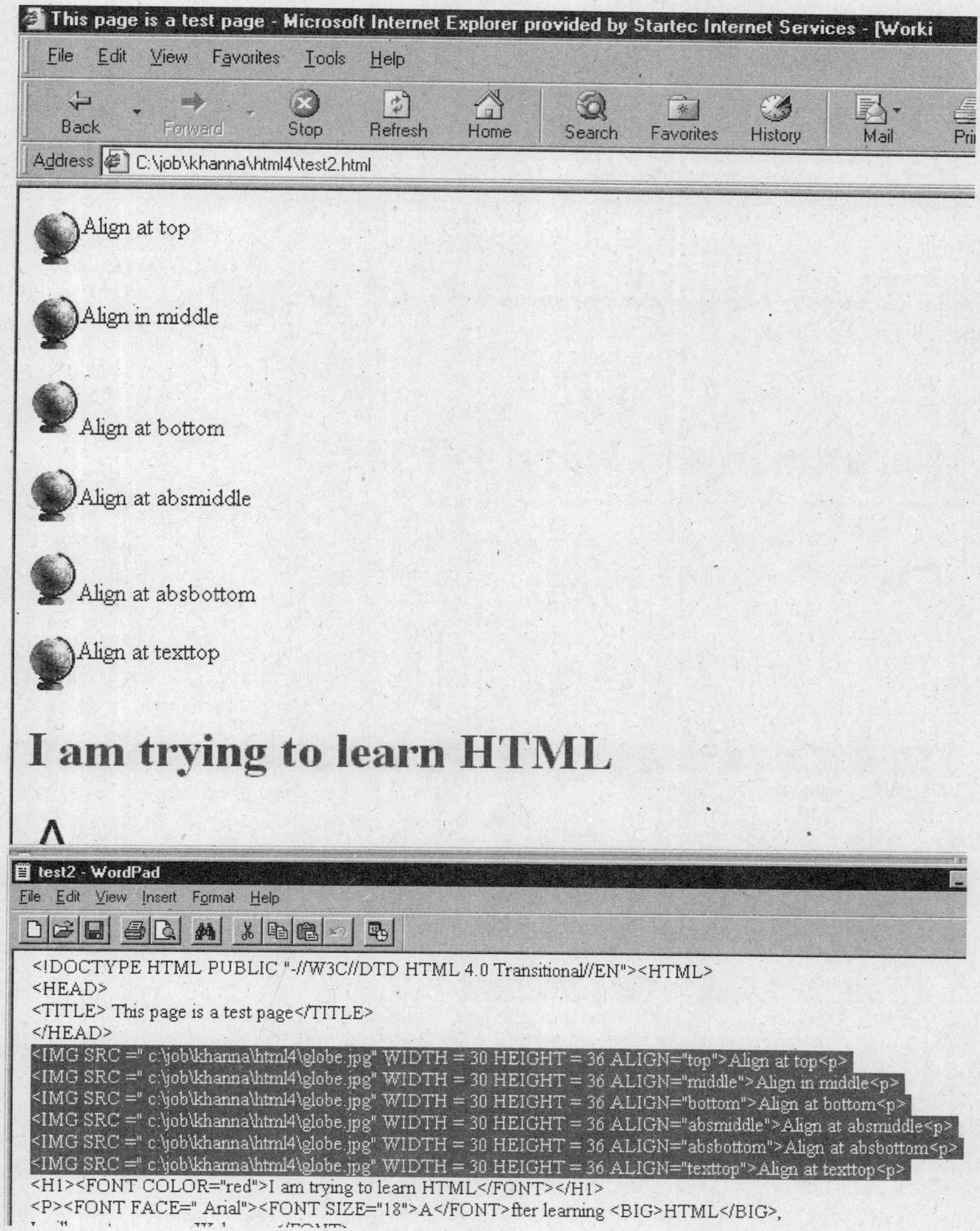

This page is a test page - Microsoft Internet Explorer provided by Startec Internet Services - [Worki

File Edit View Favorites Tools Help

Back Forward Stop Refresh Home Search Favorites History Mail Pri

Address C:\job\khanna\html4\test2.html

Align at top

Align in middle

Align at bottom

Align at absmiddle

Align at absbottom

Align at texttop

I am trying to learn HTML

A

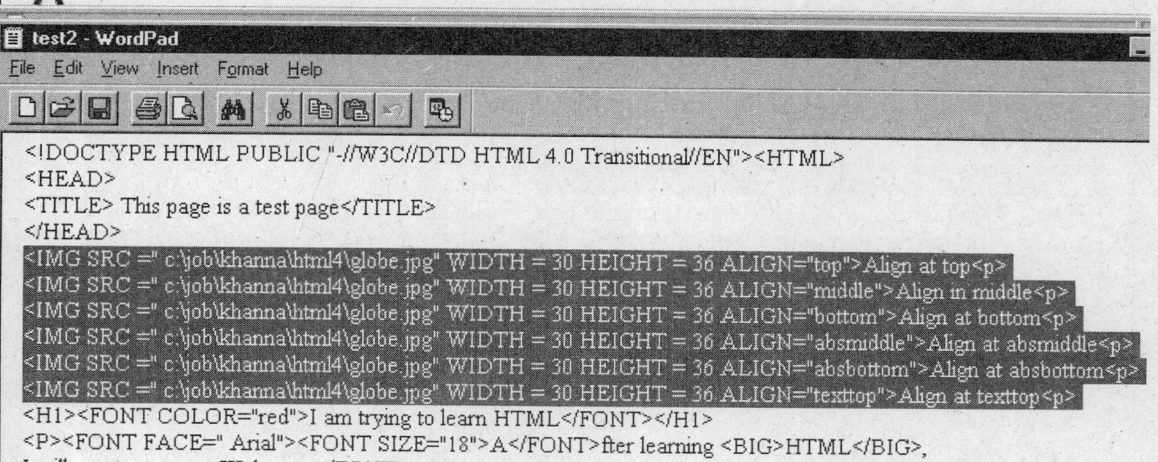


```
<!DOCTYPE HTML PUBLIC "-//W3C//DTD HTML 4.0 Transitional//EN"><HTML>
<HEAD>
<TITLE> This page is a test page</TITLE>
</HEAD>
<IMG SRC =" c:\job\khanna\html4\globe.jpg" WIDTH = 30 HEIGHT = 36 ALIGN="top">Align at top<p>
<IMG SRC =" c:\job\khanna\html4\globe.jpg" WIDTH = 30 HEIGHT = 36 ALIGN="middle">Align in middle<p>
<IMG SRC =" c:\job\khanna\html4\globe.jpg" WIDTH = 30 HEIGHT = 36 ALIGN="bottom">Align at bottom<p>
<IMG SRC =" c:\job\khanna\html4\globe.jpg" WIDTH = 30 HEIGHT = 36 ALIGN="absmiddle">Align at absmiddle<p>
<IMG SRC =" c:\job\khanna\html4\globe.jpg" WIDTH = 30 HEIGHT = 36 ALIGN="absbottom">Align at absbottom<p>
<IMG SRC =" c:\job\khanna\html4\globe.jpg" WIDTH = 30 HEIGHT = 36 ALIGN="texttop">Align at texttop<p>
<H1><FONT COLOR="red">I am trying to learn HTML</FONT></H1>
<P><FONT FACE=" Arial"><FONT SIZE="18">A</FONT>fter learning <BIG>HTML</BIG>,
```

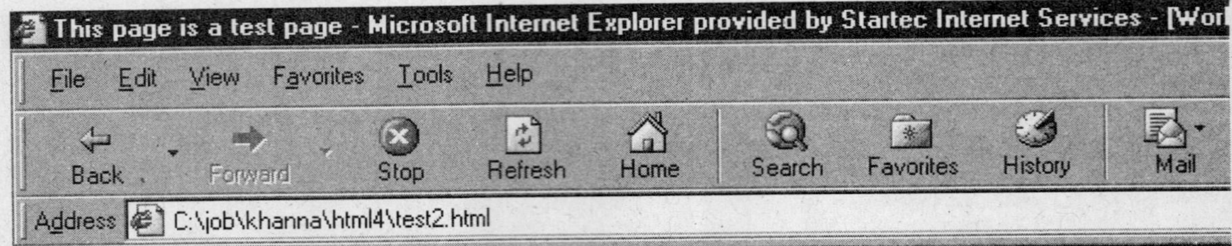

This is put on top of page

I am trying to learn HTML

After learning **HTML**, I will create my own Web page.

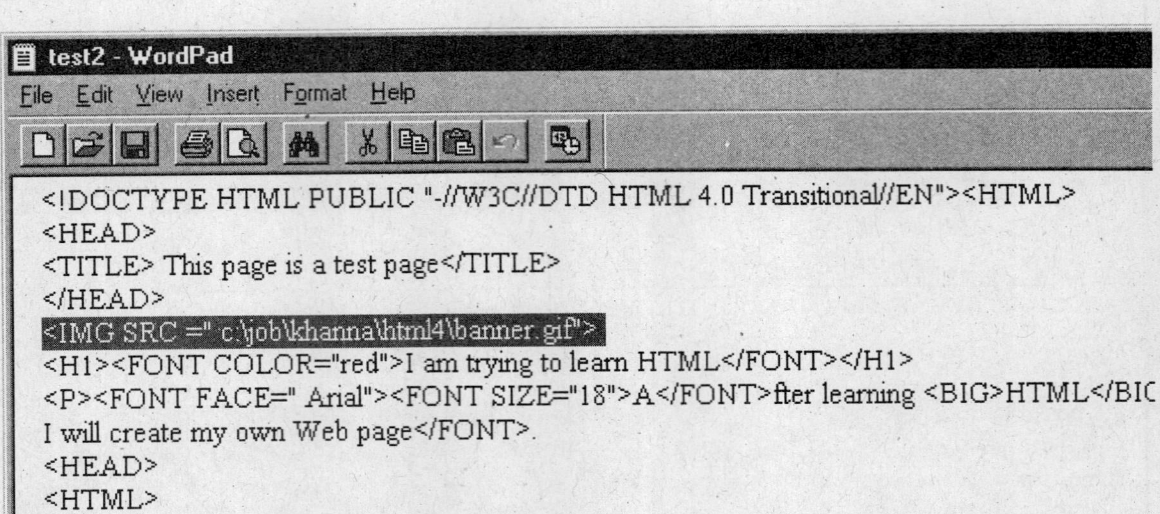

1. Type <HR where you want the rule to appear. The text that follows will appear in a new paragraph below the new line.
2. If desired, type SIZE=n, where n is the rule's height in pixels.
3. If desired, type WIDTH=w, where w is the width of the rule in pixels, or as a percentage of the document's width.
4. If desired, type ALIGN=direction, where direction refers to the way a rule should be aligned on the page; either left, right or center.
5. If desired, type NOSHADE to create a solid bar, with no shading.
6. Type the final > to complete the horizontal rule definition.

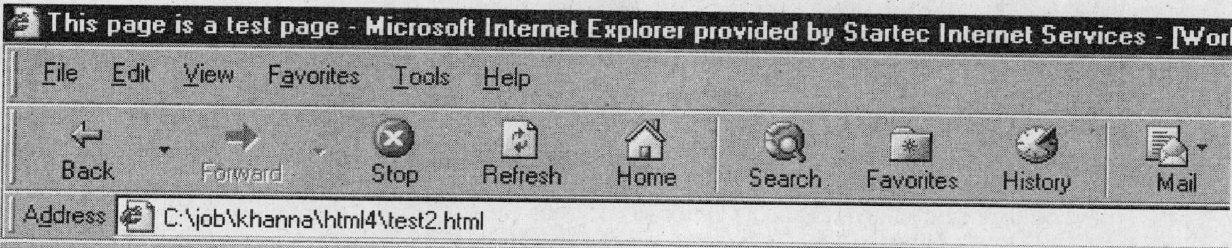

7.7.10 Using Alternate Text

It is possible that your browser may not support images at all. Or even if it does it is so slow that you wish that the graphics was not there at all. For this you can create a text that will appear even if the image, for whatever reason, does not.

Follow the following steps to offer alternate text when images don't appears:

1. Place the cursor where you want the image (or alternate text) to appear.
2. Type <IMG SRC = "image.ext", where image.ext is the location of the image.

```
<!DOCTYPE HTML PUBLIC "-//W3C//DTD HTML 4.0 Transitional//EN"><HTML>
<HEAD>
<TITLE> This page is a test page</TITLE>
</HEAD>
<IMG SRC =" c:\job\khanna\html4\banner.gif">
<HR SIZE ="10" ALIGN = "center" NOSHADE>
<H1><FONT COLOR="red">I am trying to learn HTML</FONT></H1>
<P><FONT FACE=" Arial"><FONT SIZE="18">A</FONT>fter learning <BIG>HTML</BIC
I will create my own Web page</FONT>.
```

3. Type ALT =”.
4. Type the text that should appear if, for some reason, the image itself does not.
5. Type ">.

7.7.11 Linking to External Images

Linking allows you to link instead of actually copying the image. This is done specially in the cases where the image is of a very large size. You can create an icon of the image and place it in your page.

Follow the following steps to link a small icon to your larger image:

1. Place the cursor in your HTML text where you wish the icon to be placed.
2. Type <A HREF + image.location"> where image.location is the location of the full sized image on your screen.
3. Type <IMG SRC =" icon.location”, where icon.location is the location of your icon.
4. If desired, type ALT =" alternate text" where alternate text is the text that should appear if, for some reason, the icon does not.
5. Type the final > of the icon definition.
6. Type </A> to complete the link to the full sized image.

7.7.12 Using Low Resolution Images

You can have reference to both high and low resolution versions of your image so that the low resolution image loads quickly and keeps the visitor’s interest while the high resolution version impresses your visitors, once it loads in.

Follow the following steps to use a low resolution version of an image:

1. Create a low resolution version of your image using Photoshop or any other image editing program.
2. Place the cursor where you want the full resolution image to appear.
3. Type <IMG SRC = "image.gif", where image.gif is the location on the server of the high resolution image.

4. Type LOWSRC = "imagelow.gif", where imagelow.gif is the location on the server of the low resolution image.
5. Type HEIGHT=x WIDTH=y, where x and y are the height and width in pixels, respectively of the original image. If you do not specify these values, browsers use the size of the low resolution image for both images.
6. If desired, type ALT="substitute text", where substitute text is the text that will appear if the visitor can't view images with their browser.
7. Type the final >.

7.8 Formatting Tags and Special Characters

Those of you who have worked on any word processing knows what formatting of the text is. Using this concept you make the text more presentable by making it Bold, Italics, Underline. Not only this you change the look by changing the font in use and make it bigger or smaller by changing the font size. Here in HTML you have to be careful while formatting because you do not know which browser the user is going to use. The result is different for different browser.

Let us start with font.

7.8.1 Changing Font

You have the liberty to load any number of fonts in your system. But, while using any one of them you have to make sure that the user of the web site may or may not have the same font. In that case this font would be replaced by a default font of the user's system.

Follow the following steps to change the font:

1. Type <FONT FACE="fontname1, where fontname1 is you first choice of fonts, before the text whose font you want to change. Type the complete name of the font.
2. You can even put the second font with fontname2, where fontname2 is the name of your second choice of fonts. This is used to make sure that if the first font is not available atleast this would. You can put more fonts too, but, each successive font should be separated from the previous one by a comma.
3. Referring back to example of the previous section, I choose the fontname as Arial for the line.
4. Repeat step 2 for each additional font choice.
5. Type "> to complete the FONT tag.
6. Type the text that you want to get displayed.
7. Type </FONT>.
8. Open this file in browser to see the result.

7.8.2 Changing Size

You can change the size of the text too alongwith the font. This is done to make the text stand out differently from others.

Follow the following steps to change the font size of one or more characters:

1. Type <FONT SIZE= "n"> where n is a number from 1 to 7. You may also use +n and -n to denote a value relative to the BASEFONT value (you will learn about it little later).

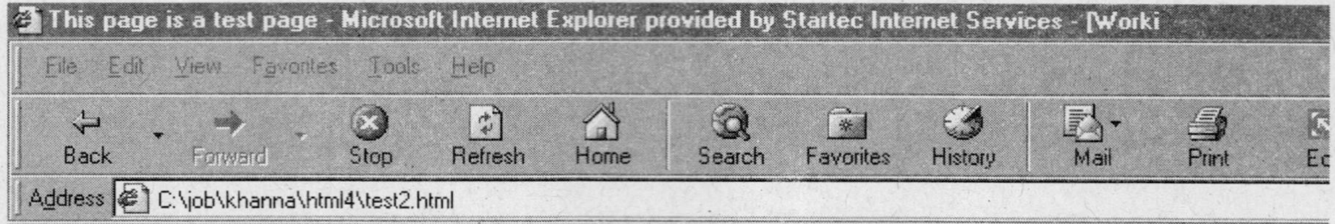

I am trying to learn HTML

After learning HTML, I will create my own Web page.

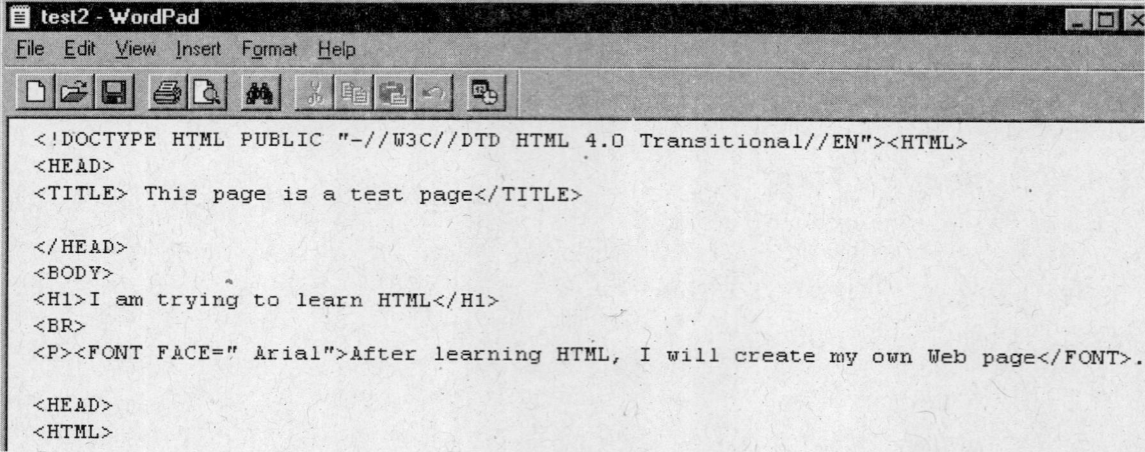


```
<!DOCTYPE HTML PUBLIC "-//W3C//DTD HTML 4.0 Transitional//EN"><HTML>
<HEAD>
<TITLE> This page is a test page</TITLE>

</HEAD>
<BODY>
<H1>I am trying to learn HTML</H1>
<BR>
<P><FONT FACE=" Arial">After learning HTML, I will create my own Web page</FONT>.

<HEAD>
<HTML>
```

2. In my case I have given the font size as 18
3. Type the text whose font size you wish to change.
4. Type </FONT>.
5. Open this file in browser to see the result.

You can even change few characters of the text. But, with all the characters whose size you have to change, you will have to give the <FONT SIZE> command in the beginning and </FONT> command to end.

In the above example, I have kept the size 18 for the first character, i.e., A and left the rest of the text to the default (which we will understand in the next topic), and see the results.

Remember

You can make designs by changing the FONT size of each letter in a word in an ascending and then descending pattern.

7.8.3 Setting Default Size

For this we have the command called BASEFONT. This changes the font of the whole text to the basefont, unless you change the size of few characters.

Follow the following steps to choose a default size for body text:

1. Type <BASEFONT>.
2. TypeSIZE= "n"> where n is a number from 1 to 7. The default is 3, which displays the font at the size the visitor has chosen in their browser's Fonts preferences dialog box.

Remember

You can choose any size of the text as the base size. But, usually a larger basefont is chosen to give more importance to the whole page. The smaller basefont is used for lengthy text-intensive pages to fit more text on a page.

You can choose only one BASEFONT tag for each HTML document. This is sufficient for all the text which precedes it. The BASEFONT tag has no effect on headers. Obviously, you would not choose the text font to be bigger than the headings font.

7.8.4 Using Relative Values to Change Text Size

Now that you have set the BASEFONT and its size. You can change the text of various characters by just saying BIG and SMALL. Remember these are relative size of a given word or phrase with respect to the surrounding text.

Follow the following steps to change the font size relative to the rest of the text:

1. Type <BIG> or <SMALL> before the text that you wish to make bigger or smaller, respectively.
2. In my case I have typed <BIG> before the words HTML and </BIG> afterwards.
3. See how it has effected the page.

7.8.5 Using Predefined fonts

There are few fonts which have been predefined by the computer in terms of codes. You can use them in your text and they will be accordingly displayed. There are several tags that are displayed with monospaced font: **CODE** (computer code), **KBD** (keyboard input), **SAMP** (sample text) and **TT** (typewriter text).

Follow the following steps to format text with monospaced font:

1. Type <CODE>, <KBD>, <SAMP>, or <TT>, as the case maybe.
2. Type the text that you want to display in monospaced font.
3. Type </CODE>, </KBD>, <SAMP>, or </TT>, the corresponding closing code for the font.
4. See how I have used them for my page and how they get displayed in the web page is shown on the next page.

7.8.6 Making Characters Bold or Italic

As you know that you can make the character Bold or Italics to give them the added advantage over the other characters.

Follow the following steps to make text bold:

1. Type <B>.
2. Type the text that you want to make bold.
3. Type </B>.

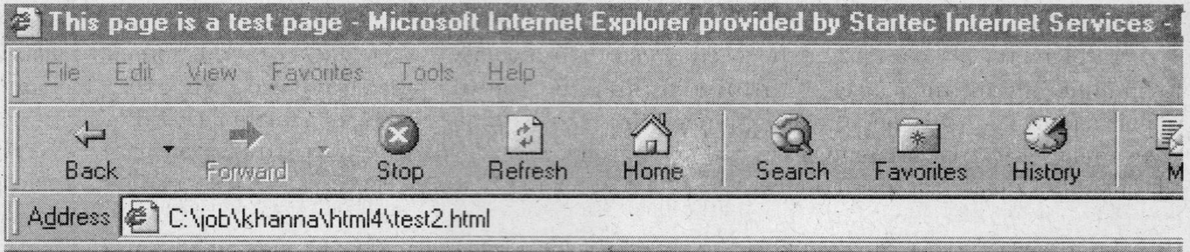

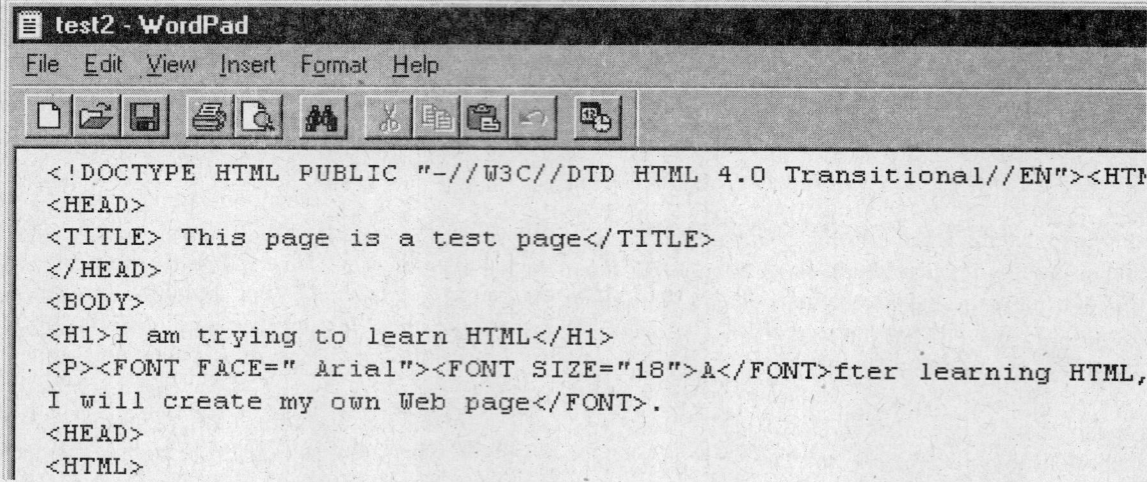

Follow the following steps to make text italics:

1. Type <I>.
2. Type the text that you want to make italic.
3. Type </I>

In the above example I have done changes to make the characters Bold and Italics, see the results.

7.8.7 Choosing a Default Color for Text

You can choose to have the text in any colour you want. The TEXT attributes for the BODY tag lets you specify a default color for all of the text on the page. You can then change the colour of individual sections (or just a word or two) with the FONT tag.

Follow the following steps to choose a default color for text:

1. Type <BODY> to start the new text line.

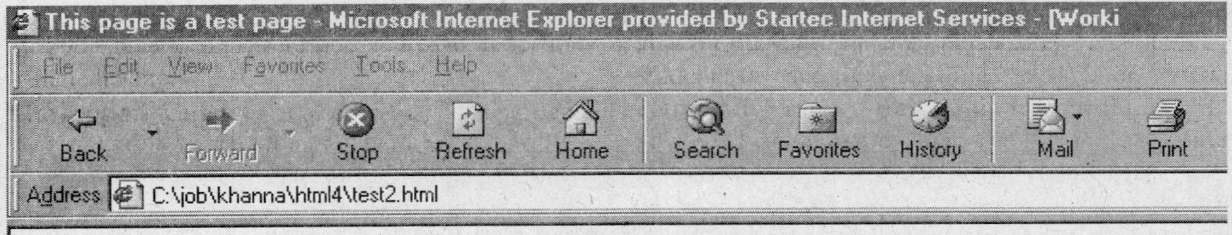

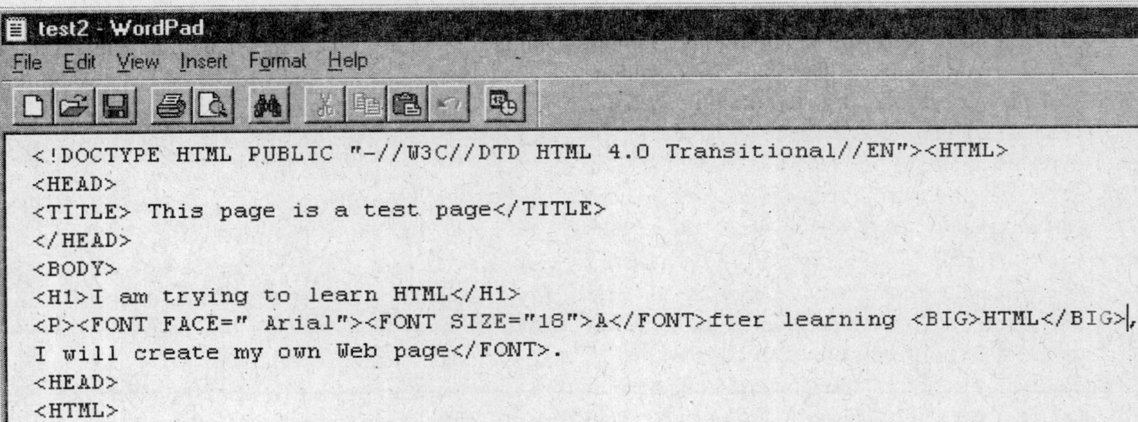


```
<!DOCTYPE HTML PUBLIC "-//W3C//DTD HTML 4.0 Transitional//EN"><HTML>
<HEAD>
<TITLE> This page is a test page</TITLE>
</HEAD>
<BODY>
<H1>I am trying to learn HTML</H1>
<P><FONT FACE=" Arial"><FONT SIZE="18">A</FONT>fter learning <BIG>HTML</BIG>,
I will create my own Web page</FONT>.
<HEAD>
<HTML>
```

2. Type BGCOLOR =" #000000" TEXT =" #ffffff", where 000000 represents the default color and ffffff represents the colour of the text.
3. Now type the text which you have to type.
4. Close the color line by putting the closing words </BODY>.

If you know the number of any other colour, you can put the same too. See the result of this on next page.

Remember

The text attributes lets you choose one color for all of the text. The FONT tag with the COLOR attribute lets you choose a color for individual letters or words and overrides the TEXT attribute.

7.8.8 Changing the Text Color

As we have seen in the last example, the colour of the whole text and the background was changed. Now we will try to change the colour of the individual text paragraphs, lines or even characters. If you want you change the colour of various characters of a line.

Follow the following steps to change the text color:

1. Type <FONT COLOR> in front of the text of which you want to change the colour.

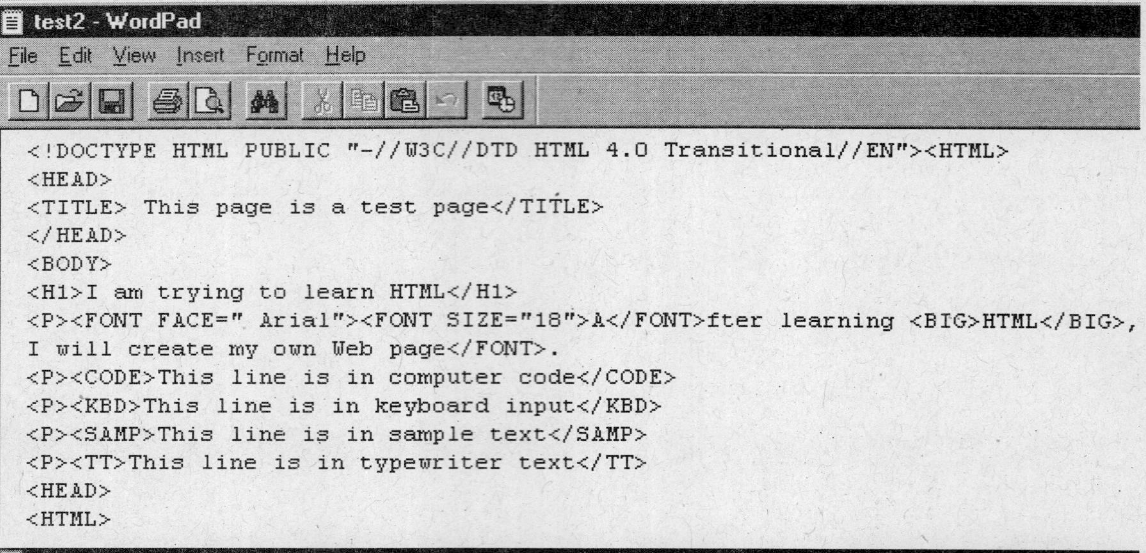

```
<!DOCTYPE HTML PUBLIC "-//W3C//DTD HTML 4.0 Transitional//EN"><HTML>
<HEAD>
<TITLE> This page is a test page</TITLE>
</HEAD>
<BODY>
<H1>I am trying to learn HTML</H1>
<P><FONT FACE=" Arial"><FONT SIZE="18">A</FONT>fter learning <BIG>HTML</BIG>,
I will create my own Web page</FONT>.
<P><CODE>This line is in computer code</CODE>
<P><KBD>This line is in keyboard input</KBD>
<P><SAMP>This line is in sample text</SAMP>
<P><TT>This line is in typewriter text</TT>
<HEAD>
<HTML>
```

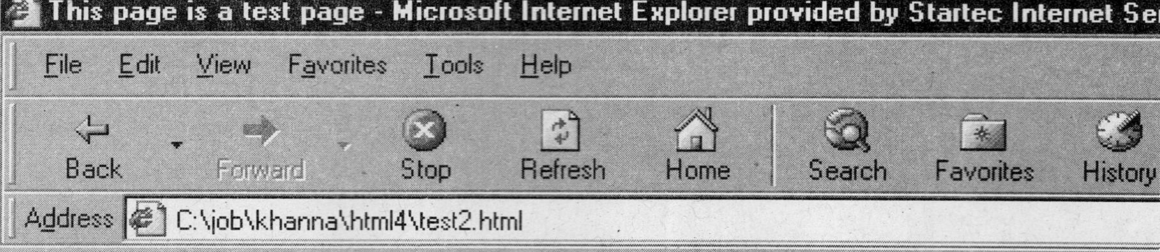

I am trying to learn HTML

A fter learning **HTML**, I will create my own Web page.

`This line is in computer code`

`This line is in keyboard input`

`This line is in sample text`

`This line is in typewriter text`

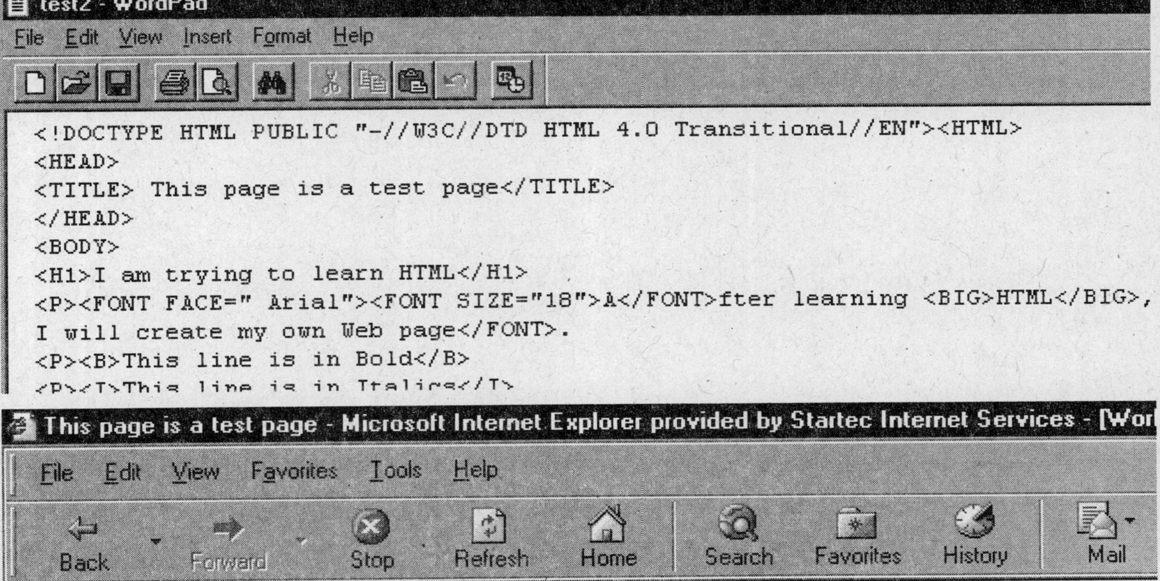

2. Type = "red", where red is the colour which I have chosen. You can choose any other standard colour from the 16 predefined colors.
3. Close with >.
4. Type the text that you wish to color.
5. Type </FONT> to close the font tag.
6. See how it looks in the browser, as shown next.

I have changed the line of the title to the red colour.

Remember

You can change all the three attributes, i.e., font, colour, size, of the text at the same time. For example, <FONT SIZE=3 FACE="Arial" COLOR= “blue”>.

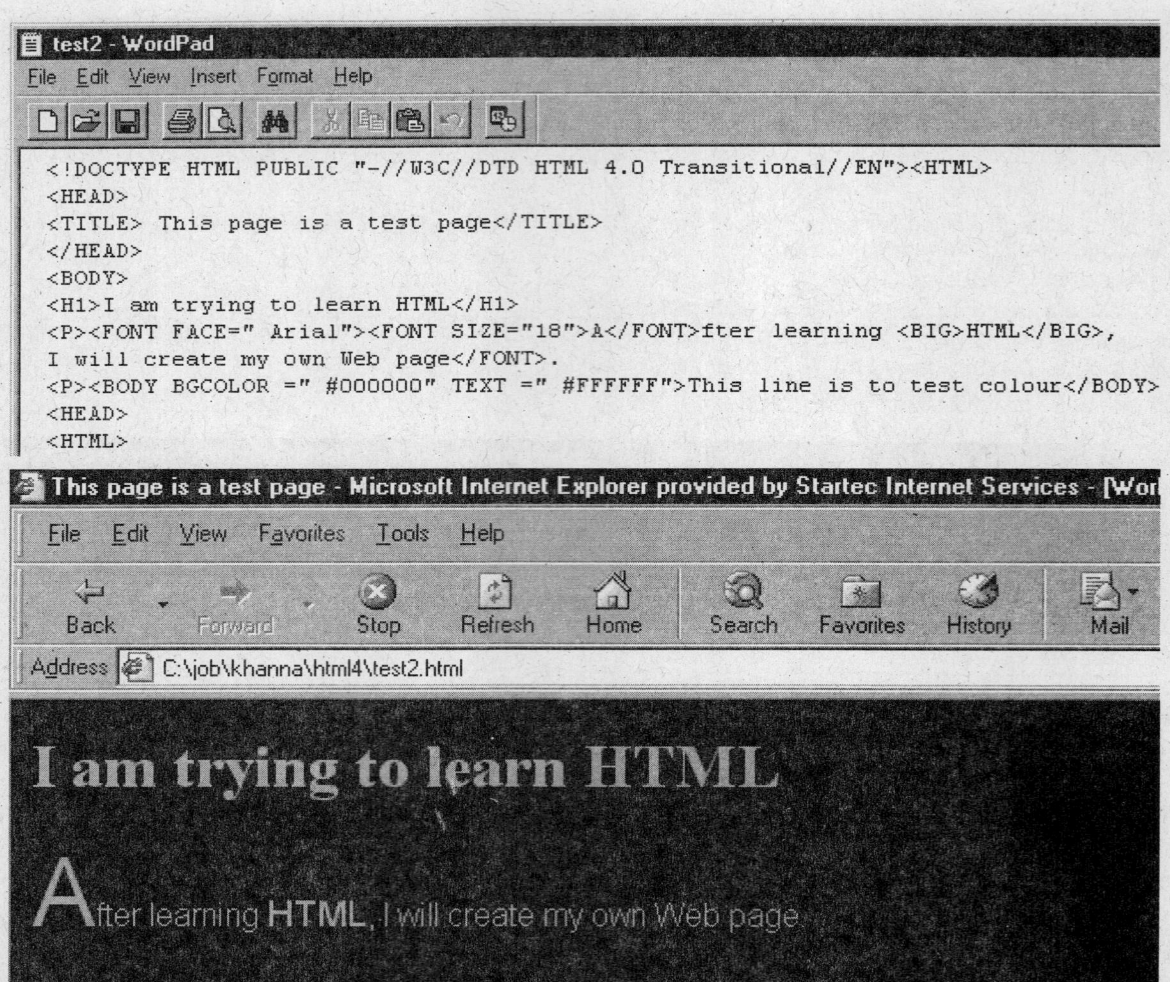

To change the color of all of the body text at once, use the TEXT attribute in the BODY as was done in the case of default colour. The FONT COLOR tag overrides colors specified with BODY/TEXT.

Sample Paper - 1

S1

Part A

Answer all questions, each of them carries one mark

Multiple Choice Questions

1. Hypertext allows you to have _________ from one section to another.
   (a) animation (b) anchors
   (c) games.
2. DVD is a :
   (a) sound device. (b) optical disk
   (c) video device.
3. A touch screen is like a:
   (a) Kiosks. (b) Printer.
   (c) Keyboard.
4. NTSC is a _________ format.
   (a) sound (b) video
   (c) text
5. Laser beam is used to store data on CD-ROM/
   (a) True (b) False
6. A font style has the following:
   (a) Bold (b) Italics
   (c) Underlined (d) All of them.
7. ASF stands for:
   (a) advanced systems format (b) advanced streaming format
   (c) advanced systems file (d) asynchonous sound format.
8. Removing blank space or dead air at the beginning or end of a recording is sometimes called:
   (a) quantizing (b) trimming
   (c) flashing (d) quieting.

9. Which of the following is not a colour specification format?
   (a) RGB (b) HSB
   (c) GIF (d) CMYK.
10. Which image file type is best for photo-realistic images?
   (a) Laser (b) Bitmap
   (c) Vector (d) All of the above.
11. Vector drawn objects are used for all the following except:
   (a) Circles (b) Photographs
   (c) Boxes (d) Lines
12. Which of the following is not a television signal format?
   (a) SECAM (b) HDTV
   (c) MPEG (d) PAL.
13. MPEG stands for:
   (a) motion picture environment group. (b) multipurpose element grid.
   (c) moving picture experts group (d) None of the above.

Part B

Answer all questions, each of them carries one mark

True False Questions

1. Hypertext is where the text of the document is linked in between for an easy access.
2. Multimedia is widely used to create Games.
3. MIDI means Musical Instrument Digital Interface.
4. Digital cameras are used to take digital pictures which can be transferred to computers.
5. Plain text is the unformatted text.
6. A relative unit is not a unit of measure that specifies a value that is relative to the font size.
7. Outline fonts or vector fonts are not collections of vector images, i.e. a set of lines and curves to define the border of glyphs.
8. Bandwidth is how much data, expressed in bits per second (bps), you can send from one computer to another in a given amount of time.
9. MPEG-1 Audio Layer 3, more commonly referred to as MP3, is a non-patented digital audio encoding format using a form of lossy data compression.
10. Accurate, high quality sound reproduction is possible with both analog and digital systems.
11. Dithering is a technique used in computer graphics to create the illusion of varying shades of gray on a monochrome display or printer, or additional colors on a color display or printer.
12. You can create user-slices with the slice tool, from a layer, from a selection (ImageReady), or from guides (ImageReady).

13. Cropping is the process of removing portions of an image to create focus or strengthen the composition.
14. Although SECAM is a 625-line, 50 Hz system, it differs greatly from both the NTSC and the PAL colour systems in its basic technology and broadcast method.
15. Auto-play DVDs work best for short movies, or movies that you want to play continuously in a loop playback mode.
16. MPEG-4 is a patented collection of methods defining compression of audio and visual (AV) digital data.

Part C

Answer all questions, each of them carries one mark

Matching Questions

A.	Graphics	1.	Combination of more than one media
B.	Text	2.	High speed printer using laser beam
C.	CD-ROM	3.	Optical Character Reader
D.	Multimedia	4.	Public places information provider
E.	Laser Printer	5.	Line drawing and images
F.	OCR	6.	Moving images
G.	Multimedia Kiosks	7.	Alpha numeric characters
H.	Animation	8.	Optical disk to store data

Part D

Answer all questions, each of them carries one mark

Fill in the Blanks

1. Computer activity where more than one media is involved is called ________________.
2. Text having line drawings and images is called ______________.
3. A ______________ typeface is a family of graphic characters that usually includes many type sizes and styles.
4. The space between the lines is called __________.
5. ___________ is the space between individual characters.
6. ________ are used to codigy printed text for direct input of printed text to computers.
7. The process of removing the blank spaces before or after the required signals is called _______.
8. The time interval taken between two samples of the original analog data, during digitizing is called __________.
9. The total number of colours that could be handled by the monitor depends upon the memory capacity of the ___________.
10. Hand tool is useful after the ________ tool to work on a part of a picture.

11. MPEG-1 uses fixed ____________.
12. Viewing a MPEG video on a micro computer requires a ____________. MPEG decoder
13. __________ video compression is used to deliver high quality picture in DVD movies. MPEG2

Part E

Answer any 10 questions, each of them carries five marks

Descriptive Type Questions

1. What is the process of Animation?
2. What role does multimedia play in development of games?
3. What are sound files known as?
4. What is the use of scanners?
5. Describe the various types of multimedia networking used.
6. Describe the working of speakers.
7. How is text used in the Multimedia?
8. Define Outline fonts.
9. Describe the various types of sound synthesis.
10. Describe how would you do the following:
    Play MIDI files using Media Player
    Play Sound files using Sound Recorder
11. How is sound digitized?
12. Define the followings:
    Audio Interchange File Format
    Musical Instruments Digital Interface
    Wave Form
    MP3
    Advanced Streaming Format
    Audio Video Interleave
13. How would you resize an image?
14. What is the use of Options Bar?
15. What are Channels?
16. Describe what type of photos can be retouched.
17. Describe the various image types.
18. Describe the various types of image compression and file formats.
19. What is video compression?
20. What do you know of the following:
    MPEG-2
    MPEG-4
    MPEG-7
    MPEG-21
21. What is cel animation

22. How would you create DVDs?
23. Describe the following broadcasting video standards:

NTSC	PAL
SECAM	HDTV
Digital video	Analog video

Part F

Answers to Objective Type Questions

Multiple Choice Questions

A.1.	a	A.2.	b	A.3.	a	A.4.	b
A.5.	a	A.6.	d	A.7.	b	A.8.	b
A.9.	c	A.10	b	A.11	b	A.12	c
A.13	c						

True False Questions

B.1.	T	B.2.	T	B.3.	T	B.4	T
B.5.	T	B.6.	F	B.7.	F	B.8	T
B.9.	F	B.10.	T	B.11.	T	B.12.	T
B13.	T	B14.	T	B.15	T	B.16	T

Matching Questions

C.A.	5	C.B.	7	C.C.	8	C.D.	1
C.E.	2	C.F.	3	C.G	4	C.H.	6

Fill in the Blanks with appropriate words

D.1.	Multimedia	D.2.	Graphics
D.3.	typeface	D.4.	leading
D.5.	kerning	D.6.	OCR
D.7.	trimming	D.8.	sampling rate
D.9.	video controller card	D.10.	zoom
D.11.	bit rate	D.12.	MPEG decoder
D.13	MPEG2		

This page left blank for rough work

Sample Paper - 2

S2

Part A

Answer all questions, each of them carries one mark

Multiple Choice Questions

1. In Animation, you run ________ at a very high speed.
   (a) frames (b) text
   (c) sound (d) food.
2. Video Parlours have multimedia ________.
   (a) Text (b) Games.
3. For putting the printed text to the computer, besides keyboard, we use:
   (a) monitor. (b) mouse.
   (c) OCR.
4. Popular operating system these days is:
   (a) DOS. (b) Windows.
5. Data on the CD-ROM will be affected by humidity and dust.
   (a) True (b) False
6. Commonly known sans serif font is:
   (a) Arial (b) Helvitica
   (c) Both.
7. Which of the following statements about MIDI audio is not true:
   (a) Files are smaller than digital audio sound.
   (b) MIDI can easily be used to playback spoken dialog.
   (c) MIDI data is completely editable.
   (d) MIDI data is device dependent.
8. We can record the sound by:
   (a) Windows Media Player (b) Sound Recorder
   (c) both (a) and (b) (d) none of the above.
9. Which of the following is a combination of text, audio and graphics?
   (a) Images (b) Video
   (c) Multimedia (d) Unimedia

10. TIFF stands for:
    (a) Temporary Instruction File Format
    (b) Total Inclusion File Format
    (c) Tagged Interchange File Format
    (d) Table Index File Format.
11. Graphic editing has to be performed:
    (a) To improve the attributes of an existing image.
    (b) To remove unwanted portions of the image.
    (c) To add special effects, not possible with actual photography.
    (d) all of the above.
12. S-video uses:
    (a) Two wires
    (b) Three wires
    (c) One wire
    (d) None of the above
13. AVI stands for:
    (a) Audio Video Interface
    (b) Audio Visual Interface
    (c) Audio Video Interleave
    (d) None of the above.
14. Which format is used in digital cameras?
    (a) MPEG2
    (b) MPEG4
    (c) MPEG1
    (d) SWF.

Part B

Answer all questions, each of them carries one mark

True False Questions

1. Animation is created using frames and running them.
2. Hardware to be used for multimedia should be such that you are not short of memory or hard disk space.
3. For video you can use available video clips or shoot your own.
4. Printers are mainly of two types: Impact and Non-impact.
5. Hypertext has no link to other text.
6. A glyph's outline is defined by the vertices of individual strokes and stroke's profile.
7. Acoustics is the branch of science that studies sound.
8. When you create multimedia, it is not likely that you will deal with file formats and translators for text, sounds, images, animations or digital video clips.
9. RealMedia is a multimedia container format created by RealNetworks.
10. 2D computer graphics are the computer-based generation of digital images—mostly from two-dimensional models, such as 2D geometric models, text, and digital images, and by techniques specific to them.
11. Tagged Image File Format – Widely-used raster graphics file format developed by Aldus and Microsoft that handles monochrome, gray scale, 8-and 24-bit color.
12. The history brush tool does not let you paint a copy of one state or snapshot of an image into the current image window.
13. The Auto-Align Layers command can automatically align layers based on similar content in different layers, such as corners and edges.

14. A digital video architecture is made up of a format for encoding and playing back video files by a computer and includes a player that can recognize and play files created for that format.
15. MPEG-1 is a standard for lossy compression of video and not audio.
16. Animation is the process of making an object appear to move by rapidly displaying a series of pictures of it, each one in it is slightly in different position; a techniques used in producing Computer-generated movies.

Part C

Answer all questions, each of them carries one mark

Matching Questions

A.	Microphone	1.	Branch of physics that studies sound
B.	AIFF	2.	KHz (Kilohertz)
C.	DSP	3.	removing dead aire or blank space
D.	Audio File Format	4.	Sound format
E	Acoustics	5.	Transducer device
F.	Trimming	6.	Digital Sound Processing
G	Sampling rate	7.	.wav

Part D

Answer all questions, each of them carries one mark

Fill in the Blanks

1. Printer which uses dots to print characters is called ________________.
2. Device which converts text into computer media is called ________________.
3. Type sizes are usually expressed in ___________.
4. A __________ is a collection of characters of a single size and style belonging to a particular typeface family.
5. The standard document format used for pages on the web is called _____________.
6. __________ is produced by the vibration of matter.
7. Sound pressure levels (loudness or volume) are measured in ____________.
8. Images that are stored as lines, arces and curves are called __________ images.
9. The __________ tool used for repair a selected area with pixels from another area or a pattern.
10. __________ holds tools for creating and editing images.
11. ___________ is the compression format used to create video CDs.
12. ____________ uses variable bit rate encoding which means that different scenes can play back at different rates.
13. _________ is used for both straming and downloadable web content.
14. Hand tool is useful after the _________ tool to work on a part of a picture.

Part E

Answer any 10 questions, each of them carries five marks

Descriptive Type Questions

1. What do you understand by Multimedia?
2. How is multimedia used in Education and Training?
3. What is Flight Simulator?
4. What is the difference between MIDI and Digital sound formats?
5. How is Digital Camera used?
6. What is the use of Touch screen?
7. What are Internation Character Sets?
8. Define the terms: Plain Text, Formatted Text, and Hypertext.
9. What are Bitmap fonts?
10. How would you add sound to your multimedia project?
11. What do you understand by Sound?
12. Define Frequency and Bandwidth
13. How would you:
    Install the software
    Uninstall the software
    Activate software
    Register software
14. Describe the various methods of selection.
15. What do you understand by Layers?
16. Describe Masks.
17. What do you understand by Computer Animation?
18. Describe the various colour modes.
19. Describe the following:
    GIF
    JPEG
    JPEG 2000
    PNG
    TIFF
    EXIF
    PS
    PDF
20. What is MPEG-1?
21. What do you understand by animation? How are they created?
22. Describe the following video recording and tape formats:
    Ampex
    VERA
    U-matic
    Betamax
    Betacam
    Video 2000
    Compact Video Cassette
    Camcoder
    Video 8
23. Describe the basics of video.

Part F

Answers to Objective Type Questions

Multiple Choice Questions

A.1.	b	A.2.	b	A.3.	c	A.4.	b
A.5.	b	A.6.	c	A.7.	b	A.8.	b
A.9.	c	A.10	c	A.11	d	A.12	a
A.13	c	A.14	c				

True False Questions

B.1.	T	B.2.	T	B.3.	T	B.4	T
B.5.	F	B.6.	T	B.7.	T	B.8	F
B.9.	F	B.10.	T	B.11.	T	B.12.	F
B13.	T	B14.	T	B.15	F	B.16	T

Matching Questions

C.A.	5	C.B.	4	C.C.	6	C.D.	7
C.E.	1	C.F.	3	C.G	2		

Fill in the Blanks with appropriate words

D.1.	Dot Matrix Printer	D.2.	OCR
D.3.	units	D.4.	font
D.5.	HTML	D.6.	sound
D.7.	decibals	D.8.	vector
D.9.	patch	D.10.	toolbox
D.11.	MPEG-1	D.12.	MPEG-2
D.13	MPEG-4	*D.14*	*zoom*

This page left blank for rough work

Sample Paper - 3

S3

Part A

Answer all questions, each of them carries one mark

Multiple Choice Questions

1. Of the following which is not used in Multimedia:
   (a) text (b) sound
   (c) odour (d) video.
2. Multimeida Kiosks are like _________.
   (a) Touch screen (b) Keyboard
   (c) Mouse (d) Speaker.
3. You can add your own sound to the computer.
   (a) Yes. (b) No.
4. Sound format more in use now-a-days is:
   (a) MIDI. (b) Digital.
5. CD ROMs are high-density memory devices.
   (a) Yes (b) No
6. A family of graphic characters that usually include many type sizes and styles is called:
   (a) typeface (b) font
   (c) point.
7. Hypermedia structures are navigated through
   (a) Keys (b) Panels
   (c) Buttons.
8. Human hearing frequency range is:
   (a) 0 to 20 Hz (b) 20 Hz to 20 KHz
   (c) 20 KHz to 1 GHz (d) 1 GHz to 10 THz.
9. Which is true about MIDI files:
   (a) MIDI files aremuch more compact than digital audio files.
   (b) MIDI files embedded in web pages load and play more quickly than their digital equivalents.
   (c) MIDI files may sound better than digital audio files.
   (d) all of the above.

10. Which file format can be used when the picture is a photograph or has lots of colours?
    (a) .jpeg (b) .tif
    (c) .bmp (d) .pic.
11. Which menu contains a command to adjust the colurs and the brightness of the picture?
    (a) Layer (b) Select
    (c) Filter (d) Image
12. Full form of PAL is:
    (a) project active line (b) program alternating line
    (c) phase alternating line (d) none of the above.
13. Which image file type is best for photo-realistic images?
    (a) Laser (b) Bitmap
    (c) Vector (d) All of the above.
14. In a video camera, CCD stands for:
    (a) colour coding data (b) charge coupled device
    (c) carbon crystal digitizer (d) none of the above.

Part B

Answer all questions, each of them carries one mark

True False Questions

1. Technology has used text and graphics to make communication difficult.
2. Sound files are not available in computer under Windows.
3. Touch screen does not allow you to get information by just touching the screen.
4. DVD means Digital Verify Disc.
5. The point unit is the traditional measurement of length is typography.
6. TrueType is a font system originally developed by Apple, Inc.
7. Digital sound is a term applied to sound that has been digitized into binary code.
8. MIDI (Musical Instrument Digital Interface), is an industry-standard protocol that enables electronic musical instruments such as keyboard controllers, computers, and other electronic equipment to communicate, control, and synchronize with each other.
9. The process by which a sound card creates music is called the sound synthesis or audio synthesis.
10. The Bitmap mode uses only two colour values to display images—black and white, while the Grayscale mode offers 300 shades of gray that range from white to black.
11. The move tool does not let you drag a selection or layer to a new location in the image.
12. You can view the color of a single area using the eyedropper tool, or you can use up to four color samplers to display color information for one or more locations in the image.
13. Four broadcast and video standards and recording formats commonly in use around the world are: NTSC, PAL, SECAM and HDTV.
14. Use the Export command to bring files—for example, still images or audio you've downloaded—that are already on your hard drive into your Adobe Premiere Pro project.

15. B-frame stands for bidirectional-frame. They may also be known as backwards-predicted frames or B-pictures.
16. The term 'Computer Animation' categories only 2D (two dimensional) animation.

Part C

Answer all questions, each of them carries one mark

Matching Questions

A.	MPEG-4	1.	The process of smoothly interpolating between two different images
B.	MPEG-1	2.	phase alternating line
C.	MPEG-2	3.	TV broadcasting standard
D.	MPEG	4.	efficient method of object oriented content based storage and retrieval of multimedia content
E.	Morphing	5.	designed for DVD applications
F.	PAL	6.	compressed format
G	NTSC	7.	designed for CD-ROM based

Part D

Answer all questions, each of them carries one mark

Fill in the Blanks

1. Sound is recorded through ____________.
2. The little decoration at the end of a letter stroke is a ___________.
3. An imaginary horizontal line on which characters rest is called ____________.
4. _________ font come in predefined sizes and weights.
5. The text in which the user has the facility to navigate in a non-linear fashion for the desired information is called ______________.
6. __________ is a device capable of changing signals from one form to another.
7. The number of computer zeros and ones (bits) required to represent a given signal in digital form is called ____________.
8. _________ is the total number of a logical pixels, in terms of rows and columns, supported by the display system.
9. _________ is a interface for obtaining images captured by certain scanner and digital cameras.
10. ________ is the extension of Photoshop file.

Part E

Answer any 10 questions, each of them carries five marks

Descriptive Type Questions

1. What is the process of Animation?
2. What role does multimedia play in development of games?
3. What are sound files known as?
4. What is the use of scanners?
5. Describe the various types of multimedia networking used.
6. Describe the working of speakers.
7. How is text used in the Multimedia?
8. Define Outline fonts.
9. Describe the various types of sound synthesis.
10. How is sound digitized?
11. How would you resize an image?
12. What is the use of Options Bar?
13. What are Channels?
14. Describe what type of photos can be retouched.
15. Describe the various image types.
16. Describe the various types of image compression and file formats.
17. What is video compression?
18. What is cel animation
19. How would you create DVDs?

Part F

Answers to Objective Type Questions

Multiple Choice Questions

A.1.	c	A.2.	a	A.3.	a	A.4.	b
A.5.	a	A.6.	a	A.7.	c	A.8.	b
A.9.	d	A.10	a	A.11	f	A.12	c
A.13	b	A.14	b				

True False Questions

B.1.	F	B.2.	F	B.3.	F	B.4	F
B.5.	T	B.6.	T	B.7.	T	B.8	T
B.9.	T	B.10.	F	B.11.	F	B.12.	T
B13.	T	B14.	F	B.15	T	B.16	F

Matching Questions

C.A.	4	C.B.	7	C.C.	5	C.D.	6
C.E.	1	C.F.	2	C.G	3		

Fill in the Blanks with appropriate words

D.1.	Microphone	D.2.	serif
D.3.	baseline	D.4.	bit-mapped
D.5.	hypertext	D.6.	Transducer
D.7.	sampling size	D.8.	Resolution
D.9.	TWAIN	D.10.	.psd

This page left blank for rough work

Glossary

G

Active Desktop The feature introduced with Microsoft's Internet Explorer 4 that enables end users to display active—that is, updateable, customizable—HTML content on the Windows desktop. Active content includes such items as channels, Web pages, ActiveX controls, and Java applets. See also Active Channel, ActiveX, HTML, Internet Explorer, Java.

Active Platform A Microsoft development platform that offers a standardized approach to incorporating Internet and distributed computing technologies in client/server applications. Microsoft Windows 9x, Microsoft Windows NT, and Microsoft Internet Explorer 4.x (and later) provide the basis for the Active Platform. On the client side, users are given a consistent interface that enables them to easily access both local and remote information. On the server side, developers can take advantage of the tools and technologies that span the client and the server. Active Platform supports development of the modular object-oriented programs known as component software and allows creation of cross-platform applications that can run on multiple chips and operating systems. Active Platform includes support for HTML and the creation of small programs in several languages through client-side scripting. See also Active Desktop, Active Server, ActiveX.

active window The open window in respect of Microsoft Windows programs which a program is being executed. In respect of Clipper debugger, window to which all key strokes (except those valid in the command window) apply.

alpha channel The high-order 8 bits of a 32-bit graphics pixel used to manipulate the remaining 24 bits for purposes of coloring or masking.

anchor 1. A format code in a desktop publishing or word processing document that keeps an element in the document, such as a figure or a caption or a label associated with the figure, in a certain position in the document. The anchored object is generally attached to another element in the document such as a piece of text (often a paragraph), a graphic, or a particular place in the document. As text and other objects are added to the document, the anchored object moves relative to the object to which it is anchored or remains stationary. 2. A tag in an HTML document that defines a section of text, an icon, or other element as a link to another element in the document or to another document or file. See also hyperlink.

anti-aliasing In computer graphics, a category of techniques that is used to smooth the jagged appearance of diagonal lines. For example, the pixels that surround the edges of the line are filled in with varying shades of grey or colour in order to blend the sharp edge into the background.

ASP.NET A set of technologies in the Microsoft .NET Framework for building Web applications and XML Web services. ASP.NET pages execute on the server and generate markup (such as HTML, WML, or XML) that is sent to a desktop or mobile browser. ASP.NET pages use a compiled, event-driven programming model that improves performance and enables the separation of application logic and user interface. ASP.NET pages and XML Web services files created using ASP.NET contain server-side (rather than client-side) logic written in Visual Basic .NET, C# .NET, or any .NET-compatible language. Web applications and XML Web services take advantage of the features of the common language runtime, such as type safety, inheritance, language interoperability, versioning, and integrated security.

ASP.NET server control A server-side

component that encapsulates user-interface and related functionality. An ASP.NET server control derives directly or indirectly from the System.Web.UI.Control class. The superset of ASP.NET server controls includes Web server controls, HTML server controls, and mobile controls. The page syntax for an ASP.NET server control includes a runat="server" attribute on the control's tag. See also Web server control, HTML server control, validation server controls.

attribute In many word processing and graphics programs a character emphasis, such as boldface and italic and other characteristics such as typeface and type size. In MS-DOS and Microsoft Windows 95, information about a file that indicates whether the file is a read-only file, a hidden file or a system file.

audio response Any sound produced by a computer; specifically, spoken output produced by a computer in response to some specific type of input. Such output may be generated using a combination of words from a digitized vocabulary or through the synthesis of words from tables of phonemes. See also frequency response, phoneme.

AVC (Audio Visual Connection) A Multimedia software from IBM that works in conjunction with IBM's Audio Capture and Video Capture boards for the *PSI* 2. It allows users to integrate sound and pictures into applications and includes in authoring language.

AVI Acronym for Audio Video Interleaved. A Windows multimedia file format for sound and moving pictures that uses the Microsoft RIFF (Resource Interchange File Format) specification.

avionics Electronic instrumentation and control equipment used in airplanes and space vehicles.

background processing The automatic execution of lower priority computer programs when higher-priority programs are not using the resources of the computer system.

backup To make a duplicate copy of a file or disk for safe keeping. A spare copy of data used for when things go wrong and to avoid the disaster which can follow the damaging or corruption of disks or data. All users should have at least one duplicate copy or backup of their program or data though more would be advisable. The ancestral file method offers additional security for data. Back-up copies may or may not be working copies of the original file.

band width The measure of the amount of information (voice, data, video) that a particular communication medium can carry. It is expressed in cycles per second (Hertz), the bandwidth being the difference between the lower and highest frequencies transmitted. Bandwidth is also often stated in bits or bytes per second.

band (1) Range of frequencies used for transmitting a signal. A band call can be identified by the difference between its lower and upper limits as well as by its actual lower and upper limits, for example, "a 10MHz band in the 100 to 110MHz range." (2) Contiguous group of tracks that are treated as a unit. (3) Printing element in a band printer.

bitmap file formats See art, cut, gif, iff, img, macpaint, neo, pcx, tga, tiff. Contrast with object file graphic formats.

bitmap font A font created by the use of bit mapping, generally these cannot be scaled or rotated.

bitmap (1) In computer graphics, an area in memory that represents the video image. For monochrome screens, one bit in the bitmap represents one pixel on screen. For greyscale or colour, several bits in the bitmap represent one pixel or group of pixels on screen. (2) Binary representation in which each bit or set of bits corresponds to some object (image, font, etc.) or condition.

bitmap A data structure in memory that represents information in the form of a collection of individual bits. A bit map is used to represent a bit image. Another use of a bit map in some systems is the representation of the blocks of storage on a disk, indicating whether each block is free (0) or in use (1). See also bit image, pixel image.

bit-mapped font A screen or printer font in which each character is composed of a pattern of dots. To display or print bitmapped fonts, the computer or printer must keep a full representation of each character in memory. When referring to bit-mapped fonts, the term font should be taken literally as a complete set of characters of a given typeface, weight, posture and type size. If you want to use Palatini (Roman) 12 and Oalatini Italic 14, for example, you must load two complete sets of characters into memory. You can't scale bit-mapped fonts up or down without introducing grotesque staircase distortions, called aliasing.

bitmapped font A set of characters in a particular size and style in which each character is described as a unique bit map (pattern of dots). Macintosh screen fonts are examples of bitmapped fonts. See the illustration. See also downloadable font, outline font, TrueType. Compare PostScript font, vector font.

bit-mapped graphics A methods of generating screen images by creating a one-for-one correspondence between bits in memory and pixels on the screen. If colour graphics, three or more bits are required in the bit map to represent the red, green and blue value of an individual pixel. Bitmapped graphics are created by paint programs and some scanners.

CAD Acronym for computer-aided design. A system of programs and workstations used in designing engineering, architectural, and scientific models ranging from simple tools to buildings, aircraft, integrated circuits, and molecules. Various CAD applications create objects in two or three dimensions, presenting the results as wire-frame "skeletons," as more substantial models with shaded surfaces, or as solid objects. Some programs can also rotate or resize models, show interior views, generate lists of materials required for construction, and perform other allied functions. CAD programs rely on mathematics, often requiring the computing power of a high-performance workstation. See also CAD/CAM, I-CASE.

CAD/CAM Computer-Aided Design/Computer-Aided Manufacturing - It is an integration of computer-aided design with computer-controlled manufacturing. The products designed in the CAD system are input directly into the CAM system. For example, after a machine part is designed in CAD, its electronic image is transferred to a numerical control programming language which generates the instructions to control the machine that makes the part.

CAI Acronym for computer-aided (or computer-assisted) instruction. An educational program designed to serve as a teaching tool. CAI programs typically use tutorials, drills, and question-and-answer sessions to present a topic and to test the student's comprehension. CAI programs are excellent aids for presenting factual material and for allowing students to pace their learning speed. Subjects and complexity range from beginning arithmetic to advanced mathematics, science, history, computer studies, and specialized topics. Also called: CAL, CAT, computer-aided learning, computer-aided teaching, computer-assisted learning, computer-assisted teaching, computer-augmented learning. See also I-CASE. Compare CBT, CMI.

cascading style sheets A Hypertext Markup Language (HTML) specification developed by The World Wide Web Consortium (W3C) that allows authors of HTML documents and users to attach style sheets to HTML documents. The style sheets include typographical information on how the page should appear, such as the font of the text in the page. This specification also directs the way in which the style sheets of the HTML document and the user's style will blend. Cascading style sheets have been proposed for the HTML 3.2 standard. Acronym: CSS. Also called: Cascading Style Sheet mechanism, CSS1.

Channel 1. A path or link through which information passes between two devices. A channel can be either internal or external to a microcomputer. 2. In communications, a medium for transferring information. Depending on its type, a communications channel can carry information (data, sound, and/or video) in either analog or digital form. A communications channel can be a physical link, such as the cable connecting two stations in a network, or it can consist of some electromagnetic transmission on one or more frequencies within a bandwidth in the electromagnetic spectrum, as in radio and television, or in optical, microwave, or voice-grade communication. Also called: circuit, line. See also analog, band, bandwidth, digital, electromagnetic spectrum, frequency. 3. A single color within a digital color space. For example, the RGB color space contains three channels—red, green, and blue—and all colors within the RGB color space are created with a combination of one or more of those three color channels. In CMYK there are four channels—cyan, magenta, yellow, and black. Color management and graphics applications rely on control and manipulation of individual color channels

CMYK Acronym for cyan-magenta-yellow-black. A color model that is similar to the CMY color model but produces black with a separate black component rather than by adding 100 percent of cyan, magenta, and yellow.

color model Any method or convention for representing color in desktop publishing and graphic arts. In the graphic arts and printing fields, colors are often specified with the Pantone system. In computer graphics, colors can be described using any of several different color systems: HSB (hue, saturation, and brightness), CMY (cyan, magenta, and yellow), and RGB (red, green, and blue).

comment A brief line of commentary embedded into a computer program. Comments aim to provide a "road-map" through a program, enabling programmers, including the original writer, to follow the overall logic of the program. Since comment occupy a line of code it is best to be brief, rather then verbose in commentary.

compile To translate all the source code of a program from a high-level language into object code prior to execution of the program. Object code is executable machine code or a variation of machine code. More generally, compiling is sometimes used to describe translating any high-level symbolic description into a lower-level symbolic or machine-readable format. A program that performs this task is known as a compiler.

desktop publishing Abbreviated "DTP". By using a personal computer to produce high-quality printed output for commercial printing. It requires a desktop publishing program, high-speed personal computer, full-or two page display monitor and a laser printer. The key feature of desktop publishing is its ability to merge and manage text with graphics and display it on screen WYSIWYG style. The program can flow text around graphic objects in a variety of ways Text and graphics may be created in the DTP program, but very few of them have full-featured word processing and graphics capability. Usually, the creation of the work is done in word processing, CAD, drawing and paint programs and then copied into the publishing system. DTP programs accept common file formats directly. DTP programs provide the ultimate in page layout capabilities, including a multitude of different type fonts, magazine style columns, rules and borders and page numbering in a variety of styles.

digital camera A type of camera that stores photographed images electronically instead of on traditional film. A digital camera uses a CCD (charge-coupled device) element to capture the image through the lens when the operator releases the shutter in the camera; circuitry within the camera then stores the image captured by the CCD in a storage medium such as solid-state memory or a hard disk. After the image has been captured, it is downloaded by cable to the computer using software supplied with the camera. Once stored in the computer, the image can be manipulated and processed much like the image from a scanner or related input device. See also charge-coupled device, digital photography.

drag-and-drop editing An editing feature that allows you to perform a block move or copy by highlighting a block of text and then using the mouse to drag the block to its new location. When you release the mouse button, the text appears in the new location.

element 1. Any stand-alone item within a broader context. For example, a data element is an item of data with the characteristics or properties of a larger set; a picture element (pixel) is one single dot on a computer screen or in a computer graphic; a print element is the part of a daisy-wheel printer that contains the embossed characters. See also daisy-wheel printer, data element, graphics primitive, pixel, thimble. 2. In markup languages such as HTML and SGML, the combination of a set of tags, any content contained between the tags, and any attributes the tags may have. Elements can be nested, one within the other. 3), HTML, markup language, SGML.

embedded In software, pertaining to code or a command that is built into its carrier. For example, application programs insert embedded printing commands into a document to control printing and formatting. Low-level assembly language is embedded in higher-level languages, such as C, to provide more capabilities or better efficiency.

embedded object In Object Linking and Embedding (OLE) an object wholly inserted or embedded, into a destination document created by an application other than that which created the destination document. The object can be text, a chart, a graphic or sound. See linked object.

Empty Element An HTML element requiring just a starting tag and not any ending tag.

end user The ultimate user of a computer or computer application in its finished, marketable form.

error A value or condition that is not consistent with the true, specified, or expected value or condition. In computers, an error results when an event does not occur as expected or when impossible or illegal maneuvers are attempted. In data communications, an error occurs when there is a discrepancy between the transmitted and received data. See also critical error, error message, error rate, error ratio, fatal error, hard error, inherent error, intermittent error, logic error, machine error, overflow error, parity error.. Compare fault.

file management system The organizational structure that an operating system or program uses to order and track files. For example, a hierarchical file system uses directories in a so-called tree structure. All operating systems have built-in file management systems. Commercially available products implement additional features that provide more sophisticated means of navigating, finding, and organizing files.

GIF 1. Acronym for Graphics Interchange Format. A graphics file format developed by CompuServe and used for transmitting raster images on the Internet. An image may contain up to 256 colors, including a transparent color. The size of the file depends on the number of colors actually used. The LZW compression method is used to reduce the file size still further. See also LZW compression, raster graphics. 2. A graphic stored as a file in the GIF format.

header 1. In word processing or printing, text that is to appear at the top of pages. A header might be specified for the first page, all pages after the first, even pages, or odd pages. It usually includes the page number and may also show the date, the title, or other information about a document. Also called: heading, running head. Compare footer. 2. An information structure that precedes and identifies the information that follows, such as a block of bytes in communications, a file on a disk, a set of records in a database, or an executable program. 3. One or more lines in a program that identify and describe for human readers the program, function, or procedure that follows.

high-level programming language A programming language such as BASIC or Pascal that crudely resembles human language. Each statement in a high-level language corresponds to several machine language instructions. Using such languages, a programmer can write programs more quickly and concentrate on the problem that the program is designed to solve, instead of how the computer will carry out the program. However, programs written in a high-level language run slower than those written in a low-level programming language.

image processing The analysis, manipulation, storage, and display of graphical images from sources such as photographs, drawings, and video. Image processing spans a sequence of three steps. The input step (image capture and digitizing) converts the differences in coloring and shading in the picture into binary values that a computer can process. The processing step can include image enhancement and data compression. The output step consists of the display or printing of the processed image. Image processing is used in such applications as television and film, medicine, satellite weather mapping, machine vision, and computer-based pattern recognition.

impact printer A printer, such as a wire-pin dot-matrix printer or a daisy-wheel printer, that drives an inked ribbon mechanically against the paper to form marks.

information Summarization of data. Technically, data are raw facts and figures that are processed into information, such as summaries and totals. But since information can also be raw data for the next job or person, the two terms cannot be precisely defined. Both terms are used synonymously and interchangeably. As office automation and data processing merge, it may be more helpful to view information the way data is defined and used, namely: data, text, spread-sheet, pictures, voice and video. Data are discretely defined fields. Text is a collection of words. Spreadsheets are data in matrix (row and column) form. Pictures are lists of vectors or frames of bits. Voice is a continuous stream of sound waves. Video is a sequence of frames.

JavaScript A scripting language developed by Netscape Communications and Sun Microsystems that is loosely related to Java. JavaScript, however, is not a true object-oriented language, and it is limited in performance compared with Java because it is not compiled. Basic online applications and functions can be added to Web pages with JavaScript, but the number and complexity of available application programming interface functions are fewer than those available with Java. JavaScript code, which is included in a Web page along with the HTML code, is generally considered easier to write than Java, especially for novice programmers. A JavaScript-compliant Web browser, such as Netscape Navigator or Internet Explorer, is necessary to run JavaScript code.

kernel The core of an operating system—the portion of the system that manages memory, files, and peripheral devices; maintains the time and date; launches applications; and allocates system resources.

layer 1. The protocol or protocols operating at a particular level within a protocol suite, such as IP within the TCP/IP suite. Each layer is responsible for providing specific services or functions for computers exchanging information over a communications network (such as the layers in the ISO/OSI reference model) and information is passed from one layer to the next. Although different suites have varying numbers of levels, generally the highest layer deals with software interactions at the application level, and the lowest governs hardware-level connections between different computers. See the table. See also ISO/OSI reference model, protocol stack, TCP/IP. 2. In communications and distributed processing, a set of rules and standards that handles a particular class of events.

magnetic-ink character recognition A form of character recognition that reads text printed with magnetically charged ink, determining the shapes of characters by sensing the magnetic charge in the ink. Once the shapes have been determined, character recognition methods are used to translate the shapes into computer text. A familiar use of this form of character recognition is to identify bank checks. Acronym: MICR.

morphing Short for metamorphosing; a revolutionary animation technique used to "fill in the blanks" between dissimilar figures so that one seems to melt into another, such as changing a man to a warewolf, a bat to a vampire or a rock singer to a panther. Morphing, a common film industry specials effects technique is related closely to another, more prosaic animation technique called tweening (short for in-betweening) which refers to the computer's capability to calculate and draw frames that are intermediate between the "key" frames hand-down by the artist. Morphing is the process of tweening to a different object.

operating system Master control program that runs the computer. It is the first program loaded when the computer is turned on and its main part, called the kernel, reside in memory at all times. It is an important component of the computer system because its sets the standards for the application programs that runs in it. All programs must work through the operating system.

optical mark recognition OMR Information processing technology that converts data into another medium for computer input by the presence of a mark in a given position, each position having a value known to the computer that may or may not be understandable to humans.

password protection A method of limiting access to program file, computer or a network by requiring you to enter a password. Some programs allow you to password-protect your files so they can't be read by others, but be sure to keep a record of the password. Many users have lost work permanently because they forgot the password and had no means to retrieve it. (If a method for retrieving a password were included in software programs, a clever cracker would quickly discover it and your data wouldn't be secure.)

Pixel Pix element or picture element – Smallest element on a video display screen. A screen is broken up into thousands of tiny dots, and a pixel is one or more dots that are treated as a unit.

Plug and Play PnP – A special fiction for rapid hardware installation and software configuration supported by Microsoft and many hardware vendors. Plug and Play is intended to relieve the user from the IRQ, DMA, BPA, etc. of PC hardware and memory problems. Plug and play support is required in the operating system, the hardware and the software drives for the hardware for it all to work. Windows 95 supports PnP; Windows NT 4.0 doesn't yet.

QuickTime Software components developed by Apple for creating, editing, publishing, and viewing multimedia content. QuickTime, which supports video, animation, graphics, 3-D, VR (virtual reality), MIDI, music, sound, and text, has been part of the Mac OS since version 7 of the operating system and is used in many Macintosh applications. Windows applications can also run QuickTime files but require the installation of special player software. QuickTime is often used on the Web to provide Web pages with video and animation. Most Web browsers support plug-ins for running these types of files. QuickTime is also part of the new MPEG-4 specification.

RAM Acronym for random access memory. Semiconductor-based memory that can be read and written by the central processing unit (CPU) or other hardware devices. The storage locations can be accessed in any order. Note that the various types of ROM memory are capable of random access but cannot be written to. The term RAM, however, is generally understood to refer to volatile memory that can be written to as well as read. Compare core, EPROM, flash memory, PROM, ROM (definition 2).

RGB Red Green Blue – Method of recording and generating colors in a video system. On a TV or color monitor, colors are displayed as varying intensities of red, green and blue dots. When red, green and blue are all turned on high, white is produced. As the intensities are equally lowered, shades of gray are produced. When all dots are turned off, the base color of the screen appears. Color printing uses the CMY or CMYK (Cyan Magenta Yellow black) sys-tem for mixing colors. In RGB, colors are added to create white. In CMY, colors are subtracted to create white.

Scanner A peripheral device that converts a printed image into digital information suitable for input to a computer. Some scanners the more expensive models, will convert text into an ASCII file, others treat text as a graphic. A flat-bed scanner uses a flat surface, similar to that found in a photocopier, whereas a drum scanner requires the image which is usually paper, to be fed into a series of rollers.

sound card A peripheral interface card providing sound reproduction support for the operating system, applications and games. There are two prevalent standards for sound on the Intel PC, the Creative Labs Sound Blaster and MIDI. The Sound Blaster and compatible cards provide basic sound synthesis (the ability to create fairly realistic musical sounds from mathematical formulas) and the ability to record and play back digital sound files (the most popular digital sound format is .WAV files (Most Sound Blaster and compatible cards also support the MIDI (Musical Instrument Digital Interface) standard.

TIFF Tagged Image File Format – Widely-used raster graphics file format developed by Aldus and Microsoft that handles monochrome, gray scale, 8- and 24-bit color. It uses several compression methods: LZW provides ratios of about 1.5:1 to 2:1. Ratios of 10:1 to 20:1 are possible for documents with lots of white space using CCITT Group III sIV compression methods (fax).

Uniform Resource Locator URL One of two basic kinds of Universal Resource Identifiers (URI), a string of characters that precisely identifies an internet resource's type and location. For example, the following fictions URL identifies a World Wide Web document (http://), indicates the domain name of the computer on which document's location within the directory structure (-toros/winerefs/), and includes the document's name and extension (merlot.html).

vector graphics In computer graphics, a technique for representing a picture as points, lines and other geometric entities.

Windows Graphics-based operating environment from Microsoft that integrates with DOS. It provides a desktop environment similar to the Macintosh, in which each active application is displayed in a re-sizable, movable window on screen. Though applications are written specifically for it, Windows also runs DOS applications and can be used as the primary operating environment from which all programs are launched.

World Wide Web WWW A global hypertext system that uses the Internet as its transport mechanism. In a hypertext system, you navigate by clicking hyperlinks which display another document (which also contains hyperlinks). What makes the Web such an exciting and useful medium is that the next document you see could be housed on a computer next door-or halfway around the world. The Web makes the Internet easy to use. Created in 1989 at the European Laboratory for Particle Physics (CERN), a research institute in Switzerland, the Web relies upon the HyperTExt Transport Protocol (HTTP), an Internet standard the specifies how an application can locate and acquire resources (such as document, sound or graphic) stored on another computer on the Internet. HTTP provides transparent, easy-to-use access to Web documents, FTP (File transfer Protocol) file archives, Gopher menus and even UseNet newsgroups, users of Web navigation software, called Web browsers, simply click on an underlined word or phrase and HTTP takes care of locating and downloading the desired documents. Most Web documents are created using the HyperText markup language (HTML), a markup language that is easy to learn and will soon be supplanted by automated tools. Incorporating hypermedia (graphics, sound, animations, and video), the Web has become the ideal medium for publishing information on the Internet. A key 1995 agreement on security protocols ensures that Web will quickly become an important commercial medium, in which consumers can browse on-line catalog and place orders without worrying about anyone intercepting the supplied credit card information.

World Wide Web Worm WWWW – A search engine for locating World Wide Web (WWW) documents that is provided by the Department of Computer Science at the University of Colorado. Relying on a automated search routine (called a spider), WWWW retrieves graphics, video and audio files as well as document titles and words in document hyperlinks.

WYSIWYG What You See Is What You Get – pronounced "wizzy- wig." Refers to next and graphics appearing on screen the same as they would print. It is almost impossible to get 100% identical representation, because screen and printer resolution rarely match.

Index

E

F

G

H

I

J

K

L

M

N

O

P

Q

R

S

T